Contents

In memory of
GEORGE JACKSON
1907–1986
Who took me backstage and showed me the magic of the theatre.

Foreword

The New Mermaid series offers a wide range of important British plays prepared by scholars for the modern reader.

This new series of Background Books has been planned to accompany the plays, and in the conviction that, as the number of historical descriptions, reader's guides and critical studies pile up, offering summaries, generalizations and evaluations, less and less first-hand material is actually within reach and fewer and fewer readers have the opportunity to read what the dramatists, actors, managers, disapproving authorities or original viewers themselves wrote. Their language is very often vivid in itself and has the flavour of its time, and is often an illuminating context for the language in the plays. Since much of this material seems to be not accessible to present-day readers, though of signal interest, and since it can be used to present a view of theatre no modern historian's survey can rival for particularity and vitality, *New Mermaid Background Books* aim to give the material currency.

Russell Jackson's collection of material in *Victorian Theatre* illuminates many aspects of the very varied drama of the time and allows a reader to trace the historical evolution of the theatre towards our own day. Further volumes are in preparation on *Restoration and Eighteenth-Century Theatre* and on *Modern British Theatre*.

BRIAN GIBBONS

General Editor, The New Mermaid Series

Acknowledgements

I am grateful to the curators and librarians of the following collections for access to material: the Bodleian Library, the British Library, Birmingham Reference Library, Bristol University Theatre Collection, Finsbury Public Library, the Folger Shakespeare Library, Harvard Theatre Collection, the Historical Society of Pennsylvania, New York Public Library, the Shakespeare Centre Library, the Shakespeare Institute, the Theatre Museum, the Furness Collection of the University of Pennsylvania. Extracts from the diaries of Charles Rice and Henry Crabb Robinson are reprinted by kind permission of the Society for Theatre Research, which publishes the editions cited.

Illustrations are reproduced by permission of the following institutions: Shakespeare Centre Library, Stratford-upon-Avon (illus. 3, 17, 23, 24, 25); the National Portrait Gallery, London (8); City of Birmingham Public Library (12–16); Finsbury Public Library (26). Other illustrations have been prepared from photographs made by the Photographic Service of the University of Birmingham Library.

Among the individuals who have given me invaluable help are Michael Booth, Susan Brock, Claire Cochrane, David Drummond, Brian Gibbons and Caroline Byard Jones. My wife, Linda Rosenberg, has been a constant source of encouragement and support.

RUSSELL JACKSON

Birmingham, 1988

Illustrations and Sources

Introduction

This anthology brings together documents of the social life of the
Victorian theatre – descriptions of the audiences, the working
conditions of Victorian actors and authors, the theory and practice
of theatre management, and the techniques of a theatre of
elaborate scenic illusion. Music-hall, which figures in these pages
as a rival of the 'legitimate' theatre, had a flourishing and vital life
which deserves separate treatment, and which historians have
begun to examine in detail and depth. I have decided to confine
this anthology for the most part to the spoken drama. But it
should be borne in mind that the 'shows' of London were
astonishingly varied, and one bill might include opera, drama,
farce and musical numbers – not unlike the range of an evening's
television. Reviews of acting and of the plays themselves – already
available in a number of collections – have not been included. My
aim here is to provide a sampling of documents that will represent
the principal features of Victorian theatre life, and complement
the authoritative historical accounts available elsewhere. With a
few exceptions, the material is from articles, reports and private
documents, rather than fiction.

In the nineteenth century the British theatre was almost
exclusively commercial and was central to popular culture and to
what may be called the entertainment industry of an urban
industrial society. Its purposes and effectiveness were argued over
by critics and practitioners, and its ability to reach a newly created
mass audience made it a prime target for social legislation.

In 1817, at the end of an essay on *A Midsummer Night's Dream*
in his *Characters of Shakespeare's Plays*, William Hazlitt remarked
on the inadequacy of the theatre's attempts to bring the play's
visions to life and concluded: 'The boards of a theatre and the
regions of fancy are not the same thing.' The Victorian theatre
was devoted to illusion, as though in an attempt to confute
Hazlitt's dictum. The romantic, visionary definition of dramatic
poetry demanded a stage that should contrive to lose its identity in
the service of this absolute illusion and make the spectators
forget – for as much as possible of their time in the theatre – that
they knew a world more 'real' than that placed before them on the

stage. Sir Herbert Beerbohm Tree, one of the great actor-managers of the period, declared that illusion was 'the first and last word of the stage; all that aids illusion is good, all that destroys illusion is bad.' (*Thoughts and After-Thoughts*, 1913, p. 57.) One version of the history of the Victorian theatre, favoured by the age itself, represents it as a steady progress in the development of the techniques that would produce a completely convincing illusory world, in which any modern, fantastic or historical event or scene could be rendered with accuracy and conviction. By the 1880s the productions of the Lyceum Theatre were being praised for fidelity to the pictorial values of fashionable painting. In the great Victorian project of reconciling a new society with poetry and romance, the theatre had an important part to play.

Charles Kean's biographer, J.W. Cole, suggested that the actor's lavish and historically 'correct' productions of Shakespeare were part of the progress of knowledge and culture:

> The time had at length arrived when a total purification of Shakespeare [i.e. by removing the additions of earlier adapters] with every accompaniment that refined knowledge, diligent research, and chronological accuracy could supply, was suited to the taste and temper of the age, which had become eminently pictorial and exacting beyond all former precedent.
>
> (*Life . . . of Charles Kean*, 1859, II, 26)

Despite the success of this technological advance, there were many who feared that the theatre, in its pursuit of illusion, might have forfeited its ability to deal directly with human feeling and behaviour. Reviewing Julia Neilson's *Romeo and Juliet*, Joseph Knight wondered whether there was not 'a growing danger that, in our regard for the dramatic grouping of figures, we may lose sight of that more important province of the dramatist, the subordination of incident to character.' (*Theatrical Notes*, 1893, p. 91.) There was even concern that pantomime and melodrama – traditionally hospitable to spectacle – might be losing dramatic qualities in favour of pictorial splendours. Although improvements in staging could be recognized as contributions to the betterment of theatrical art, there was a concern with their allegedly adverse effect on the writing of the drama – the literary achievements that would in the eyes of many commentators be a more respectable contribution to cultural life. In an essay praising Macready's qualities as actor and manager, Richard Hengist Horne insisted that 'the imagination of creative dramatists can alone call forth any new spirit and form of drama', and that 'the most profuse and admirable external aids' of scenery and costumes were detrimental in so far as they 'dazzle and mislead public judgement till it cannot distinguish the essential from the extraneous.' (*A New Spirit of the Age*, 1844, World's Classics edn, 1907, pp. 330–1.)

Another history of the Victorian theatre might show it as an institution acquiring and maintaining its social respectability, with the winning back of the middle (and, to a degree, upper) classes to the theatres, the refinement of arrangements for the comfort of audiences, and the achievement of truly 'professional' standing for actors and actresses. Macready's exclusion of prostitutes from Drury Lane Theatre in 1842, Phelps's reform of Sadler's Wells in the 1840s, the Bancrofts' management of the Prince of Wales's Theatre (and their staging of Tom Robertson's plays) in the 1860s and the knighthood conferred in 1895 on Henry Irving are the great events in this narrative. Looking back on Queen Victoria's reign from the vantage point of her jubilee in 1887, *The Era*, the leading theatrical trade paper, observed that 'the vast upper middle class has adopted the theatre as a rational means of recreation, and entertainments have had to be made more decent and more wholesome to suit its tastes.' (25 June 1887.)

A third account depicts the theatre as an expression of popular culture, in a period when the urban population increased rapidly, education and transport transformed the potential audience, and new rivals to the 'legitimate' stage asserted themselves. The very definition of 'legitimate' drama was a major cultural issue – a focus of legislation in the course of the period – and the distinction between dramatic and music-hall entertainment (together with the adequate control and censorship of both) became a subject of concern to governments. Before the 1843 act the spoken drama had been confined to the theatres that inherited the royal letters patent: Drury Lane and Covent Garden; and, in the summer, the Haymarket. In the new working-class suburbs to the south and east the 'minor' theatres outside the Lord Chamberlain's jurisdiction (then only extending to the cities of London and Westminster) were obliged to adopt such shifts as transforming popular dramas into legally permitted 'burlettas' by adding a token musical accompaniment. The inadequacy of the legislation and the poverty of the aesthetic definitions it relied on were clear. By the middle of the century the music-halls constituted something of a challenge to the theatres on artistic as well as social grounds: the best of them were comfortable, cheap and offered a variety of entertainment that the theatre soon ceased to compete with. In the evidence given to the Parliamentary Select Committee in 1866 'legitimate' managers tried to argue that drama could not be seen or heard to proper advantage when drinking and smoking were going on, but the public persisted in thinking differently. Dion Boucicault's play *After Dark* (1868) has blackface minstrels arriving at a night-shelter, complaining of their poor takings. The dialogue parodies arguments about 'legitimate' versus popular entertainment. 'Who'll paytronize the intellectual amusement when they can go into a music-hall and get rough-and-tumble with a song over their pipes and swipes,' asks a minstrel, and one of the company concurs: 'Why, for thruppence me an' the Bargee went h'into the Elysium, and we had three ballets, a selection from Il Trovytory, and we heard the great Muggings sing "A-Walking in the Zoo!"'

Yet another narrative is that of the rise of the artistically unified theatre: the demand for an overall sense of composition in staging and performance, the emergence of the independent 'producer' or (in modern British usage) director, with command over every department of the theatre and an identifiable approach to the text or the subject matter. Complementing this is the rise in status of the author, able by the end of the century to command payment and artistic control on a scale undreamed of by the playwrights employed by theatres in the 1820s and 1830s. At the end of the period 'dramatic reform' offered an agenda that included the removal of censorship, the displacement of commercial demands from their central place in artistic policy, and the establishing of an authors' theatre.

George Bernard Shaw campaigned as a critic against the theatre's current absurdities, then, after breaking into it, conducted a campaign from within to revolutionize the genres he inhabited. William Archer, champion of Ibsen and a persuasive dramatic critic, accepted as a necessary evil 'the virtuoso actor-manager, who holds that dramatic literature exists for the actor, not the actor for dramatic literature', but it was an evil whose end could be earnestly hoped and striven for (*World*, 4 June 1890). Others (notably Edward Gordon Craig) wished to replace the actor-manager with an artist who neither acted in nor wrote the text of the performance, and who would pull the theatre away from its literary and social moorings.

In all these versions of the 'progress' of the Victorian theatre there is a strong sense of the modification of the free market to acknowledge the change in the nature of society and the importance entertainment had in it. The Theatre Regulation Act of 1843 rescinded the absurd limitations of the monopolies that had dominated London theatre since the 1660s and established a reformed system of censorship and control under the Lord Chamberlain; authors' rights were protected by the 1833 Dramatic Copyright Act, the 1886 Berne Convention and the 1891 change in American copyright law; a series of acts and local authority by-laws regulated the licensing and safety of theatres and music-halls. Members of the educated middle class were beginning to call for some planned state provision for the art of the theatre, as they demanded the establishment of other cultural and educational institutions. William Bodham Donne, in an essay published in 1854, proposed the drama as 'a branch of art which delineates and appeals directly to some of the most earnest and enobling impulses in humanity', noting that 'our earnestness and our sport have travelled at railway speed during the present century'. The drama deserved support and organization, and Donne proposed a 'concordat' between theatres in London to avoid rivalry and duplication. (*Essays on the Drama*, 1858.) In 1879 Matthew Arnold urged his readers to organize the theatre, because it was 'irresistible'. Managements often appealed to a sense of the legitimate stage's dignity and the cultural centrality of the works they presented: Shakespeare was frequently an important element in these defences against the philistinism of the market-place and the religious enemies of the stage.

Whenever Victorian theatrical journals were at a loss for a topic for an editorial, or had space to fill, an article on the 'decline of the drama' seems to have been forthcoming. A representative specimen appeared in *The Stage Manager* on 4 October 1849, lamenting the drama's decline and offering hope for its resuscitation:

> The Prospects of the Drama have been but sickly for some time now; let us not only hope, but will it, that they are brightening. There is material enough to embody and to represent the noblest productions of the human mind, if the spirit of progress which actuates the public in so much, will put its shoulder to the wheel in this case.

The drama became a recognized object of reform, the scarcity of good new native plays a cause for unlimited debate and concern. It seemed absurd that the upper classes should be abandoning the

English drama in favour of Italian opera and French plays, that Drury Lane could be filled only by recourse to the entertainments that pleased the least informed taste, and that the rising middle class should feel alienated from the theatre. Progress, in hand on every side, ought to be reaching the theatre. Great poets, not hacks, ought to be writing for it; the talent that made novels the central, defining genre of Victorian literary culture, ought to be wooed back to the stage; well-behaved audiences ought to be sitting in clean, safe theatres watching pictorially satisfying productions of 'standard' plays and improving new works. Like public health, public culture should be taken in hand. At the end of the century, with the champions of Ibsen and an endowed theatre calling for new kinds of reform, there were those (notably the critic Clement Scott) who insisted that Irving, the Bancrofts and their co-workers had effected the necessary revival of the theatre – that the New Drama was a heretical and élitist pursuit that would frighten away that great middle class so recently wooed back into the playhouses. The theatre that Scott tried to defend has sunk almost without trace and it is ironic that he is now remembered solely for his invective against Ibsen: *Ghosts*, he claimed, was 'a dull, undramatic, verbose, tedious, and utterly uninteresting play' (*Daily Telegraph*, 14 March 1891).

The perspective of the late twentieth century casts such reactionaries as villains – and ineffectual villains at that – trying to resist what now seems an inevitable revolution in the theatre, but it is worth remembering that their own vision of an ideal theatre was that it should continue to be a popular art, and that 'legitimate' or 'literary' drama should hold its own within that art rather than become the province of an intellectual élite. In the event, cinema took over many of the functions of the old theatre of spectacle, and Shakespearean production, for so long a bridge between the popular and the 'legitimate', found new energy and refinement in work that combined the rediscovery of Elizabethan stagecraft with expressive, non-representational design. Panto-mime struggled on, never with that purity of delight that nostalgia had always claimed it once possessed, but still a vigorous mixture of clowning, sentiment and spectacle.

Editorial Procedure

The spelling and punctuation of the originals have been retained, with the following exceptions: italicization of book- and play-titles has replaced the use of inverted commas; the inverted commas often placed round the names of fictional characters ('Gertrude', 'William', etc.) have been removed; in some longer items I have changed the division into paragraphs. Editorial omissions have been indicated by the use of three dots (. . .). Footnotes have been kept to a minimum, and a guide to the titles of plays has been provided at the end of the book.

The abbreviations for pounds, shillings and pence have been standardized to £,s.,d. Readers unfamiliar with the two lower denominations should remember that in 1970, when British currency was altered, the shilling was the equivalent of 5 new pence, that 12 old pence made one shilling and 20 shillings one pound. Prices and salaries were often quoted in guineas (1 guinea = £1 1s.). It is difficult to give meaningful modern equivalents for the value of money in the last century: but it should be borne in mind that, during the period from 1830 to 1900 working-class wages ranged from 5s. to £2 a week (so that the lowest-paid actors received the equivalent of a skilled hand). In 1867 one estimate of middle-class incomes suggested a range from £300–£1000 a year.

Part I

Theatres for Audiences

The range of Victorian theatre was as wide as that of Victorian society, for it was the principal medium of entertainment available to literate and illiterate alike. At one end of the social scale was the Opera – frowned on among the intelligentsia as having supplanted the 'legitimate' drama on the stages of the major London theatres – and at the other end were the booth theatres. Those with faith in a fundamental unity of human character could take comfort in the similarity between what was on offer at either end of the spectrum. Dickens, after describing a melodrama at the Standard Theatre, observed that 'when the situations were very strong indeed, they were very like what some favourite situations in the Italian Opera would be to a profoundly deaf spectator,' and concluded that 'there is some hopeful congeniality between what will excite Mr Whelks, and what will rouse a Duchess.' (*Household Words*, 30 April 1850: see also Charles Booth, xxii below.)

The travelling shows offered fairground patrons hectic, truncated versions of popular dramas at low prices. Fairs were not the only sites for such entertainments (see no. v). Recitations were among the performances given in the streets, and Henry Mayhew interviewed a street performer who specialized in Shakespearean monologues. His theatrical career included acting in a 'slang' – a temporary booth – that constituted 'the twopenny theatre on Victoria-bridge, Manchester'. On a Saturday night the manager could get through six houses, starting at three o'clock, when the factory hands had been paid off. 'It was a very little stage, but with very nice scenery, and shift-scenes and all, the same as any other theatre.' (*London Labour and the London Poor*, III, 1868, p. 152.) Another kind of theatre, the so-called 'private' theatre, catered for novices who were prepared to pay for the privilege of 'coming out' in a piece from the 'standard' repertoire. Dickens described this in one of the *Sketches by Boz* (1832–6), where it is made clear that the enterprise merely preys on the vanity of the stage-struck. He quotes a list of prices charged for playing the roles quoted: 'Richard the Third, – Duke of Glo'ster, £2; Earl of Richmond, £1; Duke of Buckingham, 15s.; Catesby, 12s.; Tressel, 10s.6d.; Lord Stanley, 5s.; Lord Mayor of London, 2s.6d.'

Between these establishments and the fashionable West End houses London possessed a range of professional theatres that changed in number and nature as the century progressed. In the first three decades of the century, as London grew rapidly, the legislation that restricted 'legitimate' drama to the two 'patent' houses was less and less able to cope with the proliferation of 'minor' theatres. Some of these, such as the Surrey, were 'minor' only in the customary nomenclature: they were large, well-appointed buildings with huge audiences living near them, whose tastes and convenience they were better placed than Drury Lane and Covent Garden to satisfy. Others – notably Sadler's Wells in the years before Phelps – were indeed serving poor entertainment to an audience of the unrespectable poor. But before condemning such entertainments and their audiences as brash and inartistic, it is important to remember that the theatre was for many working-class people the only escape – apart from the public house – from a drab and laborious life. Dickens and some other humanitarian reformers of culture (notably Phelps and Henry Morley) under-stood this: in Dickens' *Hard Times* the circus is a potent symbol of life and imagination in Coketown, an acknowledgement, however tawdry, that 'people mutht be amused'. Pantomime and circus seemed to appeal across barriers of class and age. Patrons of 'high' and 'low' theatre shared a predilection for variety and colour in entertainments, and the mish-mash of drama, circus and pantomime available at such establishments as Astley's reflects a love of novelty and brightness that appears to have transcended class barriers.

The reclamation of Sadler's Wells by Phelps and the Bancrofts' transformation of the Queen's, Tottenham Street, into the Prince of Wales's were acclaimed as models of what might be achieved by way of attracting 'respectable' audiences. There were many imitators of both enterprises. In *The Drama of Yesterday and Today* (1899) Clement Scott recalled the effect of the Bancrofts' regime:

> Visitors accustomed to dingy, dirty, uncomfortable theatres, as bad, if not worse, than the ordinary Paris theatres of today, were enchanted with the light, bright, joyous little playhouse, always compared to a blue quilted 'bon-bon' box, where the very walls of the theatre seemed to welcome you, as they do today in the theatres of America.

(I, 485)

But although the establishment of a theatre for 'refined' middle-class tastes was in some sense a considerable achievement, the Bancrofts' work hastened a separation of fashionable from popular theatres. As John Pick emphasizes in his book on the evolution of the West End mentality (see *Further Reading*), theatres began to accommodate themselves to the social rituals familiar to middle- and upper-class playgoers – to the exclusion or at least marginali- zation of others. Even the experience of Phelps at Sadler's Wells may need to be reinterpreted: Pick argues that the playgoers attracted by Phelps were predominantly middle-class, and that, with the 'decline' of Islington in the 1860s, as these families moved to outer suburbs, the fortunes of Sadler's Wells also declined.

The trend was emphatically towards smaller, more comfortably appointed and socially exclusive theatres. At the same time, music-halls were growing in number and capacity: as a venue for popular entertainment a good music-hall suffered none of the inhibitions of the newer theatres, and from the managers' point of view they were cheaper to run. The 'legitimate' managements' fear of the new contenders for the mass audience was responsible for much of the testimony given before the 1866 Parliamentary Select Committee. The boom in theatre building of the 1860s firmly established the West End, and subsequent developments resulted in a large number of intimate and comfortable theatres, including the Criterion (1874), the Comedy (1881), the Avenue (1882, now the Playhouse), the Prince of Wales's (1884), the Lyric (1888), the Garrick (1889), Wyndham's (1899) and the New (1903, now the Albery). Two especially lavish new theatres from the end of the century are the Palace, built for Richard D'Oyly Carte as the Royal English Opera House in 1891, and Her Majesty's Theatre (1897), referred to by Tree as 'my beautiful theatre'. Spectacle was served by the London Hippodrome (1900) and music-hall was housed on a grand scale in the Coliseum (1904). By the end of the century central London's theatres extended from the St James's and the Imperial in the west to the Gaiety and the Aldwych in the east, with the Princess's in Oxford Street marking the northern boundary. A number of inner suburban theatres – such as the new Court (now Royal Court) in Sloane Square (1888) – amounted to outposts of the fashionable theatre-world. These were the architectural symbols of a theatre that had re- established itself as a rational entertainment for the middle and upper classes, the fulfilment of the Bancrofts' work. Provision on a corresponding scale and with similarly lavish expenditure on front-of-house facilities took place in other cities. More stringent

1 A fashionable London theatre, seen from the stage: the interior of the Criterion Theatre, from a souvenir book published in 1903

application of building regulations, simpler means of advance booking (the modern ticket-and-stub system replacing hand-written tickets) and increased foyer space made the theatre an easier, more welcoming place to go to. Such 'cleansing' as Macready's banishing of prostitutes from the precincts of Drury Lane had made it a safer place for the middle class. Even those whose religious conscience made them doubt the ethical value of playgoing could indulge in such entertainments as Mr and Mrs German Reed's Royal Gallery of Illustration (a theatre by any other name . . .).

The theatres' appeal was increasingly to middle-class taste. The comfort of those in cheaper seats was not so carefully provided for, and pains were taken in most theatres to segregate the classes of patron from the moment they came to buy a ticket. Buying tickets in advance from the circulating libraries (customary agents for booking) was sometimes an intimidating process (see Pick, pp. 81–2). The pit, whose large number of inexpensive benches occupied the space nearest the stage, was deprived of its prominence and power in the auditorium, being moved back to make way for expensive 'stalls', pushed under the overhanging dress-circle and finally banished to the upper gallery. The Bancrofts' remodelling of the Haymarket in 1880, putting a gilded picture frame all the way round the proscenium aperture and banishing the pit patrons to the upper circle, was a *cause célèbre* (no. xix; see also xi, xv). There was sometimes a real sense of rivalry and antagonism between gallery and stalls, but the desire of the poor to assert their respectability usually overcame any rowdier elements. *The Times*, reviewing the first production of Robertson's *Caste* in the issue of 11 April 1867, observed that the gallery accepted the play's unflattering portrayal of lower-class characters:

> Let it be remembered, too, that the Prince of Wales's Theatre, though it has been fashionable for two years, is by no means in a fashionable neighbourhood, and that the gallery must be peopled by many of those working men who patronized it when it was the humble Queen's. That such an assembly is pleased with an exhibition of a most un-demagogic kind is a fact worth noting by those who take an interest in the real operative of London.

The relationships between actual social class and social attitudes, and the links between both and the nature of the theatres' entertainments were never simple. The many reports of docile and enthusiastic working-class audiences enjoying Shakespeare (xiv, for example) may need to be treated with circumspection, but comparisons were commonly made between working-class and fashionable audiences – often to the detriment of the latter (nos. vii, xi, xiii, xxii). The theatres addressing themselves specifically to working-class aspirations and treating their audience with respect are one of the more attractive features of Victorian cultural life, but they were hardly centres of political radicalism. It was often remarked that working-class audiences were more likely than others to insist on the strict observance of conventional morality and decorous behaviour in plays. Phelps's Sadler's Wells was invoked as a byword for earnest, 'legitimate' popular theatre. In *London, a Pilgrimage* (1872) Blanchard Jerrold observed that 'The Stage has not progressed with the spread of education – that is not in fashionable parts of London' and that the drama is spreading through the poorer and less educated portions of society, who always crowd to the theatres where classic or sterling modern drama is played' (p. 173). A reviewer in the *Spectator* mentioned the number of copies of the play to be seen in the audience at Sadler's Wells, where each member of the audience, proud to have

Merthyr Theatre — — the Audience —

2 A working-class audience at *Macbeth* in a fit-up theatre from a *Graphic* report on the lock-out in South Wales, 6 March 1875. The theatre is 'a part of the market-place, roughly enclosed and roofed. The audience sit in semi-darkness, as there is but one gas-jet in addition to those which form the footlights.' The illustrations to this sympathetic report of the dispute show working-class people without caricature or condescension.

participated in saving the legitimate drama from destruction, was 'brought up in the faith that his sturdy grasp alone prevented the dire event from coming to pass' (4 September 1847). The appeal of Sadler's Wells and its imitators, like so much else in 'respectable' working-class culture, was populist rather than radical.

Macready's managements at Covent Garden (1839) and Drury Lane (1841–3), and the Matthews-Vestris regime at Covent Garden – ending with bankruptcy in 1855 – had been a costly last attempt to run these theatres as fashionable homes for 'the drama'. By the 1870s the two patent houses had become emblems of a class division in entertainment: Covent Garden was an opera house, and Drury Lane was known for its spectacular melodrama and pantomime. By the last decades of the century the Adelphi was the other customary home of strong melodrama, the Lyceum and (from 1897) Her Majesty's were providing sophisticated, lavishly produced 'legitimate' drama, and social comedy had a number of appropriately intimate homes. The Gaiety was where John Hollingshead tended 'the sacred lamp of burlesque', which was beginning its metamorphosis into musical comedy. The Savoy continued to offer the Gilbert and Sullivan pieces and similarly conceived works of 'artistic' light opera.

In the provinces there were now many large, well-appointed theatres whose audiences were attracted by a variety of touring companies rather than one permanent, resident troupe. Some provincial managers (Charles Calvert in Manchester, for example) established their reputation by mounting expensive 'revivals' of Shakespeare and asserting their centrality in the culture of the city. The tastefully decorated auditoria and front-of-house decorations and amenities offered middle-class playgoers the standards of comfort they were beginning to demand in other public places – especially in the newly popular restaurants. The seaside resorts had their theatres – often kursaals, winter gardens and other hybrids – and adapted to a higher level of consumer spending. With income tax around one shilling in the pound, the decades before the Great War were the heyday of the middle classes, with a corresponding rise in the living standards expected by the more affluent among the working class. The social division among audiences in theatres remained, and the facilities offered to patrons of different parts of the house were varied accordingly, but even music-hall, the distinctively working-class entertainment, was becoming 'gentrified'.

The Gallery 'Gods', 1830s

[James Grant's account of London life, *The Great Metropolis* (1837), includes this description of the gallery on 'Box-night' (i.e., Boxing Night, 26 December, when Christmas gratuities have been distributed).]

The pantomimes are a great source of attraction to young people; and as they are always brought out on 'Box-night,' when there is something in the pockets of the lower classes, the galleries of the various theatres are, on those occasions crowded to suffocation; and a more motley appearance was never assuredly presented than that which then graces the various galleries. The railing on the front seat exhibits a goodly array of all sorts of second-hand apparel. It would do the heart of a Jew old clothesman good to see it. It has the appearance of a pawnbroker's shop: bonnets broken in the crown, or without any crown at all; caps 'all tattered and torn'; shawls which were once of various hues, but which are now, for want of the application of a little soap, all pretty much of one colour; hats, coats, waistcoats, &c., &c., are all fastened to the railing along the whole front of the upper gallery. Then there are the 'gods' themselves – the name by which they have always been called since Garrick delivered one of his celebrated prologues,[1] in which, when apostrophizing that portion of the audience in the immediate neighbourhood of the ceiling, he exclaimed,

> And you, ye gods! – to merit never blind –
> A fellow-feeling makes us wondrous kind.

A very large proportion of 'the deities' on such occasions consists of chimney-sweep apprentices, who are by far, considering their limited means, the most liberal patronizers of the drama. A considerable number of their sootships are always to be seen in the front seats, where their black frontispieces oddly contrast with their tusks and the whites of their eyes, which are displayed to great advantage on such occasions. There is also a fair sprinkling of bakers' apprentices on box-night, who are sure to be seen sitting cheek-by-jowl with the youthful knights of the soot-brush. A large number of those who people the upper regions of the house appear in their shirt-sleeves: their coats are doffed because the heat of the place has become intolerable. Others are swearing and fighting; while cries of 'turn him out!' 'turn him out!' 'order, order!' 'silence there!' assail your ears from all quarters. It were impossible, indeed, to witness a more uproarious scene than that invariably exhibited on such occasions. The unlimited play which the 'divinities' give their lungs on these nights often, in fact, has the effect of drowning the voices of the actors on the stage. The truth is, that they claim a prescriptive right to be as noisy as they please on box-night, and all efforts to preserve order would be perfectly useless.

Has the reader ever seen a piece, on its first production, condemned? or, to use theatrical phraseology, 'damned', – in any of the larger establishments? No one who has not witnessed such a scene can form any idea of it. The audience, on such occasions, are in a perfect hubbub. Mr O'Connell,[2] even when in his most violent and most forcible moods, never produced so much 'agitation' in any assemblage of the 'finest pisantry in the world', as is exhibited in Drury Lane, or Covent Garden, when a new piece is undergoing the process of utter 'damnation'. The great majority of the audience seem to make the matter a personal one. They feel as if some insult had been offered to them individually by the luckless wight of an author, and the scarcely less unfortunate proprietor of the theatre. They will in such cases rise from their seats, and express their indignation, not only in loud hisses, groans, &c., but by the most violent gestures.

NOTES

1 *Garrick . . . prologues* Garrick's prologue for 10 June 1776, 'the last time of his performing', includes the lines 'To you, ye Gods: I make my last appeal; / You have the right to judge, as well as feel' (*Poetical Works*, 1785, II, 326). OED's earliest example of the usage is from 1752.

2 *Mr O'Connell* Daniel O'Connell (1775–1847), Irish politician and orator.

Theatres and neighbourhoods, 1832

[In the evidence given before the Parliamentary Select Committee on Dramatic Literature in 1832, much of what passed for evidence on the behaviour of audiences in the different kinds of theatre was little more than opinion. John Payne Collier, scholar, historian of the theatre and the Lord Chamberlain's Examiner of Plays (and thus, effectively, a censor) was an enthusiast for the drama, anxious to defend the threat to its claims as an art that might come from too liberally extending the right to play the 'legitimate' repertoire.]

423. Do you think it would be injurious to the public morals if plays were allowed to be acted on Wednesdays and Fridays in Lent, or on the 30th of January? – That entirely depends on the respect which people feel for Lent.

424. Do you think it would be repulsive to the public feeling? – Not generally; but at the same time I am well persuaded that it would be employed as a handle by a certain part of the public to attract odium to the theatres.

425. Does it attract odium at the Coburg or the other theatres out of the jurisdiction of the Lord Chamberlain, for they act every night? – Except in Passion week; I believe they did not then.

426. But on Wednesdays and Fridays during Lent? – I believe they did; but I think the theatres on that side of the water [i.e. south of the Thames] are so lawless that people are not accustomed to view them with the same eyes as those with which they look at the proceedings of the other theatres.

427. The inhabitants on that side of the water you consider are less civilized? – I never resided on that side of the water, nor am I acquainted with many people who live there; therefore I am not competent to decide. If the inhabitants of that side of the water are more ignorant and worse informed than on this side, the chance is they would be more bigoted.

428. But on the other side of Oxford-street, in Tottenham-street,* they play during Lent, they play there on Wednesdays and Fridays during Lent. Do you believe public odium has been directed against the theatre on this account, or are the people less

religious than they would otherwise be? – I am not competent to judge whether it is more or less; but as a fact I can say, that so little odium do I suppose it has excited, that it never reached me that they did perform there.

429. Do you suppose what passes between the walls of a metropolitan theatre is a complete proof of the state of morals of the people? – Not at all, for it is notorious that the morals in the neighbourhood of the theatres are always inferior to other parts of the town.

430. But if there is no complaint in Marylebone against that theatre for playing in Lent, why should there be in other places? – I am to be understood as not stating my own opinion, for personally I should feel no objection to the theatres being open on Wednesdays and Fridays during Lent, or perhaps in Passion-week either, but I only think it would give the enemies of theatrical representation a handle against theatres which they do not at present possess.

431. Who do you consider enemies to them? – That class of persons who are usually considered Methodists; in fact the descendants in opinion of the original puritans, who have been enemies to dramatic representations from all time during which we have any records of the existence of theatres.

NOTE

* *on the other side of Oxford street, in Tottenham Street* A site occupied by a succession of theatres from 1772; in 1865 the Bancrofts refurbished the existing theatre (known as the 'Dust-Hole') and reopened it as the Prince of Wales's.

'A tremendous row' at the Surrey, 1837

[The comic singer and amateur reviewer Charles Rice describes a disturbance at the Surrey Theatre on 12 August 1837. The first piece on the bill was Weber's opera *Der Freischütz* ('curtailed, botched, and all but spoiled') which passed without incident. Then followed *The Quaker* by Charles Dibdin the elder, and Auber's *Gustavus the Third; or, the Masked Ball*. The editors of Rice's manuscript note that the unusual costumes referred to in the last paragraph can be accounted for by the following announcement: 'A limited number of gentlemen from the Boxes may be admitted to join the Masquerade at the termination of the Second Act, upon application to the Box-Keeper, by providing themselves with Dominos or Character Dresses.' Rice's spelling and punctuation are retained. From *The London Theatre in the Eighteen-Thirties*, edited by Arthur Colby Sprague and Bertram Shuttleworth (1950).]

The Quaker was admirably begun, and an encore was given to Wilson's (Lubin) 'Women are will o' the wisps', and H. Phillips's (Steady) 'The lads of the village', both of which were complete gems. Just as Solomon (W. Smith) was protesting his love to Floretta (Mrs Fitzwilliam) commenced the disturbance I have hinted at, occasioned in the first instance by some boy amongst the Olympians, who render'd himself conspicuously disagreeable, being taken out by the officer, and a determination on the part of the gallery assembly that no performance should go on till the said boy should be reinstated and the officer expunged from the gallery. The row continued for, I dare say, twenty minutes, when at last Mr R. Honner, who was at the wing superintending, came forward, in obedience to the calling and beckoning of the audience, to stand and try to speak for nearly as long a period as the uproar had already occupied. At length silence was proclaimed by everybody, obeyed by nobody for some time, and at last gained by everybody but those who originally vocally desired it, and Mr Honner spoke: he said he had no doubt the officers had used all necessary forbearance before they put the boy out (hissing from the gallery) and if they would keep quiet the police should in no wise interfere; to this, a bare repetition of what they before disapproved, the gods responded with a hearty cheer, and *The Quaker* recommenced. But the officers being still at their posts in the gallery, the row was now renewed, and the performance was again suspended for a few minutes, but Mr Honner waving his hand to the leader of the orchestral band, the quintette which concludes the first act was performed in dumb show, and the drop curtain fell.

Quiet was now the order of the night till the curtain again drew up, when hissing, yelling, and all other sounds musical, appertaining to the human, demoniac, canine and feline species, were put in full force, and almost as suddenly received a check by the appearance on the scene of Mr Davidge, when the torrent of disapprobationary music was changed to a tremendous round of applause to welcome the old acquaintance, which again subsided in partial quietude. His first question was to ask the cause of their disapprobation? – which was answered thus by a would-be orator who occupied the front seat in the gallery: – 'Your officers have took a boy out for nothing, and we want him back again'; to which Mr Davidge replied, he was at any time averse to coercive measures; the audience must be aware that one individual in that gallery was enough to disturb a whole assembly; such an individual was the boy removed; were the cause of disturbance in his house gentle or simple* such should always be his remedy, and all the disturbance and clamour of the gallery company could not alter his determination; the boy should not be allowed to re-enter! He desired the audience to consider what an arduous duty is that of a manager; he was the caterer for their amusement, and he would be the guardian of their comforts; the officers had been acting under his direction; he wanted to know whether in such directions he was or was not justified; and he begged of the ladies and gentlemen to bear in mind that if any disapprobation was due, it was to him, and not to the ladies and gentlemen in the farce, that it should be shown, and he therefore hoped they would allow the piece to proceed; he threw himself on the protection of the respectable portion of the audience; whilst he was proprietor of this or any similar establishment, he would be master, the boy should not be readmitted!

This manly address was followed by great cheering, and waving of hats and handkerchiefs, and the farce concluded amidst great applause and an encore to Mrs Fitzwilliam's song 'I wish I was a lady!' *Gustavus the Third* was only remarkable for the performance of Gustavus by Lyon, instead of Yates, whose absence was unaccounted for, and the appearance about the Swedish court of several senators &c. with complete suits of modern black, whilst others figured still more characteristically in white four and ninepenny silk hats, and strapped duck trousers; but as these were not praiseworthy novelties, the present notice is at an end, since censure is all that remains, and that is no pleasant subject for the lengthening of this or any other critique. The house was so crammed last night, as to leave no view of the stage come-at-able after the end of *Der Freischütz* even in the boxes.

NOTE

*   *gentle or simple*   Of high or low rank.

iv

Enthusiasm for the play

[From *The Times*, 8 January 1842.]

A circumstance, not unworthy of record, occurred on the revival of *The Gamester* at Drury-Lane Theatre on Wednesday last. The gallery-doors were besieged by a considerable crowd at an early hour. At the shilling gallery the pressure was so great that the doors were actually forced open before the money-takers were at their posts. A number of persons entered and took possession of the seats. Expulsion would have been difficult, if not impossible; but, application being made, the money was honourably and very readily paid in every instance, the rush having been occasioned by a real interest in the performance of the drama.

Booth theatres, 1840s

[W.E. Adams, author of *Memoirs of a Social Atom* (1903), was born in Cheltenham in 1832: after training as a printer he became a journalist.]

Early in my apprentice days I came under the influence of the drama. It was the travelling, not the regular drama. I was entitled to threepence a week pocket money. Every Saturday night in the season, as I left work at twelve o'clock, I used to climb up a spout to read by the light of a street lamp the names of the plays that were to be performed the following week. It would, of course, have been intolerably tantalizing if, with the playbills about the town, I had had to wait till Saturday to learn the fare for Monday. If I was impatient to see the name of the play, it need not be said that I was still more impatient to see the play itself. Monday was my only night for the drama. Having started work at midnight on the Sunday, I was not required on the Monday to continue work till eight o'clock, the usual hour of happy release on the other days of the week. So I was always in good time for the rise of the curtain. Luckily for me, with my small allowance of coppers, there were no early doors[1] then.

The drama, as I have said, was not the regular drama. There had been no regular drama since the regular theatre had been burnt down. The ruins of the burnt building, blocked up with boards, were still to be seen in another part of the town. I had promised in my indentures that I would not 'haunt taverns or playhouses'. But a booth was not a playhouse. As booths were not mentioned in the indentures, I assumed that I was quite at liberty to haunt *them*. Anyhow, I did haunt them as often as they came round. The best known of these enterprises was Hurd's. It had its regular circuit and it came round at regular intervals. Hurd's Theatre was as famous in Gloucestershire as Prince Miller's in Scotland or Billy Purvis's in Northumberland. The booth was set up in an inn yard – the Nag's Head or the King's Arms. An outside show always drew a big crowd. It was the custom of the performers – comedians, tragedians, acrobats, and ballet dancers – to parade up and down an open platform, dressed in all their stage finery, with the view of inducing the spectators to walk up and see the wonders to be presented within. The outside show was sometimes supplemented by the offer of prizes for the boys who, stripped to the waist and with hands tied behind their backs, could soonest eat the treacle rolls that were suspended from a rope across the platform. This was before the days of paraffin lamps. The platform was illuminated by great pans of blazing grease, which had now and then to be stirred up with an iron rod, and which, when thus stirred up, threw out almost as much black smoke as it did flame, accompanied by a penetrating and suffocating stench that set the poor actors and actresses a-coughing. The inside arrangements were just as primitive as those outside. A couple of hoops, filled with sconces for eight or ten tallow candles, and hung from the roof of the booth, afforded all the light that was thrown upon the stage. As the performances proceeded, the light grew more and more dim, till the audience, scarcely able to discern one actor from another, raised loud cries of 'Snuff the candles.' Then an old super would lower the hoops by means of a piece of twine, doing what was required, sometimes with his fingers and sometimes with a pair of snuffers, and the next act of the drama could be better seen. Of course, if any of the audience stood or sat under the 'chandeliers', they ran a pretty good chance of getting their best clothes soiled and spoiled with droppings from the 'long sixes'[2] above them.

The actors and actresses who formed the company of that canvas booth in an inn yard were veritable heroes and heroines to the lads and lasses who watched and wondered in the back seats. Tommy Hurd was the leading comedian. Never did he speak without setting the house in a roar. What Tommy had said and what Tommy had done in the farce we had seen on Monday lasted me and my companions for delightful conversation the whole of the week afterwards. But the tragedian and his wife – Mr and Mrs Maclean – were held by us in special awe and reverence. If we met them in the street, as we often did, we followed them at a respectful distance, admiring every strut and movement. If they looked at us, we were proud as Punches; if they had spoken to us, it would have been heaven; if they had shaken us by the hand or patted us on the head, we should have gone clean crazy . . .

NOTES

1   *early doors*   The practice of granting early admission, at a slightly higher price, to the cheaper, unreserved seats.

2   *long sixes*   Candles (costing sixpence each).

Complaints about 'fees' (and other matters) in 1847

[A letter to the editor, printed under the title 'Imposition and Insult at Theatres,' in *The Theatrical Times*, August 1847. This makes clear the manner in which front-of-house services – as well as refreshments – were contracted out. Benjamin Webster (1797–1882) was lessee of the Haymarket for sixteen years, beginning in 1837.]

Sir, – I wish to say a few words about a system that needs reform; and request your attention for a minute. I met a gentleman the other day who said that some time ago he went into the Haymarket theatre at half price¹, and was shown into the dress boxes. The box-keeper looked at him, and the gentleman did not give him the customary fee. Whereupon the functionary asked him to come out, told him those seats were engaged, and that there was room up stairs! – I think in justice to the public, if such things are allowed, Mr Webster ought to add in his playbill that if the box-keeper is not given a shilling for shewing people to their seats they will be insulted and told to go up stairs. Such conduct is disgraceful in the extreme. A poor critic, who receives little or nothing for his articles, and who does not like the heat and (if a lady be with him) the *society* of the other boxes, is exposed to the insolence of a fellow who if he had his deserts would be well caned for his pains. But the culpability is the manager's, who allows such villainous proceedings in his theatre. If the law were enforced this establishment would be put down as a public nuisance. It is infested by the most disreputable characters, and very often I must say the pieces produced are immoral and indecent. *Mr Peter Piper* to wit. I have expressed myself warmly, but I am sure that all honourable minds will agree with me that the public should withold its countenance from a place where such proceedings are permitted.

A POOR REPORTER

[The editor comments:]

We must add a few words to the above communication. With respect to the box-keeper, his conduct was impertinent, but as he pays £500 a year for his situation, what is the poor devil to do? We think that the public would prefer giving an extra shilling for admission to putting it into the hand of the box-keeper, if it is quite indispensable that a manager should make money otherwise than by the legitimate mode of charging a reasonable sum for a good entertainment. But what can be expected from the generality of Lessees? There is hardly a gentleman among them, and they care only for their pockets. It is a pity we have not a man like Goethe at Weimar to superintend a theatre. If Sir Edward B. Lytton[2] had the St James's or the Haymarket and acted as the illustrious author of *Faust*[3] did, everything, no doubt, would be well and liberally conducted.

NOTES

1   at half-price   i.e. halfway through the programme (often set at 9 p.m.).

2   *Sir Edward B. Lytton*   (1803–73) Novelist and dramatist, friend of Macready, and active in the movement for authors' rights.

3   *the illustrious author of* Faust   Refers to Goethe's superintendence of the theatre in Weimar, from 1775 to 1783.

vii

Working-class theatres, c.1850

[The first number of *Household Words*, 30 March 1850, included an article on 'the Amusements of the People' in which the editor, Charles Dickens, insisted that the leisure habits of the working class should be viewed with sympathetic understanding, that the theatre was central to its amusements, and that 'it would be a very doubtful benefit to society' if the 'innate love for dramatic entertainment' could be 'rooted out'. The first article is about the theatrical tastes of 'Joe Whelks' and includes this sympathetic description of the Victoria Theatre (now the Old Vic) in New Cut.]

A few weeks ago, we went to one of Mr Whelks's favourite Theatres, to see an attractive Melo-Drama called *May-Morning, or the Mystery of 1715, and the Murder!* We had an idea that the former of these titles might refer to the month in which either the Mystery or the Murder happened, but we found it to be the name of the heroine, the pride of Keswick Vale; who was 'called May Morning' (after a custom among the English Peasantry) 'from her bright eyes and merry laugh'. Of this young lady, it may be observed, in passing, that she subsequently sustained every possible calamity of human existence, in a white muslin gown with blue tucks; and that she did every conceivable and inconceivable thing with a pistol, that could anyhow be effected by that description of fire-arms.

The Theatre was extremely full. The prices of admission were, to the boxes, a shilling; to the pit, sixpence; to the gallery, threepence. The gallery was of enormous dimensions . . . and overflowing with occupants. It required no close observation of the attentive faces, rising one above another, to the very door in the roof, and squeezed and jammed in regardless of all discomforts, even there, to impress a stranger with a sense of its being highly desirable to lose no possible chance of effecting any mental improvement in that great audience.

The company in the pit were not very clean or sweet-savoured, but there were some good-humoured young mechanics among them, with their wives. These were generally accompanied by 'the baby', insomuch that the pit was a perfect nursery. No effect made on the stage was so curious, as the looking down on the quiet faces of these babies fast asleep, after looking up at the staring sea of heads in the gallery. There were a good many cold fried soles in the pit, besides; and a variety of flat stone bottles, of all portable sizes.

The audience in the boxes was of much the same character (babies and fish excepted) as the audience in the pit. A private in the Foot Guards sat in the next box; and a personage who wore pins on his coat instead of buttons, and was in such a damp habit of living as to be quite mouldy, was our nearest neighbour. In several parts of the house we noticed some young pickpockets of our acquaintance; but as they were evidently there as private individuals, and not in their public capacity, we were little disturbed by their presence. For we consider the hours of idleness passed by this class of society as so much gain to society at large, and we do not join in a whimsical sort of lamentation that is generally made over them, when they are found to be unoccupied.

[The second article, on 13 April 1850, describes a visit to a 'Saloon' on a Monday evening, 'Monday being a great holiday night with Mr Whelks and his friends'. Dickens explains that 'the Saloon in question' (in fact the Royal Standard Theatre) is the largest establishment of its kind in London, is situated in Shoreditch and is known as 'The People's Theatre'.]

The prices of admission are, to the boxes, a shilling; to the pit, sixpence; to the lower gallery, fourpence; to the upper gallery and back seats, threepence. There is no half-price. The opening piece on this occasion was described in the bills as 'the greatest hit of the season, the grand new legendary and traditionary drama, combining supernatural agencies with historical facts, and identifying extraordinary superhuman causes with material, terrific, and powerful effects.' All the Queen's horses and all the Queen's men could not have drawn Mr Whelks into the place like this description. Strengthened by lithographic representations of the principal superhuman causes, combined with the most popular of the material, terrific, and powerful effects, it became irresistible. Consequently, we had already failed, once, in finding six square inches of room within the walls, to stand upon; and when we now paid our money for a little stage box, like a dry shower-bath, we did so in the midst of a stream of people who persisted in paying theirs for other parts of the house in despite of the representations of the Money-taker that it was 'very full, everywhere'.

The outer avenues and passages of the People's Theatre bore abundant testimony to the fact of its being frequented by very dirty people. Within, the atmosphere was far from odoriferous. The place was crammed to excess, in all parts. Among the audience were a large number of boys and youths, and a great many very young girls grown into bold women before they had well ceased to be children. These last were the worst features of the whole crowd, and were more prominent there than in any other sort of public assembly that we know of, except at a public execution. There was no drink supplied, beyond the contents of the porter-can (magnified in its dimensions, perhaps), which may be usually seen traversing the galleries of the largest Theatres as well as the least, and which was here seen everywhere. Huge ham-sandwiches, piled on trays like deals in a timber-yard. were handed about for sale to the hungry, and there was no stint of oranges, cakes, brandy-balls, or other similar refreshments. The Theatre was capacious, with a very large capable stage, well-lighted, well appointed, and managed in a businesslike, orderly manner in all respects; the performances had begun so early as a quarter past six, and had been then in progress for three-quarters of an hour.

It was apparent here, as in the theatre we had previously visited, that one of the reasons of its great attraction was its being directly addressed to the common people, in the provision made for their seeing and hearing. Instead of being put away in a dark gap in the roof of an immense building, as in our once National Theatres [i.e., Covent Garden and Drury Lane], they were here in possession of eligible points of view, and thoroughly able to take in the whole performance. Instead of being at a great disadvantage in comparison with the mass of the audience, they were here *the* audience, for whose accommodation the place was made. We believe this to be one great cause of the success of these speculations. In whatever way the common people are addressed, whether in churches, chapels, schools, lecture-rooms, or theatres, to be successfully addressed they must be directly appealed to. No matter how good the feast, they will not come to it on mere sufferance. If on looking round us, we find that the only things plainly and personally addressed to them from quack medicines upwards, be bad or very defective things, – so much the worse for them and for all of us, and so much the more unjust and absurd the system which has haughtily abandoned a strong ground to such occupation.

[On 4 October 1851, Dickens collaborated with R.H. Horne in an article on the transformation of Sadler's Wells Theatre into a home for the 'legitimate' drama. In this account the behaviour of the 'unreformed' audience is no longer accepted as spirited and harmless, but seems potentially and actually criminal. For the purposes of the article, the success of Phelps's management consists in the expulsion of the ruffians, leaving Sadler's Wells free to pursue its high-minded policies of respectable repertoire and ensemble playing.]

Among other good places of sound rational amusement, we hold that a well-conducted Theatre is a good place in which to learn good things. And we wish to show what an intelligent and resolute man may do, to establish a good Theatre in most unpromising soil, and to reclaim one of the lowest of all possible audiences.

Seven or eight years ago, Sadler's Wells Theatre, in London, was in the condition of being entirely delivered over to as ruffianly an audience as London could shake together. Without, the Theatre, by night, was like the worst part of the worst kind of Fair in the worst kind of town. Within, it was a bear-garden, resounding with foul language, oaths, catcalls, shrieks, yells, blasphemy, obscenity, – a truly diabolical clamour. Fights took place anywhere, at any period of the performance. The audience were of course directly addressed in the entertainments. An improving melo-drama, called *Barrington the Pickpocket*, being then extremely popular at another similar Theatre, a powerful counter-attraction, happily entitled *Jack Ketch*, was produced here, and received with great approbation. It was in the contemplation of the Management to add the physical stimulus of a pint of porter to the moral refreshments offered to every purchaser of a pit ticket, when the Management collapsed and the Theatre shut up.

At this crisis of the career of Mr Ketch and his pupils, Mr Phelps, a gentleman then favourably known to the London public as a tragic actor, first at the Haymarket Theatre under the Management of Mr Webster,[1] and afterwards at the two great Theatres of Covent Garden and Drury Lane, when Mr Macready made them a source of intellectual delight to the whole town (persons of fashion excepted), conceived the desperate idea of changing the character of the dramatic entertainments presented at this den, from the lowest to the highest, and of utterly changing with it the character of the audience. Associating with himself, in this perilous enterprise, two partners: of whom one (for a time) was Mrs Warner,[2] a lady of considerable reputation on the stage; the other, Mr Greenwood,[3] a 'gentleman of business knowledge and habits': he took the Theatre, and went to work.

On the opening night, the scene of Mr Ketch's triumphs – which may be presumed not to have been confined to that small sphere, but to have extended, in the glory of his pupils, beyond the height of the Old Bailey to the harbour of Norfolk Island[4] – was densely crammed with the old stock. The play was *Macbeth*. It was performed amidst the usual hideous medley of fights, foul language, catcalls, shrieks, yells, oaths, blasphemy, obscenity, apples, oranges, nuts, biscuits, ginger-beer, porter, and pipes – not that there was any particular objection to the Play, but that the audience were, on the whole, in a condition of mind, generally requiring such utterance. Pipes of all lengths were at work in the gallery; several were displayed in the pit. Cans of beer, each with a pint measure to drink from (for the convenience of gentlemen

3 Sadler's Wells Theatre, 1845: playbill for performances of *The Winter's Tale*, showing prices of 2s., 1s. and 6d. with half price at 9 o'clock.

who had neglected the precaution of bringing their own pots in their bundles), were carried through the dense crowd at all stages of the tragedy. Sickly children in arms were squeezed out of shape, in all parts of the house. Fish was fried at the entrance doors. Barricades of oyster-shells encumbered the pavement. Expectant half-price visitors to the gallery, howled defiant impatience up the stairs, and danced a sort of Carmagnole[5] all round the building.

[Phelps dealt with these objectionable elements one by one, and with some success.]

But the most intolerable defilement of the place remained. The outrageous language was unchecked; and while that lasted, any effectual purification of the audience and establishment of decency, was impossible. Mr Phelps, not to be diverted from his object, routed out an old Act of Parliament, in which there was a clause visiting the use of bad language in any public place with a certain fine, on proof of the offence before a magistrate. This clause he caused to be printed in great placards, and posted up in various conspicuous parts of the Theatre. He also had it printed in small hand-bills. To every person who went into the gallery, one of these hand-bills was given with his pass-ticket. He was seriously warned that the Act would be enforced; and it *was* enforced with such rigour, that on several occasions Mr Phelps stopped the play to have an offender removed – on other occasions went into the gallery, with a cloak over his theatrical dress, to point out some other offender who had escaped the vigilance of the police – on all occasions kept his purpose, and his inflexible determination steadily to carry it, before the vagabonds with whom he had to deal – on no occasion showed them fear or favour. Within a month, the Jack Ketch party, thoroughly disheartened and amazed, gave in; and not an interruption was heard from the beginning to the end of a five act tragedy.

[Subsequently, Sadler's Wells was able to offer an exemplary repertoire of Shakespeare (1000 performances by spring, 1851) and other 'legitimate' plays.]

It is to be observed that these plays have not been droned through, in the old jog-trot dreary matter-of-course manner, but have been presented with the utmost care, with great intelligence, with an evidently sincere desire to understand and illustrate the beauties of the poem. The smallest character has been respectfully approached and studied; the smallest accessory has been well considered; every artist in his degree has been taught to adapt his part, in the complete effect, to all other parts uniting to make up the whole. The outlay has been very great; but, having always had a sensible purpose and a plain reason, has never missed its mark. The illusion of the scene has invariably been contrived in a most striking, picturesque, and ingenious manner. A completeness has been attained, which at twenty times the cost could never have been bought, if Mr Phelps were not a gentleman in spirit, and an accomplished and devoted student of his art.

[The audience in 1853 is described by the critic and educationalist Henry Morley, writing in *The Examiner*. From Henry Morley, *Journal of a London Playgoer, 1851–66*, ed. Michael R. Booth (1975).]

The *Midsummer Night's Dream* abounds in the most delicate passages of Shakespeare's verse; the Sadler's Wells pit has a keen enjoyment for them; and the pit and gallery were crowded to the farthest wall on Saturday night with a most earnest audience, among whom many a subdued hush arose, not during but just before, the delivery of the most charming passages. If the crowd at Drury Lane is a gross discredit to the public taste, the crowd at Sadler's Wells more than neutralizes any ill opinion that may on that score be formed of playgoers. The Sadler's Wells gallery, indeed, appeared not to be wholly unconscious of the contrast, for, when Bottom volunteered to roar high or roar low, a voice from the gallery desired to know whether he could 'roar like Brooke'.[6] Even the gallery at this theatre, however, resents an interruption, and the unexpected sally was not well received.

NOTES

1   *Mr Webster*   Benjamin Webster (1797–1873), actor and manager.
2   *Mrs Warner*   Mary Warner (1804–64), actress.
3   *Mr Greenwood*   Walter Greenwood (1806–79), lessee of Sadler's Wells, 1842–4; Phelps's partner, 1844–60.
4   *Norfolk Island*   Used as a penal colony until 1856.
5   *Carmagnole*   Frenetic dance popular with French revolutionists in the 1790s.
6   *Brooke*   Gustavus Vaughan Brooke (1818–66), tragedian.

The iniquity of 'fees': complaints in 1855 and 1872

[From *The Times*, 1 January 1855. Advance booking regularly involved payment of a fee, and patrons of the more expensive parts of the house were shown to their seats by a box-keeper. This usher was not employed directly by the management, and in the days of unnumbered seats he had a power that could be exploited.]

The gentleman who takes seats for his family at the play is still fined 1s. by the keeper of the places, and, if he be so rash as to take seats for more than six, he is fined 2s. for such conduct. The Olympic Theatre has, indeed, the peculiar distinction of levying more blackmail of this kind than its neighbours. The 2s. fine is inflicted at the Olympic, upon any one who pays money to the management for more seats than four, and is raised to a 3s. fine, if more than eight seats are taken, and so on in proportion. Nor is even a playbill supplied in return for this shameful tax, for the expectation is that the playbill may extort another silver contribution. Surely it cannot be to the interest of managers that playgoers should be exposed to treatment of this description. If the charge for admission is not high enough (it is 5s. for a moderate amusement at the Olympic, and 6s. for no amusement at all at the Princess's), by all means raise it; but let there be a fair and single charge, and no system of vexatious perquisites appended.

[On 14 January 1872 *The Era* reprinted five letters from *The Times* on the very same topic. A playgoer complained of being charged at the Olympic a booking fee of sixpence per ticket, and of proffering threepence but being asked sixpence for a playbill by the box-keeper – and the cloakroom fee was also sixpence! The manager of the theatre, W.H.Liston, replied apologetically, but the box-keeper was less conciliatory and insisted on his independence of the manager.]

Sir – As one of the box-keepers at the Olympic Theatre, you will, I hope, allow me to say that the charge for a playbill is not left entirely to the visitor, but a demand of 6d. is made by me providing a person should offer less. As I have to pay Mr Nugent £1 16s. per week and 6d. a dozen for bills, I cannot see my way clear how I could possibly charge the public less than 6d. for a programme – sometimes, voluntarily, I get more.

As I am not engaged by Mr Liston, I really am at a loss to understand why he should take upon himself to call me one of his subordinates, well knowing, at the same time, that Mr Nugent pays him £25 per week for the saloons and the privilege of supplying the visitors with programmes. If Managers would be contented with less rent from enterprising individuals, I have not the least doubt but what all playgoers would be able to get polite attention and cheap programmes; but, until then, it is folly to blame a poor box-keeper, who only tries to get back what he has invested, with a slight interest for his trouble and outlay.

[A letter from one Martin S. Skeffington pointed out further details – and abuses – of the system, which, he pointed out, would not be dealt with properly until 'fees' were abolished.]

To me it has always appeared a deliberate piece of dishonesty that the same playbill which is sold in the pit for 2d. should be vended in other parts of the house for 6d.; and who, having purchased a dress-circle ticket unnumbered, does not know and remember with disgust the halt of the attendant before he opens the door, and the suggestive holding out of the playbill, upon the amount given for which depends entirely his position for the rest of the evening?

ix

An audience for Ristori, 1856

[On July 11 1856 Henry Crabb Robinson went to see the Italian tragedienne Adelaide Ristori in Goldoni's *La Locanderia*. From *The London Theatre: Selections from the Diary of Henry Crabb Robinson*, ed. Eluned Brown (1966).]

. . . [I] accompanied Leach then to the Lyceum – not knowing that the *Pit* begins only under the front boxes – All the rest being filled with Chairs at 20s. – I sat in a 5s. Chair behind in the dark, – I could hear nothing – And I had no pleasure – Madame Ristori in the comedy expressed only the cunning and contrivance of a lodging house keeper. She acted with spirit And there was applause from the Spectators *behind* but the fashionables before me manifested very little enjoyment – I suspect little was given – in fact with a *front seat* and a previous knowledge of the play I would willingly give a pound to see her in tragedy – her face is Jewish And through an Opera glass, the eyes of all the performers seemed large and dark – though I had no pleasure yet I am unwilling to suppose I could not have.

x

Improving the playhouses, 1866

[Henry Morley, in the preface to his collection of dramatic criticism, *Journal of a London Playgoer, 1851–1866*, suggested that the spread of literacy made it imperative that the theatre should compete with the novel, which could be read in comfort. Morley's complaints reflect conditions in theatres before strict fire regulations (prompted by such disasters as those at Liverpool in 1878 and Exeter in 1887).]

The play, if, after its kind, as good as the novel and well acted, gives a greater pleasure. But is it a pleasure so much greater as to tempt people away from their home comforts after the labours of the day, induce them to submit to the trouble of a journey to and from the theatre, and sit there during four, or sometimes five hours, bound to one allotted seat? The changes to which this question points have almost all been recognized during the past fifteen years, and for even so much progress we have reason to be thankful. One theatre after another has lost its old aspect of discomfort before the curtain; and petty exactions that interfere with perfect rest of mind are gradually disappearing, though they are not yet altogether gone. The payment for a seat should be made to secure, within the theatre, every service necessary to the right enjoyment of it. Not only the seats but the approaches to them should be easy. Seats in the pit should be cushioned, backed, and not overcrowded; in the boxes and stalls, always comfortable chairs. Desire to reap quickly the fruit of every success still tempts nearly all managers to crowd their seats together, and grudge lines of open space for movement to and fro. They crowd, if they can, with extra chairs, or sell as 'standing-room' even the few narrow pathways which they are compelled unwillingly to leave. In this they are not just to their public, and I believe also that they are less kind to themselves than the state of their treasury on any single night might lead them to suppose. First catch your customer, then truss him, and stew him four hours in a hot closet, is a recipe that involves some risk of at least not catching your rational customer a second time.

They eventually got it right and realised it was the surroundings that were objected to so cleaned up the theatres so the audience felt clean theatre = clean plays, even though ones such as Shakespeare contained obscenities

xi

An explorer ventures to the 'minor theatres' in the 1860s

[T.W. Erle's *Letters from a Theatrical Scene-Painter* (1880) offers 'Sketches of the Minor Theatres of London as they were Twenty Years Ago'. The following extracts comment directly on audience behaviour and illustrate vividly the author's sense that in visiting these theatres he was travelling 'beyond the pale of civilization' to a hostile and alien community.]

[Preface]
While extracting amusement, but in no ill-natured spirit, from some of the doings at minor theatres, the Author wishes in justice to them to say, that even the humblest of those places compared very favourably, and greatly to their credit, with the more pretentious houses, in point of the regard which was shown for propriety. Such may still be the case. For, taking, for example, Her Majesty's and Covent Garden in their characters of theatres of the highest class of all, it may fairly be laid to their charge that

the subject matter of (for instance) *Rigoletto*, and that of the *Traviata*, is open to exception, as are also, on grounds of another kind, scenes such as the cemetery dance in *Roberto*, and that of the display which is sometimes made of six coffins on the stage in the last act of *Lucrezia*. And in what terms can the quality of *Formosa*, a stock piece at Drury Lane, be described?

As for the feeling and demeanour of the high-class and low-class audiences respectively, the tempest of applause which invariably hastened to drown the conclusion of the time-honoured sentiment 'The man who would insult defenceless woman – ' used to be a more comfortable thing to note than the proceedings, with reference to some of the humbler feminine persons on the stage, of the gilded youth which filled the stalls at the West End.

Also, what are, or were commonly known as 'leg-pieces' (a term hardly requiring interpretation for even the most obtuse perceptions), with their lean allowance of drapery, would not have been at all to the taste of a Hoxton audience.

The truth is, that Mile End grows as strong a crop of good fellows, in their own way, and of well-disposed women, as Belgravia does; and a full and fair comparison might possibly disclose the fact, that the amusements of the classes which ought to be the promoters of good taste, propriety, and of the wholesome forms of enjoyment, are not, in every particular, so very much more admirable than those of their humbler neighbours after all.

[The Royal Effingham Theatre, Whitechapel]
An expedition into the partially-explored districts of Whitechapel is so serious an undertaking, that it may not be amiss to add a few details of its costs and difficulties, for the use of anyone who may happen to have an enterprise of the kind in contemplation. What with the cab-fare thither, and the cost of a disinfectant, with which prudence imperatively demands that you should be furnished, and the loss of half the value of your watch and purse (this estimate may be taken, since it is about an even chance that you are pickpocketed), the expense of a sixpenny stall at the R. E. comes altogether to much about the same figure as that of the best box at the opera. The atmosphere is very trying, the house forming a sort of *eccalabeon* [sic],[1] where 'hatching by steam' might be attempted under conditions eminently favourable to the success of the experiment. The bad quality of the tobacco smoked, and the preponderance of the Jewish element in the audience, render *Eau de Cologne* indispensable. It will be necessary to take

refreshments with you if you are likely to want any, since the staple commodity of the R.E. commissariat is pork pie. Hence it is to be feared that the Jews who so freely partake of it are renegades, unless indeed the alternative explanation be accepted, that in the 'pork' may be descried a solution of the enigma as to what becomes of the deceased cab horses and costermongers' donkeys of the metropolis. The pies in question are of a violently adipose character, and given to glisten in a manner which is apt to overwhelm the intending consumer with consternation and discomfiture. Cabs are not always forthcoming so far beyond the pale of civilization, and to have to walk through a sort of perambulatory market of costermongers' carts, which fringe the pavements in that locality, is a rather formidable ordeal to encounter . . . .

[The Royal Britannia, Hoxton. Erle comments at length on the number of damp, squalling babies-in-arms in the audience, then turns to the gallery.]
Very different from the condition of the poor babies is that of the youths in the gallery, who are gifted with a flow of exuberant animal spirits which find a safety-valve in shrill whistlings, reminding one of Virgil's account of the storm,[2] where Aeolus lets loose the wind, and 'Una Eurusque Notusque ruunt,' etc. etc.

Since the temperature up in their sixpenny heaven is so high (there was a little fat boy up there who I thought would have been melted and had to be taken home in a galipot),[3] they find it 'cool and convanient' to sit without their coats. They evince, too, a noble independence of bearing and sentiment towards the swells in the body of the house (who are in this case the counter-skippers of Kingsland and Dalston)[4] by turning their backs to the chandelier, and sitting along the gallery rail like a row of sparrows on a telegraph wire. In this position they confront their friends in the back settlements, and exchange with them a light fusillade of *badinage*, principally couched in idiomatic expressions of remarkable vigour and terseness, which is sustained with much animation during the time that the curtain is down between the pieces.

NOTES

1   *eccalabeon*   The 'eccaleobion', a patented egg-hatching apparatus invented about 1839 (OED).

2 *Virgil's . . . storm* In Book I of the *Aeneid*: the quotation is from line 85: 'Eurus and Notus [the winds] rush together . . .'
3 *galipot* Small glazed earthenware vessel.
4 *the counter-skippers of Kingsland and Dalston* Shop-workers from the north-eastern suburbs.

xii

Theatres, music-halls and public morality, 1866

[The report of the Parliamentary Select Committee of 1866 on theatrical licences and regulations showed the concern of London theatrical managers working under the Lord Chamberlain's jurisdiction to protect their monopoly of dramatic entertainment and the legislature's anxiety to control public – specifically, working-class – leisure. An article in *The Economist* (15 September 1866) provides an independent overview of the issues. The theatrical managers objected to the fact that music-halls were governed by more lenient rules concerning the sale and consumption of refreshments (instancing particularly the audience's freedom to smoke during performances), and asserted that such behaviour was incompatible with the 'legitimate' drama for which the theatres claimed a monopoly. The article points out that in Shakespeare's day no such inhibitions existed. Having disposed of this 'theoretical' claim, it proceeds to discuss the wider issues at stake.]

That by allowing music-halls to compete with theatres you may be doing injury to the theatres, can be assumed with tolerable certainty. But is there any reason why the Legislature should show the vested rights of theatres any more partiality than it shows to gas companies or other speculators? The only question about a monopoly is how far it is necessary, not how far it will injure the monopolists to throw the thing open. If music-halls were immoral, if smoking increased the chance of fires, if the drama in a music-hall produced a worse moral effect than the same drama in a theatre, we could understand the arguments of actors and managers. But what are the facts on these points? Let us take the morality first. Mr Pownall, the chairman of the Middlesex Bench of Magistrates, tells us that having known London for many years, he finds a very great improvement in the state of the streets at night, and he attributes that, in great part, to the increase of places of public entertainment. He seems to think that these places withdraw vice from the streets and concentrate it, so that they diminish the temptations of vice to those who do not seek it. We admit that this would be a very slender reason in favour of music-halls, but the admissions of others enable us to draw a truer moral from Mr Pownall's experience. Sir Thomas Henry[1] says they have had very few complaints from music-halls at Bow Street, and he believes them to be well conducted. Sir Richard Mayne[2] says the same. Mr Norton,[3] who went to see the performances when the music-halls were brought before him, was very much pleased: 'I thought it was an imitation, somewhat similar to what I have seen in the tea-gardens of Germany, only it was an improvement on them, because in addition to the music and dancing they gave a simple story.' The class of frequenters, he said, consisted chiefly of artisans, 'and I am happy to say very much with their wives and children, sitting round those little tables and enjoying the performance.' Now if vice was concentrated in these music-halls this would hardly be the effect they produced on a police magistrate. And therefore one reflection is forced upon us very strongly, that much of our vice has arisen from want of sufficient amusement, and the same cause which has removed vice from the streets has done much for its diminution. Mr Norton particularly observes that the effect of amusements which a family can join in is on the whole beneficial. 'I think that the great evil which we have to contend with is drunkenness, and drunkenness generally arises in tap-rooms of public houses, where fathers of families meet together, as the upper classes do in club rooms, and there they drink in a private manner. Now, by taking them out into public places, their families go with them. In some districts, I have been very much shocked to see that the women get drunk in a larger proportion than the men; that has been very much caused by men going to those tap-rooms from their families, and leaving the wives at home. I think that taking their wives with them to places of amusement has very much led them to neglect the tap-rooms.' This is surely enough on the general question of morality. The object we have in extending the privileges of the music-halls is, however, closely bound up with that question. If the music-halls are allowed to give a higher class of performance, they will gradually elevate their present audiences. Mr Boucicault states that in New York smoking, eating, and drinking were allowed at Niblo's Garden;[4] 'by degrees they imported the drama; the drama abolished smoking, eating and drinking.' Here is a sufficient answer to Messrs Webster and Buckstone.[5]

But this is just the answer with which those gentlemen will be least contented. They are not quite clear about their own grievance; they have a very strong notion that their attractions are not sufficient. They tell us in one breath that the music-hall will take out the pith of their performance, and that this pith will be taken out so badly that no one will come to them to see the rest. They tell us that the music-halls would snap up the actors by giving them higher wages, and that no actor worth having looks to pecuniary profit. They say that barns are hot-beds of genius, because they are patronized by the gentry, but the frequenters of music-halls are very doubtful people. But while they are zealous in arguing that the state should interfere to keep up a school of actors, they never ask the State to interfere in the only way that has proved effectual. Schools of actors are kept up by the State in other countries because there are Court theatres and subventions. If it was necessary to do anything with a view to restoring the drama, why should we stop short of this? Why should we be content to keep up a monopoly which only satisfies, and hardly satisfies, those who enjoy it? All the unprofessional witnesses admit that the state of the drama is very low. They do not indeed think it will be improved by throwing it open to music-halls, but that is not the object of the inquiry. As one of the witnesses said, the great British drama is a fine phrase, but the great British public is more important. It is more essential that the British public should be improved and refined than that the stage traditions should be kept up, and that Hamlet should not utter his soliloquy before an audience consuming chops and kidneys.

As the Committee reports that the power of dramatic censorship vested in the Lord Chamberlain has acted well, and that it ought to be extended to other places of public entertainment, the great objection to public songs, on the score of grossness and immorality, may easily be obviated. But it is rather curious to notice how much modern audiences have acted as self-appointed censors, and how many things which the Lord Chamberlain has passed have offended the nicer ears of the public. Even the music-halls have been purified by public opinion, though their frequenters are 'very doubtful people'. In theatres, the taste of the audience is sometimes more nice than accurate. At the Haymarket, they hissed Goldsmith's familiar line,[6] 'came to scoff, remained to pray,' because they thought it was taken out of the Bible. Nor has the Lord Chamberlain always deprived spectators of an excuse for unreasoning censure. His objections have not been tyrannical, but they have often been frivolous. We read that *King Lear* was withdrawn from the stage during the illness of George the Third; that Scribe's *Verre d'Eau* was refused a licence out of respect to the memory of Queen Anne; and that *Ruy Blas* was forbidden until the queen, who was in love with the hero, was changed into a princess. These scruples may be over-delicate, but at all events they show the existence of true zeal for the public morality, and for the preservation of the tender ears of lady playgoers from anything which might shock them. May not music-halls be safely trusted to the same supervision?

NOTES

1   *Sir Thomas Henry*   (1807–76), chief magistrate at Bow Street.

2   *Sir Richard Mayne*   (1796–1868), Commissioner of the Metropolitan Police.

3   *Mr Norton*   The Hon. G.C. Norton, magistrate at Lambeth Police Court, gave evidence concerning the Canterbury Music Hall to the Select Committee.

4   *Niblo's Garden*   William Niblo's pleasure gardens at the corner of Broadway and Prince Street in New York; the last theatre on the site was demolished in 1895.

5   *Webster and Buckstone*   Benjamin Webster (1797–1882) was manager of the Haymarket from 1837 and the Adelphi from 1844; John Baldwin Buckstone (1802–79) ran the Haymarket, 1853–79. Both were members of the theatrical 'establishment'.

6   *Goldsmith's familiar line*   From 'The Deserted Village' (1770).

Among the gods, 1867

[In *Some Habits and Customs of the Working Classes* (1867) 'A Journeyman Engineer' offers a description of working-class life by one who is 'really a working man – a unit of the great unwashed'.]

The regular frequenters of the gallery may be divided into the roughs, the hypocrites or snobs, and the orderlies. Of these the roughs are the most numerous division; it consists of those who come to the theatre with unwashed faces and in ragged and dirty attire, who bring bottles of drink with them, who *will* smoke despite of the notice that 'smoking is strictly prohibited,' and that 'officers will be in attendance'; who favour the band with a stamping accompaniment, and take the most noisy part in applauding or giving 'the call' to the performers. The females of this class are generally accompanied by infants, who are sure to cry and make a disturbance at some interesting point in the performance. The snobs comprise those who will tell you that they prefer the gallery to any other part of the house, and that they would still go into it if the price of admission was as high as that charged for admission to the pit or boxes; nevertheless, they seem very ill at ease in the place of their choice, and shrink from the glance of the occupants of the pit and boxes. The snob, also, is of those who stand on the back seats, and while talking loudly among themselves, but *at* the other occupants of the gallery, are at great pains to inform you that they have merely come into the gallery for a 'spree', or 'just to see what kind of place it is', but who strangely enough are to be found there two or three nights a week, and are amongst the most deeply attentive portion of the audience. The orderlies are those who, while they admit that the gallery is the least comfortable, and it may be the least respectable part of the house, and that they would much rather be in the boxes, go into the gallery because it is the *cheapest* part of the house – because they can go into that part twice for the same amount of money that they would have to pay to go into any other part once . . .

That the celestials are often noisy, and are sometimes given to discharging nutshells, peas, orange-peel, and other annoying, though harmless missiles, at the heads of the devoted occupants of the 'regions below'; and that their 'chaff' often assumes an unpleasantly personal tone, previous to and during the intervals of the performance, is but too true. But as Falstaff was not only witty himself, but the cause of wit in others, so the celestials, during the progress of the performance, are not only orderly themselves, but the cause of order in others. For instance, when those two stupid-looking and more than half-drunken 'swells,' who have come into the boxes at half-price time, begin to annoy the audience by talking and laughing in a very loud tone, and making grimaces at and trying to interrupt the actresses, is it not the gods who bring them to order? The scornful looks and indignant hushes from the pit and boxes have no effect upon them, but when, at the end of the scene, the gods give loud utterance to their well-known war-cry, 'turn them out,' the effect is instantly apparent. The swells at once subside into silence, and suddenly become very much interested in the playbill. And beside materially assisting to keep order during the performance, it is admitted by all who know anything of theatrical matters, that the gods are by far the most lively portion of a theatrical audience, and the witticisms and eccentricities of those in the gallery are sometimes quite as entertaining as any part of the legitimate performance.

xiv

'Shakespeare among the gods', 1872

[From *The Morning News*, 26 September 1872.]

It was on a certain evening last week that your contributor found himself amid the wilderness of broken bricks that now skirts the bottom of Lower Temple street. He had passed the wide portals of the pit, and had seen the throng of pittites eagerly yet quietly swarming through its doors to gratify their expectations concerning 'The Grand Shakespearean Revival' at the Theatre Royal. His object was the same, but he was pursuing it by a different path. He was going lower, and yet higher. Deserting his usual place among 'the critics of the pit', he was going among 'the gods who in the gallery sit'.[1] He therefore advanced and, casting a furtive glance around before taking the final step, made a sudden rush up Queen Street, and found himself in a long, low, vaulted passage, supplied with a very moderate amount of light. Payment was made through a small square hole in the wall. Placing his sixpence therein, he saw it snatched away by a hand (for no other portion of a human body was visible), and a metal cheque substituted. Armed with this, he pursued his path.

It was a long ascent and a steep ascent, and your contributor inhaled his breath much more frequently than is his wont before he had mounted to the top of the gallery steps. But after various stoppages to recruit his exhausted energies, behold him at last, worn out, yet triumphant; his difficulties overcome, and himself panting and perspiring, thankfully seated on the topmost row of the gallery benches!

How dark and gloomy is the house! How steep are the benches! At first sight one would say that, in case of a slip, there was nothing to prevent one falling into the pit beneath. How like a chasm it looks! As one's eyes become accustomed to the prevailing obscurity, a light iron railing becomes perceptible, sufficiently strong to prevent the most portly frame from accidentally toppling over. A legend is rife of an obnoxious policeman having been heaved over, but whether based upon anything more substantial than a vivid imagination your contributor is unable to say.

The doors have now been open about ten minutes, and the gallery is about half-full, but the vacant seats are rapidly being filled. There is little noise, and all conversation is carried out in a low tone, except when a late-comer, making a speaking-trumpet of his hands, and addressing the gallery generally, shouts, 'Bailey!' 'Hollo!' (this from a distant part). 'Got any room?' 'Ah.' The late-comer then proceeds in a business-like manner to make his way to 'Bailey'. With his hands he thrusts aside the shoulders of those immediately beneath him, and insinuates one foot on to the seat below. The process is repeated until the desired row is obtained. Then, leaning heavily on the shoulders of those beneath him, and thrusting aside the knees of those about him, he dextrously edges along the row until he reaches his friend. The presence of long-legged gentlemen, of gentlemen of Claimant-like[2] proportions, and of stout old ladies with huge baskets of provisions, renders his progress somewhat slow; but, by perseverance, all difficulties are overcome. His manner may be rough, but none take exception to it. Such incidents are regarded as an unavoidable feature of gallery life, as disagreeable necessities, and all submit to them with the greatest good-humour.

Not being so fortunate as to have a friend with a place secured for him, your contributor cautiously descends the steps, and settles himself by an exceedingly haughty-looking person, with a tall hat, and a black coat. He is evidently a swell. His open waistcoat displays a paper front (not too clean) and several studs of doubtful value. His collar is of paper with an edging of hair oil. Finding that the increasing number of the audience is causing us to be brought into too close proximity with each other, he addresses your contributor with, 'I'm a-tryin' to keep a place for a friend; that's why I'm a-sittin' so wide.' Your contributor politely offered to assist him in his endeavour, at the same time remarking that there was a probability of an exceedingly crowded house. 'Yes, and them over on that side won't be able to see anything. The pit's a-gettin' full as well. Why, I've been in the pit when we had to be changing to the lower boxes all night to see anything at all. But if I can get a good place in the gallery, I'd rather be there than anywhere else.' Your contributor hinted that, his eyesight not being so good as it had been, he had a preference for being rather nearer the stage. 'Oh, I can see everything as well as I can read this here bill. And I've tried my eyes a good deal too. Five years ago, I used to read in bed till two or three o'clock every morning. And after I'd been to sleep I'd used to wake with a start and think the whole room was in a blaze of light. And I'd see every page as I'd read as clear as if it was before me – especially if it was a good novel. I'm very fond of novels, I could read any quantity.' In reply to a question respecting his choice of authors, 'Oh, I like all of 'em. Well, certainly, there are some as I wouldn't read. They're so dull. Some of Dickens's are very good, but there's some capital authors on the *London Journal*. I'm very fond of reading Shakespeare' – this with a proper amount of veneration. 'I've read nearly all his plays, and acted 'em too. Law, bless you, I've been in a club, and we did lots of his plays; and the gentleman that's coming here – a friend of mine – he's a capital actor. You should have seen him do the Goblin Monk in *Esmerelda*. Splendid! As well as any professional. Why, bless you, I'll be bound he knows every line of the play they're going to do to-night.' Many other things he related of his friend, so that your contributor's curiosity respecting him was strung up to the highest pitch. ...

The audience was now getting impatient, and stamped the floor vigorously. The haughty gentleman was anxiously looking for the Goblin Monk, which shadowy personage was nowhere visible. 'Are there three or five acts?' he inquired, suddenly. 'There are five acts in all of Shakespeare's plays. By your asking the question, I presume that the *Winter's Tale* is *not* one of those that you have read.' 'Well, no, I haven't *read* it, but I've *got* it, mind you. I've got them all – in one volume – that thick, with a picture at the beginning of each play. I gave a shilling for it in Ann Street.'

There was no time for further talk. The band had finished the overture. The crowded house was clamorous for the commencement. The Goblin Monk had not appeared, but the bell rang, and the curtain rose.

A simultaneous 'Sh' issues from many mouths, those who fail to comply with its meaning being briefly told to 'shut up!' We are all attention. The play is evidently quite unknown, and as the plot slowly develops, our interest in it deepens, until we become quite absorbed. Not a word is lost. Each assumes a constrained attitude of attention. It is pleasant to watch the eager eye and open mouth as each listens with all his soul to the glowing, eloquent passages of the play. It is pleasant to observe the impatience manifested at any interruption. 'Why don't you go on the stage if you must talk?' is the sarcastic rebuke given to two unlucky youths who, being unable to see or hear, are whiling away the time with conversation interesting only to themselves. As each actor enters, he is received with hearty applause, and each pointed speech is received in the same manner. Perhaps there is a little too much favour shown to merely loud speeches, but this error of judgement is not confined to the gallery.

When the drop-scene descends, there is a general rush for refreshments, and each returns with bottled porter, ginger-beer, &c., for those whom he has left behind. By the bye, the amount of ginger-beer drunk is astonishing, and seems to indicate that the disciples of temperance are more numerous in the gallery than in other parts of the house. No glasses are available. The bottles are, therefore, passed from mouth to mouth, a preliminary wipe on the coat or shirt sleeve being the only preparation considered necessary.

The Goblin Monk now comes to the seat secured for him. He does not realize the expectation raised by his friend, being short, stout and puffy. Little by little his seat has been encroached upon, so that his coming incommodes us exceedingly, as two or three of his right and left hand neighbours have to sit sideways, to accommodate him. His ardent admirer at once fetches him a pot of porter, which he puts on his knees, and imbibes at intervals during the progress of the next act.

A low melodious whistle is now heard. The attention of all is directed towards the spot from whence it proceeds. The executant is immediately recognized, and hailed as 'Old Blackbird'. He is evidently a well-known character. Many of the gods answer to names which were certainly never on the register, such as Blackbird, Pudding, Park Street, Gammy, Hoppy, Elephant, &c., &c.

We all settle down for the second act. In it Paulina makes her first appearance, and her bold, scathing words give great satisfaction. 'My gad! she gives him the straight tip, any how!' is the whispered comment of an admiring auditor.

By the end of the third act we all feel somewhat cramped from sitting so long in one position. A general rise takes place. We stretch our arms, and would give a great deal for an opportunity of stretching our legs. Remarks are current as to the exceeding heat of the atmosphere. 'Ah, it's them gases,' explains a goddess behind. A perspiring god, who is mopping his face with a large red handkerchief, shouts to a friend, 'I say, Jim, this is a warm *Winters Tale*, isn't it?' There is much truth in his remark, as is testified by the almost universal removal of coats. Ginger-beer and other cooling drinks are again freely circulated. 'Take care what you're about with them bottles,' shouts a distant voice, 'it's dangerous to throw 'em in the pit.'

We are charmed with the love-making of Florizel and Perdita. 'How lovely they look! don't they?' a feminine voice exclaims, 'Oh, it's a sweet, pretty play!' We at once penetrate the disguise of Polixenes and Camillo, and when they reveal themselves are highly indignant with the former for thwarting the plan of the youthful pair.

When the final *tableau* is reached, we loudly express our joy at the happy termination. 'Well,' says one, 'I want to know why it's called the *Winter's Tale*.' 'Well I don't know,' is the reply, 'but I do know that I never see a better play acted.' He would indeed have to seek wide among the fields of literature before he found a better play, and the acting, as a whole, was far superior to what is generally seen in any theatre, London or provincial.

Rough and uncultured as are the occupants of the gallery, there was a subtle, undefinable charm pervading the play, which touched them. Without knowing anything of poetry they felt the wondrous power of the poet's genius, and their flushed faces and brightened eyes betokened the thrill which some of the magnificent passages sent among them.

Be assured, reader, that no one more truly appreciates Shakespeare than a gallery audience. Unsophisticated as they are in matters of art, the utterances of the poet of nature find among them a congenial and sincere response. If to this it be added that their language, though unrefined and ungrammatical, is neither immoral nor purposely coarse, it will be seen that for one who likes to enjoy the theatre unfettered by conventional restrictions, the gallery is no unpleasant place to spend an evening in. Your contributor, at least, will never regret his night with Shakespeare among the gods.

NOTES

1   *'the critics of the pit . . . gallery sit'*   Unidentified. Perhaps a garbled reference to the epilogue to Planché's *Olympic Revels* (1825): 'Ye critics who sit/So snug in the pit . . . '
2   *Claimant-like*   i.e. resembling the bulky figure of Arthur Orton, the butcher who claimed in the 1870s to be the long-lost Sir Roger Tichbourne.

xv

'A plea for the pit', 1875

[A contribution to the debate on the replacing of the pit , and its relatively cheap seating near the stage, with the more expensive stalls. This article by Clement Scott in *The 'Era' Almanack*, 1875, like much of his journalism, includes a strong element of nostalgia and amounts to a plea on behalf of middle-class taste.]

It is not improbable that the earliest playgoing recollections of most of us date from the pit. Canvass the steady playgoers of our time, and you may be sure that the majority of them saw their first play in this popular part of the theatre. The child, ten to one, for his first treat is taken to some popular restaurant or dining-rooms, and commences his dissipation by making believe that he is a man before he goes to the play. My first dissipation of the kind – how well I remember it! – was an early dinner at Dolly's Chop-house in the City; and great was my astonishment when my play-going patron, in order fully to initiate me into the mysteries of manhood, plunged a fork into a pile of magnificent chops piled up at the door, and selected two noble victims for the splendid coke fire which was roaring at the other end of the room. Would it have been a greater pleasure if after this excellent prologue a carriage had driven up to the door within a few minutes of the performance, and we had been ushered solemnly into the theatre at the conclusion of the overture? Not a bit. My first patron knew better. He understood the true value of initiation. He desired, no doubt, to inspire me with the affectionate sympathy of the brotherhood of playgoers. We struggled into the pit with the rest. We had all the intense pleasure of expectancy. We delighted in the pleasant chaff and quaint humour of our companions. Our ears were tuned to the cracking of nuts, and our noses introduced to the first true smell of orange peel. The time draws nearer to half-past six, and the excitement becomes intense. A mysterious knocking and withdrawing of bolts, and we all rush in through mysterious stone passages, over benches, in the dim uncertain light, and then we sit in the gloom, awe-struck with the dark green curtain, aroused with the continual arrival of guests, ever and anon consulting and puzzling over the old-fashioned long playbill, until at last the theatre becomes lighter, the music commences, the play begins, and we are lost in a delightful dream. . . . Some years after, when I was promoted to a booked seat on the front row of the dress circle, and was treated every Christmas to a view of Mr Planché's Lyceum extravaganzas,[1] it seemed to me that the little white silk gloves were rather a bore, and I certainly preferred the pit fare of nuts and oranges to the dress-circle luxury of ices and acidulated lemon-drops. When years once more rolled on, and one became more and more one's own master, every spare evening was devoted to the good old pit, which I then believed, and still believe, to be the fountain-head of all dramatic taste and appreciation.

There is no more orthodox and courteous assemblage than the pit of an English theatre. It is possible to meet there men of the highest dramatic intelligence and the keenest artistic feeling. A steady playgoer with a retentive memory may pick up scores of theatrical anecdotes from his companions, and, before now, has made there those earnest and lasting friendships which are alone formed by a complete artistic sympathy. People who go to the pit, who fight for the first row, and who linger affectionately at the doors long before they are open, show by their own conduct what extreme interest they take in the play. They are the true playgoers. They sacrifice some comfort occasionally and some time for their love of dramatic art. I believe that they are far happier when they have come in here and paid their money like men, than if they had come in by an order[2] or been passed in by a friend.

[Scott argues that it would be impossible to organize a *claque* – a paid conspiracy to give or withhold applause – in the pit.]

. . . The time-honoured honesty and dignified demeanour of the pit is perfectly safe in the hands of the pit; and I would go further and say that had not the privilege of the pit been seriously interfered with, had not the position of the pit been sadly altered, had not the conditions of pit criticism been changed, had not the voice of the pit been stifled, many of the recent scandals would have been avoided, and we should not have found, as now, a kind of civil war being waged in all matters of theatrical interest, – on the one side those who love the art, on the other [those] who view it merely as a commercial speculation, or possibly something worse. Had the pit been left in its old form and strength, had this large and generous assemblage, with no piques or prejudices, been permitted to remain and watch with eager eyes over the interests of art, the difficulties of the critic would in a great measure have been removed, and all authoritative interference would have been unneccessary. That which was once done by the loud, strong, and manly voice of the people, is now forced upon the representatives of the newspapers, whose opinion may be in harmony with that of the people but cannot be publicly endorsed by them. That which is now done by the distinct order of the Lord Chamberlain would, once upon a time, have been settled in a manner not quite convenient and comfortable for the manager. . . .

Let us see, however, what has been done with the poor old pit, what treatment has been extended to the honest gentlemen who, in fair weather and foul, have remained at the helm of the dramatic ship. They have been driven back, back, back by those ten-shilling stalls, until the place of the pit is a pen, and the pit's protection is no longer a power. Back they thrust the pit, under the suffocating roof of the dress-circle. They are huddled away anywhere out of sight. If a play be popular more rows of stalls are added – the pit is more and more reduced. In many theatres it has become the fashion to remove the pit from the ground-floor altogether, and to send its faithful members upstairs to the upper-boxes and galleries. The pit once removed or curtailed, the pit once banished upstairs, the pulse of interest which once vibrated through the theatre ceases to beat. The hum is hushed. The applause is deadened. The entertainments cease to fizz. They are like flat champagne – uncorked and *fadasse*.[3]

To look at the matter from another point of view, how, we may ask, do the artists like the changed position of affairs in the matter of the pit? Punctuality is at an end. Interest is threatened or broken. In the opening farces the stalls are all but empty. When the play begins the company has not half arrived. All through the first act there are interruptions, moving about, chattering and whispering. The swells come in full of good wine, and talkative after a good dinner; they are foggy about the plot, and they attempt to get at it by cross questions, leading no doubt to some very crooked answers. The men are too indolent to appreciate and the women too grand to applaud. How little they care for the drama or dramatic art! They come to the stalls in order to lounge away a few hours, to meet their friends, to be tickled with a gentle excitement. In the summer, when there is no opera, the play is on the way to the ball. In the winter it is a relief from the boredom of home. If this uninteresting and uninterested people make a noise and a drawling chatter, there is no corrective pit to keep them in order. They create a listlessness, and this no doubt is communicated indirectly to the artists. Actors will tell you that the difference of the atmosphere of audiences is wonderful. On some occasions a delightful sympathy exists between actors and audiences. A communicative electric chord runs between one and the other. At such times the acting is at its best. But then there come evenings when no efforts on the part of the artists can create excitement, or waken the stalls from a dead and stupid lethargy. Many actors tell you more. One sympathetic voice, one exhilarating laugh acts like quicksilver, and is instantly appreciated. A certain painful expression of countenance will unnerve an actor at times, and the other day a celebrated actor stopped in the middle of his part, and plainly told a gentleman that he (the actor) could not go on unless the gentleman stopped coughing. I have witnessed the repetition of such a scene in a church before now. The clergyman stopped and harangued the schoolchildren on the subject of coughing; he declared it was a trick, and could be stopped. And so it appeared, for there was not another cough heard that morning. It is believed by many artists that acting was never such a pleasure as when the curtain drew up to an audience crammed up to the very orchestra and footlights. It is impossible to believe that actors and actresses (but more so actors) are only occasionally sensitive. Who that is reading aloud likes the disturbance of a servant entering the room? . . .

I believe firmly and earnestly that the ten-shilling stalls are the falsest of all false economies. They look as if they pay, but they cannot pay enough in the long run. When this astounding sum is paid for a seat in the theatre, the purchaser expects very much. His evening's entertainment has probably cost him a sovereign at the lowest possible figure, what with driver, fees, refreshments, and supper. And if such a playgoer is not amused, he is the worst advertisement in the world. He thinks he has been 'taken in', and he goes about London ridiculing the entertainment, and dissuading his friends and acquaintance from 'wasting' their money . . .

It is a pity no doubt that artistic and commercial considerations are so hopelessly interwoven on the stage. It is a disgrace that, in this great country, there is not one theatre in which artistic aims can be placed higher on the shelf than the money-bags, and in which the manager, being guaranteed against a loss, can turn his attention to the higher development of the art which appeals to the whole world.

NOTES

1   *Mr Planché's Lyceum extravaganzas*   Entertainments written for the Vestris-Mathews management at the Lyceum (1847–55).

2   *an order*   A ticket for free admission (see p. 254).

3   *fadasse*   (Fr.) Flat.

'Stalls swells', 1877

[From *The Era*, 5 August 1877. *Two Roses* is a comedy by James Albery, first performed in 1870.]

In *The Two Roses* Jack Wyatt gratefully enlarges on the labour and care taken by the Swell to offer a magnificent appearance for his delectation, and the author wittily describes the humorous side of the philosophy of exquisites. In no place, however, does the Swell shine better than in the stalls of a theatre, nowhere else is Swelldom found to greater perfection or under such advantages as it gains by the contrast with other people. Be it remembered that the Swell is a much-treasured patron of the West-end Theatre; ordinary folks, who like their amusement to begin early, have been offered a farce, new or old, that has served to stop their craving histrionic appetites, to suit the conveniences of Swelldom, so that the *pièce de résistance* may come on at a later hour. Not that the Swell thinks of putting in an appearance in time for the commencement of the play, far from it; perhaps about nine o'clock, at the end of the first act or the beginning of the second, a bright and glorious presence hoves in sight; he has a long Ulster,[1] which he has taken off in the lobby of the stalls, and he holds it in such a way that it seems to measure about nine feet; he has a vast display of shirt front devoid of fold, but generally a little crumpled, a spotless neck-tie, clothes from Smalpage,[2] gloveless hands, and hair oiled to perfection and parted down the centre of his head with faultless accuracy. He is generally forgetful of a programme, but rewards the stall-keeper munificently for it, when that official respectfully suggests it to his notice. The Swell's entrance to his seat is fine, he is perfectly unconscious of anyone else in the Theatre, and if by chance he should be placed next to a gentleman, the latter's knees will most likely be the recipients of the skirts of the Ulster for the first five minutes, unless he call the attention of the owner to the inconvenience before that time, in which case the apology offered will be of the very vaguest and most unemphatic description.

The Stall Swell should by right have a male companion, without whom he is as much lost as is a conjuror debarred of his accomplice. As a matter of experience we may say that the Swell when solitary never stays until the conclusion of the piece; he will have spent the first ten minutes looking round the stalls and at the private boxes; he will, perhaps, have had his attention riveted by a pretty soubrette or a juvenile lady on the stage, and he may have been diverted for a few bars by the unseen band's performance of a familiar waltz; but, these attractions losing their power, he will soon have become bored, will rise from his seat in the middle of the most interesting scene of the play, and, with his inevitable Ulster apparently longer than ever, will beat a deliberate retreat, to the discomfort of every one he passes, seemingly unaware and regardless himself of the great nuisance he is. But the Swell is but a fragment without his brother exquisite. You might as well take Damon from Pythias,[3] or Sandford from Merton,[4] as part this youthful Aeneas from his faithful Achates.[5] Inflicting solitude upon him you deprive him of his distinctive quality – his power of speech; and what a quality it is, parenthetical no doubt, but as indomitable as it is detached.

They have possibly dined at the club, in which case they give their neighbours a broken up discussion of the *menu*, or they will talk of some fellow's bad form or refer to another acquaintance in words that to the unititiated might seem to have a reference to Walton's gentle art.[6] Perhaps a subordinate part in the play may be sustained by a lady who has assisted at an amateur performance with which they have been associated; if so, a vast amount of talk is immediately brought into action, and you will hear hypothetical suggestions that 'She sees us!' 'I think she noticed *me*!' 'By jove, I wish I had a bouquet!' and the like. Some hint may be thrown out that the people outside might send for one, but, as a rule, conversation goes off at a tangent, and kettle-drums, or receptions, or at homes push the young actress from their consideration until she happens to come on the stage again, by which time their enthusiasm very likely will have suffered a little reaction, and they will discover that her mouth is bad, or her hands large, and such disparagement will continue until oblivion mercifully steps in and criticism ceases. By the way criticism is a feature of the citizens, we should rather say patricians of Swelldom; of course it has no aesthetic lights, but is rather an *ignis fatuus* of judgement that would lead any one who followed it into hopeless, bottomless marshes of absurdity. Its only recommendation is its brevity, consisting mainly of ejaculatory commentary, such as 'Look at the fellow's coat!' 'Why doesn't that girl have her hair dressed more becomingly?' or, 'Awful slow piece.' The Swell never applauds; but, on the other side, he seldom hisses, and, when he has a companion to talk to, he betrays no impatience to go away, allowing energetic ladies and anxious railway travellers to get in front of him with imperturbable carelessness. Altogether the Swell is a pretty harmless and a liberal patron of the Stage, but we would rather not have our stall within earshot of him.

NOTES

1   *Ulster*   Long loose overcoat, fashionable from the late 1860s.
2   *Smalpage*   Smalpage and Son, Bond Street tailors.
3   *Damon . . . Pythias*   Syracusans of the 4th century BC, types of self-sacrificing friendship.
4   *Sandford . . . Merton*   Title characters in a children's book (1783-9) by Thomas Day.
5   *Aeneas . . . Achates*   In Virgil's *Aeneid* the hero's closest companion is 'fidus' (faithful) Achates.
6   *Walton's gentle art*   i.e. 'angling' – from Izaak Walton's *The Compleat Angler* (1653). The reference is to thieves' slang, 'anglers' meaning 'thieves'.

xvii

'Dress-circle gentility', 1877

[From *The Era*, 16 September 1877.]

The farce is near its end – the lover has been discovered in the cupboard, whence he has emerged to be forgiven by the passionate papa, and made happy for life with the old gentleman's daughter; or the somewhat faithless husband has escaped by the very skin of his teeth the danger of his wife's finding him out, and is about to express his intention of turning over a new leaf for the future, whilst 'click-click' go the box-keeper's keys, and *paterfamilias*, his wife, and daughters, enter in solemn procession to take possession of the seats, probably booked three days in advance. *Materfamilias* is generally stout, and, in point of fact, takes a chair and a half, which causes her eldest daughter to encroach upon her sister's share; this sister – if there be three of them present – is sure to be the youngest, as the second daughter will be certain to flank her on the side more distant from her mama, and that lady's senior pledge, the row being carefully and safely completed by the head of the family, who, be it remarked, is as much distinguished by body as well, that gentleman thus putting himself in a position to defend his party from all possible or impossible assailants. It is lucky for the scion of the house that she is thin, for what with the invasions of which her sisters have to be guilty, pushed on thereto by the bulk of their parents, and the very limited dimensions of the chairs, the evening would not promise an excess of comfort for any one of more than the slenderest of figures.

Mama wears a slightly old-fashioned brocaded dress, with an unmistakable shawl, china crape and as big as a counterpane, that has an annoying habit of slipping off that particular part of her shoulders its owner wishes it to cling to. There is a good deal of lace about the lady's throat and *corsage*, which somewhat conceals a brooch containing the miniature of a gentleman taken at a time when there was less white-waistcoat necessary than is indispensable to its original at the present time, and when the colour in his face and the quantity of hair on his head bore an inverse proportion to that which they do at present. The young ladies are dressed precisely alike, peach-coloured silk skirts with diaphanous Bernouse cloaks,[1] with three-button gloves, and an artificial white rose occupying exactly the same position in all their hairs, which are arranged in identically the same way. Indeed, they are as much alike each other as those hollow globes, one outside the other *ad infinitum*, so ingeniously manufactured by the Chinese, and really make one think that mama will pack them up in a similar manner and put them away when she gets home.

Number three opens the programme at once, and dives into the cast of the farce with an interest that the descent of the act-drop somewhat checks. Number two has a sudden and important communication to make to her mama which involves much leaning in front of her sisters, and induces the elder lady so to disarrange herself that the China crape snatches the opportunity and descends summarily to its owner's waist. The second daughter is informed that papa has got it, whether it be the number of the cab or the ticket number that will entitle them to certain street gear at present in custody in the cloak room, does not appear, for no more is said, the second daughter being apparently satisfied. Meanwhile other parties are entering the dress-circle, couples of old maids who *will* give such an elaborate analysis of the love-interest of the piece, while the curtain is down; several pairs of lovers who sustain the love interest whether the curtain be up or down, and who, doubtless in their attention to what is going on upon the stage, will be quite unaware of the propinquity of their companion's knee, or of the illustration of that law of natural selection that induces these lovers to prefer each other's hands to their own, all this being done in such a very circumspect and secret manner that only the most ill-natured could possibly remark it. Of course later in the evening will come the gentleman whose seat has been given to some one else, and whose anger will at once rise to boiling point which the offer of a private box all to himself will hardly appease, and he will have been only just quitted when the advent of two bashful ladies, whose seats are in the front row, will have to disturb about thirty people as they go blushing and stumbling to their places. This interruption does not matter so much for the back rows, as they are used to it; indeed, whenever they hear the box-keeper's keys they rise involuntarily from a habit that repetition has made second nature. The back rows, for special reasons, generally come before seven, and have a good deal to do in the cloak room, where they are often well known to the attendants. They do not get their dresses from Worth's at Paris, nor from White's in Regent-Street, and as to those single-button primrose gloves we should hesitate to say how many months they have been acquiring that dingy hue that all the care in the world cannot guard them from. For all Mr Thackeray said to the contrary in his preface 'Thunder and Small Beer',[2] dead heads are a contented class and rarely pass severe censure on the entertainment so liberally offered them. Indeed, dress-circle gentility is not critical; now and then *paterfamilias* may take alarm at a low comedian's humour or at a French joke not sufficiently adapted, but for the most part the frequenters of that portion of a Theatre, which is now occasionally styled the balcony, seem to say with Terence *Quod sors feret, feremus aequo animo*,[3] and if they do not show much mind exhibit a vast stock of patience. Looked at from the stalls they wear a somewhat overpowered appearance, as if the amusement were too much for them or the accommodation insufficient; but for all that we would ask no better than to be in the place of *mater* or *paterfamilias*, though we fear we should hardly be considered worthy to rub shoulders with Dress Circle Gentility.

NOTES

1   *Bernouse cloaks*   Also spelled 'burnous'; Arabian or Moorish
    hooded cloak.
2   *Thackeray . . . 'Thunder and Small Beer'*   A preface added to
    the second edition of *The Kickleburys on the Rhine* (1850), in
    response to criticism in *The Times* (known as 'The Thunderer').
3   *quod sors feret . . .*   (Lat.) From Terence's *Phormio*: as given
    here, the line means 'Let us bear with equanimity whatever fate
    may bring'.

xviii

The price of champagne, 1877

[A letter in *The Era*, 10 June 1877.]

Sir, – I was at the Globe Theatre on Monday night last, and
between the acts of *After Dark* sought refreshments in the saloon
of that house. A pint bottle* of Moet's champagne was ordered,
and the modest sum of *six shillings* was charged for the same. A
reasonable request to see the wine list was at once declined, and a
refusal given to serve me again, because I had remonstrated in the
first instance. Surely this is not a state of things calculated to
advance the interests of any establishment, and certainly it is not
asking too much to be made acquainted with the charges so as to
be able to purchase or abstain from an article that you do not
consider worth your money. If it is to their interest to charge the
public a hundred per cent over the original cost of what they
supply let them do so by all means, but least let the poor victim
know before he falls into the snare.

It may seem a very trivial subject to call down notice, but ask
regular visitors to theatres what are the samples of solids and
liquids they are called upon to take, and the universal reply will be,
not worth one-third of the money they have to pay for the same.

Individually, it is of no moment to me, but upon public grounds I call attention to these facts.

JUSTITIA

NOTE

*   *A pint bottle* Champagne was bottled in pint and half-pint measures for the British market.

xix

The changing audience, 1880

[When the Bancrofts took over the Haymarket in 1880 they reduced the space available as the pit in order to increase the number of stalls. In a speech made in response to a disturbance on the opening night, Bancroft claimed that the pit had not proved viable at this theatre in recent years. Frederick Wedmore, in *The Academy* (7 February 1880) took issue with this, arguing that pit takings had fallen off as a result of the Haymarket's failure to attract audiences. But he conceded that whether or not theatres could still afford a pit was open to question. Wedmore's article is of particular interest because it widens to a discussion of the tendency to 'luxury' in stage settings and in front-of-house furnishings, and to major changes in London theatre-going habits.]

If the expenses of a 'first class theatre' have of recent years greatly increased, so also have its receipts. At a period when the greatest dramatic artists were appearing together on the boards of one theatre – and that theatre not only the vast Drury Lane, but sometimes the Haymarket itself – there were no receipts whatever from stalls. The fashionable resort was that portion of the house whose name still indicates its old pre-eminence – the dress-circle.

Later, as eminent actors got fewer, and the theatre fell into comparative disrepute with the educated classes, but was increasingly frequented by the merely wealthy, two or three rows of stalls were timidly introduced. Later still – except, indeed, at the Haymarket – the three became five, six, or seven; and the Pit, driven back, was no longer the coign of vantage that it long had been, though it was still a place that might be gone to. Latest, the price for a stall – already treble that of the same seat in the pit of old days – was raised from seven shillings to ten. It is difficult to believe that theatrical expenditure has been raised in a like proportion – that the margin between reasonable receipt and reasonable outlay has not been greatly widened. But that is a matter, we admit, for the theatrical manager alone: a theatre, as Mr Bancroft said, is a place of business; and a manager may, in a business sense, be entitled to the utmost profit he can contrive to secure. If the manager of the Haymarket is mistaken in what he believes – if he and his brethren could better afford than he imagines to suffer the continuance of a Pit – we still have nothing to say to him. It is a business question for each individual manager. If the shop is found to be a dear one, the public need not buy in it.

But if, on the other hand, the statement is literally and absolutely true, then, indeed, we have something to say. For how has it come about – this overwhelming expenditure which requires so much additional provision? Is it that the art of acting has become more costly – that perfect artists who can dictate their terms are engaged by the dozen? Or is it that the exaggerated luxury of appointments and accessories absorbs so formidable a sum that the old revenues of the theatre are no longer sufficing? It is the latter alternative that is very forcibly suggested by the aspect of more than one of the newly equipped theatres; for the former there is, we fear, too little reason to decide, and this, not because of any reluctance on the part of the managers to engage excellent artists when they can discover them, but because of their scarcity in proportion to the number of playhouses over which excellent artists must be distributed. A disproportionate outlay on scenic decoration and furniture for the performances of modern comedy – nay, even on the playhouse itself – is at the root of the question. It began, no doubt, with genuinely artistic intentions, and has never been dissociated from good taste. But what was an adroit and justifiable bait to begin with ends by being hardly an attraction at all, and only a tyranny. Luxury has no limits. Its novelty ceases, but not the need it creates. The blue china and the old English furniture that were the material setting of one comedy must be capped by the porcelain of Sèvres and the finest marqueterie of Louis Quinze as the setting of another. Nay, the expenses of a first-class theatre may in time become such that a dress worn at a Drawing-Room is inadequate to the Stage, and the 'paste' of theatrical brilliants must be discarded for the treasures of the jewellers of Bond Street.

The gradual but most pronounced growth of luxurious expenditure – the addition to the attractions of the drama of the attractions of the show-house and the studio – means, sooner or later, with that manager or with this, a still further rise in the price of entry to entertainments presumably dramatic. And that means, of necessity, to most of the best lovers of the drama, less frequent visits to the theatre – it may mean almost the extinction of the older and more critical class of playgoer. It means that playgoing, instead of being a general amusement and a method of cultivation, may be but a costly indulgence for those who have richly dined. The intelligent, not wealthy, playgoer, who goes, or has been accustomed to go, very often will go so seldom that his critical opinion will not be worth having – a merely occasional visitor is not at home in the house, and can know nothing of its art. Is it for the advantage of the theatrical profession that the chance audiences drawn from every suburb and provincial town, or drawn from the haunts of only the wealthiest inhabitants of London – people generally listless, often dull – shall supersede wholly as they have already done in part, audiences who are accustomed to the habitual, and careful, and often delighted observation of the art of acting? What is done cannot be undone. As for the Haymarket pit, the local circumstances, the peculiar construction of the house, may count for something in excuse of its abolition. We make no personal matter of this question. If there is offence, Mr Bancroft is not the only offender. But it has become time to consider – and the public as well as managers have their share in the consideration – whether the expenses of our theatres shall be suffered to grow yet further in the sterile way of luxurious outlay on material things with which dramatic art has little to do. Is the Comedy to become a spectacle just as much as the Pantomime?

Playbills and programmes, 1880s

[From Dutton Cook's *A Book of the Play* (4th edn, 1882).]

Modern playbills may be described as of two classes, indoor and out-of-door. The latter are known also as 'posters', and may thus manifest their connection with the early method of 'setting up playbills upon posts'. . . . Of late years the vendors of playbills, who were wont urgently to pursue every vehicle that seemed to them bound to the theatre, in the hope of disposing of their wares, have greatly diminished in numbers, if they have not wholly disappeared. Many managers have forbidden altogether the sale of bills outside the doors of their establishments. The indoor programmes are again divided into two kinds. To the lower-priced portions of the house an inferior bill is devoted; a folio sheet of thin paper, heavily laden and strongly odorous with printers' ink. Visitors to the more expensive seats are now supplied with a scented bill of octavo size, which is generally, in addition, the

4 The new style of programmes, 1890s: *The Case of Rebellious Susan* by Henry Arthur Jones.

means of advertising the goods and inventions of an individual perfumer. Attempts to follow Parisian example, and to make the playbill at once a vehicle for general advertisements and a source of amusing information upon theatrical subjects, have been ventured here occasionally, but without decided success. From time to time papers started with this object under such titles as the 'Opera Glass', the 'Curtain', the 'Drop Scene', &c., have appeared, but they have failed to secure a sufficiency of patronage. The playgoer's openness to receive impressions or information of any kind by way of employment during the intervals of representation, has not been unperceived by the advertisers, however, and now and then, as a result, a monstrosity called an 'advertising curtain' has disfigured the stage. Some new development of the playbill in this direction may be in store for us in the future. The difficulty lies, perhaps, in the gilding of the pill. Advertisements by themselves are not very attractive reading, and a mixed audience cannot safely be credited with a ruling appetite merely for dramatic intelligence.

xxi

'The value of the pit', 1887

[Under this title an editorial in *The Era* (18 June 1887) examined the arguments in defence of the pit and argued for the preservation of this middle ground between stalls and gallery. The writer suggested that most of its proponents were thinking of 'the manners and customs of the last generation'.]

In the days when our fathers and mothers were young the habits of the 'comfortable' middle class were very different from what they are at the present date. People dined early then who possessed a social position the holders of which at the present day would be scandalized at the idea of partaking of dinner before seven; many highly respectable tradesmen thought it no shame to pass their evenings with others of their degree smoking and sipping in a tavern parlour; and people went to the pit who at present take refuge in the more genteel localities of the upper or dress circle. But there is one characteristic of the pit which we do not think it will ever lose, and which indeed is rather intensified than otherwise by the architectural construction which throws back that part of the house under the 'circle'. Youth in all ages has been an impecunious epoch of life; and in the kindly shade of the o'erhanging dress-circle the young barrister, doctor, medical student, or artist can enjoy the play without fear of his presence being perceptible to the young ladies of the families where he is invited to dine and dance, who may be witnessing the performance exactly over his head. It is, however, on first nights that the unique nature of a pit audience is most marked. Who, indeed, except a dramatic enthusiast, would encamp for weary hours before the doors of a theatre, laying siege, as it were, to the building, simply to have the pleasure of pronouncing a verdict on a new production? The first-night pittite gives weighty proofs of his love for the drama. Even as a matter of physical endurance, the first-night test is creditable to the pit patron. Mr Irving's theory that playgoers of the 'real sort' like a crush and a scramble at the doors was based on a deep perception of the characteristics of the English people. We are accustomed to attribute the docility of the French and their aptitude at forming *queues* outside theatres to the superior intelligence of the nation. But may not the superior physique of the Briton have something to do with the difference between the ways in which the public of the two countries take their pleasures? . . . Mr Irving tried the experiment of numbering the pit, and it failed. No, thank Heaven! our national characteristics are not yet obliterated. What can be a more perfect repetition of the demeanour of the English troops at Quatre Bras* than the behaviour of the crowd which encamps on a first night in the alley which leads to the pit door of the Lyceum? The patient, earnest sustentation of delay and fatigue, followed by the equivalent to the Great Duke's 'Up, Guards, and at 'em!' which is produced by the sound of the bolts being driven back, and then a wild, onward rush, and – victory!

The man who makes his entry in this manner into a theatre awaits the rising of the curtain with very different feelings from the 'swell' who strolls in full of old wine, or the languid lady who takes the play as a preceding entertainment to a fashionable ball. His blood is warmed by the difficulties he has overcome. He feels that he has sacrificed something to gain admission to the house, and this makes him doubly critical if he be disappointed, and yet doubly enthusiastic if he be pleased. The pit has no prejudices. It is an amalgam of ingredients too different and various to form a

clique. It may not possess as a whole the same amount of 'culture'
as the stalls and dress-circle; but it more than equals them in
attentiveness, in information, and in earnestness. It is a happy
medium between the stalls and the 'gods'. It is critical, yet hearty;
thoughtful, and still enthusiastic; and a manager could easier spare
a better paying part of the house than the plebeian pit.

NOTE

*   *Quatre Bras*   Engagement in the battle of Waterloo.

xxii

East End entertainment, 1889

[From the first edition of Charles Booth's *Life and Labour of the
People in London*, 1889.]

There are three theatres in the East End: the Standard in Norton
Folgate, the Pavilion in the Mile End Road, and the Britannia in
Hoxton; all homes of legitimate drama. Everywhere in England
theatregoers are a special class. Those who care, go often; the rest
seldom or not at all. The regular East End theatregoer even finds
his way westwards, and in the sixpenny seats of the little house in
Pitfield Street* I have heard a discussion on Irving's representation of *Faust* at the Lyceum. The passion for the stage crops up
also in the dramatic clubs, of which there are several. But by the
mass of the people the music-hall entertainment is preferred to
the drama. There are fully half a dozen music-halls, great and
small, in the district, and of all of them it must be said that the
performances are unobjectionable – the keynote is a coarse, rough
fun, and nothing is so much applauded as good step-dancing. Of
questionable innuendo there is little, far less than at West End
music-halls, and less, I noticed, than at the small benefit concerts

held at public houses. At one of these public houses a more than *risqué* song was received with loud laughter by the men and with sniggering by the married women, but by the girls present with a stony impenetrableness of demeanour, which I take to be the natural armour of the East End young women. The performances, whether at the music halls, or at the clubs, or at benefit concerts, all aim at the same kind of thing, and may be taken as supplying what the people demand in the way of amusement.

NOTE

*   *the little house in Pitfield Street*   Known as the Variety Theatre.

xxiii

A future radical gets to see Henry Irving, 1898

[From *The Gentle Art of Theatre-Going* (1927) by John Drinkwater (1882-1937), subsequently actor, dramatist and a leader of the Repertory Theatre movement.]

When I was sixteen I ran from my office at closing time and stood for two hours or more in a queue outside a Birmingham theatre holding ninepence with which to pay for early door admission to the gallery. This was to see Irving. When I reached the box-office window the 'gallery full' board was put out. In despair I begged to be allowed to try my luck, and at last succeeded in getting my metal token – cut, I remember, like a rosicrucian cross – for ninepence. When I had climbed the stairs, I found every inch of standing room occupied to the back wall, and could see nothing but the dimly-lit timbers of a lofty dome. After furtive and vain efforts to squeeze myself into some corner of vantage, I somehow climbed up the back wall, swarmed along a beam on my stomach, and lay the entire evening on a six-inch accumulation of dust, peering down from the roof on to a stage that seemed to be a mile away. And I would, if I could, do the same thing again to-night in order to see Henry Irving act. For there *was* acting if you like, as I may tell any young playgoer who never saw it. But underneath the glamour of that histrionic genius, what did we find after all but the one-man show *in excelsis*? Instead, however, of being frankly that, this, we were asked to believe, was the theatre that took its place among the great arts. As a one-man show it was magnificent, but as the theatre of the imagination, we sadly realized that, for all its pomp and ceremony, it did not exist. For acting, be it as rich as you will in native ability and power, does not become great acting until it is employed in the service of great drama. A man like Irving could so invest the dregs of impoverished play-writing with his own superb quality as to make us forget the wretched stuff in which he was dealing, but on reflection we realized that Irving's genius labouring against enormous odds was by no means compensation for what we ought to have had, namely, such a genius devoted to the service of yet greater and more significant genius than itself.

xxiv

Pit and stalls, 1900s

['E.F.S.' in *Our Stage and its Critics* (1910).]

It may be asked whether the ordinary playgoer exactly appreciates the position of the last rows of the stalls. Probably he believes that there is a gulf fixed between the stalls and the pit, and does not know that there is merely a barrier. Now a barrier can be removed easily – a gulf cannot. When paying his half-guinea the simple visitor imagines that the difference between the price of his seat and that of a place in the pit is to a great extent based upon an advantage of nearness – although it appears that some managers do not think that propinquity involves a gain.

As a matter of fact, a considerable portion of the floor of the house is occupied by stalls or pit, according to the nature of the business done in the theatre. If a piece is not attracting fashionable folk the barrier is moved towards the footlights, the chairs are changed to benches, and the place which at a *première* some deadhead[1] proudly occupied as a stall takes a 'back seat', and sinks to the indignity of becoming pit; and, of course, the converse sometimes happens.

It is amusing to hear the people on the other side discussing the entrance of the stall first-nighters, many of whom are identified. One hears comments upon the gowns, and sometimes severe remarks about the alleged misdeeds of professional critics, as well as unflattering observations concerning the personal appearance of some of us. We might a tale unfold that would freeze a good many young bloods, but for a question of confidence. . . .

Many articles have been written pointing out that the judgement of the pit is sounder than the opinion of other parts of the house, that the pittites are the real, serious, reflective, critical playgoers whose views are worth more than those of the playgoers either in the gallery or the more costly seats.

For a long time some of us believed in this tradition, probably, in fact, until circumstances caused us to move forward and study plays from the other side of the ambulatory barrier. One thing is certain – the pit plays a very great part in determining on a first night the apparent failure or success of a play, for on most occasions comparatively little noise is made by way of applause or condemnation save in the pit and gallery.

The stalls are remarkably frigid, though, on the other hand, they never, or hardly ever, show any active signs of disapproval. Somewhat false impressions are produced upon critics nearer to the footlights than the back seats. One of them the other day stated 'the fall of the curtain was greeted with hearty and long-sustained applause from all parts of the house.' Yet three of us noted – and compared notes – that after a little clapping, followed by one elevation of the curtain, the stalls did not contribute at all to the cheers. That evening there was a peculiarity in the pit's applause. It was 'patchy'. Here and there little groups were very noisy, and at the wings were some people from the 'front of the house', quite enthusiastic about a performance of which they could have seen very little if they had attended to their duties, whilst there were noiseless areas of considerable size.

There is no need to suggest that the pit lacks judgement merely because it is composed very largely of those from whose mouths, according to the Psalmist,[2] cometh forth wisdom; not, indeed, that in our West End houses there are present those very youthful playgoers who cause a disturbance by their audible refusal of the attendant's proposal of 'ginger-beer, lemonade, bottled ale, or . . . stout', being tired perhaps of the last-named beverage owing to the quantities they have taken – vicariously. Nevertheless, the pit on many first nights is wonderfully young; indeed, we calculated the other night that the average age of its temporary inhabitants was much less than half that of the distinguished company representing the play, and considerably less than that of the people whose late arrival caused murmurs and even words of disapproval.

It is natural for youth to be more enthusiastic than middle age, so one may easily explain the fact that the pit is more exuberant in demonstration than the stalls without the theory of the electrical effect of contact on crowds, a theory which every journalist at some stage in his career believes himself to be the first to have discovered. . . .

Probably in all parts of the house, except at one or two theatres, there is a preponderance of women in the audience, and this may have some subtle connection with the converse proportion of male and female characters in the cast; it may be observed that there is some change in the proportion of the sexes at theatres where there is no actor whose photographs sell prodigiously.

A sort of alteration seems quietly taking place in the costume of the pit, and not a few of the young ladies have come very close to a solution of a problem baffling to the Englishwomen belonging to what one may fairly regard as of somewhat higher stratum – the problem of inventing and wearing a demi-toilette.[3]

It should be added that in some theatres the critics have good seats allotted to them. Indeed as a rule the courtesy shown to us is in something like direct ratio to the importance of the management.

Speaking for a moment seriously, one may say that whilst the ordinary first-night pit is full of enthusiasts, it would be rash to attach very great value to its manifestations of opinion concerning the value of really ambitious plays, though in respect of most pieces, and performances too, its judgement may be regarded as satisfactory, since it fairly represents those aimed at by authors and players. The higher class of comedy and the severely intellectual drama demand a more mature judgement.

NOTES

1   *deadhead*   One who has not paid for his seat.
2   *according to the Psalmist*   Psalms 8:2 – 'out of the mouth of babes and sucklings hast thou ordained strength.'
3   *demi-toilette*   Clothes that will be smart without being full evening dress.

XXV

Leaving the London theatres, 1901

[Contrasts between West and East End, described vividly in an article by A. St John Adcock in *Living London*, ed. George R. Sims in 3 vols. (1901).]

Towards ten o'clock at night a breath of the drowsy quietness that has already settled down in the heart of the City seems to blow out along the West-End thoroughfares, and lull them as with some passing thought of sleep. Office windows are dark; half the shops are closed, and others are closing; 'buses, no longer crowded, are no longer in a hurry, and the conductor is saving up his voice for an hour later, when it can be used to better purpose; traffic generally has dwindled on the pavement and in the roadway until you can walk the one without elbowing your neighbours, and cross the other safely and at leisure.

Glance into the refreshment-rooms and hotels, into the fashionable or Bohemian restaurants in the Strand and round by Leicester Square, and you will see only long rows of tables, their snowy cloths neatly set with knives and forks, silver-plated cruets, folded serviettes, and branchy, torch-shaped epergnes flaming atop into many-coloured flowers; and, except for some stray visitor, perhaps, who looks lonely amid the waste of white cloths, none of the tables are occupied. The waiters gather in idle knots to tell each other privately what they think of the manager, or they doze apart as if the business of their day was finished instead of being about to begin again; the young ladies at the confectioners' shops have time to look at their hair in the mirrors; and aproned men behind the oyster bars are yawning over the evening papers.

When half-past-ten is turned, you feel the very air becoming tense with expectancy of something that is to happen. Crush-hatted men in evening dress appear in the street, singly or in pairs, with fair companions who trip beside them, bonnetless and in opera cloaks: the later items in the music-hall programme were not attractive enough to keep them; the play bored them, and they have left before the end. Commissionaires or gorgeously-uniformed attendants are bolting back the outer doors of the theatres in readiness for departing audiences; and the traffic in road and on pavement is momentarily thickening.

Now, too, if you look up almost any byway in the Strand you will see that it is lined with hansoms and four-wheelers and hired and private carriages waiting to be called. Other cabmen, arriving too late to get front places in these waiting lines, sneak into the Strand by circuitous routes, and, failing to dodge past the policemen, hover as near as they dare to one or other of the theatres, keeping a wary look-out for the playgoers to emerge and a signalling umbrella to be hoisted.

With the advent of broughams and private carriages in the byways, dapper footmen go on sentry duty outside the principal entrances to the theatres, or stand patiently amongst the ferns and huge palms that adorn box-office vestibules. Here they pose, almost as imperturbable as a row of statuary, until the strains of the National Anthem filter out to them from within, then they come to life, and peer eagerly into the passages and up thick-carpeted stairs that converge on the vestibule.

Suddenly one of them catches a glimpse of the figures he is looking for, and is out in a twinkling, and beckoning in the lamplight at the nearest corner. A carriage detaches itself from the line, sweeps smartly into the Strand, and draws up opposite the theatre. My lady and her guest, in a splendour of diamonds and low-necked dresses half-hidden under loose cloaks, trip lightly into it; my lord and his guest, plainer, but no less immaculately garbed, step in after them; the footman slams the door, mounts the box and they are gone.

In like manner come and go other carriages, and cabs that have answered to the shrill whistling of the commissionaire or have been fetched by some perspiring tout, who will gallantly hold a ragged flap of his coat over the dirty wheel while his more finely-

5   Leaving Her Majesty's Theatre, 1901.

garmented patrons are getting in, and trot a few paces alongside to catch the largesse that will be flung to him.

Men and women and a sprinkling of children – aristocrats and plebeians mingling – are now pouring steadily out of the Gaiety, the Lyceum, the Tivoli, Criterion, Her Majesty's, and all the theatres and music-halls in the Strand, the Haymarket, Charing Cross Road, and thereabouts, the swelling tide in the main thoroughfares being fed by narrower but more plenteous streams that gush into it out of the side channels from pit and gallery doors, till the surge and rush of foot-passengers everywhere, of cabs and carriages and 'buses, are denser and swifter than even at mid-day. . . .

The emptying of suburban theatres is a comparatively small matter; for the suburbs have their theatres singly, and not in clusters. There is the same rush and scattering of the audience, but on a reduced scale, and, generally, the proportion of evening dresses is very much smaller. In fact, in many of these theatres evening dress is not the fashion, and anyone wearing it is by way of being a rarity.

Come down East on Saturday night, and see how the people pass out of the Pavilion Theatre in Whitechapel.

Whitechapel Road has scarcely begun to think about sleep yet. Not only do all the provision shops remain wide open, but tailors' and drapers' and toy and furniture-shops, with many others, are open as well; costermongers' barrows stand thickly by the kerb; in the middle of them a huge brass weighing machine towers up, flashing dazzlingly in the light of the naphtha lamps, and near beside it is a hooded whelk-stall similarly illuminated. A baked-potato merchant passes and repasses, sowing sparks from the big black can on his barrow. The public-houses are full; the pavement is covered with men and women and children, well-dressed, shabby or disreputable, shopping or leisurely promenading. The curtain has not fallen in the Pavilion yet, but there is as much life here as there is in the Strand when the theatres are emptying.

It is five minutes to eleven. Two ancient four-wheelers and a single hansom have driven up, and are standing, forlornly hopeful, opposite the theatre. An attendant bolts the doors back, and a moment later a dark mass surges up the long bare passage from the pit, and a second less compact crowd simultaneously flows by the broader exit from the stalls and boxes.

As the earliest to emerge from the gallery door round the corner are batches of rampant, hooting boys, so the first hundred or so to burst into the open air from the front entrances are all men. One, a seedy, melancholy-looking man, breaks out, solitary, stares round as if he were dreaming, and, with his hands in his pockets, pushes through the promenaders and makes for home, taking his dreams with him. The huge poster that leans against the lamp-post opposite, and represents a scene from the play, has a strange fascination for many; they cross straight to it, and stand regarding it critically. 'We never see that!' objects a lady carrying a sleeping infant. 'Yus, we did, silly!' declares her husband, carrying an elder child, who is also asleep. 'Ain't that where 'e's a-savin' of 'er from that Russian chap?' 'Oh, ah! But they didn't do it like this', she insists, and follows him still protesting.

The general inclination, especially among the fairer sex, is to discuss the play as if it had been sheer reality, and to pour scorn and loathing on the villain, a tearful pity on the distressed heroine, and unlimited admiration on the hero, but a select few of the male sex, who are habitual attendants at the theatre, concern themselves less with the play than with the merits of individual actors, old favourites, to whom they refer in familiar, even affectionate, terms.

So, for some ten minutes the crowd streams out from the front and round from the gallery door, and the larger crowd moving up and down Whitechapel Road easily absorbs it. Passing trams or 'buses are besieged; a weedy young man is regaling his much be-feathered sweetheart at the baked-potato can; two men in tall hats and a miscellany of less-imposing persons congregate around the whelk stall, and hand the pepper and vinegar about with gusto. There is an influx of trade to the public-houses; the boxes of an adjacent fried-fish shop are full of hungry revellers, and faces of men and women peer in increasing numbers over its counter, demanding 'middle pieces' well browned. You meet these customers strolling a little later eating fried fish out of scraps of newspaper, or carrying it wrapped up to be eaten more comfortably at home. Nobody has hired any of the cabs, but the drivers linger still, on the chance of finding a fare among the actors and actresses.

The illuminated arch of coloured glass goes out suddenly over the main entrance to the theatre; lights within are dying out; here, as in the West-End, doors are being closed up with a clanging of bolts and bars; players are filing into the street from the stage exit; while, in the desolate interior, attendants potter about, covering up boxes and dress-circle, and the fireman, swinging his lantern, tramps over the darkened stage, taking a last look round.

6 Leaving the Pavilion, Whitechapel, 1901.

Part II

The Actors' Life

In *Nicholas Nickleby* (1838–9), Dickens gave an affectionate, hilarious and only slightly exaggerated account of a touring company. The actors depend in the most direct way on the patronage of their audience – for their benefit nights they have to go round selling tickets. The habitual and ludicrous self-promotion that Dickens turns to such good account in describing the Crummles family is a necessary tactic for survival. Mr Vincent Crummles ('of Provincial Celebrity') stands for the personality that found its natural outlet in the imposing deep-black three-inch-high roman block capitals and fervid exclamation marks of playbills and in the exuberant rhetoric of curtain-speeches and announcements. On their way home from the theatre,

> Mrs Crummles trod the pavement as if she were going to immediate execution with an animating consciousness of innocence, and that heroic fortitude which virtue alone inspires. Mr Crummles, on the other hand, assumed the look and gait of a hardened despot . . . (ch. xxiii)

Dickens often dwelled on the contrast between the actor's public persona and the sometimes dingy realities of his life. In one of the *Sketches by Boz* (1833–6) he describes 'the class of people, who hang about the stage-doors of our minor theatres in day-time'. They have 'indescribable public-house-parlour swagger, and a kind of conscious air, peculiar to people of this description. They always seem to think that they are exhibiting; the lamps are ever before them.' A 'young fellow in the faded brown coat, and very full light green trousers' who wears shabby clothes with an ostentatious air is 'the walking gentleman who wears a blue surtout, clean collar, and white trousers, for half an hour, and then shrinks into his worn-out clothes.' He 'has to boast night after night of his splendid fortune, with the painful consciousness of a pound a week and his boots to find . . .' It is clear that the high spirits in the face of private desperation fascinated Dickens, and that as a gifted amateur actor he understood the actor's deep-seated need to perform. His friend William Charles Macready, the

'Eminent Tragedian', had no sentimental attachment to his calling. On 21 February 1840 he noted in his diary that he was visited at Drury Lane by one Mr Esdaile, 'Wishing for instruction to aid him in going on the stage'.

> I with kindness and earnestness dissuaded him from following so unprofitable and demoralizing a calling, and told him I had rather see one of my children dead than on the stage. He left me, very grateful for my advice.

The account of Macready's efforts to rescue his father's fortunes (Part IV, no.i) goes a long way towards explaining this attitude on the part of one of the century's greatest and most respected actors. One reason for the low status of actors in the first half of the century was the fragmentation of that solid centre of support for the theatre known as 'The Town', which was reflected in the lack of a secure relationship between theatres and their prospective audiences. The establishing of the new West End to cater for a middle- and upper-class audience meant that by the end of the century the profession had found a new kind of recognition. Henry James wrote:

> [Actors] appear in society, and the people of society appear on the stage; it is as if the great gate which formerly divided the theatre from the world had been lifted off its hinges. There is, at any rate, such a passing to and fro as has never before been known; the stage has become amateurish and society has become professional.
>
> (*The Nation*, 1879)

The receptions given by Irving in the Beefsteak Club and on the stage of the Lyceum were part of a general acceptance of successful actors and actresses in society as guests rather than entertainers, although ambiguities remained. It is clear that the actress, with her unusual degree of financial and expressive independence, remained a puzzling and even frightening figure for most Victorian men and women: a paradoxically respectable deviant from the social and (in conservative Victorian accounts) biological norms of class and gender. Actors became club-conscious. The Garrick, founded in 1831, was a means of bringing actors in touch with the best (male) society; other clubs, some more bohemian than others, were especially favoured as exchanges of gossip and sources of 'contacts' among the more successful. At the lower end of the scale were the agents' offices (see no. xxx) and the theatrical pubs and wine bars.

More tangible than evidence of the profession's change in status are the signs of its greater complexity and the organization it required in the last decades of the century. Railway travel, with special trains for individual companies and their scenery, had made touring rapid and gave Sundays at Crewe a special meaning in the profession. To keep abreast of who was playing what and where was not always easy. The two major trade papers, *The Era* and *The Stage*, began publication in 1838 and 1880 respectively. *The Entr'acte* (1870–1907) carried similar information, though with nothing like the density and comprehensive coverage of its main rivals. Through the columns of these, actors could keep in touch with each other and with the wide world of managements and agents. The 'cards' indicating whether they were working or were 'available' were a valuable channel of self-publicity; legal cases concerning the stage were reported in full; provincial and London theatricals reported on. The nineteenth-century columns of these papers are closely packed in a way that reflects the intensity and scope of the theatre in the period. At the same time, journalism publicizing the theatre to its audiences became more personal in tone. The new magazines of the 1880s and 1890s (*Black and White*, *The Sketch*, *The Strand Magazine*, *The Idler*, etc.) published interviews with actors and actresses of a domestic and personal turn absent in most earlier journalism. *The Theatre* (1877; edited, 1878–97, by Clement Scott) and *Dramatic Notes* (1879–93) gave detailed reviews of plays and found room for discussion of current theatrical topics. *The Illustrated Sporting and Dramatic News* (from 1879) placed the theatre squarely in the smoking-room world. The actor's career was now mediated by a popular press avid for personalities.

In the course of the decades between 1830 and 1914, the working conditions of actors underwent radical changes. A career on the stage that began before the middle of the century would typically include work with a company that prided itself on being able to play any combination of a large repertoire of familiar pieces, including pantomimes, musical pieces and farcical come-dies, as well as more or less 'legitimate' drama. This was regarded as providing the actor with a comprehensive training, even if it was limited by the routine manner in which the standard plays would usually be performed. By the end of the century touring companies offered a far more limited range of plays: an actor might spend weeks, months or even years in a handful of plays, chosen because of their appropriateness to the talents of the company's leading performers. In some cases, the 'road' versions of London successes would offer employment that consisted only of repeated performances of a single production, based as closely as possible on the original staging. A kind of 'finish' and accomplishment was achieved in the repetition of a handful of roles but the experience did even less than the old, conventional presentation of 'stock' pieces for the actor's personal development. At the same time, the actor was less likely to find himself providing costumes for his 'line' of parts (although practice in this matter varied according to the prosperity and artistic principles of the companies) and could no longer assume that 'usual moves' would obtain for such perennials as the Shakespearean plays and the comedies of Sheridan. But this does not mean that routine was miraculously banished from the actors' profession. George Arliss, who went on the stage in the 1880s, recalled in *Up the Years from Bloomsbury* (New York, 1927, p.77) how he was met off the train by the stage manager of a company he was joining:

> He showed me the part I was to play next Monday: it was the leading juvenile in *Just in Time*, a long part written in long hand on innumerable sides of paper. On each page there were two or three phrases underlined in red ink. I asked what that meant, and he told me that those were rounds of applause. The words thus underscored had to be spoken with such force as to compel the audience to respond.

Arliss was on one of the lower rungs of the ladder, but even in high-class companies it was still customary at the end of the century for actors to be given no more than their own parts – the speeches and the cues for them – rather than the whole play.

Like Nicholas Nickleby, actors in the 1830s who did not come from theatrical families, but who showed some aptitude for the stage, learned their craft by working in a company. They might need some tuition in elocution and fencing and would have to invest in the purchase of the appropriate 'props' (as the actor's wardrobe was called). By the end of the century definite moves had been made towards the establishment of a regular system of training, although entry to the profession remained remarkably open – especially in comparison with present practice. Several private coaches offered specialized instruction to would-be actors, and there were some companies – notably Frank Benson's

Shakespearean touring company – that were considered to offer an appropriate training. Herbert Beerbohm Tree began what is now the Royal Academy of Dramatic Art at His Majesty's, moving it to Gower Street in 1905 and passing control to a council in 1906. Elsie Fogerty's Central School of Speech and Drama was founded in 1906 and was notable for its special emphasis on speech and voice training. Fogerty's teaching – in person and through her books – was enormously influential. The establishment of a recognized path to the stage and the recognition of the need for skills that required training made it easier to claim that acting could be called a profession by more than courtesy.

The items collected here reflect the actors' working conditions: terms of employment; haphazard methods of training; the demands made on the performer's stamina. The longest piece, Leppington's account of work and wages in the lower reaches of the profession (xxvi), is written in the spirit of sociological enquiry. Other documents derive from actors' memoirs and books of advice to those aspiring to the stage. The account of the rules of provincial theatres, given by Leman Rede in 1827 (ii), is of particular importance as an account of the customs that governed theatrical life from the eighteenth century and well into the nineteenth. Leppington's article, and (for example) Robertson's account of the actress's career (xii) reflect the quasi-industrial organization of the Victorian theatre in its heyday. Side by side with the bettering of the actors' status (which Mrs Kendal celebrated in her 1885 address to the Social Science Congress – xxii) went a redefinition of the terms of employment. At the same time, evidence before the various Parliamentary Special Committees connects the matter of wages and social rank with such issues as the 'freedom' of the London theatres and the distinction between theatres and music-halls.

Two book-length studies of the acting profession in this period have appeared recently: Michael Baker's *The Rise of the Victorian Actor* (1978) and Michael Sanderson's *From Irving to Olivier* (1984). Baker's account of working conditions includes a reminder that the much vaunted growth of prosperity and respectability in leading members of the profession should be set against the relative lack of 'progress' in earnings and standing among lesser actors. Sanderson cites figures from 1908 that indicate how little margin could be left to an actor whose annual income, from 35 weeks' employment at £2 a week, amounted to £70; after meeting various outgoings to the tune of £37 6s. 4d., there remained 1s. 9½d. a day for food (£32 13s. 8d. total). The absence of national insurance and pension schemes made it difficult for actors to provide for retirement, and 'Only the forty or fifty pound salaries admit of making any capital possible to retire on' (Sanderson, 1984, p. 86). Professional charities and the notorious generosity of the profession provided something of a safety-net, but the fate of an actor prevented by illness or age from working was very hard. This should be set against the comfortable – sometimes opulent – lifestyle enjoyed by some Edwardian actors and the substantial sums recorded in some wills: Sanderson cites, among others, the £197,035 left by Sir Charles Wyndham in 1919, Tree's £79,984 in 1917, and Sir George Alexander's £90,672 in 1918 (pp. 81–2).

The 'official' biographies and autobiographies often make successful actors seem unbearably stuffy and complacent: the desire to represent acting as suitable for virtuous men and women resulted in some distorted perspectives. The need to separate the actor's calling from Edmund Kean's brilliant dissipation makes for much dullness in J.W. Cole's *Life and Times of Charles Kean, F.S.A.* Helen Faucit's resplendent womanly virtues shine numbingly through the biography by her husband, Sir Theodore Martin. The second part of Bram Stoker's highly informative life of Irving (1907) seems to consist of guest-lists and honours. But in Max Beerbohm's obituary of the first theatrical knight, the magnetism of the actor is celebrated. Beerbohm describes how he saw Irving in a carriage passing by Marble Arch on his way to Paddington Station, the day he was to be knighted at Windsor:

> Irving, in his most prelatical mood, had always a touch – a trace here and there – of the old Bohemian. But as I caught sight of him on this occasion – a great ocasion, naturally, in his career . . . he was the old Bohemian, and nothing else. His hat was tilted at more than its usual angle, and his long cigar seemed longer than ever; and on his face was a look of such ruminant, sly fun as I have never seen equalled. I had but a moment's glimpse of him; but that was enough to show me the soul of a comedian revelling in the part he was about to play – of a comedic philosopher revelling in a foolish world. I was sure that when he alighted on the platform at Paddington his bearing would be more than ever grave and stately, with even the usual touch of Bohemianism obliterated now in honour of the honour that was to befall him.

> (*Saturday Review*, 21 October 1905)

7   The actor-manager as cultural icon: postcard commemorating the career (from cottage to Abbey) of Sir Henry Irving, 1905. Irving was appearing in Tennyson's *Becket* on the night of his death.

Somehow Irving conveyed to Beerbohm the touch of raffish glamour that made Vincent Crummles so impressive, and which no amount of respectability could quite take away.

A warning to the would-be actor

[From the preface to Leman Thomas Rede's *The Road to the Stage; or, the Performer's Preceptor* (1827).]

A country actor in a small company, and aspiring to a first-rate situation, will invariably have to study about *five hundred lines per diem* – it is astonishing how many persons are cured [of a desire to be an actor] by this alone; this will occupy the possessor of a good memory for six hours – his duties at the theatre embrace four hours in the morning and six for rehearsal, and about five at night; here are sixteen hours devoted to labour alone, to say nothing of the time required to study the character, after the mere attainment of the words. Let the stage-struck aspirant endure this, and, if a radical cure be not effected, he has the scenic *phobia*, and had better be given to the stage at once, for he will never fix to anything else.

ii

General regulations of the principal provincial theatres, 1827

[As given by Leman Thomas Rede in *The Road to the Stage; or, the Performer's Preceptor* (1827). The system of fines is representative of practice in the Georgian and Victorian theatre. Some of these regulations anticipate disruptive behaviour, others relate to the operating practices of stock companies with their repertoire of pieces that might be given at short notice. Benefits were an important source of income for actors, whose contracts stipulated their frequency and nature (minor actors shared benefit nights, some actors were given benefits that were 'clear' and bore no house charges). The rules printed by Rede are obviously designed to protect the managers' interests by limiting the expenses of such occasions.]

[GENERAL RULES]

First. – All engagements are terminable by four weeks' notice from either party.

Second. – Salaries are not paid when theatrical performances are suspended on account of any public calamity.

Third. – Performers exercising their talents for the advantage of any other establishment, where money is taken for admission (by subscription or otherwise), without permission of the manager, incur a penalty of one week's salary; and a repetition of the offence will be held a forfeiture of their engagement.

Fourth. – Every performer is expected to go on the stage and assist in all the processions and choruses, where it has been customary in London for principals to be engaged, as in *Macbeth*, *Pizarro*, Juliet's dirge, Alexander's entry, &c. – non-compliance with this regulation subjects the party to a fine of ten shillings.

Fifth. – Every performer is required to go on the stage, if in the theatre, or within call, whenever it is deemed expedient, to sing the national airs, except such airs are introduced in the dramatic performance, or forfeit ten shillings.

Sixth. – Any performer refusing to act a part, cast by the manager, incurs the forfeiture of one guinea.

Seventh. – Performers are not to go into the front of the house during the performance of a piece in which they act.

Eighth. – Dresses apppointed to be worn are not to be changed without the consent of the manager.

Ninth. – In the Birmingham company Saturday is considered the first day of the week, as in the London theatres.

Tenth. – On benefit nights, performers are expected not to go into the front of the house without the permission of the person whose benefit it is.

RULES OF REHEARSAL

First. – Notice of pieces to be rehearsed to be posted in the green-room, and the time of beginning, before the end of the play on the previous night of performance; and it is the call-boy's duty to give notice to every performer who does not perform that evening.

Second. – Ten minutes' grace allowed for the commencement of the first piece rehearsed, but not for any subsequent one.

Third. – Every performer absent from rehearsal (without having previously assigned a sufficient cause), to forfeit for the first scene one shilling, and for every subsequent one sixpence; but not more than five shillings for a whole play, and half-a-crown for a farce.

Fourth. – For standing on, or walking across the stage, when not engaged in the scene, sixpence.

Fifth. – For not being reasonably perfect at the last rehearsal (sufficient time having been given for study), five shillings.

Sixth. – Music-room rehearsals subject to the same regulations in regard to time as those on the stage. The duets, glees, choruses, &c., to be played before the songs, and each absentee to forfeit sixpence for every concerted piece, but not for songs.

Seventh. – Apologies for non-attendance at rehearsals of every description must be delivered, before the party has incurred the penalty.

RULES DURING PERFORMANCE

Every performer liable to the following forfeits.

First – For not being ready to begin at the time announced in the bills, five shillings.

Second – For keeping the stage waiting after having been called, two shillings and sixpence.

Third – For going on or off the stage in any other place than that settled at rehearsals, one shilling.

Fourth – For opening the stage door[1] when not required in the business, two shillings and sixpence.

Fifth – For standing in the wings in sight of the audience, or sitting at the wings, two shillings and sixpence.

Sixth – For being obviously intoxicated when engaged in the performance, one guinea.

Seventh – For omitting, or introducing a scene or song without the permission of the manager, five shillings.

Eighth – For not attending to perform the part allotted, one guinea.

*** None but the performers, or persons engaged in the business, permitted to be behind the scenes, either at rehearsal, or during the performance, on any pretence whatever.

BENEFIT REGULATIONS

First – Previous to the benefits a notice will be placed in the green-room, for three days, for the signature of those performers who intend taking benefits – and those who do not sign within the time will be considered as having declined one.

Second – The charges of each night to be as follows: ** security

---

**   These sums of course differ according to the size of the theatre, &c. At Liverpool the charge is sixty guineas for the house.

for which must be given before any advertisement can appear: – the manager allows the customary stock printing, property bill,[2] and not more than twenty supernumeraries. The manager has a discretionary power of restraining the performances within a convenient length.

Third – Performers are not permitted to curtail pieces; but any piece that has been compressed in either of the patent theatres in London, may be acted from the same copy at Birmingham.

Fourth – No alteration in the price of admission at benefits, on pain of forfeiture of the benefit and the engagement.

Fifth – No comic pantomime allowed but to the harlequin, columbine, and clown, who shall throw for precedence, and only take such pantomimes as have been acted in the stock business during the season.

Sixth – No play, or farce, to be acted for a benefit, unless appropriate scenery, dresses, &c. are already in the stock, or furnished by the performer.

Seventh – Performers, and others, taking tickets, to take them on such nights as the manager shall fix for that purpose, and give security if required.

NOTES

1 *the stage door* Here, the doors on either side of the proscenium arch, giving on to the forestage.
2 *property bill* List of properties.

iii

Edmund Kean's salary at the Haymarket, 1830–2

[David Edward Morris, proprietor of the Haymarket, testifying to the House of Commons Select Committee on Dramatic Literature, June 1832. The point at issue is the claim of the 'minor' theatres to offer a suitable home for 'legitimate' performances. The Haymarket's position was unusual in that it had a licence for spoken drama during the summer months when Drury Lane and Covent Garden were closed.]

2416.   Does not Mr Kean perform at your theatre? – He has been engaged for 12 nights, 10 of which he has played.

2417.   Do the public appear as well satisfied with his representation of Richard, or any other character on your stage, as at the great theatres? – Quite as well satisfied.

2418.   Does he ever complain himself that he does not perform as efficiently as at the large theatres? – Never; I think I have heard him say that the size of it is more congenial to his wish.

2419.   How many persons does the theatre hold? – About 1,600 or 1,700.

2420.   What sum of money does it take? – £320 when it is full.

2421.   What salary do you give Mr Kean? – £30 a night; I had given him £50 the year before last.

2422.   Did you engage him last year? – Yes.

2423.   At the same salary? – Last year he got £33 6s. 8d. a night.

2424.   Then it appears that Mr Kean varies his terms? – He has varied them for the last three years; at first they were £50, afterwards they were £33 6s. 8d., and the present year £30.

2425.   The Committee understand from Mr Kean that his terms were always the same? – I believe that he has taken less at other theatres.

Town and country actors, 1832

[The standard pattern of a career on the stage was to appear – briefly, at least – in London at one of the patent theatres, and then to go back to the provinces (billed as 'of the Theatre Royal, Drury Lane' or 'Covent Garden'). With any luck, a return to London would follow. In evidence before the 1832 House of Commons Select Committee on Dramatic Literature, the actor E.W. Elton reflected on the effects of the patent houses' monopoly on the supply and training of actors throughout the country, and argued, not for a removal of the hierarchy of theatres, but a rationalization of it.]

4169.   Are there any general observations you wish to make, especially with regard to actors? – I think the present laws affect the exertions of actors very materially. There are so many theatres in the country which demand the first-rate talent, that not one-sixth part of these actors of first-rate talent that are necessarily demanded by provincial theatres, can ever hope to get engagements at Covent Garden or Drury Lane; and yet a country actor's life is considered but as a state of necessary probation, and in most cases is one of positive endurance and deprivation. The highest salary I know paid in a provincial theatre of the very first class, is three guineas a week, and very few receive so much as that, and have to pay their own travelling expenses from town to town, and frequently to provide their own stage dresses; yet it is expected a man receiving that salary shall be able to embody the first characters of Shakespeare.

4170.   Do you happen to know any particular instance of clever leading actors of undoubted talent who try to appear before a London audience, who have not been able to obtain engagements at the large theatres? – I do.

4171.   Are those instances many? – Not perhaps many.

4172.   Have you any objection to name them? – I cannot say I know such facts; I do not know of actors of talent having applied to Covent Garden or Drury Lane and being refused engagements, as such repulses would not perhaps be confessed to; but I have known actors and actresses of the first-rate talent exhibiting their talents in the country very much against their will. I have always observed a strong wish amongst provincial performers that there should be more markets in London for talents, for country actors are always looking to the metropolis as the end and aim of their ambition, and their provincial engagements are considered by them merely as a means of attaining that end.

4173. Is it your belief that those individuals have remained in the country merely on account of the difficulty of getting engagements in London? – I am sure of it. I do not know whether it will be considered improper if I mention my own case. I have been for eight years a provincial actor; I have filled situations of first-rate importance in Liverpool, Manchester, Norwich, and other theatres, not quite of so much importance as those but nearly so, and I have always found the provinces utterly inadequate to my support and that of my family. I have made applications to the large theatres for a mere trial of my talent, and those applications have been wholly unnoticed, not even answered. I at last had applications made to me from the London minor theatres, and observing, with other actors, that those theatres had of late years, with the sanction and encouragement of the public, made great strides towards attaining nearly the same respectability and excellence as the large houses, I was at length induced to accept those offers.

4174. What parts in the country theatres did you most excel in? – Richard the Third, Othello, Hamlet, and parts of that class.

4175. Did you offer probationary to play any of those parts in the London theatres? – I once did; I wrote at the same time to Mr Charles Kemble of Covent Garden Theatre, and Mr Alexander Lee of Drury Lane. Mr [Edmund] Kean at that time had seceded from the stage for a time. I made an offer, certainly a very bold one, to undertake Mr Kean's characters, or make a trial in them, at a moderate salary, for the remainder of the season. I expressly offered to do so at a very moderate salary. I never received an answer to either application.

4176. Did you state the sum? – I did not.

4177. And you believe others are in the same situation? – I believe so.

4178. You now perform principal parts at the Surrey Theatre? – I do.

4179. If those small theatres were not existing you would have no engagement in London? – If the legitimate drama was not played at the minor theatres I should certainly have had no engagement in London.

4180. You would still be performing at the provincial theatres? – Yes; I would not have accepted an engagement at a minor theatre had it been otherwise than it is. . . .

4192. . . . I give it as my opinion as an actor . . . that the right of playing the legitimate drama in London should be given to other theatres as well as the large theatres, unrestrictedly; that I think it would be advantageous to the proprietors of the great theatres such should be the case. It has been stated, and it is well known, that the actors at the great houses are generally obtained from provincial theatres. The provincial theatres have been the school for the actors at the large theatres in London; but it happens frequently that upon recommendations of persons known by the managers of the large theatres, actors and actresses are brought from the provincial theatres, and fail after they have made long engagements. There have been instances of actors and actresses making engagements for three and even five years, at large salaries at the patent houses, who have failed on their first appearance, and the managers have been consequently saddled with those engagements, although the performers were useless. Now, if the legitimate drama were acted at the minor theatres, they would become the finishing schools, instead of the provincial theatres, and actors and actresses being then placed before the eyes of the public and of managers, and their talent and popularity matters of notoriety, no such mistakes could be made. . . .

Disappointments in Bath, 1835

[William Charles Macready's diaries reflect the temperament of
the actor – passionate, earnestly critical of himself and others and
full of a sense of his vulnerable dignity. In Bath and Bristol
Macready was in partnership with James Woulds, a provincial
actor. From *The Diaries of William Charles Macready, 1833–1851*,
ed. William Toynbee (2 vols., 1912).]

Bath, January 8. Acted Othello with a feeling of having no
sympathy from my audience; thought myself deficient in
earnestness and spirit, but do not regret having done it, as it was a
useful rehearsal for me. I never saw the Senate put so well upon
the stage. I think I may play Othello well, but the prescriptive
criticism of this country, in looking for particular points[1] instead
of contemplating one entire character, abates my confidence in
myself. Mr Woulds told me that he had heard from Mr Field of
general discontent at the prices being restored. The house tonight
was wretched, but what could be expected at such a time?

January 9. My [land]lady brought me up her bill, and began some
enquiries about my stay – the number of my family and some etcs.
which showed a disposition to impose; she added that Mr Woulds
had not mentioned my *profession*. My blood rose at this
impertinence, and I was foolish enough to be so angry as to
observe that there was no person in Bath, whether titled or not,
that could claim a higher character and that I would relieve her of
the inconvenience of such an inmate. She attempted to excuse
herself, but I cut the matter short. Heard from Mr Woulds the
account of the first week's balance, which was very satisfactory.
Read the newspaper, and to my astonishment and satisfaction saw
Talfourd[2] member for Reading.

January 10. Expedited the rehearsal as much as possible, but it
proceeded slowly owing to the inattention of the actors. What a
calling is this! How deeply I feel the degradation of belonging to
it, which yet for my dear children's sake I will endeavour
cheerfully to pursue. . . .

January 17. In going through the box-office heard a woman
inquiring for something entertaining for children. Brownell

mentioned that Mr Macready and Dowton would play on Monday. 'Oh, no,' she replied, 'they are very good actors, but I want something entertaining for children; when will *Alladin* be done?' So much for Bath taste! Acted King Lear unequally – wanted the sustaining stimulant of an enthusiastic audience – wanted in them the sensibility to feel quickly what I did, and the ready manifestation of their sympathy; some parts I did tolerably well; acted with some degree of vivacity and nature in Puff.[3]

NOTES

1 *points* Strongly marked (and often traditional) moments of emphasis in action and declamation.

2 *Talfourd* Sir Thomas Noon Talfourd (1795–1854), Irish lawyer and dramatist, author of the classical tragedy *Ion* (1836).

3 *Puff* The dramatist in Sheridan's burlesque *The Critic; or, a Tragedy Rehears'd* (1779).

vi

Should actors read reviews? – 1836

[Helen Faucit, new to the stage, was upset by hostile reviews. Her diary, with its sentimental and earnest accounts of her feelings, is quoted extensively in the biography written by her husband, Sir Theodore Martin, and published in 1890. On this occasion she was appearing as Belvidera in Otway's *Venice Preserv'd* – still part of the standard repertoire.]

Thursday, Jan. 28th Oh, these horrid newspapers, they tell me, have cut me up in fine style. I amused myself with fretting the whole morning, until I could scarcely see out of my eyes. This was very wise, knowing I had got this part to act again at night. It was very silly, I know, for they have written against a thousand times better actors and actresses than I can ever hope to be; but I felt weak and ill, and could not help it. I wish I had made up my mind to do what Mr [Charles] Kemble asked me to promise him before I appeared, which was *not to look at or think of a newspaper*. He said I should save myself a great deal of annoyance, and that no good could be attained by it; for, put them all together, and see how generally the one contradicts the other, and condemns you for what the next you take up very likely praises you for. Which are you to be guided by? In the end you must fall back upon your own resources and judgement.

I was so rejoiced to find this evening that the audience did not seem prejudiced against me from the newspaper reports, but received me, oh! so kindly, that I felt the sudden revulsion of feeling almost too much for me, and as I leant my head upon Mr Kemble's (Jaffeir's) shoulder to recover myself, he whispered most kindly in my ear, 'Do you hear, my poor little child? Does that sound as if the papers had done you much harm?' I looked up at him, and, smiling through my tears, blessed him in my heart for giving me a small portion of what I then so sorely needed, confidence in myself. I felt a new creature, and entered into my part with all my heart. 'Don Felix' (in *The Wonder*) says 'What wondrous magic lies in one kind look?' What wondrous magic lies in one kind word! At least I always feel it so. I certainly acted much better tonight than last night. No doubt there was a great deal of truth in what was said against me, but still I think it is rather hard that critics should see you and judge you so severely on a *first* appearance, when young people, most particularly, from their over-anxiety and nervousness, cannot have that coolness and self-possession which are so necessary in embodying a character. Why not go on the second?

But why do I not go to bed instead of scribbling nonsense, when I am so thoroughly tired and worn out with one thing and another? Mr Kemble took me on again [i.e. to acknowledge applause] at the end of the play. How very good and kind he has been to me! I wrote to Hetty [her sister] this morning and told her all my troubles.

In the Green-Room, 1840s

[From George Vandenhoff, *Green-Room and Stage* (1865). Vandenhoff (1813–85) describes the 'patent' theatres in the 1840s, and refers to the management of Covent Garden by Elizabeth Vestris and her husband Charles Mathews. The author's desire to emphasize the gentility of the theatres may have coloured his account.]

It must be understood that in Covent Garden and Drury Lane Theatres, there were a *first* and *second* Green-Room: the first, exclusively set apart for the *corps dramatique* proper, – the actors and actresses of a certain position; the second, belonging to the *corps de ballet*, the pantomimists, and all engaged in that line of business – what are called the *little people* – except the principal male and female dancer (at that time, at Covent Garden, Mr and Mrs Gilbert), who had the privilege of the first Green-Room.

The term Green-Room arose originally from the fact of that room being carpeted in green (baize, probably), and the covering of the divans being green-*stuff*. But the first Green-Room in Covent Garden Theatre was a withdrawing room, carpeted and papered elegantly, with a handsome chandelier in the centre, several globe lights at the sides, a comfortable divan, covered in figured damask, running round the whole room, large pier and mantel-glasses on the walls, and a full-length, movable swing-glass; so that, on entering from his dressing-room, an actor could see himself from head to foot at one view, and get back, front, and side views by reflection, all round. This is the first point to attend to on entering the Green-Room, to see if one's dress is in perfect order, well put-on by the dresser, hanging well, and perfectly *comme il faut*. Having satisfied him or herself on these interesting points, even to the graceful drooping of a feather, the actor or actress sits down, and enters into conversation with those around, which is interrupted every now and then by the shrill voice of the *call-boy* 'making his calls'. The call-boy is a most important 'remembrancer'; – he may be named the prompter's devil, as the boy in a printing office who calls for copy is yclept the printer's devil. His business is to give the actors and actresses notice, by calling at the door of the Green-Room (he is not allowed to enter those sacred precincts in a London theatre) the names of the persons whose presence is required on the stage. This he does by direction of the prompter, who about five minutes, or three lengths (120 lines) before a character has to enter the stage, finds marked in his prompt-book of the play a number thus {3} He then says to his attendant imp, who has a list in his hand (a call-list – very different from a New Year's call-list), 'call *three*'; – the boy looks at his list, walks to the Green-Room door, and calls the character marked {3} in that act; or the prompter orders him to call 4, 5, 6, 7: he consults his list for the act, finds these numbers, and at the Green-Room door calls the characters they represent, thus: –

> HAMLET,
> HORATIO,
> MARCELLUS,
> GHOST.

The gentlemen who represent these characters, on being thus called, leave the Green-Room, and go and stand at the wing – the side-scene – at which they are presently to enter. All the calls are made at the Green-Room door, and it is at an actor's peril to take notice of them; it is only on a change of dress that he is entitled to be called in his dressing-room, except *stars*, and they insist on being always called there, as well as in the Green-Room; and the point is conceded to them.

In many theatres the calls are made by the name of the actor or actress representing the character called. It was so, I recollect, at Covent Garden; at the Haymarket it is otherwise; and generally throughout the theatres of the United States, the calls are made by the names of the characters: and it is the safer plan, and less liable to mistakes on the part of the call-boys: each way has its own advantages and disadvantages.

The Green-Room was exceedingly comfortable during the Mathews and Vestris management. Indeed I must pay them the compliment of saying that their arrangements generally for the convenience of their company, the courtesy of their behaviour to the actors, and consideration for their comforts, formed an example well worthy to be followed by managers in general; who are not, I am sorry to say, usually remarkable for these qualities. In fact, the reign of Vestris and her husband might be distinguished as the *drawing room management*. On special occasions – the opening night of the season, for example, or a 'Queen's visit,' – tea and coffee were served in the Green-Room; and frequently between the acts, some of the officers of the guard, or gentlemen in attendance upon the royal party, would be introduced, which led, of course, to agreeable and sometimes advantageous acquaintances.

A dispute with an actress, 1848

[From the *Theatrical Journal* 1848: reports of cases such as this are common in the 'trade' press, and usually include accounts of transactions between actors and managers.]

At the sitting of the County Court in Hull, on Thursday week Mr Raines, the judge, decided a claim of salary, brought against Mr George Egerton, the lessee of the Amphitheatre, by Mrs Stoneham, an actress, better known by the name of Miss Adelaide Cooke.

The sum claimed was £12 15s., for seven weeks' services, at the rate of 35s. per week. On the part of the plaintiff, who was represented by Mr Moss, Solicitor, it was proved that, on the 5th of February, Mr Egerton wrote to Miss Cooke, who was at that period in Newcastle, offering her an engagement, and asking her to state her salary. In this letter he said, 'I know well your professional reputation, and have been introduced to you in London; what are your terms, and when will you be at liberty?' To this letter Mrs Stoneham replied; and, on the 22nd of February, Mr Egerton again wrote, agreeing to give the plaintiff 35s. per week, and stated that was the highest sum paid on his establishment. In this letter Mr Egerton said, 'My season is until September, but I expect my licence to be continued, and of course my season will be continued also.'

In consequence of this letter the plaintiff went to Hull, and began playing on Wednesday, the 1st of March. For the first piece cast for plaintiff, she was required to assume male apparel, but as she was not the proper figure, she requested Mr Egerton to allow some one else to play that character. This, however, Mr Egerton could not do, as he had no one in his establishment who could assume that attire, and a military cloak was suggested to conceal the defect. Accordingly, Mrs Stoneham played it with the military cloak on, and continued playing the different characters assigned to her until the 17th of March, and was paid up to that time. Mr Egerton finding it inconvenient to keep the plaintiff on his establishment, in consequence of her not being able to take male characters, gave her a written fortnight's notice to quit. This, however, Mrs Stoneham would not agree to, and claimed the payment of her salary in full, until the end of the season, which was the 16th of May, amounting to £12 15s.

On the part of the defendant it was contended that the plaintiff was engaged with the understanding that she was to leave, if necessary, on the usual fortnight's notice being given, and Mr Egerton had given her notice in consequence of her figure not being suitable to all the characters necessary to be played.

The Judge: My opinion is, that Mr Egerton ought to have found that out before. It was his own fault; he should have gone to her before he made the engagement. He forgets that young people sometimes grow stouter.

Verdict for the plaintiff for £12 15s., the amount claimed.

ix

A beginner in the 1850s

[Ellen Terry began her stage career as the Spirit of the Mustard-Pot in a pantomime in a Scottish town. Her next engagement, and the first in which she had a 'part', was as Mamilius in Charles Kean's spectacular production of *A Winter's Tale* at the Princess's Theatre, London, in 1856. She was eight at the time. In *The Story of My Life* (1908) the actress describes her audition, and her excitement when her part, 'bound in green American cloth', arrived.]

Why was I chosen, and not one of the other children, for the part of Mamilius? some one may ask. It was not mere luck, I think. Perhaps I was a born actress, but that would have served me little if I had not been able to *speak*! It must be remembered that both my sister Kate and I had been trained almost from our birth for the stage, and particularly in the important branch of clear articulation. Father, as I have already said, was a charming elocutionist, and my mother read Shakespeare beautifully. They were both very fond of us and saw our faults with the eyes of love, though they were unsparing in their corrections. In these early days they had need of all their patience, for I was a most troublesome, wayward pupil. However, 'the labour we delight in physics pain', and I hope, too, that my more staid sister made it up to them!

The rehearsals for *A Winter's Tale* were a lesson in fortitude. They taught me once and for all that an actress's life (even when the actress is only eight) is not all beer and skittles, or cakes and ale, or fame and glory. I was cast for the part of Mamilius in the way I have described, and my heart swelled with pride when I was told what I had to do, when I realized that I had a real Shakespeare part – a possession that father had taught me to consider the pride of life!

But many weary hours were to pass before the first night. If a company.has to rehearse four hours a day now, it is considered a great hardship, and players must lunch and dine like other folk. But this was not Kean's way! Rehearsals lasted all day, Sundays included, and when there was no play running at night, until four or five the next morning! I don't think any actor in those days dreamed of luncheon. (Tennyson, by the way, told me to say 'luncheon' – not 'lunch'.) How my poor little legs used to ache! Sometimes I could hardly keep my eyes open when I was on the stage, and often when my scene was over, I used to creep into the greenroom and forget my troubles and my art (if you can talk of art in connection with a child of eight) in a delicious sleep.

At the dress-rehearsals I did not want to sleep. All the members of the company were allowed to sit and watch the scenes in which they were not concerned, from the back of the dress-circle. This, by the way, is an excellent plan, and in theatres where it is followed the young actress has reason to be grateful. In these days of greater publicity when the press attend rehearsals, there may be strong reasons against the company being 'in front', but the perfect loyalty of all concerned would dispose of these reasons. Now, for the first time, the beginner is able to see the effect of the weeks of thought and labour which have been given to the production. She can watch from the front the fulfilment of what she has only seen as intention and promise during the other rehearsals. But I am afraid that beginners now are not so keen as they used to be. The first wicked thing I did in a theatre sprang from excess of keenness. I borrowed a knife from a carpenter and made a slit in the canvas to watch Mrs Kean as Hermione! . . .

There is something, I suppose, in a woman's nature which always makes her remember how she was dressed at any specially eventful moment of her life, and I can see myself, as though it were yesterday, in the little red-and-silver dress I wore as Mamilius. Mrs Grieve, the dresser – 'Peter Grieve-us,' as we children called her – had pulled me into my very pink tights (they were by no means *tight* but very baggy, according to the pictures of me), and my mother had arranged my curls on each side of my head in even more perfect order and regularity than usual. Besides my clothes, I had a beautiful 'property' to be proud of. This was a go-cart, which had been made in the theatre by Mr Bradshaw, and was an exact copy of a child's toy as depicted on a Greek vase. It was my duty to drag this little cart about the stage, and on the first night, when Mr Kean as Leontes told me to 'go play', I obeyed his instructions with such vigour that I tripped over the handle and came down on my back! . . .

From April 28, 1856, I played Mamilius every night for one hundred and two nights. I was never ill, and my understudy, Clara Denvil, a very handsome, dark child with flaming eyes, though quite ready and longing to play my part, never had the chance . . .

It is argued now that stage life is bad for a young child, and children are not allowed by law to go on the stage until they are ten years old – quite a mature age in my young days! I cannot discuss the whole question here, and must content myself with saying that during my three years at the Princess's I was a very strong, happy, and healthy child. I was never out of the bill except during the run of *A Midsummer Night's Dream*, when, through an unfortunate accident, I broke my toe. I was playing Puck, my second part on any stage, and had come up through a trap at the end of the last act to give the final speech. My sister Kate was playing Titania that night as understudy to Carlotta Leclercq. Up I came – but not quite up, for the man shut the trap-door too soon and caught my toe. I screamed, Kate rushed to me and banged her foot on the stage, but the man only closed the trap tighter, mistaking the signal.

'Oh, Katie! Katie!' I cried. 'Oh, Nelly! Nelly!' said poor Kate helplessly. Then Mrs Kean came rushing on and made them open the trap and release my poor foot.

'Finish the play, dear,' she whispered excitedly, 'and I'll double your salary!' There was Kate holding me up on one side and Mrs Kean on the other. Well I did finish the play in a fashion. . . . How I got through it, I don't know! But my salary was doubled – it had been fifteen shillings, and it was raised to thirty – and Mr Skey, President of St Bartholomew's hospital, who chanced to be in a stall that very evening, came round behind the scenes and put my toe right. He remained my friend for life. . . .

8   Ellen Terry as Mamilius, with Charles Kean as Leontes, in *The Winter's Tale*, Princess's Theatre, 1854.

During the rehearsals Mrs Kean taught me to draw my breath in through my nose and begin a laugh – a very valuable accomplishment! She was also indefatigable in her lessons in clear enunciation, and I can hear her now lecturing the ladies of the company on their vowels. 'A, E, I, O, U, my dear', she used to say, 'are five distinct vowels, so don't mix them up all together as if you were making a pudding. If you want to say, "I am going on the river", say it plainly and don't tell us you are going on the "riv*ah*"! You must say *her*, not *har*; it's *God*, not *Gud*: remo*n*strance, not remu*n*strance', and so forth. No one ever had a sharper tongue or a kinder heart than Mrs Kean . . .

One of the most wearisome, yet essential details of my education is connected with my first long dress. It introduces, too, Mr Oscar Byrn, the dancing-master and director of crowds at the Princess's. One of his lessons was in the art of walking with a flannel blanket pinned on in front and trailing six inches on the floor. My success in carrying out this manoeuvre with dignity won high praise from Mr Byrn. The other children used to kick at the blanket and progress in jumps like young kangaroos, but somehow I never had any difficulty in moving gracefully. No wonder then that I impressed Mr Byrn, who had a theory that 'an actress was no actress unless she learned to dance early.' Whenever he was not actually putting me through my paces, I was busy watching him teach the others. There was the minuet, to which he used to attach great importance, and there was 'walking the plank'. Up and down one of the long planks, extending the length of the stage, we had to walk first slowly and then quicker and quicker until we were able at a considerable pace to walk the whole length of it without deviating an inch from the straight line. This exercise, Mr Byrn used to say, and quite truly, I think, taught us uprightness of carriage and certainty of step.

'Eyes right! Chest out! Chin tucked in!' I can hear the dear old man shouting at us as if it were yesterday; and I have learned to see of what value all his drilling was, not only to deportment, but to clear utterance. It would not be a bad thing if there were more 'old fops' like Oscar Byrn in the theatres of to-day. That old-fashioned art of deportment is sadly neglected.

Advice to the actor, 1860s

[From *The Actor's Art: its Requisites, and How to Obtain Them; its Defects, and how to Remove Them* (undated, *c*. 1867) by Charles William Smith. Most of Smith's advice is directed at actors in a theatre dominated by custom and routine, which set a premium on basic efficiency in the execution of generalized effects of behaving and speaking on stage. The naïvety of some of the advice (such as not knocking off an actor's wig when he is carried offstage) reflects the book's anticipated audience, but it is valuable for spelling out what would be taken for granted by experienced – if somewhat old-fashioned – actors in the middle of the century. It is notable that Smith proposes methods that will produce a 'natural and effective' impression within the terms of a conventionalized theatre.]

ENTRANCES AND EXITS. – These are of the greatest importance. A novice, who, from nervousness, want of practice, or absolute carelessness, makes a bad entrance on the stage, will find it very up-hill work during the scene, to overcome the ill impression which he made at first; while a very indifferent actor, who has acquired the art of making an effective entrance, prepossesses the audience in his favour, and, at least, is listened to with attention. A good exit is of still more importance. It will frequently cover many defects, and obtain applause after a badly acted scene; while, on the contrary, a bad exit will frequently obliterate the effect of good acting, and bring a fine scene to a 'most lame and impotent conclusion'.

Entrances and exits are arranged by the 'Star' or Stage Manager, when any alteration is made from the usual printed directions, but as an actor will often have his choice of different ways and amateurs are free to do as they please, we give the following hints: –

Always be at the 'wing' some minutes before the time for your entrance, so that you may become perfectly collected, and assume the character fully before you appear on the stage. Avoid all hurrying from your dressing room. Do not talk before going on, but let your mind be entirely occupied with your acting.

In entering, and taking up a position on the stage, the first consideration should be to get into a natural and effective attitude, free from all constraint, stiffness, and mannerism. A novice almost invariably takes up his position with the leg nearest the audience covering the one farthest from the audience. He will also generally get into the same attitude in kneeling or advancing to another person. The leg nearest to the audience should never be advanced in front of the other; nor should an actor stand sideways to the audience, with his legs close to each other, like a soldier standing in line. The leg farthest from the audience should always be in advance of the other, more or less, according to circumstances. This is a most important point for a novice to attend to. Practise entering and taking up a position in your own room frequently. Although a lady's dress conceals her legs, it is equally essential for her to attend to this rule, in order to preserve a natural and graceful attitude.

In making a rush on to the stage, commence the movement several feet from the point where you will come in sight, and take particular care that your steps are firm and decided, unless you have to represent indecision, fear, or any similar feeling. See that there is nothing to impede you, such as an awkwardly slung sword, or badly arranged drapery. Practise entries of this kind again and again, until you can fix your attitude, easily and effectively, exactly at the desired spot.

When leading on others, or pursued by an enemy, your face should be directed towards the entry, but your body should have its full front to the audience. Let the head be a little thrown back. Entrances of this kind are most effective when made from the Left, because the right hand, especially if grasping a sword or baton, can be used most effectively, and the whole figure can be displayed to the greatest advantage.

In many cases, the second entrance is preferable to the first. Actual trial of both in various cases, will show the student the advantages of each entrance, better than written instructions alone.

Entrances from the back of the stage have become very common, and are, doubtless, the most effective and natural in many cases, giving the actor great advantages, but they should not be so much used as they are in many plays; for the actor is often obliged to make his exit by the same way that he entered, and an exit from the back of the stage is, generally speaking, nothing like so effective as when made from the first entrance, if expression of face, or power, or delicate modulation of voice, be important to the passage . . .

In playing the character of an old man, be careful to assume the walk, stoop, and entire manner before you go on the stage. To do this properly, you must begin to walk three or four feet from the point where you will come in sight.

Where the actor should not at first be seen by those on the stage, entrances from the back or upper entrances are the best.

When the actor makes his exit or is about to do so, just as the drop scene descends, or where a picture is formed at his exit, it is best made at the back or upper entrances.

In making an exit through the first or second entrances, take care to retire, apparently without studied object, a step or two up the stage, when within three or four paces of the wing and a few lines before the last, so as to make your exit *diagonally* with the wing, by which your face and figure are almost full front to the audience as you make your exit.

When a person is carried off the stage in a faint, or dead, great care is necessary to keep up the natural representation. . . . These exits should be carefully rehearsed, and not, as they usually are, be left to chance at night. The position on the stage, and the distance from the wing, should be properly calculated. If possible, the person selected to bear off the actor should be sufficiently strong to do so, without faltering, but if, as must frequently be the case, this actor should have to carry off a much heavier person than he can bear he should have one to help him, and by a little contrivance at the rehearsal, he may appear to support the person who is in reality sustained by the other. Take care that the dress is clear of the wings. By proper rehearsal and arrangement, the folds of robes may be made to fall picturesquely, adding greatly to the effect of the exit. Be particularly careful not to touch the head of the actor you are supporting or his wig may come off . . .

KEEPING UP THE STAGE. – It is a very common fault with novices to keep too far up the stage, by which the expression of the face is, in a great degree, lost, and the power of the voice wasted by its ascending more among the 'flies' than penetrating into the front of the theatre. This arises, generally, from nervousness. Besides, the other actors speaking to him are thus obliged to act with their backs more or less turned towards the audience, by which their faces are concealed from the spectators, and their voices being directed towards the back, or farther sides of the stage, are but indistinctly heard in front. Old actors frequently keep up the stage, though not so far up as novices, purposely to display themselves to the exclusion of the other actors. This, which is allowable to a certain extent in a great actor, should be moderated by good judgement and fairness to the other actors. You should give and take, displaying yourself to the greatest advantage, whenever you have a fair opportunity, and allow others to do the same. Whenever you can act under the proscenium without interfering with the general grouping and effect, do so, especially when you have to delineate character by fine touches, as delicate modulations of the voice, and minute and transient shades of expression will be better heard and seen there than far up the stage.

THE STAGE WALK: – In tragedy the steps should be longer, the tread firmer and heavier, and the walk more massive and stately than in representing ordinary life and comedy. Tread evenly and easily on the ball of the foot, and avoid all unnatural swinging of the shoulders or the lower part of the body. Do not bend the knee . . .

STAGE COMBATS: – In stage fighting and fencing, skill in the use of the broadsword and foils, although of great service when backed by a knowledge of stage effect, is of comparatively little use without it. Perhaps the best way to become proficient is, to first take lessons from a good teacher of Fencing and Broadsword; practising as often as you can with those who are skilful, and avoiding practising with novices who may lead you into bad habits; and when you have acquired considerable knowledge of the capabilities, and skill in the use of your weapons, to take a few lessons from a good stage swordsman and fencer; who will instruct you in stage effect, fighting attitude and gestures. The old fashioned fighting swords with which 'terrific combats' were wont to be fought, are now almost out of vogue, and Macbeth frequently fights with a genuine claymore. This causes the fight to appear much more natural as well as more effective, but it is a very dangerous practice, even for skilful swordsmen to fight with sharp and full-length weapons. The best plan is to keep a sword specially for fighting, a little shorter than a real sword, made of very good steel, with thick, round edges and tip. It should have a strong guard for the protection of the hand and the hilt should be proportioned to the size of your hand. By always using this, you will become accustomed to it, and feel easy and confident in wielding your weapon. This fighting sword should be exchanged for the stage sword and placed in your scabbard before you go on the stage for the scene in which you have to fight . . .

REHEARSING: – It is a great and general mistake with actors at rehearsal to mutter over their parts in a hurried and inaudible manner. Some do this from carelessness; others with a mistaken purpose of preserving their voices for the actual performance at night. It has been said that the best method of strengthening the voice and keeping it in order for night, both for actors and singers, is to speak or sing as loudly at the rehearsal as you would at night. We consider this to be a great error. The quickest and surest way to ruin the voice is to fatigue it by too much wear. The actors who play the subordinate characters might rehearse aloud without being fatigued in voice at night; and advantageously, in so far as improving the voice by practice; but such a method is certain to beget constraint and an unnatural style of action and elocution. It is most difficult, and to most actors very unpleasant, to 'get up the steam' in rehearsing even a leading character full of the most impassioned and poetic language. To compel an actor to act a minor part at rehearsal as he ought to do at night, *à la* Macready and his copyists, for the edification of his fellow-actors, and a few scene-shifters, is converting the stage into a school for unnatural, conventional acting and elocution, and making a rehearsal a mental torture to the sensitive . . .

The careless, muttering mode of rehearsing is equally bad, and begets a slipshod style of elocution, imperfection in the words, and uneven acting. 'All right at night, my boy', has spoiled many a promising actor.

The best mode of rehearsing, combining all the advantages of the first method, such as thoroughly understanding the business of the play, the proper positions, and effects to be produced, and perfectness in the language, with a more natural style, and also freedom from the defects of both methods, is this: To rehearse with the same *quality* of feeling or passion as you would express at night, but with a less *quantity*, that is, equally true to nature but more subdued; with assumption of character, but not so strongly drawn; with the same emphasis and elocution, but less loud. The rehearsal should be to ascertain that the actors are perfect in the language and business of the play, and also in some cases to test or try the effect of the coming representation; and to do this well, the actor should be so far from the excitement of the actual performance before an audience, that his mind is constantly on the watch to correct, to improve, to develop and to perfect. The rehearsal should be to the actual representation, what the correct and spirited sketch of a master is to the finished and highly coloured picture.

'Treasury', matinées and salaries: the Bancrofts' reforms, 1860s

[Squire Bancroft and Marie Wilton (subsequently Sir Squire and Lady Bancroft) took over the Prince of Wales's Theatre in Tottenham Street in 1865. Their transformation of it from 'the dust-hole' to a mecca for middle-class comedy is emblematic of Victorian ambitions for a respectable theatre. The improvements included measures calculated to better the status of actors. The following is taken from the 1909 edition of the Bancrofts' joint autobiography, *The Bancrofts: Recollections of Sixty Years*.]

Of all the changes which were inaugurated by my wife and myself at the little Prince of Wales's Theatre, I, personally, was proudest of, perhaps, the simplest of them. I had endured much mortification in my early days upon the stage from the old method which then prevailed of paying the actors engaged in the theatre. Every one of them had to assemble on Saturday mornings outside the treasury at a certain hour – carpenters, ballet girls, cleaners, players, musicians, mixed up together. I found, to my profound surprise, that things were just the same in London, and claim the privilege of having been the first to alter the obnoxious custom. It was, in fact, the initial reform made by me when I came into authority, to order that all members of our company should henceforth be waited upon by the treasurer instead of their having to wait upon him. I record the fact because actors of the present day can have no idea who made the change, or of the former habit . . .

A brief history of the commencement of morning perform- ances may have some interest to-day. In the early days of our management they were things unknown, except for pantomimes and occasional big charity entertainments. We first tried one of *School*, in the height of its great success, with only a moderate and not sufficiently encouraging result. Five or six years passed before we repeated the experiment, and then with the sole object of gratifying an earnest wish expressed by Sothern to see my wife act in *Sweethearts*. To complete a short programme, Ellen Terry, who was then a member of our company, appeared with me in a charming one-act play, called *A Happy Pair*, which we studied for this solitary occasion. The theatre was crowded. In the following year we acted *Peril* a considerable number of times on afternoons; but it was not until we produced *Diplomacy*, in 1878, that what are now called *matinées* – afternoon representations of the regular evening performance – were really established. At the beginning they were much more costly than now, frequent and separate advertisements and announcements being necessary to make them known. Morover, it was our custom, and one we maintained throughout our management, to pay full salaries to everyone concerned in these afternoon performances – a rule which applied not only to actors but to business managers, booking-clerks, hall-keeper, firemen, in fact to all to whom the performance practically involved the equivalent of an evening's labour. These afternoon performances have long since become a large source of income to the managers; but I am told that in most of the theatres other systems of payment now prevail. It seems to me hard that the actor should not be given his full share, and harder still upon the ballet-girls and poorer members of a company, who can ill afford the least deduction from their pay, and who are not in a position to protest.

In what were called 'the palmy days' of the drama – days, in my remembrance, of much slovenliness and dingy solemnity, as well as of most useful and hard work – salaries were lamentably small, and the rewards to which even eminent actors could aspire in former times were pitiful indeed. I know no more plaintive story than the desperate struggles made by so great a man as Macready to secure for his retirement an income of a thousand a year to support and educate a large family, even that fortune involving banishment from London for the remainder of his life. We may claim without arrogance to have been the first to effect a reform which should secure a proper reward for the laborious life and special gifts demanded of the actor, and make the stage a worthy career for refined and talented people. The pay was small enough, and on the old lines, when we began; in a few years things were very different. As an instance, John Hare's[1] first salary when he was but an unknown youth, was only two pounds weekly, nor did he ever reach with us the high figure subsequently paid, as it never exceeded twenty pounds – a large sum then. The advance came soon by leaps and bounds: four years afterwards [in 1879] we gave George Honey[2] sixty pounds a week to take the part in *Caste* which he had previously acted for eighteen, while Mrs Stirling,[3] when she played the Marquise in our final revival of that comedy [in 1883], received eight times the salary we had paid to the original representative of the character. To Charles Coghlan,[4] who only received nine pounds a week with us when he replaced Montague,[5] we paid, on later occasions, fifty, and then sixty pounds; and without multiplying examples, I may say that such rates were maintained proportionately throughout the company.

NOTES

1   *John Hare*   (1844–1921), actor and, later, manager: engaged by the Bancrofts to play the gasfitter, Sam Gerridge, in the first production of *Caste*.

2   *George Honey*   Comic actor whose line of parts included Eccles in *Caste*, Graves in a revival of Bulwer-Lytton's *Money* and Cheviot Hill in Gilbert's *Engaged*.

3   *Mrs Stirling*   Fanny Stirling (1815–95): actress, famous for performances in soubrette roles.

4   *Charles Coghlan*   (1842–99) After considerable success as a comic actor in plays by Robertson and others, he sought to extend his range: Shylock (in 1875) was thought by some to show the inadequacy of 'cup and saucer' technique for impassioned Elizabethan roles.

5   *Montague*   H. J. Montague played Lord Beaufoy in the first production of *School* (1869).

'Leading ladies, walking ladies and heavy women', 1860s

[By T.W. Robertson, *The Illustrated Times*, 13 February 1864. Articles in the series, 'Theatrical Types,' include some fictionalized biographical sketches (here omitted) and the general aim is to present a true picture of life in the theatre.]

The first time that a sensitive and impressionable lad, above thirteen years of age, visits a theatre and sees a play, the most vivid image he carries home with him, is that of a stately creature, with high forehead, haughty mien, and thrilling voice; clad, not dressed, in heavy, massive, black velvet, or white aërial, floating, breezy muslin. In theatrical parlance this grand and noble divinity is the Leading Lady, or, in the cant translation bred of cheap return tickets and the desire to avoid simple English, the Tragédienne . . .

The love of acting spreads over so wide a surface of society that Leading Ladies are recruited from all classes. Daughters of wealthy men who have bent their knees imploringly to *soi-disant* Siddonses;[1] daughters of ruined gentlemen forced to seek their bread, and insufficiently accomplished for the dreadful trade of 'governessing'; daughters of actors, born and reared to it; and daughters of publicans who keep theatrical taverns, where the portraits of popular actors and actresses are framed, glazed and enriched with autographs. All these are the raw material which time, tact, and the horse labour of a rising barrister[2] manufactures into dramatic heroines. While speaking of portraits, it is impossible not to remark on the blessing of photography to small celebrities seeking publicity.

But though tragic actresses of genius are born, not made, good tragic actresses are made, not born. It is but seldom that they rush from mamma's frowns to the stage-manager's sneer; and when they do, they usually fail. . . . Leading Ladies begin by playing what is called, in greenrooms, dressing-rooms, and dramatic agents' address-books, first and second Walking Ladies.

Walking Ladies have been said to derive their appellation from the fact of their always being ready to escape from their father, aunt or guardian, and walk off with their lover . . .

This sort of dramatic infancy being endured for two or three years, in various country theatres, the walking lady casts off the sash of farce, the wings of ballet, the hood of melodrama and the hoop of comedy, and assumes the toga, robe, and crown of tragedy; and then what weight of work, what worlds of words are piled up for the aspirant! A Colonial Secretary leads a lazy life compared to the poor Leading Lady. And a deceived public believes the actor's life is *play*. A tragic actress must 'study' – that is, learn by heart, as it is called, the text of the characters of Desdemona, Imogen, Cordelia, Lady Macbeth, Constance, Miranda, Rosalind, Beatrice, Portia, Juliet, Hermione, the two Katherines of Padua and Aragon, Julia, Virginia, Belvidera, the ladies Teazle, Townley, and Randolph, Mistress Jane Shore, and a host of heroines of dramas such as Black-eyed Susan, Rachel Heywood, Miami, Cynthia, and the like . . .

The leading actress in the country theatre will rise at nine, and, after laving her hot forehead and pale face with water, snatch a cup of turbid, provincially prepared coffee, rush to the theatre, for the 'call' for the rehearsal at ten. The drama of *Susan Hopley*, in which she sustains the character of that pattern of domestic young ladies in service, occupies her till past twelve. She then waits till two, for the eminent tragedian, Mr Lara Thunderstone, who is to 'star' as Macbeth that night, does not rise early, and always keeps rehearsal waiting. The 'eminent' having at last arrived – bilious of stomach and fastidious of taste – protracts the rehearsal, and at half-past-four, faint, sick, and tired, the sinking actress reaches her lodgings. Her dinner has been waiting two hours. It is half cold and wholly clammy. She is past appetite and orders tea, which is prepared as detestably as was the morning's coffee. Dresses have then to be looked out, unpacked, altered, trimmings changed and gold lace ripped off and 'run on'. The basket, that wondrous mystery, is packed, and the actress follows it to the dressing-room, where she is installed by six. For five hours and a half she acts, and acts, and acts, speaks, speaks, and speaks, changes her dress, changes her dress, and changes her dress; and all this time she never sits down for a moment. Home by midnight, she eats and enjoys her supper, the only meal hard fate permits her. 'She sleeps well, after that', might say an unbelieving reader. Sleep! She sits up till daylight, studying Evadne, in Sheil's play; for the eminent tragedian, Mr Lara Thunderstone, of the Theatres Royal Everywhere, has chosen to play Colonna on the following evening. Ladies at the head of establishments, schoolmistresses, governesses, shopgirls, milliners, cooks, housemaids, laundresses and charwomen – what is your work to this?

The power that sustains the actress through her enormous daily and nightly task is the artiste's nervous irritability, love of applause, and the hope of future fame – that hope so delusive that, in green-room diction, it is called 'The Phantom'.

Six or eight years passed in the dreary drudgery of provincial theatres, the Leading Lady at last gets an appearance in London. If she pleases her audience – that is, if the manager of the theatre permit her to appear in a part she *can* play, and does not compel her to appear in one for which she is unfitted, she is a great success, and, as dramatic slang has it, 'her wood is made'. Her income is at once raised from £2 or £3 per week to £20 or £30; her dismal lodgings changed to elegant apartments; her shabby black silk gown for new and lustrous moire antique; her old listless, half-resentful, half-despairing manner for a winning grace and proud consciousness of power; her relatives, particularly those who held her adoption of the stage in the strongest horror, call on, fawn, flatter and borrow money of her; and four-and-twenty photographers all of a row besiege her door determined not to move on under a sitting . . .

When the L.L. (Leading Lady) makes a failure she returns to the provinces; or, if she be gifted with a matronly figure and deep voice, drops into what is called 'heavy business' – that is, she plays Emilia in *Othello*; the Queen in *Hamlet*, &c. 'Heavy Women', as they are elegantly and delicately designated, have often large families and rickety husbands, and support both with a heroism far more admirable than that of the wordy and blatant personages they represent. Those who know but little of theatres and their belongings, often regret that actresses in private life so little resemble the heroines they portray. If they could look on them, not by the false medium of batwing burners, but by domestic daylight or economical composites,[3] they would regret that heroines did not often idealize the real virtues of actresses – virtues intensified and polished by the cultivation of the most emotional of arts. Though all leading dramatic heroines do not become the wives of baronets, the practice of their education so refines and educates their sentiments that they are always ladies.

NOTES

1   soi-disant *Siddonses*   Self-styled tragedy-queens (claiming to be successors of Sarah Siddons, 1755–1831).

2   *the horse labour . . . barrister*   i.e. in a play written in his spare time by a barrister.

3   *batwing burners . . . composites*   Gas lights and candles.

Actors: supply and demand, 1866

[Horace Wigan, manager of the Olympic, testifies to the House of Commons Select Committee on Theatrical Licences and Regulations, May 1866. The Committee's deliberations concentrated on the effects on the legitimate theatre of the growth of the music-halls and the kind of entertainment that should be allowed in the halls.]

4580.   Do you think that there is room for a good many more theatres in London? – I think that the present number of theatres is amply sufficient for the actors, and for the theatrical public; but I am not prepared to say that if there were more theatres it might not create a wider taste in the English public; I think perhaps it would.

4581.   Would it create actors? – I do not think that they require creating; I think that there are plenty of actors.

4582.   Do you think that there are plenty of actors to supply the whole of the theatres that you might have? – Plenty.

4583.   Are the salaries as high as they used to be? – They are very much higher, particularly in the country, where they have increased 30 or 50 per cent within a few years. I remember the time when a guinea a week was considered a good salary in the country; but there are very few men at the present time in the country, with any responsible duties to perform, who would not get three times that amount.

[H.J. Turner, theatrical agent, appears before the same body. E.T. Smith, manager of Drury Lane, had already commented on the eagerness of young actors to become comic singers: 'A man can go and get £6 a week from a music-hall, and he will sing over the water, or he will keep his brougham and go up to the Oxford, and then he will go to another music-hall again; he will go and get his four or five turns a night, and earn £20 or £30 a week.' (Qu. 3862.)]

5044.   You are a Theatrical Agent, are you not? – I am.

5045.   Can you tell the Committee what business that involves? – Receiving from managers their instructions with regard to what actors or actresses they require, and furnishing them with them. . . .

5049. I suppose there is no man who is more acquainted with the general scale of salaries of actors and actresses than you are? – I should say that few men are better acquainted with them than I am.

5050. Do you act for the provinces? – I act both for town and the provinces.

5051. Now, on the whole, have the salaries of actors risen or fallen within the last few years? – I should say, in the provinces they have risen from one-third to one-half.

5052. And there is a great demand for both actors and actresses, I suppose? – There is a great demand. I find a very great difficulty in supplying the managers, either in town or in the country, with the ladies and gentlemen they require.

5053. There is not a large number of unemployed actors and actresses, is there? – I think there are very few good actors or actresses unemployed.

5054. If there were many more theatres, would it be difficult to supply that larger number with actors and actresses? – I think it would.

5055. Do the numbers increase in the theatrical profession? – I should say not. There are a great many theatres built, but the numbers of the profession have not increased in the same ratio.

5056. Are there many actors taken away by the music-halls? – There are a great many subordinate ones; young men who can sing a song. The payment is much better in music-halls than in theatres.

Prices for Charles Kean's tour, 1867

[The insistence on their dignity by leading Victorian actors may sometimes seem pompous, but (then as now) reputation and livelihood were inextricably joined. Kean here writes from Liverpool to James Rodgers, lessee of the Theatre Royal, Birmingham, who was managing a tour of the Midlands for him. MS letters in Birmingham Public Library (Local Studies Collection). The abbreviations for currency have been added.]

17 May 1867

My Dear Sir, Are we to play *two* or *three* nights in Worcester? It is now time that I should know. And what is the *precise route* you mean to take after Nottingham [?] Do not put us up for *three* nights in Worcester unless you feel certain of the success. Better *two great* than three middling.

We are doing fine business here & it is likely to continue till the end – Friday 31st.

Can you tell me whether there is any store rooms or Warehouse in Birmingham where I could deposit my boxes for three month or so? If you know of such a place please send me the name and address.

They have issued throughout Liverpool & the neighbourhood some thousands of printed circulars which have done good service. Hundreds read them who never look at the newspaper advertisements or the play bills – I will send you a copy in a day or two.

18 May 1867

Dear Sir, Your suggestion about Nottingham prices has startled me. Had I been aware that there would have been any opposition to the usual scale at which I play elsewhere, & more especially considering it will be my 'farewell', I would not have engaged to visit that city at all.

I never have acted *successful* engagement anywhere to low prices. My party altogether amounts to 8 and sometimes nine persons – my expenses average £100 a week and how can one shilling and one sixpence with three shillings pay me?

When I was at Nottingham with you before the prices were 5s. dress [circle] – 2s. Pit & 1s. Gallery. This should have been arranged long before this & the bills & advertisements might now be out if you purpose *great* business.

You do not say a word to me in your letter of today whether you wish me to play *two* or *three* nights in Worcester. I think two quite sufficient – namely Thursday 6 June & Friday 7th, but all this ought to be published now. You are getting behind hand in time & these engagements will break down if you don't be quick about announcing us. Worcester 5s. Dress, 2s. Pit and 1s. Gallery.

No half price any where and no children admitted.

The lowest prices I will play to in Nottingham are 4s. Dress, 2s. 6d. Upper [Circle?], Pit 1s. 6d., Gallery 1s. But if on conferring you find the feeling strong in favour of the 1 Pit & sixpenny gallery, I will give my clear understanding that [? name illegible] has the power of *limiting* the numbers. But assuredly not less than 4s. D[ress] Boxes and 2s. 6d. Upper [Circle].

I enclose you the copy of the circular which will benefit the engagements if you have printed with the alterations & circulate. Of course altering dates & names to suit your Towns. Send me a *proof*. I cannot act after the 21 June.

xv

An actor's stock-in-trade, 1872

[When the veteran actor Walter Montgomery died, his wardrobe of costumes was sold. The report in *The Era* (10 November 1872) gives an idea of what a touring actor needed to own in the middle decades of the century, the roles of the 'standard' legitimate repertoire, and the extent of his travels.]

On Monday last the theatrical wardrobe and other valuable effects of the late Walter Montgomery were submitted for sale by auction at Messrs Puttock and Simpson's Gallery, Leicester-square. The attendance was by no means so large as had been anticipated, but we nevertheless noticed among the costumiers and dealers who surrounded the rostrum of the auctioneer a number of gentlemen of eminence in the theatrical world, evidently anxious to secure a *souvenir* of one who, both by his talents as an actor and by his personal good qualities, had endeared himself to all whose privilege it was to know him. The first lot submitted to competition was a costume for Hamlet, consisting of shirt, tabard, belt, pocket, striped drapery, shoes, hat and feather, and black disguise cloak, which realized 25s. A costume for Othello went for 40s.; Claude Melnotte,[1] second dress, 40s.; third dress, 35s.; Richard the Third, first dress, 36s.; second dress, 22s; third dress, 45s; Julius Caesar, first dress, including amber merino undershirt, Roman back and breast plates, helmet and plume, sword, shield, wristlets, scarlet-cloth toga, and under shirt, 60s.; Macbeth, including three surcoats, spangled gauntlets, neck-piece, head-piece, crimson-cloth robe with jewelled bosses, red and black drapery, 60s. Costumes for Coriolanus, Louis the Eleventh, Shylock, Romeo, Don César de Bazan, Master Walter, the Stranger,[2] &c., realized prices of which 30s. was the average. The best prices were secured for a number of pairs of worsted and silk tights. The travelling case and leather portmanteau, which accompanied the deceased in his wanderings, and which still bore the labels of railway companies in far distant lands, was purchased by a well-known and popular comedian for one guinea. Two stage claymores were sold for 34s., and a jewelled sword and dagger for 30s. The double-barrelled breech-loading gun, by Westley Richards, used in the field by Mr Montgomery only a week prior to his death, went for £10. The sale realized altogether about £80; several lots beings purchased by Mr H. Melton, of Regent-street, a very old and sincere friend of Mr Montgomery. His intimate friends said there were various articles (especially a collection of books) belonging to the deceased scattered about at Liverpool, New York, Boston and Melbourne.

NOTE

1   *Claude Melnotte*   Leading character in Bulwer-Lytton's play *The Lady of Lyons* (1838).
2   *Master Walter, the Stranger*   Characters in James Sheridan Knowles' *The Hunchback* (1832) and English versions of Kotzebue's *Menschenhass und Reue* (as *The Stranger*, 1798, etc.). Louis the Eleventh and Don César de Bazan are the title characters of popular plays adapted by Dion Boucicault from French originals.

'Trials of the ballet', 1877

[Two letters in *The Era* on the pay and conditions of ballet girls in London theatres.]

16 December 1877

Sir, – Will you give me space in your valuable columns to show a few of the trials, troubles, and temptations of those whose lot it is to belong to the ballet. In the first place it is not generally known that we have to practise for four to six weeks, for which in London we get not a single penny-piece. I ask why we should not be paid for that time as well as when the night duties commence? We often get promises from the Manager that he will give us half-pay for rehearsals, but when these rehearsals commence he shuffles out of it with some lame excuse. Surely the rehearsal time is the time we want money most to obtain food and other necessaries. As soon as the rehearsals are complete we have a night or two before the production of the ballet to go to the Hall or Theatre at twelve o'clock at night and rehearse until five or six o'clock the next morning. Now, why is this necessary? Could it not be done as well in day-time? It is all very well for the principals, who have their friends to treat them to what they like, but not for the ballet. There are more girls annually that I know who have been brought to shame and trouble through midnight rehearsals than through any other cause. The Press generally is ever ready to crush us poor wretches. No one has a good word for us, because the world does not know one half our trials and troubles, or they would have pity instead of disgust. Hoping that some kind friend will take up the matter and remedy the evils of the ballet in its present state, I enclose my name and address, and I subscribe myself,

Yours obediently,

A POOR BALLET GIRL

23 December 1877

Sir, – Seeing *The Era* of last Sunday, I beg to say it is true about rehearsals, and that is not all. I am what they call an extra lady, and at the Theatres on this side the water – the Surrey side – we only get 8s. per week, and at this time of the year we have to find everything for the Pantomime, as they say they can't afford to pay for them. So we must, or go. We mustn't speak out, or we go at a moment's notice. Tights, shoes, and muslin dresses take over one pound to pay for out of our money. We have to do all this for nothing. We have rehearsals from ten in the morning until five, then sometimes in the evening; and then you have your own dresses to make. What time have you, except when you ought to be asleep? If you are five minutes late in the morning you are fined, and at the same time you are starving, and have to depend on your landlord to let you run on a bit, or pawn all you have got, or do something else, and that is our lot in life. This is how us poor girls are treated that want to get a honest living, as I and hundreds more do. If the public did but know half our lot they would pity us, I think, and we might get a little more and the Proprietor might buy our things, as it is for their good, not ours. All this is true, I am sure, and a deal more. If you think proper to publish this, or any of it, you would have the thanks of many poor girls, who would ever pray for your welfare.

Yours obediently,

A BALLET GIRL

xvii

Terms on a sliding scale for a 'star', 1876

[Letter (28 August 1876) from Edward Saker, manager of the Alexandra Theatre, Liverpool, to 'Mr Rogers' on terms for an American performer, evidently of some standing. MS letter, Harvard Theatre Collection.]

The best terms I can offer Mr Rigg* is [sic] should the receipts be under £500 per week, I would share with him after £180 per week – should the receipts be over £500 and under £700 I would share after £125 per week. And should the receipts be over £700 per week I would share after £100 per week – for twelve nights to commence 16th April 1877 – the earliest date I have – Easter being already engaged.

NOTE

*   *Mr Rigg*   Unidentified.

xviii

Terms proposed to Hermann Vezin, 1880

[Vezin, an American-born actor famous for his elocution, never rose above secondary roles in London: in this letter (22 September 1880) W.W. Robertson offers him a contract to appear on tour with a season to follow in London at the Gaiety. 'Mornings' are matinée performances. MS letter, Bristol University Theatre collection.]

I understood we were arranged from Oct 11th till Dec 10th or thereabouts terms £30 and travelling expenses. That you would be able then to join us for mornings at Gaiety commencing Jan 8th on previous terms you having [?right to three] Evenings. From Oct 11th to Dec, We shall mostly play *As You Like It* but at Glasgow purpose letting you shine in something big if business in former drops at all.

At the Gaiety we produce *Much Ado*. Benedict you would be cast for.

A novice's guide to backstage organization, c.1880

[*The Actor's Handbook, and Guide to the Stage for Amateurs*, by 'the Old Stager', was published by Dicks in the mid-1880s. Much of the advice on acting – especially the description of gestures and expressions for the different emotions – seems to relate to an earlier theatre and is of doubtful value to the historian. The section below deals with responsibilities backstage in old-fashioned 'stock' theatres.]

THE LINE OF CONDUCT TO BE OBSERVED ON FIRST ENTERING A THEATRE

The first person you should inquire for . . . is the prompter, to whom you make yourself known, and give your address. The prompter will introduce you to the stage manager, who will conduct you to the green-room and introduce you to the rest of the company. The part assigned to you, and a notice as to the rehearsal, will be sent to you according to the address given, or delivered to you at the theatre by the call-boy or prompter's assistant. As you read your character, you will ascertain what properties are required in the different scenes you have to act – such as a purse, books, keys, bottle, &c., &c. Of these things you will make memoranda, and on the night of the performance, hand the list to the property man, or ask him for them. In a properly conducted theatre the performer is saved this trouble, as at the last rehearsal and at night the call-boy brings him the properties required when he makes each call. It is essential that these things should be returned immediately, as they may be wanted in the next scene; but if you have to deliver them to any person on the stage, the responsibility for returning them rests on the person so receiving them from you.

After the rehearsal, your next care is to find the wardrobe-keeper, whose permission you should ask to look at your dress. Then try it on, and show the wardrobe-keeper what alterations (if any) are necessary. It is a rule in every well-regulated theatre that no dress be worn that has not been approved of by the manager; in light comedy, however, where you provide everything, this is left to your own discretion. Still, in such pieces it will be wise to consult your fellow-performers as to what costume they intend to assume. From a neglect of this precaution, I have seen, at one of our first provincial theatres, Sir Benjamin Backbite* and Charles and Joseph Surface habited exactly alike, a thing destructive of scenic effect, and therefore displeasing to the eyes of the audience.

In the dressing-room, to which the prompter's boy will conduct you, you will find your name written at that part of it assigned for you to dress in, and thither the articles provided by the theatre for you to wear will be sent by the wardrobe-keeper. It is no part of the duty of the dresser of a provincial theatre to clean the shoes or boots you wear upon the stage; but this is usually done by him, and for this he expects some little remuneration. A few years since it was understood that the things worn in the play should be washed for you by the establishment, but in the provinces this custom is falling into disuse. Neither is it now usual for a hair-dresser to attend at the manager's expense, so the performer must therefore be prepared to look after himself in this particular. It may be well to remark in this connection that one of our greatest actors has said – 'Wear your own locks whenever it is not absolutely improper; the best wig is not so good as the worst head of hair' . . .

At rehearsal, if there is any particular movement or action, technically called 'business', for you to perform, the stage-manager or prompter will explain it to you and show you how to go through it.

Having rehearsed one scene, should you have another, or anything farther to do in the piece, retire to the green-room until you are again called. Never, under any circumstances, leave the theatre, or be out of the way, when you are liable to be called for the stage. It is the duty of the call-boy to summon you from the green-room only, unless your presence is required in the music-room for some especial purpose. Operas, ballets, pantomimes, and some particular pieces are generally called for by the act – that is, all concerned in the piece are summoned at the commencement of each act, and are expected to be at their place of entrance, &c., without further notice.

Should there be any changes made with your entrance or in anything else at rehearsal, always mark your part according to such alterations, and also make a memorandum of the stage properties which you are to carry on or use at night, in order to avoid trouble or difficulty in case the call-boy should forget or neglect to hand them to you. The first thing after you receive a part is . . . to become perfect in the words as soon as possible. In a new piece, never be seen at the last rehearsal with the book or MS in your hand. Should the play be in manuscript, it will be read to the company in the green-room, to which you should pay particular attention . . .

I have now, I believe, given you all the instructions, rules, &c., concerning a rehearsal that can be communicated by means of the pen; and when you have gone through it with the zeal of a student and the demeanour of a gentleman, the next subject which should claim your attention is that of your dressing-room. It is usual at the commencement of the season for the stage-manager to place a list upon the door of each dressing-room, containing the names of the persons who are to occupy the apartment; but should this not be done, you will consult the stage-manager at once. Having settled all these matters, go home and select such articles and private properties as you will need for the night, and then read your part over, or, if perfect in that, peruse some good book on the profession, the lives of eminent actors, works on the customs of different nations, on elocution, &c., or any standard literary productions calculated to expand the mind, and to improve and refine the taste.

NOTE

* *Sir Benjamin Backbite* . . . In Sheridan's *The School for Scandal*.

A beginner in the 1880s

[In *Mainly Players: Bensonian Memories* (1926) Constance Benson, wife of Sir Frank Benson, recalls her first engagements. She began with small parts in a provincial tour by the Lyceum company, 'walking on' as Rosaline in *Romeo and Juliet*, and appearing as a page in *Ruy Blas*. Hugh Moss, referred to as a source of advice, was stage-manager with the company and played a servant in the opening scene.]

Following this engagement with the Lyceum Company, I joined the John Chute's Company on tour. . . . Several Shakespearean plays were in the repertoire, also *La Dame aux Camélias, Lady of Lyons* and *A Night of Terror.* . . . I was engaged for 'boys' and 'second old women', and had to provide my own dresses at a salary of a guinea a week. One night, on account of the leading lady's indisposition, I was asked by Chute to play Juliet at a few minutes' notice. I had only been six weeks on the stage, but, through nightly watching the play from the wings, while with the Lyceum Company, I knew every word of the part, and so was able to get through without any catastrophe. After the play, I received an offer from Chute, to play Vera, in *Moths*, which I was wise enough to refuse, knowing I had not enough experience for leading parts.

Engagements followed with the Hemming Farcical Comedy Company, the late Gerald Moore's *Our Regiment* Company on tour, and matinées at the Criterion and Toole's Theatre.

My next engagement was as Dulcie in *Vice Versa*, and then with Ada Swanborough,[1] playing in the 'Strand Comedies', both at the old Strand Theatre (now demolished) and on tour. It was during one of these performances, at the Strand Theatre, that the celebrated Mrs Keeley[2] most graciously spoke kind words of approval and encouragement to me.

After this, on Hugh Moss' advice (which was, that every actor should have a short course of Pantomime, 'to teach him to shake hands with the audience'), I took an engagement with the late Fred Neebe, of Exeter, in his Christmas pantomime of *Aladdin*. What an experience! but how invaluable it was, in teaching one to move on stage, to gain self-confidence, and to 'face the audience!'

I was cast for the 'third Boy'. I, who was so miserable at wearing tights in *Ruy Blas*, was clad in a tight satin costume, covered with spangles and perfectly hideous. I was never so depressed in my life.

Hugh Moss had told me that, when a girl wore boy's clothes, she should disguise her figure by winding a towel round her waist. This device I had employed in the Lyceum Company, so I tried it again as the 'third Boy'. But my manager would have none of it, and sent me on to the stage, looking a very fair imitation of an hour-glass.

The part I was cast for consisted of about six lines, which I know I delivered abominably. In the third Act, I had to wear a black cloth 'Masher' coat, and satin breeches, and strut round the stage, singing the while the following ditty:[3]

> I'm a strut up the Strand-ity
> Cane in my hand-ity
> Cutting the Deuce of a Fellah!

This song evidently suited my style, for I was given the 'principal girl', owing to the star's absence through illness and played the part for three or four weeks. That pantomime was a wonderful experience, and one that I have never regretted.

I found the chorus-girls kindness itself; few of them would have been engaged for their morality, but they had the greatest admiration for virtue in others . . .

After the pantomime, I joined the late William Gomersal's stock season company in Worcester, where we played a different play every night.

This was in the days (even then dying fast) when the most primitive effects were not despised. I remember a melodrama being put up, in which there was the most thrilling railway accident. The train was a cardboard one (in profile) and the whole strength of the Company was enlisted to run this locomotive across the stage. The fact that our feet were visible did not seem to detract from the tragedy of the situation, and a piercing shriek from the wings, announcing the heroine's awful end, brought the curtain down with storms of applause.

NOTES

1   *Ada Swanborough . . . 'Strand Comedies'*   Ada Swanborough (1845–93) appeared in a succession of comic roles at the Strand Theatre from 1861 to 1879.

2   *Mrs Keeley*   Mary Ann Keeley (1806–99), actress, notably
     successful in comic parts. With her husband Robert Keeley she
     managed the Lyceum from 1844 to 1847.

3   *the following ditty*   Apparently indebted to one of Gilbert's lyrics
     in *Patience* (1881).

xxi

Herbert Beerbohm Tree states his terms, 1881

[E.W. Godwin had evidently invited Tree to join one of his
experimental enterprises, but Tree's letter (21 September 1881)
shows that the terms proposed were not adequate. Tree had been
a professional actor since 1878. MS letter, Theatre Museum (papers
of E.W. Godwin).]

My dear Godwin,
I now send you my engagements for the last two years – I may
remark, in addition, that I refused a second year's engagement
with Bruce* at £20 per week, as I was told to keep myself open
beyond the first year in order to join the theatre with which we
both contemplated being connected – you will observe that last
Xmas I was already in receipt of £15 per week at the Criterion
Theatre, and as far back as March, 1880, I was in receipt of £14
14s. per week in *Madame Favart* Coy., having at that time not
been two years on the stage – It would therefore be absurd on my
part to join the 'English Society of Players' upon a lower basis
than £20 per week upon the calculation of full salaries. That is my
decision.

                                        Your Sincerely,

                                        H.BEERBOHM TREE

NOTE

*   *Bruce*   Edgar Bruce (1845–1901), actor and impresario.

Johnston & Hoffmann.

1139 B   MR. AND MRS. KENDAL   ROTARY PHOTO. E.C.

9   The actor-managerial couple as eminently respectable:
postcard showing Mr and Mrs Kendal, *c.* 1905.

Mrs Kendal on the actor's status, 1885

[From a paper, 'The Drama', read by Mrs Kendal at the Congress of the National Association for the Promotion of Social Science in September 1884 (1885).]

Perhaps the most remarkable change that has come over the condition of the Drama is the fact that there is at last a recognized social position for the professional player. Formerly actors formed a little body in themselves. The Theatrical Profession was considered outside, if not beneath, all others, and was regarded with something like contempt. It was a wrong, cruel, and an absurd state of things, for even then the Theatre was popular, and was doing good work. . . . [In Garrick's day] members of all the other professions were glad enough to come and amuse themselves with the outcome of the actor's genius; his ability was recognized; it was, as it is now, the subject of universal conversation and of much newspaper comment; but the door of 'society' was closed to him. Now all that is altered. The Theatrical Profession is acknowledged to be a high and important one, and the society of the intelligent and cultivated actor is eagerly sought after. Just at present, indeed, the new state of things, having become universally known and recognized, has become also a little embarrassing.

One is always hearing or reading in the papers that the professions are 'overstocked' – that there are too many clergymen, too many lawyers, too many doctors, and the fact that the terms of actor and of gentleman may now be regarded as synonymous, seems to have sent the 'overdraft' of all these other professions headlong on to the stage.

How many younger sons of well-born but not too well-to-do parents have hailed the present social position of the actor with delight? How many educated girls, finding themselves, through force of circumstances, suddenly compelled to face the world on their own account, have turned with a sigh of relief from the prospect of the stereotyped position of 'companion' or 'governess' to the vista that an honourable connection with the Stage holds out to them? From these, and from other sources, the theatrical Profession also runs the risk of becoming 'over-stocked'.

These young aspirants rush to the Stage as to a promised land. The would-be actors congratulate themselves on the fact that there are no 'stiff' examinations to pass; they complacently regard their handsome young faces in the looking-glass; they contemplate with satisfaction the latest efforts of their West-End tailors, and think themselves on the high-road to fame and fortune.

A young man of this stamp not long ago called upon a London manager, sent in his card, and being admitted to his presence, informed him that he had made up his mind to 'go on the stage', and was prepared to accept an engagement. The manager not unnaturally asked some questions as to his qualifications for the career which he proposed for himself. 'Had he any experience as an actor? Had he studied the dramatic art?' 'No,' was the reply, 'but he had decided to "go on the stage", and all that he wanted was an engagement.' The manager led him to the door, and, returning his card, pointed to a building on the opposite side of the street. 'That,' he said, 'is a bank; go and present yourself there. Say that, without knowing anything about the business, you have made up your mind to be a banker's clerk, and ask for a situation. If you succeed in getting one, come back here and I will engage you as an actor.' The young gentleman took his departure, but *he did not return*!

The would-be actresses are more diffident, and are certainly more disposed to devote heart and soul to their work; but neither the one nor the other has the slightest idea of the amount of study, of labour, and of devotion to the art – to say nothing of natural aptitude – that is necessary for success.

[Claims are made for the didactic power of the drama; then its influence on the actors themselves is described.]

. . . The playing of many parts naturally gives to the actor and actress a curious insight into the sentiments and passions that sway and bias human nature. The earnest actor, who has heart and soul in his work, and conscientiously studies the various parts he is called upon to play, is compelled to think, more than the mere man of business, of human strength and weakness, of hate and love, of joy and sorrow; for in their turn he has to portray them all, and to judge by results, the effect upon his nature is to make him very charitable.

Where, I may safely ask, is charity more openly or more cheerfully practised than among the members of the Theatrical Profession? I do not allude to mere almsgiving – the readiness with which an actor will in that way help a comrade who has fallen by the way has become proverbial; but to charity of a very different and more valuable kind . . .

The Theatrical Profession . . . offers chances to all men and women, no matter what their past has been; and it is in this way that I maintain it to be a more charitable one than any other. A sad and undeserved consequence of this is, that actors are liable to suffer as a body for the very charities they so unselfishly practise, for they give the outside world opportunities of indulging in that scandal about the Stage which apparently forms one of its chief delights. The Puritanical-minded point to some too well-known 'backslider' who is endeavouring to earn a living in a theatre, lift up their pious hands in horror, and condemn the whole profession. It would be well, indeed, if these worthy people would take the trouble to look a litle further into the matter, and ascertain how cruelly unjust such condemnation is.

xxiii

An actress's luggage, 1886

[A list from the diary of Mrs Scott-Siddons, 1886 (MS, Folger Shakespeare Library).]

2 travellers Baths
Large trunk
    ,,   leather bag
    ,,   'Stuttgart'
Little 'Stuttgart'
Kitchen Hamper
Lunch   ,,
China   ,,
Weide-Korb [Hamper]
Blck. covd. dress basket
   ,,   ,,   round hat basket
Music hamper
Gladstone bag of S.M.W.
Leather hat box   ,,
Tin bonnet box M.Y.S.S.
1 Bird cage.

A beginner and his salary, 1880s

[Jerome K. Jerome, in *On the Stage – and Off* (1891), describes his financial rewards after the period of probation, and compares them with provincial salaries in general.]

I expected about three pounds a week salary after giving my one month gratis, and I did not get it. My agreement stipulated that I should receive a 'salary according to ability' at the end of that time, but the manager said he did not think there would ever be enough money in the house to pay me at that scale, and suggested nine shillings a week instead, generously giving me the option of either taking it or leaving it. I took it.

I took it because I saw plainly enough that if I didn't I should get nothing, that he could find twenty other young fellows as good as I to come without any salary at all, and that the agreement was not worth the paper it was written on. I was wrath at the time, but, seeing that the nine shillings was soon raised to twelve, and afterwards to fifteen and eighteen, I had really, taking things as they were, nothing to grumble at; and, when I came to know a little more about professional salaries, and learnt what even the old hands were glad to get I was very well satisfied.

The company was engaged at summer prices, which are a good deal less than winter ones, and these latter average something less than the wages of an industrious sweep. The public, who read of this actor receiving a hundred and twenty pounds a night, of that actress making eight hundred pounds a week, of a low comedian's yearly income being somewhere about six thousand pounds, and of a London manager who has actually paid his rates and taxes (so he says), can scarcely have any idea of what existence at the bottom of the stage ladder is like. It is a long ladder, and there are very few who possess a personal experience at both ends. Those who do, however, must appreciate the contrast. Mr Henry Irving, speaking somewhere of his early days, mentions his weekly salary, I think, as having been twenty-five shillings; and no doubt at the time, he thought that very good, and can most likely remember when he got less. In the provinces, thirty shillings is a high figure for a good all-round 'responsibles', and for that amount he is expected to be equal to Othello or Sir Peter Teazle at a moment's notice, and to find his own dress. A 'lead' may get three pounds in the winter, and a young 'utility' thinks himself well off indeed on a guinea. Now and again, the latter will get twenty-two or three shillings, but this only leads him into habits of extravagance, and he suffers for it afterwards. At the minor London theatres, there being no expenses connected with travelling, etc., the salaries are even less, and from eighteen shillings to two pounds are about the sums *promised*.

XXV

Advice to a would-be actor, 1891

[A letter (5 January 1891) from the actor Hermann Vezin to a 'Mr Weatherby' evidently in response to a request for advice on going on stage. Vezin warns that in some companies 'Beginners are often asked to pay a premium, or at least to come for no salary'. MS letter, Historical Society of Pennsylvannia, Philadelphia.]

Your *best* way would be to try to get a 'walk on' at a good London theatre, meantime taking lessons in Voice Production of Miss Bchanks[1] 18 Earls Court Square, Fencing of Mons. Bertrand, 10 Warwick St., Regent [?] & elocution of Miss Bchanks or any other good teacher. Then get some small parts in the provinces, & get your practice & apply what you have learnt in London. [Another] plan is to join a good company like mine or Ben Greet's or F.R. Benson's & get your practice without previous training. The former plan is *by far* the better one. You can always ensure some months' practice by paying Miss Sarah Thorne[2] (Theatre Royal, Margate) a fee, I think it is £25 for 6 months.

NOTES

1   *Miss Bchanks*   No Miss Bchanks or Banks has been found at a corresponding address, so the name may be incorrect.
2   *Sarah Thorne*   (1837–99), actress and manager of the Theatre Royal in Margate, famous as a trainer of aspiring beginners.

Conditions and wages, 1891

[This important article, 'The Gibeonites of the Stage', by C. H. d'E. Leppington, appeared in *The National Review* in 1891. Gibeonites were the biblical 'hewers of wood and drawers of water' (Joshua 9:27).]

[Supernumeraries]
The word super is an abbreviation for supernumerary. These men are recruited by the super-master, who keeps a list of the names and addresses of men whom he can send for as occasion requires. They have to be drilled like a regimental company to teach them the manoeuvres they have to go through in each scene. The super has generally no opportunity of showing any originality in the part allotted to him. His every gesture is prescribed for him beforehand, and all he does is in dumb show. He has simply to do precisely as he is told. Consequently there is little chance in first-rate theatres of his rising to be anything better than a super. [Leppington's note: For the purposes of this article, theatres whose minimum charge of admission is a shilling are styled first-rate; those described as minor theatres having a lower scale of charges.] In the minor theatres, where a less rigid standard of manners and education is demanded, a super may now and then have a chance of rising. Perhaps the utility man[1] breaks down, and, as his place has to be supplied at a moment's notice, the smartest of the supers is picked out for the purpose. Now is his time to show what metal he is made of. If he carries out his part satisfactorily, he may be promoted to 'under-study' a subordinate character, so as to be prepared to act if a change in the cast has to be made. And thus he may at last become an actor, though he is not likely to rise very high in his profession.

Supers are drawn from all sorts and conditions. They almost always follow some other principal calling, if it be but the humble one of sandwich-man or market-porter. But it is said that in a few first-rate theatres young men of a superior class, stage-struck, for whom, through want of training or ability, no opening in the higher ranks of the profession offers, may be found serving as supers.

Though the general custom is for each theatre to engage its supers through its own super-master, still the enlisting of supers and letting them out to theatres is said to have become of late an independent, though not as yet, it seems, a very extensive business.

[Chorus-singers]

The chorus-singer is a person of increasing importance in these days of Gilbert and Sullivan. Though not actors, these artistes appear in costume, and often have to illustrate their songs with more or less action. Now and then some members of the chorus may have to take a more conspicuous part. They may have to speak a few sentences, and the lay mind will then find it hard to decide whether they are minor actors or leading chorus-singers. Chorus-singers often add to their incomes by singing in churches and elsewhere in the day-time and on Sundays.

[Ballet-dancers]

The ladies of the ballet are divided into several grades. With the *première danseuse* and the *coryphées* we have little concern, except in so far as their position forms the goal of the aspirations of each ambitious young débutante in the back row. Their salaries range from five guineas a week upwards. Next to them come the 'front eight', then the middle rows, and, lastly, the back rows and 'extras', though these last are not strictly members of the ballet. A dancer's position in the rows is determined by her proficiency, and by her personal appearance. The back rows are composed of the beginners, the *passées*, and the unskilled. So long as a dancer retains the necessary amount of agility, she can remain on the boards, in spite of advancing years, well on into middle life; mother and daughter have danced in the same ballet before now. The dresser's art is quite equal to supplying the necessary appearance of youth.

The ballet girls are sometimes married women with families of their own, though more often they are girls living at home and supporting their parents, or else lodging by themselves or with some of their companions. They are frequently children of poor parents, and the rooms even of the well paid, from the few specimens I have seen, strike one as being by no means above the average working-class home in point of neatness or comfort. Perhaps their constant presence at performances or rehearsals leaves them little time or inclination to attend to household duties. Those who are skilful enough and fortunate enough to get into the *corps de ballet* of a house such as the Alhambra have pretty regular employment all the year round; but a great number can only obtain temporary engagements in the pantomime or other busy seasons. At other times they go on tour in the country, live with their parents, or turn dressmakers and needle-women, and sometimes, probably, have recourse to less reputable modes of obtaining a livelihood. It is only fair to add, however, that the appearance of the ballet-girls as they leave the theatre very much resembles that of any other body of young women leaving a respectable place of business. The corps of one large house has organized a benefit club for the help of its sick members. The subscription is 3d. or 6d. per week, according to earnings. Full sick-pay is 15s. a week and lasts ten weeks, followed by half-pay. Any balance in hand at the end of the year is shared out among the members. This fund has been in existence for many years.

In reckoning the earnings of a ballet dancer we must remember that she has generally to find her own tights and shoes, though in one or two places both these are found for them. Common worsted tights may be had for 8s. or 10s., but really good silk tights cost from 30s. to 40s. As in the legitimate drama, character costumes are found by the management. Shoes cost from 2s. 6d. to 5s., and last three or four weeks; this, however, depends very much on the condition of the flooring, and on the wearer's step, a heavy tread wearing out the shoes sooner than a light one. Feathers, ribbons, and such-like articles are usually found by the artiste, and this rule applies to actresses as well. A week's notice is usually given to terminate an engagement where it has not been made for a fixed period.

To qualify for a ballet dancer requires a long training, and there are several training-schools where children are apprenticed by their parents. These training-schools contract with the management of theatres to supply pantomime children and ballet-dancers. As the children become too old for the pantomime they are taken to train for the ballet. There appears to be no difference in the rates of payment of pantomime children and dancers engaged through contractors and that of those engaged directly by the management itself, assuming the class of theatre and the nature of the performance to be the same in both cases. But the contractor naturally favours his pupils, who have in this way a better chance of regular employment than other children. In addition to this, the more proficient pupils are set to teach the others, and for this they receive extra pay of from 10s. to 20s. a week.

A pantomime generally lasts from two to three months, but performers are engaged for a certain number of weeks 'and the run', that is to say, for as much longer as it may answer to keep the piece before the public. A week or two's notice is given if the pantomime has to be withdrawn sooner.

The pantomime season opens on Boxing night, but daily rehearsals will have been going on for from three to six weeks previously. The performers are paid for their attendance during the last week (sometimes the last fortnight) of the rehearsal. It is no easy task to drill a troop of perhaps two or three score of youngsters (some stupid, some recalcitrant, and the bulk of them just about the age described[2] in *Tom Brown* as the most mischievous of British boyhood) to a faultless performance of long-continued concerted action; and as the weeks fly past, and the spectre of the opening night looms nearer and nearer, rehearsals follow quicker and last longer, till (to quote one case I heard of) the troupe is summoned for four o'clock on Christmas Eve, and kept at it for the next twelve hours straight off, in view of opening on Boxing Night.

[Children on the stage]
Children employed in theatres come, like others, within the scope of the Public Elementary Education Acts. So long as these children are only engaged during the short pantomime season, they may be able to put in the number of attendances required by law during the rest of the year. But when the pantomime has an extraordinary run of several months, or the children are pretty constantly engaged throughout the year in theatres or in training-schools, the case alters. The exigencies of rehearsals and matinées will not allow of their attending at the normal school-hours. This difficulty is met to some extent, as in the case of choristers in cathedrals, by holding classes specially for the attendance of such children at such times as they are disengaged. How far such an arrangement is generally adopted is hardly to be ascertained, but it has been estimated by the advocates of legislative intervention to affect about 5 per cent. of the thousand children engaged on the stage. An Act passed in 1889 (52 & 53 Vict., c.44) absolutely prohibits the employment of children under seven on the stage in any capacity and on any terms, and a licence is required for the employment of children between seven and ten. The opinion of the theatrical world as to the advisability of this enactment is probably not unanimous, but it may be safely assumed that legislative interference with their freedom of action in the selection of artistes is not popular with lessees and managers. At the same time, I have heard the measure approved of on the ground that by forbidding the employment of very young children the position of the elder children will be improved, since they will

be freed from a competition which was seriously damaging their own prospects.

Here I should mention that for some years past a club has existed at Macready House, in the vicinity of the theatres, where young women, and children of both sexes, can rest and amuse themselves during the intervals of their appearance on the stage. Refreshments are provided, and in the basement is a gymnasium for the boys.

The earnings of children employed on the stage vary greatly . . . Many are mere supers; some dance, some sing, a few act. A child would have to display very considerable talent to earn the two pounds a week specified . . . as the maximum salary of the child-actor. One youth of thirteen, for instance, has made 12s. a week in a West-End theatre. His rôle required him to appear twice or thrice at an evening, for a few minutes at a time, and indulge in a scuffle with some other boys. He had obtained the appointment on his own application, and his father thought that if he could have accompanied him, his son's talent would have commanded a more liberal recognition. This young gentleman was designed for the low-comedy line, and had already been three years on the stage. He was a plump, rosy-cheeked boy, evidently on extremely good terms with himself.

A good deal has been said on the question of the healthiness, or otherwise, of the theatrical life for children. Apropos of this, the mother of two grown-up daughters, both of whom had been pantomime children, told me they had not suffered in health, and seemed to think it was mainly a question of wrapping-up the children warmly enough, and conveying them straight home on leaving the theatre.

The parents of these children are often themselves engaged in the theatre, and it is probably best in every way for the children when this is the case. They are better looked after and protected, and they are, beside, serving their apprenticeship, as it were, to their ultimate profession, for they generally retain their connection with the stage through life, and their parents can, of course, aid them in their advancement. The father of the lad I have just alluded to was himself a theatrical employee.

For the rest, I have been told that it is seldom that a mechanic's child[3] takes an engagement at a pantomime. In the West-End theatres the parents are often small clerks and shop-keepers; while the children in the cheaper theatres come from the labouring class; so, at least, I should judge from the appearance of a crowd of thin, poorly-clad children whom I watched one bright December morning thronging the stage-door of a theatre of varieties, at which the manager stood picking out the most likely-looking specimens. Many of them were evidently old acquaintances of his, performers in previous pantomimes, for he called them to him by name, and they evidently knew him well. A few of these children had been brought by their mothers, but most of them seemed to have come by themselves. They were evidently very eager to be taken on. The children attending rehearsal at a West-End theatre were of a much higher class, and seemed to be in much better circumstances . . .

[The actor's training]

It remains to give the reader some idea of the conditions under which the lower strata of the [acting] profession itself pursue their avocations, reminding him at the same time of the limit already assigned to this part of the article, and that we have very little concern with the mass of actors whose names figure on the casts of fashionable theatres.

And first I will deal with the actor's education. Actors are a migratory tribe, and for this reason, perhaps, among others, there are no such centres of training for the drama as exist for music and painting. What is known as the stock company system has of late years given place more and more to the system of touring companies and of long runs. In the former system, the bond of union which holds a company of actors together is local; it is the theatre to which they are attached, with its repertory of plays in which they are all versed, and which they represent in succession at brief intervals. In the latter system, the bond is not the place but the subject; it is the piece which the company has been formed to represent, whether in one given locality, or in a succession of localities.

The old stock company system has been credited with possessing greater merit as a school of acting than the system now in vogue. The frequent change of the plays put on the stage gave the actor more opportunity of developing his powers than he can have in a single character, to the exclusive representation of which he is bound for several months, or even for a year or two. Still, even here, some scope for training is afforded by the system of 'under-study'. On the principle of having two strings to one's bow, each part is not only studied by the actor to whom it is expressly assigned, but is also 'under-studied' by one of the less prominent actors, in addition to his own part, so that he may serve as a substitute in case the other man breaks down. Such posts, too, as the one offered in the following advertisement afford a useful apprenticeship: 'Wanted, aspirant to support touring star. Small premium and salary.' And it is not unusual for actors to take dramatic pupils.

Beyond this, there is no definite course of training. An actor advances gradually as he has abilities from insignificant parts to more important ones. He learns by constantly watching others. But he can, of course, increase his proficiency by going through a course of lessons in elocution, dancing, singing, fencing, &c.

This leads us up to our next point, the method of obtaining engagements; for the instruction I have just alluded to is often given in connection with agencies for this purpose. The fee payable at these agencies varies, being sometimes a matter of special arrangement between the agent and his client, but it usually consists of a small sum (from 5s. to a guinea) paid down, and a commission of 5 per cent. on the first fortnight's salaries. The payment of this commission is, of course, conditional on the client's being actually employed during that time. The agent is in no way responsible for the financial soundness of the management to which he introduces his client, and actors have often suffered serious losses through the dishonesty or insolvency of their principals. Of the existence of bogus agents and managers the police reports from time to time remind us. As soon as these worthies get too well known in the profession under one name, they change to another, which serves as fresh bait. It is generally advisable to enter one's name at several agencies simultaneously in order to increase the chances of success.

Besides going to a theatrical agent or making direct application to the management, advertisements in professional journals afford a means of communication between employers and employed, as widely used in the actor's vocation as in any other. . . . Actors on tour in the provinces take the precaution of advertising their successive addresses, and the dates for which they are open to fresh engagements, so as to keep themselves in touch with the world of lessees and managers.

[Terms of employment and salaries]
Costumes, in the technical sense of the word, that is, clothes which are not worn in every-day life, are found by the management; but such clothes as are ordinarily worn in private life, the actor provides for himself.

The practice as regards extra payment for matinées varies; it is sometimes at the same rate as for evening performances, and sometimes half as much. The latter is the general rule; occasionally no extra pay at all is given. Rehearsals are considered as all in the day's work, and accordingly actors attend them *ad libitum* without further remuneration, the practice as to panto-mime rehearsals previously alluded to being an exception to this rule. Assistants engaged by the day are paid extra wages at the full rate for dress rehearsals. These dress rehearsals are so called because at them the actors appear in costume, and the play is gone through with all the adjuncts used at the public performance; a few spectators too, are invited in order to discuss flaws and suggest improvements.

Actors are sometimes subjected to a good deal of annoyance from blackmailing. As they pass into the theatre they are accosted by loiterers at the stage-door, who politely offer to applaud them during the performance – for a consideration. The actor well understands that the offer is merely a thinly-veiled threat to hiss him down unless he 'squares' them with *backsheesh*. How serious a matter it is to him is plainly shown by the statement of a leading actor, made as a witness in a recent law-suit, that less than half-a-dozen men acting in concert could make such a disturbance as to render it wholly impossible for an actor to go on with his part.

The remuneration of the class of actors we are here treating of forms a subject not easily dealt with. The same actor's pay will vary immensely, not only according to his own capability, which may fluctuate greatly at different stages in his career, but according to the character he assumes, and the theatre or company in which he is acting. From 30s. to £4 or £5 a week is, I think, as accurate an estimate as can be given. If an actor has not made a reputation by the time he is forty, his market value is pretty sure to decrease as age approaches. A sort of club, with a superannuation benefit for theatrical employees, exists in the Royal Theatrical Fund, and for actors in distress there is the well-known Actors' Benevolent Fund;[4] and, besides these societies, a very considerable sum is given away privately, for members of the dramatic profession have the reputation of being very open-handed to professional brethren in distress.

NOTES

1   *utility man*   Actor playing minor speaking roles.
2   *the age described* . . .   i.e. eleven and twelve. See Thomas Hughes, *Tom Brown's Schooldays* (1857), ch.8.

3   *mechanic's*   Workman's.
4   *Royal Theatrical Fund . . . Actors' Benevolent Fund*   The
     Royal General Theatrical Fund was begun in 1839: relief was
     provided to members who had paid a subscription when in work;
     the Actor's Benevolent Fund, founded in 1882, aimed to help those
     who did not qualify for support from the RGTF and derived its
     money from patrons (initially Irving, Wyndham and other
     successful actors).

xxvii

Financial 'customs', c.1899

[From Leopold Wagner, *How to Get on the Stage* (1899).]

Some details of the time-honoured customs governing financial
matters in the dramatic profession may be usefully set down in this
place. Rehearsals are not paid for, though an actor may have to
put in an attendance at a London theatre, or travel down to a
provincial town, many days prior to the production of a new play.
Even when the play is enjoying a successful run, the stage-
manager may post up a 'call' for all concerned, with the object of
improving certain scenes or rehearsing one of the parts for which
a new performer has been specially engaged. In the case of a
musical play the orchestral conductor often calls the company
together in broad daylight for the introduction of a new song or
concerted piece, while the 'second edition' of a pantomime
imposes similar inconveniences upon the artistes. Non-attendance
at rehearsal, strolling in after the usual half-hour's grace, coming
late to the performance or keeping the stage waiting at night,
'fluffing', *i.e.*, cutting another actor out of his lines or making an
entrance at the wrong moment, or standing in the 'prompt
entrance' when the performer has no business to be there, results
in a fine. Half-salaries for morning performances obtain everywhere, unless the terms of the agreement stipulate for a weekly
matinée. During the pantomime season the stated salary generally
includes so many day performances.

'If the curtain does not rise,' the ladies and gentlemen of the company lose a night's salary. This is very convenient for the manager, who often dismisses a scanty audience rather than play to bad business. The actors may be fully dressed and waiting to 'go on'. No matter; it is 'the custom of the theatre', against which there can be no appeal. The rising of the curtain, however, does not affect the bandsmen; provided they have struck up the overture, they are entitled to their full night's salary. At times the astute manager does not definitely arrive at a decision until it is too late to shirk the claims of his orchestra. Still, he effects a considerable saving when the fiat goes forth behind the curtain that there is to be 'no show'.

Another old-fashioned custom is the fortnight's notice to terminate engagements. In London . . . engagements are made 'for the run of the piece', unless the manager chooses to release an artiste who has received an offer elsewhere, or else 'lend' him to a brother manager for a brief season. In a touring company every actor is subject to the usual fortnight's notice, and of course the notice works both ways. It is quite a common thing for a manager who wishes to rid himself of a particularly obnoxious member of the company – the obnoxiousness may arise from his persistence in claiming arrears of salary – to post up the following notice: 'The ladies and company are hereby informed that the season will terminate on Saturday evening . . . This notice does not affect Messrs. — nor the Misses — .' Obviously, there would not be the slightest need for him to act in such an underhanded manner if his desire to terminate an individual engagement was a legitimate one; in that case a private note, conveying a fortnight's notice, would suffice.

xxviii

Salaries, c.1899

[Extracted from Leopold Wagner, *How to Get on the Stage* (1899).]

Touring salaries: 25s.–35s. for a small part.
                 £2–3 'for a line of business'
                 £5 (maximum) 'for heavy or juvenile lead'
                 35s.(maximum) for choristers (less for 'show-girls' in a burlesque company)

London salaries: 1 gn for a 'walking part'
                 £2–5 'the average salary of a subordinate actor in a West-End theatre'
                 £2 (maximum) for a chorister
                 £7, £10, £12 or £15 for secondary parts

Leading actors' salaries vary considerably, and some make a private arrangement at a rate lower than that on their 'stamped' engagement – the contract registered at Somerset House.

xxix

A rehearsal for a new play, c.1900

[In Leonard Merrick's novel *The Actor-Manager* (1898) the hero, Oliphant, joins a company which is a leading actor's first venture into management.]

The stage was dark and draughty. When Oliphant reached it nobody had come but the prompter, who stood by a small table, overlooking the empty orchestra and the auditorium swathed in holland.* His hands were plunged in the pockets of his overcoat, and he shivered. He paid small attention to the other's advent, because he was to be described on the playbills as 'Assistant Stage-manager', and Oliphant was playing a small part. In the position that he had filled [in another company] on tour, Oliphant would have joined him at the table; in the position that he filled here, theatrical etiquette forbade it. He walked up and down in the wings, and questioned for the hundredth time if, with such a part as this, Edmund Kean himself could have created an effect.

The other subordinates continued to assemble, and to hang about with him. They watched the principals arrive and stroll to the table unabashed; and tried to hear what they talked about, and envied them their lustrous boots, which showed that they had come in cabs. The villain recounted a funny incident to the leading lady, and she laughed merrily without having grasped the joke: his salary was understood to be thirty pounds a week, and *she* was only beginning. Besides, the celebrated actor under whom she had studied, and who had obtained the engagement for her, had always declared that her laugh was her strong point. The low comedian demanded of the prompter when they were 'going to have the floats'. There was considerable delay about this, and general expectancy; and then the footlights ameliorated the gloom a little, and the leading lady, who was very charming, bent over the blaze of light in a pretty attitude to warm her hands. The 'small part women' in the wings looked additionally miserable, as they gazed at her, and the men inquired irritably among themselves 'why the devil they were called for eleven.' Only one, a youth who had twenty words to deliver, affected to be oblivious of his surroundings. He sauntered to and fro, muttering and gesticulating, stimulated by the secret thought that somebody of importance might comment on his enthusiasm.

A little man, with a hopeless expression, crept down to the footlights, and was greeted with cordiality – especially by the young leading lady. He was the author. He had a roll of manuscript in his hand, which represented the alterations he had been urged to make at the last rehearsal. He was wondering what further misfortunes would befall him and his drama to-day.

Signs of impatience might be detected on the faces of the principals also now; but the actor who had a theatre for the first time felt it due to himself to keep the company waiting. He strode through the wings presently, ignoring the minor members – who scattered to let him pass – and, reaching the prompt-table, raised his hat about half an inch.

'Morning, ladies and gentlemen', he said curtly to the group about him. He made some remark to the author about the weather, and turned to the assistant stage-manager, whom he

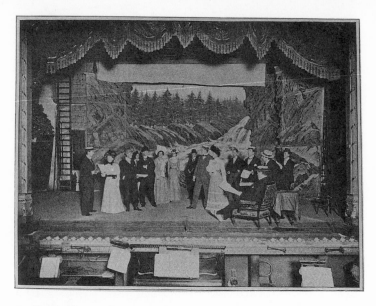

10 Rehearsing a play on stage, 1901.

addressed as 'Mr Mote'. He was fat, and held himself stiffly erect, endeavouring to palliate by his carriage the loss of his figure. In manner he was arrogant, and he had frequently the air of swelling – as often as he wished to assert his dignity in private, or to express emotion in a part.

'Clear the stage, please!' cried Mr Mote, clapping his hands twice. 'Act two, scene one! Sentry! Come on, Mr – er – Williams, please – Act two, scene one!'

The youth who had been immersed in study huried nervously to that part of the stage where he fancied he was supposed to be pacing battlements bathed in moonlight; but he was not certain that he wasn't meant to be in a corridor, looking out of a window. This lent indecision to his movements. He said:

'It's a fine night. How quiet it is!'

At the same moment concealed carpenters began to hammer furiously. The youth looked disconcerted, but nobody else took any notice.

'How quiet it is!' repeated the assistant stage-manager. 'Enter the Colonel. "Colonel", please! Mr – er – Fowler! "How quiet it is!"'

'I beg your pardon!' The Colonel rushed forward. The rehearsal proceeded, and some of the women in the wings found chairs, and chatted in undertones . . . The Adventuress discussed her baby's first tooth, and the danger of convulsions, with the low comedian, who, as a family man, spoke authoritatively; and by the side of the author, who sucked his umbrella handle, the Hero sat, shouting comments, and rising from time to time to bluster with more violence.

NOTE

*   *holland*   Linen covers for seats and furnishings.

xxx

The agent's waiting-room, c.1890

[Elizabeth Fagan's autobiography, *From the Wings*, by 'the Stage Cat', 1922. The actress went on the stage in the 1890s.]

Looking for an engagement is the nastiest part of theatrical life – I mean for the small fry, the beginners, and provincial stage folk. When one has 'made good', and gained even a small London reputation, there is generally no need to hunt for work; it comes along, and one is sent for by managers, but before this, for the less favoured beings, it is cruel work. The starting out in the morning, in best clothes, whatever the weather (and best so soon gets second best under these conditions). The waiting with crowds of others bent on the same errand in the agent's office, hoping that he will at least see one, even if he has no suitable engagement to suggest; the trying to catch his eye if he happens to pass through the waiting-room; the 'being nice' and smiling to the horrid office-boy – or girl – who takes one's name to the great man (or doesn't, as the case may be). They are all horrid as a species, these

11   At the theatrical
agent's office.

'officials', though, no doubt, individually they may be excellent
children, for they hold the keys of bread and butter, if not of life
and death, for the anxious applicant, and are nearly always head-
swollen with the knowledge of this power.

Blackmore's in Garrick Street was the biggest agency in my
time, and unless one arrived very early in the morning, there was
nearly always a crowd of other Theatricals waiting there, and
sometimes the room got so full it was difficult to move. On arrival
perhaps one felt quite brave, and resolved to carry things off with a
swagger, as if it did not matter in the least whether an
engagement came along or no; so, with a high and mighty air,
intended to give the impression that one was a leading London
actress, who had just 'drifted in', one went to the desk of the
'horrid boy', and this sort of thing took place: –

ANXIOUS APPLICANT (with great hauteur): Just take my name in to
  Mr Blackmore, will you? Say Miss — , please.
HORRID BOY (rudely): Got an appointment?
ANXIOUS APPLICANT (a tone lower): Well, not exactly an
  appointment, but he told me to be sure and look in again.
HORRID BOY (with meaning): Oh! Indeed! You'd better wait. I'll
  see about it later.

And wait you did – perhaps for an hour, perhaps longer, with
the courage oozing out of your boots and the conviction growing
stronger that you'd never get a 'shop', till at last you could bear it
no longer, and you again approached the horrid little imp behind
the desk. This time, though, you walked delicately, like the
gentleman in the Bible, and smiled sweetly, even though you had
murder in your heart.

'Don't you think you could get him to see me now?' you'd coo
in your most dove-like voice, and the H.B. (unless he was very extra
H.B.) would relent – if you were pretty – and condescend to tell you
that: –

'The gov'nor wasn't coming at all that morning. It wasn't no
good your waiting', or even perhaps that: – 'He'll be coming in
directly; you'd better stand by the door and catch 'im'.

You stood by the door, and then shortly a harassed and busy
little man would attempt to hurry through the room – of course he
was hurried; hadn't he been all the morning trying to satisfy the
demands of insatiable London managers requiring high-salaried
actors? That at least was what we were meant to think: perhaps we
did.

You pounced and caught him. Cornered like that, he was
probably kind, if you were good to look upon (again that same
'if'); after all, one never knew: you might pay him huge sums for
commission on engagements some day! So, though he didn't
remember you from Eve – how should he, seeing so many girls
every day – he would press your hand and say, 'Nothing today,
dear, but I'm bearing you in mind; look in again when you're
passing.'

So it was of no use waiting any longer. The morning was over,
and one went to lunch, generally a scone and butter and a cup of
tea in an A.B.C.,* not a very good foundation for a further hunt for
work in the afternoon.

No, it is not a pleasant thing looking for an engagement, and it
is as well to take this side of the life into consideration when
deciding to go on the stage; but of course it has its humorous side,

too, and it is exciting enough when one has sufficient money in one's pocket to lunch decently and be smartly dressed.

The great secret of dressing in my time was a Silk Petticoat – petticoats were worn then – rustling ones; the more they rustled the better, they gave such an impression of wealth and the uselessness therefore of offering one anything less than £20 a week as salary.

White kid gloves and a rustling petticoat were really indispensable when going out to seek an engagement. There was an enormous amount of confidence to be got out of a silk petticoat. A hansom to the managers, too, was money well spent, I always thought – one felt so much less like a servant looking for a situation if one arrived in a hansom than if one came, with the mud of the streets on one's shoes, by the humble bus or train. (Even in those days minor actresses were less in demand than domestic servants.)

Stage life, no doubt, is not the only life in which the plums go to those who need them least, and one can understand the manager's, or agent's, point of view. Obviously a girl who has got – or can get – enough money to dress well, is a more attractive, and therefore better, proposition than an ill-dressed one.

This all sounds very trivial and rather ugly, I'm afraid, but remember, I am speaking now only of the bottom of the ladder; no doubt it is real merit which climbs to the top in the long run – at least, I hope it is – but, all the same, a 'Silk Petticoat', both mental and material, is not an unuseful adjunct to the climbing. Please note that I do not say a moral silk petticoat, though – well, one has heard – ! But, anyway, the morals of the stage are no worse than those of most other places. I'm sure of that.

---

*   A.B.C.   Teashop run by the Aerated Bread Company.

Part III

Behind the Scenes

This section deals with the means by which stage effects were achieved, from the apparently simple matter of getting on and off stage to the destruction of houses by fire and the elaborate 'transformations' of pantomime.

At the beginning of the Victorian period the backstage workings of the theatre were still by and large those of the Georgian playhouse: scenery consisted largely of flats, wings and borders – painted perspective sets made up of canvas stretched on wooden frames and running in grooves set parallel to the front of the stage. Scenery still changed in full view of the audience at the command of bells and whistles. Gas had superseded oil as a lighting medium, and new sophistications of lighting effects and trapwork had been achieved, but the technology of counter-weights and windlasses had changed little.

In 1894 the scenic artist William Telbin commented on recent developments in stage technique:

> The appliances connected with the stage have within the last twenty years been greatly changed. The stage is now in most theatres a big box, in which you can set up a picture in any way you please at any angle. The grooves, the flats, the wings made by the dozen pairs, are all gone – electricity has taken the place of gas, as gas did that of the oil-lamp. In the auditorium stone, marble, brick, concrete, and iron are now used instead of timber, which became a harbourer for dirt and dust, and greatly added to the possibilities of fire.
>
> (*The Magazine of Art*, XVII, 44)

Increasing sophistication in lighting, the greater use of 'built-out' or modelled scenery, and the retreat of the forestage until the entire stage-picture could (as at the Haymarket in 1880) be contained within a seeming picture-frame, meant that by the last decades of the century audiences would no longer have been convinced by the scenic devices accepted as adequate in the 1830s. By now rooms on stage were expected to have ceilings, and side walls set at an angle to the footlights, forming the 'box set'

12 This and the following three photographs were taken at the Theatre Royal, Birmingham, shortly before the demolition of the building in 1901. The first one shows the cleared stage, viewed from the auditorium.

interior (the exact date of whose arrival is not certain). In plays with a modern setting the suppliers of the costumes and household furnishings used on the stage were often the firms that the stalls audience would expect to patronize. Much of the credit for implementing this break with older stage conventions of dress and scenery can be given to the Bancrofts' management at the Prince of Wales's Theatre. Sir Squire Bancroft, reflecting on the impact of his innovations in staging and dressing modern comedy, made explicit the social significance of his work:

> I do but echo unbiased opinions in adding that many other so-called pictures of life presented on the stage were as false as they were conventional. The characters lived in an unreal world, and the code of ethics on the stage was the result of warped traditions. . . . [Robertson], it was truly said, . . . rendered a public service by proving that the refined and educated classes were as ready as ever to crowd the playhouses, provided only that the entertainment given there was suited to their sympathies and tastes.
>
> (*The Bancrofts*, 1909, p.83)

Reflecting middle-class life accurately was an essential part of this, coming under the jurisdiction of 'stage-management'. After the 1860s the conventional dressing and setting of plays, reflected in the lists of costumes prefacing old acting editions and sometimes included in manuals of advice for would-be actors, were no longer generally accepted. The 'stage swell' (for example) had given way to the accurately rendered swell.

In the course of the century, the functions of the stage-manager, responsible for the rehearsing of the company and the setting of the stage, changed out of recognition. In the older dispensation, a strong emphasis on custom and tradition facilitated the rapid turnover of 'standard' plays and novelties. Special preparation was necessary for spectacular entertainments, especially the Christmas and Easter pantomimes. But the vogue for authentic historical detail entailed employing specialists who insisted on ignoring cherished conventions of costume. If scenery and costume were to be specific to particular plays, there was no way of continuing the old system, allowing exchange of sets and dresses between one piece and another. The staging of Shakespeare was favoured as the occasion for displays of authenticity, and 'revivals' (implying a freshly mounted and accurate *mise-en-scène*) dominated the work of such managers as Charles Kean. A number of Shakespeare's plays were given by Kean without any extraordinary or novel staging, but it was the elaborate (and expensive) 'revivals' that gave the Princess's its reputation. Such production values demanded a degree of organization and unity of effect – from the performers as well as the technicians – that made inevitable the concentration of authority in one person, and the diminishing of the artistic responsibility of the stage-manager, whose role began to resemble that of his modern equivalent, answerable for the efficient running of performances rather than any artistic decisions. Planché's account of his employment as an adviser on historical matters (no. i) refers to the discomfiture of the actor customarily given sole charge of the spectacle in Charles Kemble's theatre. At the same time, it is clear from such accounts as Telbin's article on scene-painting (xvii) that in the 1880s and 1890s the heads of some departments still had considerable artistic freedom: the scenic artist, responsible for executing the work, was not yet a functionary carrying out the instructions of a designer. The costume designer, on the other hand, was unlikely to make the dresses himself. C. Wilhelm, one of the most influential costume designers of the late decades of the period, is an important figure in the 'rise of the director', for he insisted on a degree of control over the whole visual effect that made him virtual designer-director of the ballets he was engaged on (see xx). The need for some functionary with overall artistic responsibility grew out of improvements in staging techniques, but there followed a separation between technical and artistic work that resulted in the appearance by the 1900s of the 'producer' – a man who did not act, paint scenery, or sit in the prompt corner with the book.

A move of a different kind, but also leading towards the establishment of the independent director, was taken by Henry Irving and other actor-managers who supervised every aspect of their productions. At the Lyceum, in the period between 1879 and 1899, the sense of unity was achieved through Irving's careful superintendence of every department, and his skilful delegation of responsibilities. The organization of the Lyceum under Irving was particularly well documented – partly because Irving was remarkably adept at what would now be regarded as publicity and public relations. Such accounts of his work as the description of a rehearsal (xix) or Bram Stoker's article on lighting at the Lyceum (x) should not be allowed to suggest that Irving was the only actor with an interest in such matters – Herbert Beerbohm Tree, in many respects his rival and successor, had similar artistic aims and

13 The prompt corner, with electric lighting board above.

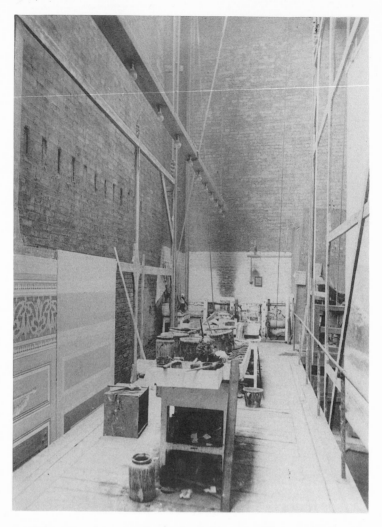

14 The paint frame at the back of the stage. The winches in the background are to move cloths up and down on the frames (L. and R.) and the painters' benches are in the centre of the gallery. The stage is to the right.

methods – but the Lyceum represents the most advanced techniques of British staging in its day. The description of a Lyceum rehearsal also suggests that, whatever care might be taken to achieve unity of effect and the avoidance of absolute error or inadequacy on the part of the performers, how an actor arrived at a characterization was still very much his or her business. It might be said that the Victorian theatre's 'progress' in the production of plays consisted almost entirely in moving away from a theatre of tradition and custom, and in achieving newly defined conventions of stage realism. It was a series of developments in the achievement of pictorial effects rather than in the psychology of impersonation. The most internationally prominent British contributor to the 'rise of the director' is Edward Gordon Craig, whose contribution to the debate on the psychology of acting was an urgently expressed desire to do away with it as soon as possible. William Archer's thoughtful *Masks or Faces?* (1888) is a study by an observer rather than a proposal for developments in technique. To move towards a sense of ensemble in the psychology of character and relationships was another step, not yet taken in the British professional theatre of the 1890s. A convincingly unhistrionic representation of 'normal' behaviour was achieved by such actor-managers as George Alexander and Charles Wyndham, but the kind of investigation undertaken by Stanislavski had not yet arrived in the British theatre. It seems that, in a spirit of pragmatism thought to be characteristically British, Alexander and his peers could elicit appropriate acting in their fellow performers without what would later be recognized as theoretically self-conscious 'directing'.

In some quarters – notably in melodrama and in some Shakespearean performances – the older theatre of obviously conventional acting and staging survived. The guides for amateur actors or would-be professionals, in so far as they offer advice on acting technique, list conventions or rehearse prescriptions that can be traced back to eighteenth-century sources. Against the stylized and schematic effects demanded by most melodrama can be set the apparent realism of Robertsonian domestic comedy. It was not easy to find a place in this range of techniques for a decorous 'legitimate' style: to avoid melodrama on the one hand and 'low' realism on the other. The dilemma was concisely expressed by George Henry Lewes:

> The supreme difficulty of an actor is to represent ideal character with such truthfulness that it shall affect us as real, not to drag down ideal character to the vulgar level. His art is

15 The 'star' dressing room. The notice over the fireplace announces 'The circle bar will be kept open for half an hour after the end of the performance for the convenience of the artistes.'

one of representation, not of illusion. He has to use natural expressions, but he must sublimate them; the symbols must be such as we can sympathetically interpret, and for this purpose they must be the expressions of real human feeling; but just as the language is poetry, or choice prose, purified from the hesitancies, incoherences, and imperfection of careless daily speech, so must his utterances be measured, musical and incisive – his manner typical and pictorial.

(*On Actors and the Art of Acting*, 1875)

The 'ideal'/'real' opposition that informs this summary is common to much Victorian writing on the principles of stage effect, as to aesthetic theory in general, during the period.

Throughout the century runs a constant regard for pictorial effect, nowhere more apparent than in the careful arrangement of 'strong curtains', tableaux, and what were called 'pictures'. *The Stage* in 1881 (19 August) identified the Stage Picture as 'one of the most delicate and trying tasks of stage-management'.

16 Staging a train crash: *The Whip* at Drury Lane, 1908.

To intensify a particular climax forming a picture in which each character takes a different attitude, though at the same time, one exemplifying the dominant idea, or a portion of it, is a task to fulfil which successfully taxes the imagination, ingenuity and general perception of effect of the person responsible for it.

A picture should elicit applause and the demand for a second picture: a 'call' which would advance the action further, not give actors an opportunity to acknowledge the audience's favourable response to them. Much Victorian drama was written to allow for such effects – sometimes to the exclusion of other considerations – and they were among the most powerful elements in the physical language of the theatre. The point at which strong dramatic emphasis became sensationalism – the spectacular crisis for its own sake – was not always easy to define, and it was one of the leading critical issues of the period. But there was a consensus that melodrama should include some ingredients of powerful situation and spectacle, and that this constituted a distinctive resource of the Victorian theatre. Scenes that reproduced familiar and famous sights on stage were the theatrical equivalents of such paintings as Frith's *Derby Day*, just as the apocalyptic vision of John Martin and the tradition of moral narrative painting could be found on stage. The values and even some of the techniques of Victorian stage spectacle and visual story-telling informed early cinema, the medium which replaced it, and made historical pageant and fantasy transportable at a rate cheaper than any road company could manage.

The advent of 'archaeology', 1823

[James Robinson Planché, Somerset Herald, was the author of many extravaganzas and an expert on the history of costume. In his supervision of the costuming of Charles Kemble's production of *King John* at Covent Garden in 1823 he confirmed the movement towards elaborately realized historical accuracy which reached its apogee in Charles Kean's 'revivals' of Shakespeare at the Princess's in the 1850s. A passage in Planché's autobiography (*Recollections and Reflections*, 2 vols., 1872) describes his work for *King John*.]

In 1823 a casual conversation with Mr Kemble, respecting the play of *King John*, which he was about to revive for Young,[1] who had returned to Covent Garden, led to a step, the consequences of which have been of immense importance to the English stage – and not less valuable because, as in all other great changes, excess and abuse have occasionally entailed misfortune and merited reprobation. I complained to Mr Kemble that a thousand pounds were frequently lavished on a Christmas pantomime or an Easter spectacle, while the plays of Shakespeare were put upon the stage with make-shift scenery, and, at the best, a new dress or two for the principal characters. That although his brother John, whose classical mind revolted from the barbarisms which even a Garrick had tolerated, had abolished the bag wig of Brutus[2] and the gold-laced suit of Macbeth, the alterations made in the plays founded upon English history in particular, while they rendered them more picturesque, added but little to their propriety; the whole series, *King Lear* included, being dressed in habits of the Elizabethan era, the third reign after its termination with Henry VIII, and, strictly speaking, very inaccurately representing the costume even of that period. At that time I had turned my attention but little to the subject of costume, which afterwards became my most absorbing study; but the slightest reflection was sufficient to convince anyone that some change of fashion must have taken place in the civil and military habits of the people of England during several hundred years. I remembered our Life-Guards in cocked hats, powder and pigtails, and they were at that moment wearing helmets and cuirasses. It was not requisite to be an antiquary to see the absurdity of the soldiers before Angiers, at the beginning of the thirteenth century, being clothed precisely the same as those fighting at Bosworth at the end of the fifteenth. If one style of dress was right, the other must be wrong. Mr Kemble admitted the fact, and perceived the pecuniary advantage that might result from the experiment. It was decided that I should make the necessary researches, design the dresses, and superintend the production of *King John, gratuitously*, I beg leave to say; solely and purely for that love of the stage, which has ever induced me to sacrifice all personal considerations to what I sincerely believed would tend to elevate as well as adorn it . . .

[Planché was helped generously by the antiquaries Samuel Meyrick and Francis Douce.]

In the theatre, however, my innovations were regarded with distrust and jealousy. Mr Fawcett,[3] the stage manager, considered his dignity offended by the production of the play being placed under my direction. He did not speak to me, except when obliged to by business, for, I think, nearly three years; but I lived it down, and remained very good friends with that excellent actor to the day of his death. Mr Farley[4] – dear old Charles Farley – also took huff. He was the recognized purveyor and director of spectacle, and dreaded 'the dimming of his shining star'. The expenditure of a few hundred pounds on any drama, except an Easter piece or a Christmas pantomime, was not to be tolerated. 'Besides,' he piteously exclaimed, 'if Shakespeare is to be produced with such splendour and attention to costume, what am I to do for the holidays?' He was not quite so openly rude to me as Fawcett, but he didn't like me a bit better *then*, though he also came round in the end, and was one of the warmest admirers of *my* Easter pieces. Never shall I forget the dismay of some of the performers when they looked upon the flat-topped *chapeaux de fer* (*fer blanc,*[5] I confess) of the 12th century, which they irreverently stigmatized as *stewpans!* Nothing but the fact that the classic features of a Kemble were to be surmounted by a precisely similar abomination would, I think, have induced one of the rebellious barons to have appeared in it. They had no faith in me, and sulkily assumed their new and strange habiliments, in the full belief that they should be roared at by the audience. They *were* roared at; but in a much more agreeable way than they had contemplated. When the curtain rose, and discovered King John dressed as his effigy appears in Worcester Cathedral, surrounded by his barons sheathed in chain mail, with cylindrical helmets and correct armorial shields, and his courtiers in the long tunics and mantles of the thirteenth century, there was a roar of approbation, accompanied by four distinct rounds of applause, so general and so hearty, that the actors were astonished, and I felt amply rewarded for all the trouble, anxiety and annoyance I had experienced during my labours. Receipts of from £400 to £600 nightly soon reimbursed the management for the expense of the production, and a complete reformation of dramatic costume became from that moment inevitable upon the English stage.

That I was the original cause of this movement is certain. That without fee or reward, and in defiance of every obstacle that could be thrown in my path by rooted prejudice and hostile interest, I succeeded in the object I had honestly at heart, I am proud to declare; but if propriety be pushed to extravagance, if what should be mere accessories are occasionally elevated by short-sighted managers into the principal features of their productions, I am not answerable for their folly.

NOTES

1 *Young* Charles Mayne Young (1777–1856), tragedian.
2 *the bag wig of Brutus* . . . Refers to the 18th-century practice of dressing characters in contemporary costume.
3 *Mr Fawcett* John Fawcett (1769–1837), actor.
4 *Charles Farley* (1772–1859), comic actor.
5 *fer blanc* (Fr.) tin.

Incompetence at Drury Lane, 1838

[Alexander Ducrow, manager of Astley's Royal Amphitheatre, and a famous equestrian performer, writes to the management of Drury Lane to protest against the inadequate arrangements for a show involving some of his performing animals. The letter was in the possession of Douglas Jerrold, and is quoted in the biography of him written by his son, W. Blanchard Jerrold, *The Life of Douglas Jerrold* (2nd edn, n.d.).]

ROYAL AMPHITHEATRE,
October 23rd, 1838

My Dear Sir,

I suppose Mr Bunn,[1] nor any of the authorities, will be at the theatre till late today, as there is nobody called till twelve or one, which is not a fit call for such requisites required for tonight's performance, as it is not the performers, but the scenery, gas, arrangement of the animals' cages, and such scandalous inattention to the above matters that caused the disapprobation of the audience at all times at such disgraceful bungling. I must request for my own reputation, as well as that of the theatre, that those departments may be called and looked to, viz., the Cataract Scene set immediately, to have it simplified, to be enabled to have it set and worked. The wood decorations on the top of the lions' cages requires cutting away, and merely sufficient to hide lights.

It is a disgrace to Drury Lane, after the first act receiving three rounds of applause, at the drop descending and being the heaviest, that the second part should be spoilt by bungling in placing the cages, &c., which I informed them in the first instance would be the case. The Fire Scene was scandalously attended to, lit with pitch torches, and smothered the audience with all kinds of nuisances of lime and smoke. As the piece is short I suggest that it be put in three acts; the second act finishing with the Fire Scene, and thus allowing the time for setting cages in the third act. The dresses were not fit for Richardson's;[2] and, if I had not had some few of my own to furnish the piece, it would have been obliged to have been stopped; and, as you have no act drop, and the audience not knowing when the performances are over, it will be necessary to state in the bills that the whole of the entertainments of Monday and the new spectacle having concluded before eleven, it has been found essential, to facilitate the extensive arrangements, to present it in three acts, or divisions, thus each bearing distinctive points of attraction. I shall expect the contents of this attended to, as I will not be liable for the neglect and faults of others. I will thank you to call someone to attend to the alteration and setting of the scenery of second act, as great *alterations* must take place, as well as that of the band. If Mr Bunn should not be there, desire the carpenters to set the Cataract Scene directly, and make the front flats work. I shall be there at twelve to give any instructions necessary.

Yours truly, with respect,

DUCROW

N.B. – The gentlemen who play the Arabs in the second act are to be informed that their faces must be coloured tonight to a certain degree.

NOTE

1   *Bunn*   Alfred Bunn (?1796–1867), impresario: cf. Part IV, no. ii.
2   *Richardson's*   A famous fairground booth theatre.

iii

The dramatists' guide to staging, 1840

[Edward Mayhew's book, *Stage Effect: or, the Principles which Command Dramatic Success in the Theatre* (1840) is addressed to would-be playwrights, but it includes advice on the scenic devices of the theatre. Mayhew approaches this via the customary romantic opposition of the ideal (or poetic) and the real.]

Falstaff's figure, Bardolph's nose, Launce's dog, to such as are of capable fancies, can never perhaps be perfectly realized; but there are others, who are only entertained when the objects are bodily represented to their view, and who have no previous conception whereby to test the sufficiency of the assumption.

Properties should always be quiescent. It argues a want of perception to make them actors, or to entrust them with action; for, if this is done with an appearance of success, such things invariably distract the attention, by claiming applause separate from the real interest of the scene; besides which, they are apt to be ludicrously unreal, or so much the contrary as to stand away from the general truth.

To make this more clear, let us imagine some incident in a piece depends upon the appearance of an eagle. To heighten the effect, the author describes the terrible aspect of the bird and kindles the fancy of the audience; immediately on which the property-man lowers his stuffed effigy of the creature, which, though it shall be an admirable resemblance, and shall move its head and flap its wings, must obviously have so little the appearance of life, that the actors shall stand apart from it. On the other hand, living animals have too strong a sense of reality to blend in with the scene. The actor's art consists chiefly in forgetting his personality, and assuming a character and feeling foreign to his real one, – a delusion these simple creatures are incapable of abetting him in. The player may take on, but the horse is an honest, bona fide horse, without any love for hypocrisy; he will snort when the prince is talking, will make the canvas trees give way to his curvettings, and though a whole army may be perishing in a desert, he will look sleek and comfortable, and persist with his hoofs that the ground is made of wood. Animals, however well trained, perform their parts with so much composure, that it has the appearance of ludicrous condescension, and places the performers in miserable contrast. All the vanity and frivolity of the stage is made apparent by the test of reality, and the reason is provoked into criticism upon the meanness of, as it were, so gross an attempt at actual deception.

Properties should be quiescent. It is true Shakspere, in one of his earliest plays, has introduced a dog. Yet, if caught at as a licence, the reader must observe, this is done, first, in the comic portion of the drama; and, secondly, in such a manner, that however badly the animal might behave, the effect would only be heightened.

Next in practical importance to the properties, are the scenes of the theatre. An author will best please the painter, and certainly consult his own interest, by studying variety in his directions; not confining his incidents to chambers, but occasionally introducing streets and landscapes.

There are but three different kinds of scenery; known by the terms, *drops* or *cloths*, *flats* and *set scenes*. The rest, as wings and side pieces (houses, bowers, rocks, etc., which, when a change takes place, are pushed on and joined to the wings) being adjuncts. Formerly, the chief part of all stock scenery consisted of *drops*, as is still the case in most country theatres; but these are now seldom used in London, flats having superseded them; except close to the proscenium, where they are lowered, when any extraordinary space is required to display the scene which is to follow.

Further from the footlights than the middle of the stage, *flats* are seldom used, the remaining half being devoted to *set-scenes*, which, in the painter's and manager's estimation, are the first kind; and a piece is generally cared for by the theatre in proportion to the number of set-scenes bestowed on its production. Any scene, however, written 'A Palace', 'A Cottage', can be made a set scene; but there are some which cannot be well represented in any other form – those wherein any part is required to be practicable; as staircases down which the characters have to descend; bridges, across which the actors have to pass, etc.; or where machinery is necessary to aid the effect, as torrents, waves, etc.; and in general all, which are other than a picture on a flat surface, may be reckoned *set-scenes*.

It was once desirable an author should so construct his plot, that *flats* and *set-scenes* might alternate one with the other; and this, for authors not intimate with the theatre, is still a good plain rule, though the improvement of machinery now enables the carpenter to work several *set-scenes* consecutively; but it needs some acquaintance with the capabilities of the theatre to do this with effect, and the accidents and delays, common on the first nights of pantomimes, are cautions not to be disregarded.

There are two terms frequently occurring in stage directions, *discovered* and *closed-in* – the importance of which it may be necessary to explain.

' *A Discovery*' is where the act-drop ascends and shews a party at tea, etc., or a front-scene is drawn aside, and a council, etc., seen behind it. Some depth of stage is usually given to scenes in which these occurrences take place; because, unless the footmen are sent to clear the stage (a practice now disapproved of), the chairs and tables must be 'closed in', or shut from view, by the scene which follows; therefore in no instance ought a set-scene to follow one in which there is 'a discovery' requiring these 'properties'. Neither should a death take place in a front scene, unless it be the ending of an act, or the action is directed so as to remove the body – for the footmen would not look well walking away with the corpse.

Concerning *traps*, etc., no directions can be of any value, the carpenter of the theatre being the only person who need study these mysteries. Let the author give his imagination free scope, and he can hardly write directions which cannot be fulfilled.

It may be well, before leaving this part of the subject, to endeavour to ascertain the value of scenes and properties to an author. Actors and managers regard these aids very proudly; and for 'the getting up of a piece', often assume the merit of its success; forgetting the many yearly brought out, with lavish expenditure, which are condemned on the night of their production. Though a weak piece, especially of the melodramatic cast, may gain support from the splendour of the accessories, the fact proves, that no help an author can obtain from the theatre will render a *bad* drama successful. He should never sacrifice his feeling to suggestion from the management, by cutting for this effect, or elongating for that. Above all, he should never write what are called *carpenters'-scenes* – little scenes of dialogue introduced to give time for mechanical arrangements. To have his piece performed, is but a means – the end is its success. His interests are those of a theatre. But vanity is more powerful than interest; and nothing is more common than to sacrifice the author rather than inconvenience the carpenter. Actors are too apt to look on authors as people who need their instruction, and to resent, as obstinacy, any resistance to the theatrical laws which regulate the scenes and properties. The worth of their suggestions will be easily ascertained, by considering the effect such aids to a drama have on the minds of the audience. No art can give reality to *the scenes*. Reality is only acknowledged when the reason is convinced; and in the theatre, the instant the reason questions, illusion ceases. Spectacle is a toy to amuse the senses, and, through them, lull the reason. Scenes, also, have other uses; they spare long passages of mere description, and may be rendered suggestive. This is their highest merit. It seems 'as gross as ignorance made drunk',[1] to talk of their giving *reality*. Illusion can only be perfected through the feelings. All *really feel* with Lear; but who ever felt for scenes and properties? Stanfield's[2] art excites admiration; Bradbury's[3] claims applause; each in his province pleases our sensations – but it is in *the passion only, the drama is a reality*; and it has justly fallen into contempt, in proportion as it has lowered its power for the exaltation of its inferiors.

NOTES

1   *'as gross as ignorance made drunk'*   Cf. *Othello* III. iii, 408–9:
     'fools as gross as ignorance made drunk'.
2   *Stanfield*   Clarkson Stanfield (1793–1867), scene painter and
     artist, especially noted for marine subjects.
3   *Bradbury*   Not identified.

iv

A 'hard-working theatrical life', 1850s–70s

[In August 1877 Thomas Harris, a dresser at the Princess's
Theatre, was arrested and accused of stealing 'some small pieces of
soap . . . valued at 8d.', together with some fake banknotes and
coins, used in the play *After Dark*, and a towel belonging to
Clarkson's, the wig-makers. Detectives had been called in to
investigate some thefts from the dressing-rooms, and Harris had
the misfortune to be challenged as he left the theatre. Although
the value of the articles in question was paltry, and the actor
William Terriss spoke up in Harris's defence, the dresser was
committed for trial at the Central Criminal Court. His defence
counsel argued that used soap was widely regarded as a dresser's
perquisite. The case was dismissed. A letter from Harris printed in
The Era (9 September 1877) gives an interesting account of the
dresser's varied career.]

Sir, – Will you allow me, through the medium of your valuable
journal, to give an epitome of my connection with the Profession
for the last twenty-three years, and leave your numerous readers
and the Profession generally to judge if they think it probable I
should now, having borne an unimpeachable character through
my life, jeopardize my poor (but honest) name and reputation for
some paltry pieces of used soap valued at 8d. (but actual value at
the utmost 4d.) Now, Sir, in 1854, through unforeseen circumstances – viz., fraudulent trustees and a relative who ruined me and

blasted my prospects in life – I was thrown friendless, almost homeless, on the wide world. I then entered the Princess's Theatre, under the late Charles Kean's management, as a supernumerary, and remained with him in various capacities until the expiration of his management, August 1859, when, through the late Mr George Ellis, Stage-Manager, I received a gratuity of £2 as acknowledgement of my attention to my various duties. In January, 1860, I was engaged by the late Mr S. May,[1] Bow Street, as dresser, and sent to the St James's Theatre, then under the management of Mr F.B. Chatterton. Within three months I was also appointed super-master at the same theatre, in which I continued until the expiration of his management, August, 1860. In September I was sent by Mr May with some £300 worth of wardrobe in my care, on a tour with Mr Charles Dillon[2] through the chief provincial towns. With him I also first played speaking parts. On my return I joined Mr Chatterton again, at the Theatre Royal, Rochester, as wardrobe keeper and general utility at 21s. per week, playing old men and character business.[3] The affair proving an utter failure in eleven weeks, we in January 1861 returned to London (not being able to exist on 8s. 1d., which we shared the last week) with Mr Chatterton's best wishes for my future, having, as I believe, given him every satisfaction.

For many months I was laid on a bed of sickness, and had only my wife's labour to support us. I then determined, if I could get any light employment, to abandon the profession. Failing to do so, I again, in 1862, was sent as wardrobe keeper to the Royalty Theatre, then under the management of Mr Eliot Galer, where I stayed until he relinquished it. In September 1862 I was sent to the Theatre Royal, Manchester, with *The Peep o' Day* (its first production in the Provinces) as wardrobe keeper at £1 1s per week. Was then appointed super-master by Mr Chatterton over 102 men, and also played parts until Christmas 1862, when I travelled all through the West of England for Mr May with Addison's English Opera Company, also fulfilling the duties of prompter until March 1862, when, being left at Torquay I started a musical entertainment in conjunction with a Mr Edmund Elliston, with which I continued at different periods, with varied success, until December, 1865. (I enclose bills of the same to verify my statement.) When in London, I had been employed in the winter season since 1858 by the Sacred Harmonic Society, Exeter Hall,[4] assisting to fit up the orchestra for their concerts. From 1866 to the present time I have had the management of the same myself, and given satisfaction to Sir Michael Costa[5] and all concerned. In the summer season, when in London from 1860 to 1870, I was engaged at Covent Garden Theatre (Italian Opera seasons) in various capacities – wardrobe, armoury, assistant super-master, etc. From 1871 to '73 I was out of any Theatre, my time being fully occupied at the Royal Albert Hall, Exhibition '71 and '72, Crystal Palace, etc.

Since 1874 I have been engaged as dresser at Drury Lane, except last season, when, my health again failing me, I obtained lighter employment – theatrical copying and doing business for an auctioneer and estate agent (whose card I enclose) – until June, this year, when I was engaged at the Princess's Theatre to dress the principal room, which I continued to do until this charge was brought against me. . . . At other spare intervals which I have not mentioned from 1860 I have been employed at other theatres, viz., Sadler's Wells (attendant on the late Captain Horton Rhys), City of London (super-master), Surrey, Lyceum, Adelphi, etc. Such, Sir, is a plain, unvarnished statement of my career from the time I entered the Profession – showing the struggles and shifting scenes of a hard working theatrical life . . .

NOTES

1   *Mr S. May, Bow Street*   Samuel May, theatrical costumier, with premises at 35 Bow Street.
2   *Mr Charles Dillon*   (1819–81), popular tragic and melodramatic actor.
3   *character business*   Engaged to play secondary roles, with distinctively performed (but not necessarily comic) characteristics.
4   *Sacred Harmonic Society, Exeter Hall*   A famous amateur choral society, founded in 1832, which performed at the Exeter Hall (demolished 1907) in the Strand.
5   *Sir Michael Costa*   (1808–84), conductor, founded Royal English Opera at Covent Garden in 1847.

Charles Kean consults an antiquary, 1856

[George Godwin, FSA, advised Kean on the 'archaeology' that was a prominently advertised feature of his revival of *A Winter's Tale*. This was one of the triumphs of his management of the Princess's, and was the production in which Ellen Terry played Mamilius (see p.100, above). In these letters (MS letters, Folger Shakespeare Library, Washington, DC) the actor-manager asks for information and indicates his awareness of the demands of stage effect and publicity (the 'fly-leaf' and the 'bill').]

[?9 February 1856]
I am very anxious about the said Palace of Polixenes. I should like to make a grand display in this situation but cannot find a *cause* – A Banquet would not do, as Leontes has one in the 1st Act & a Procession would be too like *Sardanapalus*[1] – Can you think of any *reason* for an effect –

I should like to have one Greek chamber – an interior – for though we are giving a Greek play we have not one scene of this description.

As our last scene of the piece, the statue scene, has pillars all round, & thereby in no degree resembles the one arranged for the opening of the 2nd Act when Hermione is discovered at work with her women, don't you think it might be introduced with good effect in this situation?

Don't forget about the tomb of Midas if you please for the carving is so beautiful on that that I should like, if possible, to introduce it in the Palace of Polixenes, and I can't imagine we can be wrong as Midas was a King of Phrygia.

[?11 February 1856]
I find the *Theatre* was often the place for religious & civil ceremonies, & Dr Smith[2] the other day (the author of the Classical dictionary) asked me why I did not select that locality for the trial of Hermione – At first I hesitated but reflection makes me think it would be advantageous, and afford me an extra line for my fly-leaf – it would add to the interests of the play by giving a *real* scene instead of an imaginary one – I have asked Mr Grieve[3] to make a model & submit it to you . . .

17 Princess's Theatre, 1854: triple playbill for Charles Kean's production of *The Winter's Tale*, showing prices of 2s.6d., 2s., 1s. and 6d., with 'orchestra stalls' at 6s., and details of arrangements for booking places in private boxes and stalls. Kean's account of the production's historical background occupies the first leaf of the bill. Compare illustration 3.

[11 February 1856 following 'a brief and hasty note this morning']
I had the positions of the stage tried the other morning with
regard to the Banquet scene, but found the Couches, Tables, &
Candelabras, left no room for my Pyrrhic Dance, which I consider
one of the features of the piece.

How may I raise a third of the Stage (at the back) & place the
Banquet there leaving the front for the dancers? This would of
course necessitate a change from an open Hall to an *interior
room* . . .

I wish Grieve also to get on with the first scene of the Temple
of Minerva – but he does not appear to know how to paint the
background.

I have recommended the Fountain of Arethusa in the
perspective & the city wall. The Fountain would be a feature in
the *bill* – to this I think there could be no objection, as it was in
the same part of the city as the Temple –

I am very solicitous also about your idea of the *Theatre* for the
Trial which would give me a good line in the Fly leaf. The
construction of our house would not allow of a front view & we
should be obliged to place it sideways –

Don't think me too troublesome I beg of you, but I cannot help
being very anxious until these points are finally settled.

NOTES

1   *Sardanapalus*   Kean's spectacular staging of Byron's play ran for
     93 nights in 1854.
2   *Dr Smith*   Sir William Smith (1813–93), editor of a *Dictionary of
     Greek and Roman Antiquities* (first published 1842).
3   *Grieve*   From the family of scenic artists, the Grieve in question
     is Thomas (1799–1882).

vi

The stage manager as a dying breed, 1866

[In his evidence before the 1866 Parliamentary Select Committee, Charles Kean spoke of his regret at the passing of the provincial stock companies, with their dependence on custom and tradition in the staging of plays. One consequence was the loss of the old-fashioned stage manager, whose functions and authority Kean describes. His reply to question 6711 implies that the stage manager was a valued and well-paid functionary.]

[6705] ... There is one system in the theatrical world which has done great harm, and that is the loss of efficient stage-managers; formerly, every theatre had a respectable stage-manager, who knew everything connected with the profession, and who had seen all the old actors before him, and that gentleman directed the minds of the younger actors, and he had an authority which none of the stage-managers of the present day seem to possess. For economy's sake, when the patent theatres were done away with, managers dispensed with them, and combined the duties with those of the prompter.

6706.   Sometimes the stage-managers used to perform as well, did they not? – Sometimes, and sometimes not; a brother of Mr Farren[1] was stage manager at the Haymarket when I was a young man; he did not act, but he had been an actor. Mr James Wallack[2] was the stage-manager at Drury Lane when I came out, and he was a very good actor.

6707.   Have the theatres no stage managers now? – They have prompters, promoted to that rank; but they can hardly be called stage-managers, they have not the same authority.

6708.   How was a stage manager educated? – From long use and practice with previous actors. Mr Wallack knew all the business of the old comedies, and what was done by Mr Kemble or Mr George Frederick Cooke,[3] and he could direct any rehearsal in consequence of that knowledge and his own natural ability.

6709.   But with regard to the country it would be difficult to have stage managers when there are no stages, would it not? – But all the theatres are not closed; Liverpool has four theatres and another one building.

6710. They have a stage manager there, I suppose? – No, not a regular stage manager; there is one actor appointed to look after the stage business, perhaps.

6711. How do you account for that? – It is economy; throwing the theatres open [i.e., ending the monopoly of patent theatres in the provinces] forced managers to draw in their expenses, and the stage manager was an expensive gentleman.

NOTES

1   *Mr Farren*   William Farren the younger (1786–1861), retired in 1853; his son, also William (1825–1908) is referred to here.
2   *Mr James Wallack*   The elder (1791–1864), an actor and manager popular on both sides of the Atlantic.
3   *Kemble...Cooke*   John Philip Kemble (1757–1823) and George Frederick Cooke (1756–1812).

vii

'The mask-maker', 1868

[From a story in *The Mask*, a periodical edited (and for the most part, written) by the dramatist and designer Alfred Thompson. The speaker, Chawker, is a property master and mask-maker. The title of the pantomime and its scenario and property-plot (of which only two sections are given here) are fictional but typical.]

I am a property man at the theatre, and it is impossible to write too fully upon the supreme importance of my position, and the intellect necessary to fill it properly.

   High up in my room among the sky borders[1] – up some three hundred stairs, rickety and narrow, the latter portion very steep, with ropes for bannisters – gas and fire always burning, glue always boiling, size and paint always smoking, with the roar of the rehearsal going on on the stage below during the day, and the roar of the performance going on during the night . . . it is there I humbly prosecute my peculiar and important labours, ignored by the authors and abused by the management. I am unknown to the public, but it is I who make up all the articles, or, as it is technically called, the 'properties', used in the performance of the plays – tragedy, melodrama, farce, ballet or pantomime – upon the stage. Oh! what triumphs I have had! Oh! what I have done for the authors, whose pieces I have furnished! Oh! what would the drama be without me! Let me, without egotism, if possible, state a case: – A new piece comes into our theatre. It is written by a celebrated author. It is read in the green-room. No one can make very much out of it. The parts are cast. The whole of the actors and actresses grumble over them. The language is nothing. The opportunities for the display of acting emotion of a high order is nothing.

'Ah!' but says the author to the manager, 'there's the scenery and the properties; that'll make it go. Where's young Skipper? and where's old "Muffins"?' Skipper, I may incidentally say, is the scene-painter, 'old Muffins' is an opprobrious description of myself. Suppose the first act is a snow-storm, with a murder in it. It is I who snows the snow. It is I who makes the little horses and carts in pasteboard which go across on the bridge at the back. It is I who loads the weapon which is the instrument of the deed – always having a second pistol in the wings ready to fire, in case the murderous weapon refuses to go off, which it invariably does. It is I who provides the victim's blood.

Suppose in the second act there is a ballroom scene, followed by a conflagration. It is I who sees to the tables and chairs, and makes the ices that are handed round; it is I who fills the bottles with toast-and-water,[2] off which the hero gets drunk; the cards with which he plays, the money and bank-notes which he loses; it is I who provides and burns the red fire[3] in the wings, and which sets the house on fire; and it is I who provides the falling bricks and shower of sparks, and sees to the proper and vigorous thunder of the crash.

Suppose in the third act there is a railway collision upon the stage. It is I again who designs and arranges the locomotives and carriages; who lights the fires, and makes the smoke come out of the funnel; and when the carriages have come into collision, both the boilers burst, and all the passengers are blown into the air, it is I who fires the retorts at the back, provides the 'dummy bodies', and throws them from the flies.

The piece runs five hundred nights, of course; but it is the snowstorm, the fire, and the collision which make it run. And who has produced them? Who is the real author of the dramatic success? Why, it is old Chawker, the property man. In the future gallery of British dramatists shall I not have a place? 'Shakespeare, Sheridan, and Chawker' would read well; and still, without egotism, may I not claim the position?

Ah! but it is at Christmas time that the greatest exhibition of my industry and ability takes place. Getting up the pantomime is the thing to bring out your capacity, and to prove whether you are really a man of genius or an impostor. Well do I remember one particular pantomime we had at our house. It was called *Polly Put the Kettle On; or, Harlequin King Cricket, the Demon of the Red-Hot Poker, and the Fairy of the Enchanted Hearthstone.* It was a very heavy production for the property department, for it was full of properties, and the management was very late with it. When our stage-manager, Mr Pincher, issued to me 'my plot', by which I refer to the list of things I had got to make for the pantomime, and only about three weeks to do it in, I must say that even I, accustomed as I had been to works of a gigantic character, I must say even I staggered – although never given to drink – like an intoxicated carpenter. It was all written out on long slips of paper, like the bill of fare at the coffee shop where, in the slack season, I take my meals; and the list, in its entire length, measured exactly seven yards. I hung it up in my room, and sat down, and contemplated it in speechless amazement . . .

The first item on my programme was as follows: –

1st scene, Demon Cave

It was in this scene that the Demon revel took place, followed by the sudden appearance of the Demon King in his car, who, after consulting the magic cauldron, despatched the Red-hot Poker to earth by a favourite sprite. This was the list of things I had to make: –

Twelve demons' heads; ditto three-pronged spears; ditto wings; ditto tails; and one dragon to vomit fire, with tail to move. One cauldron, to burn blue; demon king's head; one red-hot poker; four owls, with lighted eyes, to change to green imps; twelve squibs, to light on demons' tails; red fire; head to fit Mr Gruffs.

And here I may observe that there is nothing like demons in a pantomime. They make a great mistake when they cut out the demons. Nothing like the smell of lots of squibs and red fire early in the evening. It's more fragrant to the children than Rimmel's perfume.[4] It's true it makes the old people choke; but don't it recall to them the memories of their youthful days, and what can be more interesting?

The next scene in the pantomime was of course the Fairy Scene. A gorgeous affair, painted by young Skipper, and here, of course, the Ballet, by the young ladies, took place, followed by the appearance of the Fairy Queen, who determined to protect the lovers, and having summoned some Christmas properties as indications of the season, another short ballet took place, and the scene closed on Tableau. This was on my list: –

> 2nd. Scene – Fairy Scene.
> Twenty-four silver helmets for ballet, eight superior; twenty-four javelins for ditto, eight superior; twenty-four shields, eight superior; twenty-four garlands of flowers, eight superior; twenty-four tails of false hair, eight very superior; a cupid's bow and arrows; one dove to fly off; one plum-pudding to walk; one wedding-cake to walk; one round of roast beef to sing and dance; white fire.

I have ever felt great pride in being called upon to contribute to the proper turning-out of our young ladies, only I could never understand why Mons. Anatole, our ballet master, always showed such a determination to make them carry heavy properties while they were dancing. It is not pleasant to have to dance with a quantity of implements in your hands, and it was always very distracting to myself, for it is difficult to make twenty-four giddy young creatures, eight, however, superior, understand where their properties are, and then to get them to take on the right ones. Over the eight superior I took always great pains. These were for our eight leading young ladies, who did all the dancing in the front, and who were handsome young ladies, and very beautifully formed, and who, in the ballet, completely shut out all the other young ladies who couldn't dance over much, but who made tremendous pretence at the back that they were accomplished performers, which altogether, gave a liveliness to the scene, and made the audience think that they were all superior young ladies, instead of there being only eight worthy of the designation.

NOTES

1   *sky borders*   Strips of painted cloth across the top of the stage
    setting, concealing the upper regions of the stage.
2   *toast-and-water*   Water coloured with burnt bread to represent
    alcoholic drinks.
3   *red fire*   Coloured flash powder, used in representing explosions
    and fires, and to accompany magic transformations and sudden
    appearances in pantomime.
4   *Rimmel's perfume*   Eugène Rimmel (d. 1887) established a
    successful perfumery business in London, from the 1830s. The
    firm's products were often used to perfume theatre programmes.

viii

Painting and lighting a sunrise effect, 1875

[From Frederick Lloyds' *Practical Guide to Scene-Painting and
Painting in Distemper* (1875). Lloyds had been scene-painter at
Sadler's Wells during Samuel Phelps's management.]

Transparent cloths have a fine effect when well managed. They
are painted on union[1] or linen if the scene is not too
large . . . entirely in transparent colours, and by means of
successive glazings either in oil or size colour. Oil colour is to be
preferred when the transparent cloths are not more than about
twenty feet square; but beyond that size, they had best be painted
in size colour, which is rather a difficult process to manage, as the
colour sets faster than the cloth can be painted, and, in the case of
a sky, it is not easy to make it look smooth. The best plan, I find,
is to mix the size a little stronger than half-and-half, letting it cool
into a jelly; and then, when required for use, to put an equal
quantity of cold water to it, mixing the two with a large sash tool[2]
thoroughly together by twirling it rapidly round and round. The
size will thus become a thin jelly, and, when mixed with your
colour, will work almost like oil paint. But observe to keep your
colour constantly stirred to prevent its setting into a complete
jelly, in which state you could not use it freely. Whenever you may

want the light to be entirely blocked out, use thick body colour with size, on either the oil or size colour cloth . . . Paint the face of your cloth with very thin size colour . . . and very lightly as it will be lighted from the front only with all the blue mediums over the gas battens, the wing or sidelights down, green glass on the footlights, and gas lengths at the sides with green glasses on them. With this amount of light the slightest stain of colour on the sky will be sufficient. Commence with a slight tinge of yellow lake and scarlet lake at the bottom of your sky; then work up to crimson lake, and afterwards add a little blue, continuing to add blue till it is all blue from about one third up the sky to the top. The warm tints must be so faintly laid in that the blue colour from the mediums may be able entirely to overpower them, producing all the effects of moonlight on the sky. Now paint the landscape portion of the cloth, from distance to foreground, in a manner suitable for a night view, and so light that the subdued and coloured light in front may not cause your scene to look black . . .

The work of painting must then be carried on at the back of the cloth, and as you proceed you can observe the effect of the transparent oil or size colour that you are using . . .

Now paint the sky – on the back of the cloth . . . beginning at the top with Prussian blue, and then working down the sky with crimson lake, continually added to the above till the colour is all lake; then with the scarlet lake with a little yellow lake in it, finishing at the bottom with Indian yellow and a little scarlet lake with the yellow lake. Next throw in such clouds as you think will be effective, taking care that the edges of them are lighted up with a warm colour, lighter than the sky. Let the distant hills and part of the landscape be lighted in the same way, and paint the shades and shadows with a cool, purple tint. Strengthen up the whole subject, and, in parts, block out the transparencies altogether, so that the lights may tell out more strongly and warmly. Now you can lay in freely, and where you want the lights to tell out well, you can wipe them out with a piece of calico or cloth of any kind, before the colour hardens.

The next thing to do will be to prime a piece of canvas, about three-fourths the depth of the cloth so as to exclude the light; and to the bottom of that have a piece of crimson silk, about four or five feet deep, sewed on, softening the edge of the silk into the primed cloth with priming. Then have a piece of yellow silk, about four feet deep, sewed to the crimson silk, into which you must soften the edges of it with some crimson lake colour. These silks should have been varnished before being joined to the canvas.

To work the effect, have the cloth and the silks hung close behind the transparent cloth, a part of the crimson silk only appearing above the horizon. Behind this, again, let there be two or three rows of gas, which must be turned quite down at first. When the day is supposed to break, gradually turn up the gas in the lowest row, and there will appear a faint glow of crimson light, which will, of course, grow stronger as the gas in the bottom row is turned on to the full.

The gas last alluded to being full on, let the cloth with the silks be slowly raised. While the yellow begins to appear, and the crimson is rising higher and higher in the sky, the gas behind must be gradually turned up to the full, the mediums in front being worked round from blue to red, and then to yellow, in unison with the change at the back, and the green lights at the wings being gradually turned down and the white lights partly up. The cloth with the silks will by this time have worked up out of sight, and the whole of the painting at the back of the cloth will be seen, in consequence of the strong light at the back of it, to help which the white lights in front have been kept subdued. If lime-lights are used, the glasses will then change from blue to crimson, and next to yellow, in unison with other changes of colour. By reversing the movement, the same painting and arrangements will serve to represent the change from sunset to moonlight.

NOTES

1   *union*   Composite fabric.
2   *sash tool*   Brush used by glaziers (in constructing sash windows).

A call for scenic reform, 1875

[E.W. Godwin, father of Edward Gordon Craig, was an architect whose involvement in theatrical design led him to campaign for harmony and accuracy in stage scenery – and, consequently, to argue for the vesting of authority over such matters in one expert. This article from *The Architect* (24 April 1875) is one of a series on the designs appropriate to Shakespeare's plays. In the same year Godwin prepared a production of *The Merchant of Venice* for the Bancrofts, who staged it at the Prince of Wales's with Ellen Terry as Portia.]

Our business in *Twelfth Night* is to compose or design the architecture in harmony with that which obtained in a Venetian town on the eastern coast of the Adriatic about the year 1600. This is the work of an architect as well as of an antiquary, and there are various ways of doing it; but there is more than this, for in planning the scenes it is necessary that the architect should understand something of the requirements of the stage, and of the *business* of the action, or the best design in the world may result in failure. Stage management, or the 'business', as it is technically called, is one of the colours on which the dramatic picture depends; scenery is another; costume another; and the choicest tints, the high lights, the jewels of the picture are to be found – or should be found – in the expression of the actor's voice, face, and figure. But the *whole* batch of colours and tints must be as one in their treatment, if we wish to see a play rendered fitly. For one man to design an interior for Olivia's house with no control of or understanding as to the stage management; another to arrange the stage business in total ignorance of the inner arrangement of an Italian mansion, or of the uses of its several parts; for one to paint the walls knowing nothing of the colours of the costume; another to design the dresses utterly indifferent to the colours of his background; are the happy-go-lucky processes usually employed on the English stage, and any success that may result from the adoption of such ways and means must necessarily be of the nature of a fluke. If we really want to progress in these matters, the first step is to accept the dictum of Macready: – 'No actor should be a manager.' This strikes at the compound system of ignorance, mystery, envy, and egotism under which the dramatic and histrionic arts languish; flickering up now and then by the special help of some exceptional individual with, I will not say false, but misleading brightness.

x

Changes in lighting: the Lyceum, 1878–98

[Bram Stoker's article, 'Irving and stage lighting' (*Nineteenth Century – and After*, 69, 1911) claims that 'the history of the Lyceum Theatre during Henry Irving's management . . . is the history of modern stage lighting.' Stoker's article is useful because it describes the normal practices of the 1870s, as well as Irving's innovations. An omitted paragraph refers to alterations made during his tenancy by Charles Fechter, and Irving's removal of the old stage machinery and accumulated rubbish in 1878 and 1881.]

When the reconstruction of 1878 was in hand special care was taken to bring up to date the mechanical appliances for lighting the stage. In those days gas was the only available means of theatre lighting – except, of course, 'limelights', which were movable and the appurtenances of which had to be arranged afresh for every play done. But for ordinary lighting purposes gas was used; and, in order to ensure safety, certain precautions were, by Irving's direction, adopted. Instead of having all the gas to be used in the theatre – both for stage and auditorium – supplied from one main, as had been theretofore done, he had supplies taken from two different mains. Thus, in case of explosion, or any other cause of interruption outside the theatre, it was possible to minimize the risk of continued darkness. To this end a by-pass was made connecting within the theatre the two supplies. Of course, an explosion in a gas main, no matter where occurring, is apt to put out all the lights fed from it – if lit. This used in those days to be the great source of danger from fire, for with the enormous number of burners in use in a theatre all turned on, and the gas escaping, the introduction of a naked light was an immediate source of danger. . . . In the Lyceum Theatre a large number of men were employed to look after the gas, to light and turn it off as required. The rules regarding this work were very strict. Each gas-man had to carry (and use for his work) a spirit torch. Under no circumstances was he allowed to strike a match except in places suited for the purpose. After all, it was not a very difficult job to light up a scene, so far as the carrying out of the appointed way was concerned. To make this apparent to a reader not well versed in stage appliances it may be as well to explain the various mechanical appliances for lighting used on the stage:

(1) Footlights, or 'floats', as they were called in the old days of oil-lamps, the name being retained when the special applicability for it had passed away; (2) battens; (3) standards; (4) lengths; (5) ground rows; (6) all sorts of special form and size, made to suit particular pieces of built scenery.

Of these lights, the only kind directly observable by the public are the footlights. That is, they are in front of the stage, but it is essential that they be not themselves seen; otherwise their glare would entirely destroy all distinctions of light. What the public sees are the backs of the reflectors which hide the glare from the audience and send it back upon the stage. These lights are of great power. In the present time, when electric light is used for the purpose, these lamps vary from twenty to a hundred candle-power. To realize this blaze of light it must be remembered that an ordinary domestic light of the 'Swan' or 'Edison' pattern is of some eight candle-power. In Irving's time – at the close of his personal management of the Lyceum – the footlight lamps were of sixty candle-power, modified occasionally for artistic purposes, as I shall show further on.

Battens are long frames that run across the top of the stage from side to side. These contain a large number of lamps, placed side by side so as to show a very strong line of light. The battens are hung with such fittings as allow them to be raised or lowered at will. In the gas days the batten was a wooden frame to which was attached, in such a position that the light could not come into contact with anything inflammable, an iron gas-pipe, in which were fixed at regular intervals a multitude of burners. The special burners used for this purpose were what were known as 'fish-tail' burners, which allowed the flame to spread laterally, and so were, by securing good combustion, effective for lighting purposes. This gas-pipe was connected with the main by flexible leather tubes, so that provision could be made for altering the height above the stage without interfering with the supply of gas. At one end of the

pipe was a burner fed by quite another tube, so that it would keep
alight when the main supply of that pipe was turned off. This jet
was known as the 'pilot', and was specially lit in readiness before
the beginning of the play. When the supply of gas was turned on
to the batten pipe, the pressure sent the flame along. . . . To
ensure readiness, alterability, and safety in these and other lights,
all along the stage from front to back, behind the line of the
'wings' which mask in the scene, were special water-taps
connected with the gas mains of the theatre, so as to ensure a
constant supply up to these points. The flexible tubes had metal
ends which fell easily into place in the taps and left no leakage.
Then the gas-man with his key turned on the tap so as to make
lighting possible. All these taps were so arranged that the supply
at each batten could be turned on or off at the 'Prompt', where the
'gas-table' was fixed vertically. There was a batten for each
portion of the stage, from front to back. For a stage is divided for
working purposes by measured distances which are the continuance of the old 'grooves' by which the 'flats' in the old days used
to be pushed out or drawn off. All stage hands understand No. 1,
No. 2, No. 3 and so on.

The standard is a vertical pipe, set on a strong, heavy base, so as
to be secure from accident of lateral pressure. The gas supply
enters through a flexible tube at the base, arranged with the taps
in the same manner as are the battens. The top of each is a cluster
of very powerful burners; thus each standard is in itself a source of
intense light, which can be moved when required.

Lengths are battens of convenient size, and are made adaptable
for almost any use. As the purpose of the lighting is to throw the
light from front and back of the stage, these are often arranged to
be hung on the back of the scenic piece in front. Hooks are
provided for the purpose. Lengths can be placed in any position or
shape; and, so long as their direct light is concealed from the
audience, can be made to enhance or supplement any volume of
light.

The ground rows are a length applied to a special purpose.
Stage perspective differs somewhat from the perspective of nature,
inasmuch as it is much stronger; and it is therefore necesssary at
times to even-up this extra strength to eyes accustomed in
ordinary to a different perspective focus. In fact, in proper stage
lighting – that which produces what seems to be the ordinary
appearance of natural forces – it is not sufficient to have all the
lighting from one point. The light of nature is so infinitely
stronger than any artificial light, and so much better distributed,

that science and art have to be requisitioned to produce somewhat similar effect.

As to special lighting pieces for 'built' scenery, these have on each occasion to be made to serve their present purpose. In 'built' scenery it is sometimes difficult to avoid throwing objectionable shadows. The lights are so strong, and the space available is so small, that there is hardly room at times for simple effects. So, when there is a shadow which cannot be avoided, it is generally possible to build in some piece of seemingly solid work, behind which a light can be so placed as to destroy the shadow.

Now, in 1878, all this had practically to be done by gas. Of course, what are known as 'limelights' were in use. These are exceedingly powerful lights, produced by playing burning gas heavily charged with oxygen and hydrogen on a fragment of lime. The light is so concentrated that it is easily adaptable to the localizing of strong light. The appliance for producing the light being small, it can easily be placed in a specially-made box, whose face is a lens of strength suitable to the work to be done. The effect is, of course, proportionate to the amount of concentration. In fact, the general scientific law applies that what is gained by direction is lost in force, and *vice versa*. In a well-equipped theatre many different kinds of limelights are now in use, the lenses being in such variety that a skilful operator can select that best adapted to the special occasion; 'open limes', 'spot lights' of varying focus and intensity, lights so constructed as to cover a certain amount of space, and so on. The moon, the lights from the windows of the 'old home', the convenient ray which follows the hero about the stage, so that the audience may never forget that he is present, and nearly all such aids to the imagination of the spectator are produced in this way . . .

Now as these two methods of lighting – gas and lime-light – were already in existence when Henry Irving managed a theatre for himself, his part in the general advance was primarily to see that both these means were perfected. To this effect he spared no expense. The equipment of the Lyceum Theatre so as to able to use gas-light most readily and to the best advantage was a costly job. . . . But when the mechanism was complete it was possible to regulate from the 'Prompt' every lamp of the many thousands used throughout the theatre. This made in itself a new era in theatrical lighting. By it Irving was able to carry out a long-thought-of scheme: that the auditorium should be darkened during the play. Up to this time such had not been the custom. Indeed, it was a general aim of the management to have the auditorium as bright as possible. The new order of things was a revelation to the public. Of course, when the curtain came down the lights went up, and *vice versa*. In the practical working of the scheme it was found possible to open new ways of effect. In fact, darkness was found to be, when under control, as important a factor in effects as light. With experience it was found that time could be saved in the changing of scenes. It used to be necessary, when one 'full' scene followed another, to drop a curtain temporarily so that the stage could be lit sufficiently for the workmen to see what they were doing. But later on, when the workmen had been trained to do the work as Irving required it to be done, darkness itself became the curtain. The workmen were provided with silent shoes and dark clothing, all of which were kept in the house and put on before each performance. Then, in obedience to preconcerted signals, they carried out in the dark the prearranged and rehearsed work without the audience being able to distinguish what was going on. Later on, when electric power came to be harnessed for stage purposes, this, with different coloured lights, was used with excellent effect . . .

It was not till about 1891 that electric-light was, even in a crude condition, forward enough to be used for general lighting purposes in British theatres. Irving had it then put in by degrees, beginning with the footlights, which formed a test of suitability. Electric-light differs from other lights in that when it is lowered in degree it changes colour. This is perhaps due to the fact that it is not in the ordinary sense a light at all, but a heat visible *in vacuo*. In order to allow the footlights to be turned down it was necessary in those days to have a liquid resistance, which was a wasteful as well as an expensive mechanism. In addition, the light even then afforded was an unpleasing one for the stage, unless the vacuum lamps were tinted. Therefore considerable consideration and experience were necessary before a satisfactory result could be achieved. The purpose of lowering footlights is to create a scenic atmosphere of night or mystery or gloom. Now in nature night and mystery and gloom are shown in tints of blue; but as electric light is produced by red-hot carbon the atmosphere was warm instead of cold, cheerful instead of gloomy. In those days coloured lights on the stage were in their infancy, and the best device we were able at first to adopt was to cover the lamps of the footlights with bags of thin blue paper . . .

[Stoker explains that the licensing authorities thought these paper bags dangerous. He mentions the need for some kind of heating in the auditorium – now cooler because of the use of electric stage lights. Then he turns to Irving's use of the technology described.]

All that I have said of lighting in the theatre is merely with reference to the mechanism. The part most noteworthy, and which came from Henry Irving's incomparable brain and imagination, was the production of effect. In the 'seventies, as I have said, there was very little attempt to produce fine gradations of light and shade or of colour. Henry Irving practically invented the *milieu*. When he became a manager the only appliances were what were called 'mediums', which were woven films of cotton or wool or silk drawn between the lights and the stage or scenery which they lit. The finest stuff we used then was 'scrim', a thin silk which gave certain colour without destroying or suppressing an undue amount of the illuminating quality. This stuff, dyed only in a few rudimentary colours, could be used to go beneath the battens and encompass the standards, wire guards being affixed everywhere to prevent the possibility of conflagration. It was also used occasionally to cover the bull's eyes of the limelight boxes. But it was impracticable to produce colour effects, except generally. The stage could be fairly well reduced to one dominating colour, but that was all.

Accordingly Irving set himself to work in his own quiet way, and with the help of his employés, had various mechanical processes devised. He had transparent lacquers applied to the glasses of the limelights, and, when electric light came in, to the bulbs of the electric lights, and thus produced effects of colour both of intensity and delicacy up to then unknown. Instead of rudimentary colours being mentioned on the lighting 'plots' – by which the operators work – 'blue', 'red', &c., the plots began to direct the use of certain fine distinctions of colour, so that before long the men themselves became educated to finer work and would no more think of using 'dark blue' instead of 'light blue', or 'steel blue' instead of 'pale blue', than they would insert a slide of any form of red instead of any form of blue.

Then came quite a number of colours new to this use, as the possibilities of lacquer for the purpose became known and enlarged. Shades began to take the place of colours in matters of choice, and soon even the audience became trained to the enjoyment of fine distinctions of colour . . .

[Irving also divided the footlights into sections of lamps of different colours, so that lighting effects could be concentrated and selective – 'it became an easy matter to throw any special part of the stage into greater prominence – in fact, to "vignette" that part of the stage picture which at the moment was of greater importance'. Irving 'began to use the media of coloured lights as a painter uses his palette.' In conclusion, Stoker describes the actor conducting a lighting rehearsal.]

It was most interesting to see him setting about the lighting of a scene. There were, of course, certain rudimentary matters which had to be observed in all scenes; but it may be useful to describe the *modus operandi*. This work, especially in its earlier stages – for it was a long process, entailing many rehearsals – was done at night, when the play of the evening was over. The stage workmen, after a short interval for their supper, got the new scene set. While this was being done, Irving and I, and often the stage-manager if he could leave his work, took supper in the 'Beefsteak Room', which was one of Irving's suite of private rooms in the theatre. When the scene was ready he went down – usually sitting in the stalls, as the general effect of the scene could be observed better from there than from the stage. The various workmen employed in the lighting 'stood by' under their respective masters – with, of course, the master machinist and the property master and *their* staffs ready in case they should be required. There were always a large number of men present, especially at the experimental stage of lighting. The gas engineer, the limelight master, the electrician, all had their staffs ready. Of these the department the most important was that of the limelights, for these lights had to be worked by individual operators, all of whom had to be 'coached' in the special requirements of the working of the play before them; whereas the gas and electric lighting was arranged with slow care, and was, when complete, under the control of the prompter – or the masters under the direction of the prompter – who took his orders from the stage-manager. It was seldom indeed that any member of the company was present at a lighting rehearsal; never in the earlier stages. It was only when some special requirement made the presence of one or more of the actors advisable that such actor attended, and then only by request. The rule did not apply to Miss Terry, who, as a privileged person, could attend whenever she chose. But in fact, she was never present at the earlier rehearsals when the scheme of lighting was invented and arranged. These were late at night, or rather, early in the morning, long after – generally hours after – she had gone home. Let it be clearly understood that the lighting of the

Lyceum plays was all done on Irving's initiation and under his supervision. He thought of it, invented it, arranged it, and had the entire thing worked out to his preconceived ideas under his immediate and personal supervision . . .

xi

Transformation scenes, c.1880

[From Percy Fitzgerald's *The World Behind the Scenes* (1881).]

All will recall in some elaborate transformation scene how quietly and gradually it is evolved. First the 'gauzes' lift slowly one behind the other – perhaps the most pleasing of all scenic effects – giving glimpses of 'the Realms of Bliss', seen behind in a tantalizing fashion. Then is revealed a kind of half-glorified country, clouds and banks, evidently concealing much. Always a sort of pathetic and at the same time exultant strain rises, and is repeated as the changes go on. Now we hear the faint tinkle – signal to those aloft on 'bridges' to open more glories. Now some of the banks begin to part slowly, showing realms of light, with a few divine beings – fairies – rising slowly here and there. More breaks beyond and fairies rising, with a pyramid of these ladies beginning to mount slowly in the centre. Thus it goes on, the lights streaming on full, in every colour and from every quarter, in the richest effulgence. In some of the more daring efforts, the *femmes suspendues* seem to float in the air or rest on the frail support of sprays or branches of trees. While, finally, perhaps, at the back of all, the most glorious paradise of all will open, revealing the pure empyrean itself, and some fair spirit aloft in a cloud among the stars, the apex of all. Then all motion ceases; the work is complete; the fumes of crimson, green and blue fire begin to rise at the wings; the music bursts into a crash of exultation; and, possibly to the general disenchantment, a burly man in a black frock steps out from the side and bows awkwardly. Then to shrill whistle the first scene of the harlequinade closes in, and shuts out the brilliant vision. Some of the more ambitious of these transformation scenes, notably those of Covent Garden, are remarkable works for the daring spirit in which they are conceived and their genuine magnificence. The variety of resources brought into play, the bold use made of the opportunities offered on so fine a stage, the enormous quantity of auxiliaries to be marshalled, the variety of design presented year after year, are significant of English energy, and cannot be approached in foreign theatres.

The ingenuity exhibited in the aerial displays – girls apparently floating in the air at great heights – has to be supplemented by extraordinary precautions to prevent accidents. These 'irons', as they are called, to which the performers are strapped, are made of the finest, best tempered metal, and their shape must be ingeniously contrived to supply strength in company with the artistic requirements. This element is generally secured by extending them below the stage in the shape of long levers, which take their share of the weight. But large platforms, or *équipements*, as the French call them, are the essential portions of every 'transformation', consisting of a vast stage rising slowly from below, and suspended by ropes and counterpoises, and so nicely balanced that a couple of carpenters can raise them, although burdened by a score of *figurantes*, each strapped to her iron. This is the principle which underlies all these effects, but it is infinitely varied, and there are even platforms upon platforms, which rise in their turn after the first has arisen. The allusion has been made to the 'crowning of the edifice' at the close of the transformation, when, perhaps, a semicircular group of fairies will rise, and from out this group a central figure will mount slowly, becoming the apex, as it were, of the whole. Then it will be noted that the semicircle begins to open, the group to separate, and the figures to glide down and forward by some mysterious agency. It is contrived by ingenious machinery, called by the French a *parallèle*. This consists of a number of light pedestals, about twelve feet in height, which are ranged closely around a centre pedestal, the tops being drawn close to it by cords brought down and secured to a windlass worked by a man who ascends with the machine. At the proper moment he 'lets go', and the weight of the figures, checked by counterpoises, allows the pedestals to open out, exactly as the ribs of an umbrella would do. The whole machine is complete in itself, and is kept 'in stock', as it were, and can be fitted to many varieties of effect.

'The hive of pantomime', 1880

[An article signed 'Feraldt' in *The Theatre*, January 1880.]

'Perhaps you would be good enough to come down to the rooms and see if you are satisfied with the ballets – Signor Bacolo has completed the first, and thinks the second is just what you would like.'

'All right. I'll be there at eleven sharp.'

We are getting near Christmas, and have only another fortnight to complete everything connected with the 'Gorgeous Original Christmas Pantomime, entitled *Harlequin Ali Baba and the Wonderful Lamp, or the Wizard Bluebeard and the Little Fairy Cinderella*' – (I may say by way of parenthesis I detest this mixture of simple fairy stories, and should never think of muddling young heads with such a tissue of complicated incidents; but the title is only imaginary, and will do as well as any other) – a pantomime which is to eclipse, we hope, everything yet seen in fun, beauty, and all the rest of it.

People who take their children to pantomimes have little or no idea of the time, thought, and labour it takes to put on to the stage of one of these elaborate entertainments. A manager who looks after the production of pieces he brings out in his own theatre must be everywhere and everything at once. He may have the best coadjutors, the cleverest master-carpenter, the most artistic scene-painter, a genius as a property-man, and an experienced author whose work is interpreted by the best available talent; but if he does not give an eye to all departments there will be hitches too evident, and mistakes too palpable, which only the good-humoured criticism of Christmas will overlook.

'Let me see, that ballet-master wants me at eleven. Send for Mr Ossidew (the property-man) and Mr Rowe Spink (the scenic artist). Oh, here is Mrs Tarlatan,[1] the wardrobe-mistress. Well, have all the costumes arrived?'

'Good-morning, sir. There's three cases arrived from Arisso's, which I've opened. All the principals' except the king's boots and the princess's hat and feathers. They say the twelve pages is there, but I only count eleven. They look splendid, sir, and I should like you to see 'em.'

'I'll come up to the wardrobe at two without fail. How about the demon ballet?'

'There is only half of 'em come, and the tights ain't finished yet. But they've promised them by next Thursday.'

'Dear, dear! that's very late! Any boots arrived?'

'Not likely, sir. Them's always the last. Cavis[2] makes first-rate boots, but he do make one nervous at the end.'

Here the master-carpenter enters, and Mrs Tarlatan retires. The master-carpenter, who always looks like a general officer with a grievance, has come to say that the scene-rehearsal will be ready at midnight as soon as the usual night performance has been disposed of. Also:

'Mr Appythort, the hauthor, wants a new trap for the demon queen's first entrance. We shall have to cut away a lot of joists, and might as well use the bridge in the third entrance.'

I run up with Mortice at once and inspect the stage – the trap can easily be made, and two men are put on to it at once. The spirits of the demon queen and the author's will both rise on the opening night to their individual satisfaction.

'Ah, Mr Rowe Spink, I hope I haven't taken you away from your work?'

'Not at all, sir. I was coming down to ask you if it would not be better to add another border in the palace scene. You'll see tonight. Mortice thinks we can do without it. By the way, Mr Irons[3] will be here tomorrow to try the transformation.'

'So much the better. Where's Haresfoote?[4] Oh, Mr Haresfoote (the stage-manager), mind all the ballet-ladies and the extras are here tomorrow night for the transformation scene.'

'The extras are not all chosen yet, sir. I've got thirty or forty girls waiting now in the hall to be selected when you are at liberty'.

'Very well, I'll come at once. I shall come up to the paint-room, Mr Spink, this afternoon, and – ah, you're here, Ossidew. How are the properties getting on? Is the practicable[5] cannon ready?'

'All right, sir; everything will be there by the opening-night.'

Now there is no more fatal rock than this behind the scenes. 'All right' on the opening night generally means all wrong. If a man tells me a dress or a property, or, if it comes to that, a part will be all right on the opening-night, I say it will be all wrong, and must be specially provided for. Of course, when I get up to the property-room, the practicable cannon, out of which a whole regiment of small soldiers is going to be shot, apparently into space, is not commenced.

'What do you think of them heads, sir?' says Mr Ossidew, when he has been sufficiently lectured on the necessity of being

18 The spectacle of pantomime and the mask-maker's art: scenes from
the 1861 Christmas entertainments.

beforehand with all his productions. 'They wants just a little bit of hartistic treatment to be first-rate.' The heads are enormous *papier-mâché* (or 'paper-mash', as Ossidew calls it) effigies to be worn by the king's body-guard; and the supers who have been recruited for their particular regiments may be heard on the stage below stamping about under the drilling of the stage-manager, Mr Haresfoote. I can hear coming up from beneath me like the ventriloquist's 'man in the cellar', a voice shouting 'Confound it all! How many more times are we to do this over again? Didn't I say, after crossing the bridge and coming down the rake, you are to march two and two down to the centre of the footlights, where you see the conductor in the orchestra, and then, half turning right and half left, you will circle round into the places I showed you? Now then, pay attention! We can't stay all day at this!' But to return to the properties. The heads are all waiting to be painted and varnished; the armour is being cleaned up; the comic halberds are being fixed; the banners are all arriving at completion, and the property horses and wolves (there is a comic scene recalling the thrilling ride of Mazeppa)[6] are being tried by some of the property-men to see if they will work their tails and roll their eyes with some semblance of reality. Everything seems tolerably forward, and after repressing Ossidew's desire to make all the hand-properties – that is, the accessories carried by ballet-girls, such as wreaths, torches, or assegais – twice as large and three times as heavy as is necessary, I again return to the stage, which I now find swarming with boys who are to be drilled into an attack on some ogre's castle or who represent imps and tadpoles in the opening. . . . The boys are using their swords and guns for the first time today, and well they take to them. Meanwhile I must go and select the extras.

.　Some forty or fifty young women in various costumes, from the imitation sealskin coat and hat with a dyed feather in it, to the rusty black merino of some poor widow, are to be seen chatting and waiting in hope of being chosen to represent Peris of Paradise or Inhabitants of the Moon as the transformation scene may require.

Some few are eligible at a glance – smart, well-formed, tidy-looking girls; some are equally certain [not] to be 'cast' – drag-gled, disreputable and impossible. There is no doubt about these; but the unpleasant part of selecting is the elimination of some respectable women who are hoping, in spite of all, to add a weekly pittance to their homes, and yet possess nothing – neither height, charm, nor any personal qualifications – fitting them to appear as a decorative item in the *Houris' Home of Eternal Happiness*, where the houris, too slightly clad, are passing a very unpleasant quarter of an hour, strapped to irons, and inhaling the fumes of magnesium and red fire.

However, it has to be done; and, after all, those not chosen will go to some minor theatre where the houris are happier and the gods not so difficult to please. Our thirty extras have been selected, and will appear on Boxing Night in all the glories of gold tissue, enhanced by the limelight's rays . . .

[The manager goes to an 'Academy of Dancing' to consult the ballet-master; then he returns to the theatre.]

After visiting Mr Rowe Spink's domains in the painting-room – where cloths, i.e., canvases, are hung on both sides of a long slice of a room, lighted by skylights and encumbered with long tables down the centre, covered with large jam-pots full of horribly-smelling colours – extolling the *Moonlight Caverns*, and looking at a little model of the *Murky Mansions of Mandragora*, the last scene as yet unpainted – I wend my way across the flies, which in a large theatre like this, look something between the deck of an old man-of-war under action and an *annexe* in some exhibition for the show of looms and spinning-machines. Carefully threading the drums and windlasses, and avoiding the counterweights, I get to a small staircase, which takes me to the wardrobe. Here Mrs Tarlatan is in her glory. Cupboards to right of her, cupboards to left of her, display some three hundred or more costly dresses, all glittering with spangles and foil. Baskets of chorus-dresses and tarlatan skirts stand about; while on a broad table are sundry parcels, tied up, of wings, head-dresses, and other accessories to the costume department. Some twenty women are here at work – some at sewing-machines, some with their needle, altering fits, adding fringes, or repairing dresses continually in use.

Every day, for three or four weeks, before a pantomime is brought out, some such personal supervision as has been sketched out here, has to be gone through. The work itself has been going on for months. The author has written his dialogue, but is still on the look-out for puns, topical allusions, and new or effective songs, for the latest improvement of his piece. The scenery has been modelled, and now only wants the rehearsal, which is to take place at night, to fit, set, and complete the beautiful pictures, which form such a feature in the entertainment. The properties have all been noted, old ones restored and made young, fresh ones invented and carried out. The wood and canvas has been stretched and hung, the profile and scroll work is now being finished, and in another week complete rehearsal will be the order of the day and night; for the work has to be completed by a certain time, and to ensure perfection, the only way is to stick to it and to make the others follow your example.

Nothing, perhaps, is more tedious than a scene-rehearsal. You sit with the scenic artists in the stalls or the circles – sometimes in one, sometimes in the other – to judge of the artistic effect, and to dispose the lighting of the various sets or pictures. The fly-men (that is, the carpenters up aloft), the cellar-men (those below the stage), and the stage-carpenters have never yet worked together; and it appears almost marvellous, looking at the crowded cloths and borders, wings and ground-pieces, with the complicated ropes and pulleys above, and cuts and bridges in the stage, not to mention the traps and sliders, gas-battens and ladders, how a series of fifteen or sixteen scenes, besides the elaborate transformation scene, which, perhaps, demands the united skill of fifty or sixty men to work its marvels and develop its mysterious beauties, can even be worked with such systematic regularity and unerring correctness. A good master-carpenter is a general, and all his men depend on his head in time of action. Then there are the gas-men, who have to raise or subdue the floats or footlights, the ground-rows, the wing-ladders, the battens or border-lights, and the bunch-lights or portable suns, which are required to give one effect to a brilliant tropical landscape on [or?] a bewilderingly luxurious palace. The limelights also have their special guardians. Each head of a department makes his special list of effects and changes, and notes the alterations or indications made at rehearsals; in fact, a large theatre at Christmas time, or whenever a spectacle of unusual splendour is to be produced, is a little world in itself, and no ant-hills, no bee-hive can be busier or more occupied . . .

To judge really of the hive a theatre becomes during pantomime season, go to Covent Garden or Drury Lane, and when you watch the masses of actors, actresses, and figurants on the stage, think of the labourers you do *not* see, and the mouths that annually depend on these shows to make both ends meet before the spring comes again.

NOTES

1   *Ossidew . . . Rowe Spink . . . Tarlatan*   'Ossidew' may represent the Fr. *assidu* (assiduous, painstaking); 'rose-pink' is a pigment of pinkish hue, associated with stage cosmetics and 'blood'; 'tarlatan' is a kind of thin open muslin, used in ballet-dancers' skirts.

2   *Cavis*   Untraced.

3   *Irons*   Refers to the 'irons', or brackets, supporting performers suspended above the stage in transformation effects.

4   *Haresfoote*   A hare's foot was a traditional implement for applying make-up.

5   *practicable*   Capable of being used, e.g., a three-dimensional (rather than painted) door that can be opened.

6   *Mazeppa*   The popular dramatization of Byron's poem of that title, first seen at the Coburg in 1823. The actress Ada Isaacs Mencken was one of the most famous exponents of the title role, in which, seemingly half-naked, she was tied to the back of a horse and chased across spectacular mountainous scenery by 'ravening' wolves.

xiii

The basics of scene-painting, 1880s

[From Dutton Cook's *A Book of the Play* (4th edn, 1882).]

Some few notes . . . may be worth making in relation to the technical methods adopted by the scene-painter. In the first place, he relies upon the help of the carpenter to stretch a canvas tightly over a frame, or to nail a wing into shape; and subsequently it is the carpenter's duty, with a small sharp saw, to cut the edge of irregular wings, such as representations of foliage or rocks, an operation known behind the curtain as 'marking the profile'. The painter's studio is usually high up above the rear of the stage – a spacious room, well lighted by means of skylights or a lantern in the roof. The canvas, which is of course of vast dimensions, can be raised to the ceiling, or lowered through the floor, to suit the

19 The paint-frame at a London theatre, 1901.

convenience of the artist, by means of machinery of ingenious construction. The painter has invariably made a preliminary water-colour sketch of his scene, on paper or cardboard. Oftentimes with the help of a miniature stage, such as schoolboys delight in, he is enabled to form a fair estimate of the effect that may be expected of his design. The expansive canvas has been sized over, and an outline of the picture to be painted – a landscape, or an interior, as the case may be – has been boldly marked out by the artist. Then the assistants and pupils ply their brushes, and wash in the broad masses of colour, floods of light, and clouds of darkness. The dimensions of the canvas permit of many hands being employed upon it, and the work proceeds therefore with great rapidity. But the scene-painter is constant in his supervision of his subordinates, and when their labours are terminated, he completes the design with numberless improving touches and masterly strokes. Of necessity, much of the work is of a mechanical kind; scroll-work, patterned walls, or cornices are accomplished by 'stencilling' or 'pouncing' – that is to say, the design is pricked upon a paper, which, being pressed upon the canvas, and smeared or dabbed with charcoal, leaves a faint trace of the desired outline. The straight lines in an architectural scene are traced by means of a cord, which is rubbed with colour in powder, and, having been drawn tight, is allowed to strike smartly against the canvas, and deposit a distinct mark upon its surface. Duty of this kind is readily accomplished by a boy, or a labourer of little skill. Scenes of a pantomime order, in which glitter is required, are dabbed here and there by the artist with thin glue; upon these moist places, Dutch metal – gold or silver leaf – is then fixed, with a result that large audiences have never failed to find resplendent and beautiful. These are some, but, of course, a few only, of the methods and mysteries of the scene-painter's art.

Music in drama, 1887

[Editorial in *The Stage*, 16 September 1887.]

To say that music is the handmaiden of the drama sounds like anything but an original statement; indeed, there is a ring of familiarity in the words which almost induces us to put the usual indication of quotation against them. Perhaps it is not too much to say that were the drama bereft of its handmaiden altogether, it would also have to submit to the loss of one of its sturdiest limbs. The strong, hardy member known as melodrama owes a very large part of its robustness and its perennial fascination to the fostering care of St Cecilia, that 'heavenly maid', whose sweetness and whose power form a combined force of impregnable strength. Within the past year or two in the provinces, and more recently in London, there have appeared several healthy signs of a large access of public favour towards strong drama as against the long run enjoyed by all the lighter forms of the art . . .

All present indications seem to point to an era of nature upon the stage. It would be too bold to assert that melodrama, as we have hitherto had it, is the counterfeit of nature; but we think it pretty safe to state that a new style of melodrama – taking its incidents from, and having its dialogue and general bearings suggested by, nature – is gradually getting a hold upon our stages. In this form, as it did in the old periwigged form, music will hold an important place. And the more leisurely we reflect upon the diverse effects music has upon the human mind the more certain does it seem that the addition of music to a drama which is intended to touch our stronger sentiments is the very wisest way of enhancing the powers of the drama itself. But a superabundance is to be rigorously avoided, while a continual iteration of one strain is so great a blot as to amount to absolute disfigurement.

In the old melodrama both these grave faults were common. The heroine, the hero, the villain, the good old man, never made an entrance without the accompaniment of the particular air which was identified with each of these parts. Of course, with our modern ideas of art this became very ridiculous – although we should not have to go many miles out of town to find the same sort of thing now occurring nightly – and it got severely handled in some of the burlesques of a generation ago. The vital use of music as an adjunct to a play is to increase expectation, enhance apprehension, work upon the sympathies. But where the situation itself is not strong and makes no special appeal to our senses music is of no avail to make it what it is not. Therefore it is only in strong situations that music should be used. And this applies also to entrance music. If the character whose entrance is preceded and accompanied by music has something strong to say or do immediately, then the music is artistic. But if it is merely in place of the servant's announcement of a visit then it is absurd and inartistic. In domestic drama the strains of the old popular and national melodies, heard at the right moments, are irresistible; they affect the whole of the audience, although the stalls and dress-circle are apt to deny the soft impeachment; but the artiste must be fully able to sustain, by acting, the impression caused by the music, or all will be spoilt. It is the conjunction of acting and music under the guidance of pure art that makes the effect which goes to the heart at once. There is one very charming effect, more than half made by music, which when skilfully arranged always touches even such hardened hearts as our own. It is the result of pathetic dialogue – a tender parting for example – while some light-hearted character is supposed to be in an adjoining room innocently playing the cheeriest and brightest of music. This is a serio-comic effect of the highest order. But if the dialogue and situation take a turn towards the tragic, instead of only the pathetic, then the effect is more greatly heightened by the performance of such a homely, plaintive melody as 'Home, Sweet Home'; but it must still be supposed to be played innocently of all knowledge of the parting which is being acted.

All stage-managers who know their work can be fully depended upon by authors in this matter of dovetailing music into a drama; but woe to the author who puts his faith in a stage-manager who does not know his work. A drama overburdened with music drags most fearfully, and disheartens everybody at a first performance. Of course, it is altered afterwards, but the immediate danger is hardly repaired by subsequent alteration in all cases.

'On stage management', 1887

[From an article in *The Theatre*, November 1887. Although the author seems very much an outsider, his observations of a stage-manager at work, and of errors in what would now be called direction are of interest. In the final section he moves to advocacy of municipal repertory theatres.]

In a letter which appeared in *The Era* shortly after my article in the September number of this journal, the writer, while admitting the truth of what I had said as to the want of sufficient preparation on the part of young actors, added that I had unaccountably omitted to say anything about stage management. That I said nothing about it is true, simply because I have had very little opportunity of watching stage managers while at work. The only time that I had the chance of witnessing day by day the rehearsal of a couple of plays in London I was much struck by the skill and rescource shown by the stage manager, who was ready and able to teach his or her business to every member of the company, and showed himself most fertile in resource and able to cope with any difficulty that presented itself. 'How lucky the company to have so good a stage manager,' said a friend of mine to me. 'How smoothly everything will go,' and everything did go very smoothly and well, and the result, so far as the piece was concerned, was extremely satisfactory. But how about the actors? How much did they learn? In my opinion, very little, if anything. The brains and thought which they ought to have brought to the study of their parts were supplied by the stage manager. Instead of playing their own conception of the characters, they played another man's, and, as each part was in great measure conceived by the same brain, there was of course in the rendering of each a certain amount of sameness which would not have been there had the actors engaged thought out their parts for themselves. It struck me at the time that had the stage manager, instead of showing the actors what they should do, contented himself with seeing first that they thoroughly understood their respective parts, and then, when anything went wrong, had he said, 'You are not giving the proper expression to the words you are using,' or 'Your business is not what is required by the situation,' while leaving them to find out for themselves the tones or business required, the result would have been infinitely more satisfactory.

Of course, the answer to this is obvious. It would take far too much time to rehearse a piece if actors, particularly young actors, were to be left alone to discover what to say and do. But if actors had taken the trouble to prepare themselves for the stage in the manner suggested in my last article, their intelligence would be so much quickened that they would commit much fewer errrors than they do now, and when they did commit any, they would, on their being pointed out to them, find it much easier to rectify them. In the case to which I have been alluding the stage manager was a singularly able one. But I suppose that there are stage managers who are not able, who cannot detect errors either of conception or execution, and what is still worse, who are unable to see any excellence in acting which does not conform to their own particular views; at least this is the inference I am compelled to draw from the fact that I have more than once noticed men and women whom I have known to be more than ordinarily intelligent play in a very unintelligent fashion.

[Two illustrations of the point are offered, of which the second is as follows:]

. . . In the scene in *The Red Lamp* in which Demetrius visits the room in which conspirators are assembled, what takes place? The conspirators, instead of moving about unconsciously and displaying the most profound indifference to Demetrius's doings, which is the only possible way of disarming his suspicions, remain fixed in one spot and one attitude, and display an amount of uneasiness, if not of terror, which would have satisfied a much less astute person than Demetrius is represented as being that there was something to be found if only he searched carefully. Certainly when Demetrius bids his men move the sofa, and Zazzulic walks across the stage with terror depicted on his face and his legs almost giving way under him, anyone who had been in the secret police for six months only, would have felt so satisfied that something was wrong that he would have arrested everyone present there and then. . . . Of course, in the scene in *The Red Lamp* the quiescence of the other performers brings Demetrius much more prominently before the audience, and enables him to concentrate all attention upon himself, but he does this at the expense of all probability – nay, in my opinion, he does it to his own detriment, for the result of the scene is very materially to impair the belief of the audience in his capacity as a member of the police . . .

[Hervey discusses the inadvisability of actors 'stage-managing' plays in which they take a leading part. He then turns to a wider question of theatrical politics:]

. . . By and by, when people have grown to understand how important a part healthy amusement plays in the life of a nation, we shall have theatres in our various large towns established. . . by the municipalities. In these the stage management will be placed in the hands of competent actors, who must on no account be allowed to act themselves, nor to introduce into the theatre their brothers and sisters and cousins. The parts should be distributed solely with regard to the competence of the actors to fill them, and authors should be listened to and their advice taken when any question arises as to whether a character is being rightly or wrongly conceived. Long runs should not be allowed, or, if they are, a couple of nights a week should be set apart for the performance of other plays. The actors would be paid by the municipality, and would, as servants of the public, retire upon pensions after a certain length of service. As for myself, I would sooner see the actors paid by the State, and have them transferred each year to a different theatre in a different town, so that they might not be perpetually playing to the same audience. The Duke of Meiningen,* I believe, insists upon his company's playing for several months of the year in towns other than Meiningen; he knows very well what a wholesome effect it has upon an actor to have to play before an audience not consisting exclusively of friends and admirers . . .

NOTE

* *The Duke of Meiningen* George II, Duke of Saxe-Meiningen, whose court theatre set standards of ensemble and seriousness of purpose throughout Europe. The company visited London in 1881.

Proposals for fire prevention, 1889

[Eyre M. Shaw, the 'Captain Shaw' appealed to by the Fairy Queen in *Iolanthe*, was chief of the London Fire Brigade, and prepared detailed reports on a number of individual theatres for the Metropolitan Board of Works. In *Fires in Theatres*, first published in 1876, Shaw proposed more stringent regulations governing access to exits, the use of a fire-proof curtain, etc. In 1878 a fire at a theatre in Liverpool prompted an Act of Parliament licensing provincial theatres . A disastrous fire at the theatre in Exeter in September 1887, in which 150 people died, gave fresh impetus to the movement for stricter legislation. These extracts are from the second edition of Shaw's book, which appeared in 1889.]

In a theatre there are some parts which cannot be divided, as, for instance, the stage, and again the auditorium; and this it is which makes the danger of such places inseparable from their very existence; but there is no corresponding reason applicable to the whole structure. On the contrary, there are many why it is desirable in the interests of true economy, and especially for the safety of life, to divide the whole building into as many distinct and separate risks as possible, of course without at all interfering with the business to be carried on. For this purpose the first and most obvious point is that at which the curtain falls, as the opening on that spot is much reduced by the partial cross walls and the supporting wall under the front of the stage. In short, at this point the whole house should be divided into two distinct parts by means of a firewall commencing in the basement and going through the roof and to a height of from 4 to 6 feet outside. This wall should be perforated at the sides on each landing, and at the bottom under the stage near the orchestra, and fitted at the perforations with wrought-iron doors; and it should, of course, have the usual large opening to the stage, but with these exceptions it should be complete; and at the great opening an effectual protection could be obtained by means of a metal curtain which could be dropped at a moment's notice. The metal curtain should be supported and worked by steel or iron chains. Such curtains, it is true, have before now been tried and have not found favour with managers of theatres, but that does not at all affect the subject under consideration. They may have been badly made, badly fitted, or badly worked; but, even so, it must be obvious that, in the event of a fire happening, they would have done *some* good.

At all events, in the present condition of mechanical skill and knowledge it is simply monstrous to say that the thing is impossible, and it is quite certain that there are thousands of the first engineers of this and other countries who would not hesitate to accept an order for such a curtain, and, if not hampered by restrictions, would guarantee that the fire would not get through or by it under any circumstances whatever in less than an hour or so, which is much more time than would be required for saving first the audience, and afterwards the auditorium and other parts of the building. In all other parts of a theatre separations can be effected by means of iron doors, and in places where iron doors cannot be fitted, wooden doors will be found better than none at all. The great object to be attained is the division of the whole building into the greatest possible number of distinct and separate risks . . .

As to the subdivisions behind the curtain, it is most desirable to have passages between the dressing-rooms and the stage, and these passages should be fitted with iron doors where they open on the stage. Such passages and all the dressing-rooms should be of strong masonry, well arched over and capable of standing the shock of anything likely to fall on them in case of fire; they should also have a safe outlet either to the open air or to some safe spot not in the risk of the stage. The stage itself cannot be subdivided, and must always be in one risk, but it can be effectually shut off from the dressing-rooms by passages, as above shown, and it should on no account be in direct communication with the workshops or the store-rooms, nor should these latter communicate directly with each other.

There are certain operations carried on within a theatre which form the special and legitimate risk of such a building, but there are others which, though best carried on in the immediate neighbourhood, need not necessarily be done within the walls; both kinds will be considered separately, and it so happens that it is in some of the latter that the greatest danger lies.

The quick shifting of light scenery in the immediate vicinity of powerful gaslights, the intense heat caused by the lights in the upper parts over the flies and the slides, the rapid manipulation of gas, oil, lime, and other lights for scenic effect, and the occasional use of explosives in the midst of a vast quantity of highly desiccated wood, a labyrinth of cordage, and a quantity of hanging drapery moving about with every draught and blast of wind –

these, and some others hardly sufficiently important for special notice, as for instance, trifling carpentering repairs, or glue-pot work on a small scale, constitute legitimate risks which may sometimes be capable of reduction, though they cannot be altogether abolished; and of them it need only be said, that they are generally well known among all engaged in a theatre, from the artists to the carpenters and other operatives, and that consequently very great caution is commonly used to prevent ignition of even the most trifling article of any kind, as they are well aware that the result would almost inevitably be the sudden blazing up of the whole.

The operations which need not necessarily be performed within the walls of a theatre are carpentering on a large scale, scenery-making, scene-painting, and decorating; and these, if carried on away from the building, are by no means specially dangerous. When, however, they are done within the walls, and subject to high temperature and desiccation as before explained, as well as to the chance of other materials suddenly blazing up near them, they increase the danger to a very serious extent. When again to these operations is added the storage of large quantities of timber, clothing, furniture, lumber, and the thousand articles known in theatres as 'property', it will be seen that the danger is infinitely increased. The remedy here is, as before, a separation of the risks, first into two great divisions, the necessary and legitimate forming one, and those operations which can be carried on outside the walls the other. Then come the subdivisions, which unfortunately cannot affect the former, at least to any appreciable extent, but which can be freely and with great advantage applied to the latter. The workshops should be effectively separated from the lumber-rooms, the lumber-rooms from the clothing-making department, the latter from the property-rooms, and so on.

These rooms should be floored and ceiled with well-burnt tiles laid in good cement or plaster; or, if preferred, the floors and ceilings might consist of cement or plaster alone; but it is essential that they should be solid, and not, as generally found, hollow, with air passages inside . . .

Care should be taken to prevent an undue accumulation of heat in any one spot, particularly over the principal light of the auditorium, and no wood or other inflammable material should be permitted in the immediate vicinity of this or any other place in which the temperature is necessarily high.

It may perhaps not be known to everyone that in many theatres the carpenter's shop is situated in the roof over the main gas light, an arrangement wholly incompatible with the safety of an audience in case of fire.

Where there is glass round or over lights there should be a metal grating underneath to prevent broken fragments of glass falling and injuring persons, or setting fire to the place.

All lights of every kind should be protected by hanging shades above to disperse the heat, and by cages or gratings round to prevent anything being blown on them, or coming in contact in any other way; and the footlights should, in addition to this, have a strong wire at a distance of about eighteen inches to prevent the actors coming into danger.

After the performance the lights of the auditorium should on no account be lowered until the whole of the audience has left. No excuse should be given for any one to light matches.

In every part of the theatre there should be a few oil or candle lamps kept lighted to prevent a panic in the case of the gas being accidentally or otherwise extinguished . . .

xvii

The painting of scenery, 1889

[From an article by William Lewis Telbin in *The Magazine of Art*, 1889. Telbin's father (also William) died in 1873.]

In the past the scene-painters must have been a happier class of men; their lives were spent from week to week in a less anxious state than is now the case. The majority of theatres then kept a resident artist or artists. Now only two do so. Drury Lane Theatre in Macready's time employed many: Stanfield, Danson, Marshall, Tompkins, and my father, besides others, were retained during the entire season. Covent Garden and Her Majesty's, also, employed for many years the Grieves, father and sons, and Marshall. Now, with the system of 'contract' – that is, painting each scene for so much – the painter has increased, as the manager has decreased, his responsibility. We in our turn have become managers on a small scale. With the rent of the vast studio, the gas and colour bills, the assistants and the servants – our expenses are heavy. We must push on early and late, or time and outlay will defeat us and absorb all our income. There is no leaving off nowadays and listening, brush in hand (in hand always), to an amusing anecdote or to some long and interesting personal experience . . .

Then again, few of the more recently-built theatres have painting-rooms that anyone who valued health and sight would care to paint in; hence any painting that has to be done is painted outside in rooms specially built and fitted with all the necessary apparatus for raising the scenery and stretching the large canvases. There are three very fine rooms in the older theatres – Covent Garden, Drury Lane and Her Majesty's (the latter for some reason is the most agreeable to paint in of the three, as there is no thoroughfare through it; across Covent Garden and Drury Lane rooms workers in other departments have a right of way). The room at Covent Garden is of vast proportions (ninety feet long by thirty feet wide and about fifty-five feet high), and possesses four separate stretching-frames – the largest, forty-two feet by seventy feet. This enormous stretcher is worked up and down by means of a very powerful windlass with multiplying gear, and hung by iron chains. The canvas to cover such a frame would cost about £15 with the sewing. The physical strain in covering so large a surface, and in walking backwards and forwards from one end of the room to the other to judge of the effect, is exceedingly severe. Perhaps this great physical exercise is conducive to a healthy action of the liver, and compensates to some extent for the loss of purer atmosphere.

The present arrangements in England are a great advancement upon the older method of spreading the canvas out upon the floor, and painting it standing up with long-handled brushes reaching to the ground. Scenery in France, and on the Continent generally, is still painted so; in the old Her Majesty's the painting was done on the floor over the auditorium. Within half an hour of the opera opening, the scene-setters used to arrive and roll the scene up to light the chandelier, the circular opening above which had been during the day filled in to make an even and sound surface upon which to paint . . .

I may now, perhaps, be expected to devote a few words to the financial aspect of our profession, though it is, of course, impossible for me to say in a general way whether we are well or ill paid for our work. This I may say, however – that the income of the most successful scene-painter is certainly very much smaller than that of a very second-rate cabinet-picture painter, or even of a tolerably successful draughtsman for the chief illustrated journals. Yet, considering the amount each scenic picture costs the management – for it must be borne in mind that the frame-maker, the canvas, and the scene-setter are all included in the cost of the picture – it will be readily understood that the scenic picture would not amount to less than the work of a highly-successful picture-painter. Thus a heavy 'set' at Covent Garden or Drury Lane would cost £700 or £800, and at other theatres in proportion, according to their size. Then, again, we never paint on speculation as a picture-maker does; we only paint when we receive a commission, the monetary risk remaining with the management. Whence, I take it, considering all the circumstances of the case, we are paid according to our deserts – often escaping the proverbial whipping through the leniency of our critics and, maybe, the indifference of the public.

On a fine summer's morning passing through the stage-door the heart is heavy at leaving the sunshine and the fresh air, and having to dive into a zone of comparative darkness, where the atmosphere is gas-polluted and excessively dry and hot. But in the winter-time the condition of things is entirely reversed; for passing from the damp, cold and foggy streets, the visitor who ascends to the painting-room finds much to interest him (where all is warmth, light and glitter) in these realms of 'eternal sunshine' or 'perennial greenness'. In all corners of the room plenty of foil paper is to be seen, if the subject in progress should be a transformation scene. This is a paper with a highly reflective surface of every tint, capable of producing much excellent effect when used as colour with painting upon it. The subject to be represented with its aid gains greatly in effect when in bas-relief, for with them are to be obtained an elaboration and a richness of colour as the one surface is reflected in the other. I recollect seeing a Scotch artist illustrating the wild poppy with foil paper. It was an exquisite piece of work, as, with delicate touches of colour, he emphasized the petals of it, and made them look as fragile and tender as the real thing – showing me for the first time of what foil paper was capable. But it is an expensive material, as may be judged when I say that the paper used upon the scene so decorated at Covent Garden would cost about £200.

When the scene-painter receives his commission from the manager, he receives with it some sort of particulars of what is wanted. Some managers can graphically illustrate their requirements; others, not possessing this happy faculty, give the key to the idea and requirements of the situation by word of mouth. Others can only explain the situations and 'practicabilities', leaving the artist absolutely free-handed, reserving to themselves the right of alteration when they have a tangibility before them, either in the scene itself or in the model. But, when all is said, the material generally furnished us is of the slightest – perhaps all the better for that, for it is extraordinary how little will influence the mind and hamper the imagination.

The most satisfactory way to proceed is to spend time upon the model (which is a representation of the stage to scale), and thoroughly to understand from it what you propose doing – not only the 'practicabilities', but also your composition, colour, and scheme of lighting. Any alterations considered necessary are then easy to make. For according to the scale – perhaps half an inch to the foot, pieces of paper in the model representing canvas and framework – a piece which in the model represents, say, a tree or a column fifteen inches high, would, in the actuality, be thirty feet high; to re-make or to alter and re-paint this would mean considerable labour and expense. . .

The creation of the scene in the model is certainly one of the most interesting of the many processes that in the aggregate constitute the scene-painter's art. Here all is under your finger and thumb; you can place your trees at any angle, light the scene with much delicacy and point, and besides being your own painter you are without much exertion your own carpenter and scene-shifter.

The model completed, after being duly inspected and approved by the management, the master-carpenter comes in to see it with respect to the construction of it mechanically, and to hear your suggestions as to setting and striking it in something like reasonable time. . . When all is understood he traces the various portions of the model, and from the duplicates constructs the actual scene, one foot to every half-inch of the model.

A few days after, almost acres of framework and bales of canvas are brought in; one great surface is stretched on the frame, and [the canvas] having been duly prepared, upon it you first start – this generally represents the back portions of the scene. Then you paint the different pieces in order till you arrive at the foreground, gaining in strength as you advance.

A splendid material distemper – of what is it not capable! For atmosphere unequalled, and for strength as powerful as oil, in half an hour you can do with it that which in water or oil would take one or two days. But how little we understand the merits of this beautiful material at our service; our greatest mistake in using it is that we make no mistakes, or rather admit none by sweeping our work out and getting a base upon which to model and build up. One may say to a thinly-painted landscape, or perhaps a sky and sea with high horizon, that the stage is forty feet deep, ignoring entirely the deception intended. If the colour is thick and the sky has really been manipulated and 'gradated' by the artist, and not blue-washed by the painter's labourer, it would be most difficult to guess how far it recedes or the proportions of the stage upon which it was set; but the material capable of producing such effect plays sometimes very strange antics with its greatest admirers. With the amateur it appears to be devoid of all sense of responsibility. Leaving it after diligent and well-intentioned work of three or four hours, he returns to find a singular and most unintellligible surface of smears and mildewed greys; the entire plan of his work in the process of drying has been reversed, most painful, most ludicrous to witness; the foreground all disintegrated, over the sky patches of dense fog have spread; when wet the effect was capital – the work of one who knew at what he was aiming; but this treacherous distemper has robbed his work of all evidence even of a good intention.

The model completed, the scene painted, for a day or two the stage is given up entirely to the artist for the scene to be set and lighted. This setting is the most anxious time of all, and the most experienced of us cannot help asking himself, how will it come together? For by the most earnest work in the painting-room we can but deserve, not command, success upon the stage. What a weary time it is sitting and standing about while the many necessary carpenters' fittings and connections are being completed, and the canvas portions hung by the fly-men! At last, after dawdling about perhaps from nine in the morning until nine at night, the 'setting' is begun, and if happily it comes quickly and well together, the artist may proceed at once to 'light' it; if it does not – why, it must be completed tomorrow. If it *is* all right, order follows order: – 'Light away', 'Turn up the light', 'Put out the light', 'More light', 'Where is the limelight?', 'Turn on the limelight', 'Is the light full on?', 'Yes, sir!' And the end of it all is that the artist determines that it won't do at all. All round one sees elaborate and interesting bits of painting; but, notwithstanding that, the general effect is weak and meagre in the extreme. The best scene ever designed and painted can be ruined by injudicious lighting; for the illumination is the last and most important touch to the picture – its very life. Oh, for a hint from Henry Irving (the

much-praised, and justly so, 'gas-man' of the Lyceum is no less a
person than the manager himself); no one knows how to light a
scene as he does, veiling its defects and enhancing its merits
. . . 'If I cannot have more light,' thinks the painter, 'perhaps it
is that I had too much, and that the painting is bleached by it – if,
indeed, the lighting is not too even.' Now he begins to turn down
some lights, and finds how the scene gains in force. Other lights
remain full on, and by contrast their power is doubled. After
much weary work of running about between the stage and the
front of the house to see the effect of his experiments, shouting
from there till he is hoarse, an agreeable and telling effect is at
length arrived at, and he leaves the theatre weary of foot and
husky of voice, into the deserted streets.

xviii

New developments in lighting and scenery, 1892

[From Percy Fitzgerald, *The Art of Acting* (1892). Fitzgerald was a
prolific journalist, specializing in theatrical matters, particularly in
articles describing production techniques. This book includes
information on staging on the pretext that it is necessary to an
understanding of the actors' art – although the author seems
anxious to fill out an otherwise slim volume.]

The [electric] light has become so profuse and glaring that all
distance and mystery is lost, while the scene painters are
compelled, in self-defence, to make their colours as fiery as
possible. There is one theatre, however, where true feeling and
mystery and illusion is carried out under the most poetical
conditions. I allude, of course, to the Lyceum. Here we find a
most accomplished artist, Mr Craven, worthy descendant of the
line of Beverley and Stanfield.* The Lyceum system is worth
considering for a few moments, as here is cultivated the sense of
illusion in the most perfect way.
    The system in use there, is like most systems of the day, an

eclectic one; it selects and combines what will best carry out its purpose. It is a mixture of the old 'border' and 'flat' systems, and the 'built-up' one. *Any* method, in short, that will carry out the end, is adopted. There is a great advantage to start with in the beautiful and well-designed stage, well-suited to set off the pictures of the artist, which are most welcome to the eye. But the charm is in the judicious control and subordination of all these agents to the general effect.

There is also another element used here with extraordinary effect, namely, an elaborate system of varied lights, which is brought in aid of the colouring. These are apart from the usual gas 'battens'; and are contrived by a complex series of coloured glasses or 'mediums' which are changed and experimented upon till the effect is found. Mr Craven once explained some of his views, and they are interesting. 'A particular art of painting,' he said, 'has to be applied, by which seemingly hopeless combinations are made to appear as one harmonious whole – giving height, breadth, distance, space, light, and colour; the effects of day, night, wind and rain; the general hurly-burly of the tempest and the calm of the mid-day sun.' In the scenes for *Romeo and Juliet* at the Lyceum [in 1882], and afterwards in *The Mikado* [Savoy, 1887], he succeeded in portraying a bright, clear, blue sky by the introduction of an entirely new colour; the result was abundance of light, air, and colour. This subordination of detail to the general effect is carried out in every direction. The lighting is subdued so as not to reveal details, the changes of scene are effected in obscurity; the painting and colours are in low, rich, tones, so as to throw out the figures. Every one will recall the original and strikingly effective use of the 'gauzes' for supernatural effects in *Faust* [1885]. Another element at this house is the abundant use of modelled architectural pieces, such as statues, sculptured pillars, the door of the monumental cathedral in *Faust*, and the elaborate temple that was exhibited in Tennyson's *Cup*, the pillars of which were adorned with classical figures in high relief. All which prodigies, I may say, were wrought in pasteboard; that is, the design was moulded in plaster, and sheets of paper were pasted over it until the desired thickness was reached. Thus was ingeniously secured all the effect of stone – in a material excessively light and portable, and enduring any amount of what is called 'knocking about'. Beautiful and satisfactory as these results are, they are not withhout drawbacks. This elaborate modelling affects the painted portions by contrast, and imparts a flatness to painted details. An opening scene at the Savoy Theatre (also Mr

Craven's) represents in the most perfect way 'the last word' of scenery. Here we have sky borders, and building up, and coloured lights, and modelled portions, all with the most brilliant and satisfactory result. It requires, however, extraordinary efforts to unite these systems, which are really irreconcilable, as any one can see, who in a drawing-room scene will note 'borders' used as a ceiling in combination with side walls, for edges of both cross each other at a right angle . . .

[Fitzgerald argues that it was easier to reconcile the actual space of the stage with the scale of the scene to be implied when scenic artists depended on painted perspective scenery.]

I can fancy, however, that in time we may revert to this wholesome system, where the relief and distances will depend on the skill of the painter. It is indeed possible, as a painter knows, to make a distinct art of the simulation of raised surfaces. Foreign artists make this imitation of relief and distance quite a study, and in Italian churches we see figures in relief so high as to deceive the eye. At the same time it would be impossible to revert to the old baldness of flats and side scenes without due modernization. The glare of light in which our stages are bathed is fatal to all illusion – it reveals everything, the rifts in the boards, the texture and creases in the canvas, the streaks of the paint. The light, playing on the edges of the side scenes, would show us that they were mere screens; but with subdued lighting, and low, rich tones and colours, the edges would be softened away, and all made into one whole . . .

[In the final pages, Fitzgerald discusses the contribution to illusion that can be made by drops and curtains.]

It is becoming the fashion to have divided curtains [i.e. 'tableau curtains' or 'tabs'], that fall between the acts, made of real or simulated tapestry. These close imperfectly, and nearly always indicate the 'super' behind, who has to rush to hold them together. But does this suggest the idea of the great barrier that should always exist between the mystic scene and the hard practice of life? It imparts a sort of trivial drawing-room association. We feel almost that we might step up on the stage and peep in. But it is otherwise with the old traditional heavy green curtain, which floats downwards with slow and solemn folds. Both curtain and drop-scene represent the barrier between the real and the ideal world. The floating green curtain, on which the eyes of the audience rest during the interval before the performance, has a special significance and a dramatic meaning.

Again, the drop-scene, which marks merely a suspension of the dramatic interest, should not have the solemn finality of the green curtain. It is a subject of speculation what should be portrayed on its simple surface. Sometimes we have seen landscape, by Telbin or Beverley, enclosed in a border, or it may be a grouping of painted draperies and curtains. Garnier, the architect of the Paris Opera House, holds that this is the most fitting treatment, as it represents the function of the canvas, which is to be a curtain – and if these draperies be skilfully executed with pleasing colours, the effect is good. An objection to the landscape is that it impairs illusion, as it is in fact only another scene; and when it rises, some of the effect of surprise is lost when the regular scene appears. This may seem a trivial point, but by being attended to, it fosters illusion.

NOTE

*   *Craven ... Beverley ... Stanfield* Hawes   Craven   (1837–90); William Roxby Beverley (c.1814–89) and Clarkson Stanfield (cf. note 2, p.171 above): scenic artists.

Lyceum rehearsals, 1893

[From an article by G.B. Burgin in *The Idler* (March 1893). Irving is 'like an ideal general' who 'leaves nothing to subordinates'. William Terriss (1847-97) first appeared at the Lyceum in 1880, but was best known for his portrayals of the manly, uncomplicated heroes of Adelphi melodramas. In 1897 he was assassinated by a madman as he entered the Adelphi.]

[Irving at rehearsal]
The theatre itself is deserted save by some ghostly caretaker who glides noiselessly through the shadowy gloom, sliding a brush over the upholstery without looking at it, and replacing each covering as she goes. On the stage are two gentlemen wearing picturesque soft hats, and long coats which reach to within half-a-foot of the ground. The taller of the two, Mr Henry Irving, wears a light drab-coloured coat and dark hat; Mr William Terriss is attired in a light hat and dark coat. In the centre of the stage, close to the footlights, stands a screen; behind the screen is a chair. To the left of the stage (as you look at it from the stalls) is placed a small table with a big gilt cross on it. On the extreme right there is another small table laden with papers, plans of the stage, and letters. At the back of the stage are grouped numerous male 'supers' clad in ordinary morning costume and wearing the inevitable 'bowler' hat, which does not harmonize very well with the huge spears they carry. It is the scene in the second act of the late Poet Laureate's *Becket*, 'The Meeting of the Kings', and Mr Irving is busily engaged in grouping some fifty people who are required to pose as barons, French prelates, and retainers. When he has done this, there is still something wanted to complete the picture. Two pages are lacking. 'Where's Johnny?' asks Mr Irving, and 'Johnny' appears. Mr Irving eyes him critically. 'I'm afraid you're too big, Johnny,' he says, and 'Johnny' disappointedly makes way for a smaller boy.

Mr Irving stands well in the centre of the stage, absorbing every detail. The French bishops are huddled too near together, and he groups them more naturally. Becket's mortal foes, Fitzurse, De Brito, De Tracy and De Morville, are moved lower down towards the audience, so that they can go 'off' with greater effect when jeering at Becket.

The cameo-cut outlines of Mr Irving's fine serious features are plainly visible as he turns to look at the wings. 'I don't see any necessity for having these "wings" so forward,' he declares, and the wings at once slide gently back, moved by some invisible agency. In response to Mr Irving's request for another alteration in the scenery (he speaks with an utter absence of effort in a voice which can be heard at the other end of the theatre, although it does not appear to be raised above a conversational pitch), a middle-aged gentleman, attired in a frock coat, his brows carefully swathed in a white pocket handkerchief, comes forward, yardstick in hand, and measures the stage with great assiduity. When this has been done, Mr Irving sits down with 'Please go on.' Then he turns to Mr Terriss: 'Shall we go through it first without the dialogue?' 'Yes,' answers Mr Terriss; and the whole action of the scene is gone through, Mr Irving and Mr Terriss exchanging their direction of the various groups for the assumption of their own parts with an ease and rapidity born of long practice, Mr Irving moving about from group to group until he is satisfied with the effect of the whole. Mr H.J. Loveday, the stage manager, being at present ill, Mr Terriss is kindly assisting Mr Irving with rehearsal. After the entrances and exits have been arranged for the twentieth time, Henry's magnificent voice rings out as Louis enters:

'Brother of France, what shall be done with Becket?'

As this is one of the early rehearsals, the actors are not yet word perfect. Each holds his part in his hand, and refreshes his memory as he goes on. When Henry and Louis have finished their dialogue, and Becket is about to enter, Mr Irving suddenly pauses. 'Make a note that before Becket's entrance there should be a slow chant – a Gregorian chant – and flourishes. Where are the gentlemen who sing?' The 'gentlemen who sing' come on, and practise the chant. 'Not quite so loud.' Mr Irving claps his hands (the stage signal for stopping people) and decides to try the effect behind the scenes. 'That will do: very good,' he declares, as the solemn chant steals slowly in, and then, merging the manager in the actor, kneels at Henry's feet.

At this juncture, Mr Irving becomes the stage-manager again, and turns to the group of Henry's followers. 'You, gentlemen, are to come up here. You are rather startled, and listen attentively; that's the spirit of it.' King Henry's followers move up, and jeer at Becket, who curses them. Then come the voices of the crowd without:

'Blessed be the Lord Archbishop, who hath withstood the two kings to their faces for the honour of God.'

20 Henry Irving at a Lyceum rehearsal, 1891, drawn by Bernard Partridge.

But Mr Irving is not satisfied with the crowd. 'Slower and more gravely, please. I want the emphasis on "the Lord Archbishop". So! That will be very good.'

After this, there is an interval, and Mr Irving and Mr Terriss disappear. Before they return, the stage carpenters begin to prepare for the murder scene in the last act. A number of what appear to be canvas-covered trunks are brought in and laid down to represent stones in the choir of Canterbury Cathedral.

Meantime, some of the gentlemen who represent the monks in this scene playfully spar at one another, or lunge with walking-sticks at imaginary foes. The carpenters are busy measuring the stage in all directions with tapes in accordance with a plan which one of them holds in his hand. Before Mr Irving returns, the 'supers' group themselves 'left' and answer to their names. When he reappears, they look at him expectantly. 'I am not going to rehearse this scene today,' he says, 'but will just arrange it. Those who sing, go over to the right (left from the audience). You sing the vespers. I want six more with you. Then, twelve of the shortest. You follow them. All the short ones you have, please. Yes, you're short (to a diminutive 'super' who is standing on tiptoe and trying to look seven feet high at least). Don't be bashful. You're none the worse for being short. Come along'; and with unfailing memory Mr Irving calls each man by name, and indicates his place. Where a man fails to quite realize what is required of him, Mr Irving takes him by the shoulders, and gently moves him along to the required position, very much as if the individual in question were a pawn about to be played in a game of chess. As soon as the monks are grouped to his satisfaction, he steps back. 'That's it. Now, you all come down from the choir. There is a loud hammering against the door. I go to open the door, and all of you rush right by me.' Then Mr Irving opens the door to his murderers, and is borne back by the crowd of terrified monks. Five minutes afterwards, he has returned to life, and is rehearsing a scene from *King Lear* with Miss Ellen Terry's understudy, in as natural and unembarrassed a manner as if he had not been working hard for three hours previously.

Especial care is bestowed by Mr Irving with regard to every detail of the murder scene. On another occasion, the scenery is not ready, but a flight of steps, essential to the action, is placed far back in a position to the left of the stage. As *Becket* has never been played before, there are no traditions whatever to guide actors or scenic artists, and each movement, phrase, gesture, and intonation, must be 'created'. Mr Irving picks up a huge battle-axe and

21 View of a Lyceum rehearsal from the auditorium, 1891.

22 Irving listens to the orchestra.

hatchet, and carefully plans the details of his own murder. Having decided how to die, he thoughtfully surveys the steps up which the frightened monks are supposed to rush. 'They won't do,' says Mr Irving. 'They are too steep; there is no hand-rail; and the monks will fall over and hurt themselves. Take off four steps. It would be too dangerous if anyone fell down. Now then, Salisbury and Grim, I enter, forced along by you. Catch hold of me, and put your arms around me this way. That's it. No; I don't like those steps.' . . .

[Ellen Terry at rehearsal]
But where is Miss Ellen Terry? The question answers itself as soon as asked, for a gliding, graceful feminine presence appears on the stage. Miss Ellen Terry is attired in black, with a white fichu at her breast to relieve the monotony of this sombre garb. In her hand she carries a little black basket, and there is a glimmer of steel at her side as if she wore a reticule containing the hundred-and-one trifles which ladies like to carry about with them. So much has been written and said about Miss Terry that it would seem at first utterly impossible to say anything new. In five minutes, the difficulty is to say enough. The supreme unconsciousness of Art, or Nature, enables her to assume a hundred changing attitudes; her voice is heard without effort from one end of the theatre to the other; she possesses the most exquisite tact. Watch the skill, for instance, with which she induces some young actor to realize the true meaning of a passage in the play. She seems to be thinking it out to herself as if a new idea had been presented to her. 'Yes,' she says, musingly, 'I wonder if that is what Tennyson meant?' Or, 'Wait a minute,' she adds brightly. 'How would this do?' Then she repeats the passage with the right emphasis, action, and intonation, giving the meaning clearly and fully. 'Don't you think that must be what is meant?' she asks questioningly. 'Hum-m,' says the actor, looking at the lines. 'Ah, very likely. Perhaps it is.' It is agreed that it shall be spoken that way, and the actor gives a delicate and truthful reading of the part, which will procure him a pat on the back from the critics when the play is produced. In the presence of her intuitive perception, the members of the cast instinctively become energetic and animated. At one moment she bends over to Mr Meredith Ball [the musical director] in the orchestra, her long black skirt sweeping the stage in graceful folds; at another 'moves up' to test a portion of the scenery and confer with Mr Irving, or, with chair lightly dragging after, walks to the wings, sits down, and cons her part. Three minutes after, she has crossed the stage, and is writing

a letter. Before the letter is finished, something else claims her attention. Then she comes back, finishes it, and is consulted by Mr Irving and Mr Terriss as to how he (Mr Terriss) is to jump over a table without forfeiting his kingly dignity . . .

xx

The designer in the theatre, 1895

['C. Wilhelm' (William Pitcher) was an inventive and stylish designer of costumes for ballet and spectacle. He regarded his responsibilities as far reaching, including supervision of lighting and general design and choreography. By rejecting convention and custom, and insisting on retaining control over the whole visual effect of the performance, he was a forerunner of the independent director. The following extracts are taken from two articles on 'Art in the ballet' contributed by Wilhelm to *The Magazine of Art* in 1895. The first article begins with a brief account of the French *ballets de cour*, and then describes romantic ballet in the mid-century years.]

I

This was *par excellence* the reign of the 'white muslin parasol, with two pink handles', and all [ballerinas] appear to have been similarly equipped. Occasionally a slight variation in the picture shows us the fair creature plunging from giddy heights (above a singularly parallel cataract) into the arms of a slim and curly gentleman in a zouave jacket and a sash. These facts, taken in conjunction with an indication of palm trees in the 'wings', lead one to infer that the subject of the ballet may have been a romantically Oriental one. But, as a rule, no very subtle distinctions appear to have existed in the stage costume of dancers at that particular period, or they might possibly have escaped the pencil of the chronicler. A wreath of roses, or a star (and a wreath *was* a wreath, look you, in those days, and there was no mistake about the star!) coupled with small pear-shaped tinsel wings, being apparently considered an ample allowance of accessories to indicate the realms of Sylphland. At this time no ballet appeared to be complete without its special *Pas de Fascination*,[1] and to some extent convention – which dies hard – has preserved for our delectation this relic of bygone glories. The *Pas* is with us still (alas!) but the *Fascination*, speaking from a personal experience, which I can scarcely persuade myself to be altogether exceptional, is surely a thing of the past.

If the ballet is to survive as an art, or if, to put it in another way, the Fine Arts are to be awarded more generous recognition in the ballet, it should be reformed altogether and purged of the many absurdities that must vex and perplex the soul of the spectator with weird problems. Why should the *première danseuse* start her acrobatic gyrations from the angle of the usual 'hollow-square' [formed by the *corps de ballet*] with beseeching glances and outstretched palms; why should she snatch up her skirts (a quite superfluous action this) to bestow a smirk of surprised recognition on the foot rather than the supporting one; following up this inspiriting exercise with a series of hopping plunges, alternated with a movement compounded in equal parts of actions suggesting a swimmer's side-stroke, and a cat performing its toilet. The 'business' is a little difficult of description, but anyone who has suffered (I use the term advisedly) the exhibition of it, will be enabled to fill up the blanks. The whole action of the ballet is suspended for the purpose of these gambols, which are indulged in with greater or less precision and grace by every *prima ballerina assoluta*, irrespective of place and period, and the character she is supposed by popular delusion to be representing. Meanwhile the *corps de ballet*, disguised, as a rule, in wigs of a uniform colour that halts mid-way between ginger and mustard, stand around, and look on unmoved; it does them great credit, and is a thrilling spectacle.

To touch on my own personal experiences as a designer of spectacular ballet, I may say that they have to no great extent differed from those already recounted by other writers . . . though with perhaps the sundry additional vexations and inseparable difficulties to be encountered when coping with the fads of the *danseuse* – more often than not over-generously dowered by Nature as to her physical proportions – whose beau ideal of costume for all occasions is an abbreviated perversion of a modern *débutante's* ball-dress, shorn of two-thirds of its length and *décolleté* to exaggeration. This attire, which has been so graphically described as 'beginning too late and ending too soon', is completed by a ribbon knotted round the throat, and by a corresponding bow in the hair (a favourite 'finishing touch') and is insisted on, in spite of its glaring inappropriateness to the character, say, of an evil temptress . . .

Design for the ballet and the various spectacular *divertissements* and entertainments akin to it – pantomime, extravaganza, what you will – calls for a special skill in device other than historical drama requires; and in addition to a very necessary knowledge and correct judgement of all the possibilities of combination of colour, together with a sufficient, if not necessarily an intimate or exhaustive, acquaintance with the archaeology of the modes and manners of various periods, invaluable as a basis of fact for the most airy fabric of fancy one may desire to rear thereon. And it will, I think, be readily granted that this class of entertainment emphatically demands a far greater exercise of ingenuity and freshness of invention than any more serious appeal to a cultured audience; inasmuch as the reasoning powers and sympathies being less stimulated by ballet as spectacle, the appeal to the more superficial sense of sight is the more direct, imperative, and absorbing than when the stage situation insists on a due recognition of – let us say – the heroine's fortunes rather than her frocks.

[Wilhelm refers to the difficulties of persuading performers – ballerinas in particular – to wear costumes designed to harmonize with a stage picture rather than to show off their own figure in conventional lines and colours.]

It is assuredly worth a struggle to prove the courage of one's convictions, and to stamp out the smouldering, menacing fire of what is more often than not an expression of obstinate and unintelligent caprice. Such a course of action may cost one something of the satisfaction of working smoothly; but it is, in the great majority of instances, amply justified by the result. It would be stirring up troubled waters to particularize by name several cases that rise to one's recollection at the moment; though it would be easy enough to cite them. Your 'leading lady' receives with distrust your assurance of an actual fact, that the colours assigned to the chorus and supernumeraries are arranged of a set purpose to accentuate or lead up to *her* costume, which is naturally chosen to display her to her best advantage, so that one may, so to speak, bask modestly in the reflected glory thereof, though she hesitates to believe it. She persists in a feminine method of argument, and when condescending to discuss the matter at all, does so on the lines that she supposes she is to be sacrificed to the rank-and-file, and wants to know why she can't have the style of cap she prefers in a sketch for some of the chorus, or the colours allotted after careful consideration to some other character. Were her tastes to be consulted as she would wish, a rearrangement of one's entire scheme would be necessitated, and the issue would, I am sure, be the same; for with delightful inconsistency she would veer round to one's original way of thinking, under the delusion it was her own idea. I have known one lady, of Junoesque proportions, dissolve in tears at the notion of being arrayed entirely in white – *cap-à-pie*.[2] And I may add that, being induced to defer to my judgement in the matter, she can now be scarcely persuaded to wear anything else.

II

The development of the designer's work, its translation from a creation of the brain into fabric and fact by more or less able and willing hands, of widely differing skill and perception, and by workers in many branches of industry, is a far more complicated and delicate business than many might imagine. It involves an amount of personal supervision only limited by one's conscientiousness, and the degree to which one is sensitive to a perfect (in so far as may be) accomplishment of one's ideal. I am happy to avail myself of this opportunity of placing the reader in possession of facts bearing on the actual responsibilities of the one person who, I trust I may be allowed to assert without being accused of undue arrogance, is certainly the most important factor in any theatrical production of artistic pictorial pretensions. Managers resort to the costume designer – at least I have found it so – for suggestions which, if adopted, are bound to affect some other preconceived plan; or again, such a plan, if adhered to, requires at the designer's hands so much modification to fit it for the stage, and to avoid a repetition of effect, that the original is scarcely to be recognized. Yet, so long as there is a shred left as an excuse, it is the author who receives the credit of the amended scheme, and not the artist, who has practically 'licked it into shape' and given it life. As an offset to this view of the matter, the designer has often the mortification of seeing a pet scheme, in which he has every faith, spoiled for present and future use, through being attacked in a half-hearted way that denies him the necessary sole control of its setting to ensure its best fulfilment, and through a short-sighted policy refusing him the support of managerial authority on certain points where he himself is powerless to make terms.

Where, however, the work of a costume designer of proved experience and well-tested resource is recognized, as it should be, as of paramount importance in the staging of any spectacle dependent for effect on the judicious employment of masses of people, then I maintain that his requirements should be the first consulted, and his judgement be accepted as final; every consideration being, of course, on both sides accorded to the practical aspect of the subject and to the advisability (only this is of ·minor importance, so long as the result is successful) of amicable collaboration. It cannot, however, be too distinctly set on record that the success of one stage picture – grouping and background – depends on its initial conception *as a whole*; and this must undoubtedly emanate from one brain. It will be allowed that, in a ballet or spectacle, the play of colour in the dresses constitutes the dominant feature. If the scene itself be but moderately good, it can be largely animated by well-chosen dresses and groupings; or again, however fine the scene, it may be entirely wasted if the costumes are ineffective and inharmonious . . .

[Wilhelm describes some of his recent work for Augustus Harris at Drury Lane, and mentions the difficulties encountered in getting the performers' co-operation.]

Let me not, in this connection, withhold my testimony to the patience and skill I have known devoted to my designs, at various times, by such experts as Alias, Auguste, and notably Miss Fisher,[3] whose enterprise in carrying out daring suggestions, including the actual fabrication of material in sundry experiments, has deserved all the acknowledgement that can be implied in these lines. With the best intentions in the world, however, a costumier will sometimes fail to grasp the full scope of one's idea, so that one must always be prepared with a technical suggestion for the practical solution of some artistic problem: such as simulating in a hanging sleeve of silk the enfolding undulations of a lily-of-the-valley leaf, or casting about for the best method of representing, on an extended scale, the gossamer plumage of the bird of paradise; this latter was a poser for a time – in a Drury Lane pantomime scene, 'the Kingdom of the Birds', which some of my readers may recall – until it occurred to me to try the effect of a mass of strips of fine ivory silk gauze, deepening to yellow, as in the real feathers, and I was rewarded by a complete success: the effect, seen across the footlights, of the floating filmy fabric being remarkable in its absolute identity of resemblance. For the humming birds in the same scene, played by children, I found specially-made spangles an excellent substitute for the irridescent lustre of these feathered gems. Such subtleties of contrivance and invention quicken one's interest in design and give an added zest to the realization. On one occasion I was desirous of imitating in some costumes for a ballet, the colour-effect of the wild hyacinth; all attempts to obtain a material of the exact tint were fruitless (though I am convinced that the far-reaching enquiries I prosecuted caused the rage for 'cornflower' blue, which set in the following season – an instance of demand creating supply). I could find nothing to answer my purpose, until I hit on the happy idea, as it fell out, of going direct to Nature for inspiration; and there found the flower not of a uniform colour, but a delicate blending of two or more distinct tones. Trial-trips in shot silks and fine stripes of these tones alike failed to convey the beautiful hue of the blossom, until absolute success crowned the veiling of a full sky-blue silk with an outer ample robe of lilac gauze; and I was satisfied, and the public applauded. I wonder how many of them gave a second thought, or even a first, to the evolution of a pleasing result! . . .

[Stage lighting also needs more attention than it is usually given.]

I want to see a stage illuminated with a suggestion of real sunlight, with shadows from the figures in one direction only. In processions and big spectacles, the habit of reinforcing the fiery furnace of the footlights with enormous lime-boxes; and of supplementing these by others at the various entrances, is utterly destructive of light and shade; and drapery subjected to this searching glare loses all its beauty and meaning. Again, a partiality for the use of coloured rays of light threatens to extinguish all colour in the dresses, and is greatly to be deplored. They are susceptible of effective employment, under certain rare conditions, to intensify the mystery or heighten the prominence of a group; but they should be used very sparingly and discreetly and it is distinctly fatal to allow oneself to become a slave to their cheap and facile sway . . .

I think the 'unities' should be observed in ballet that is not altogether 'fancy-free', and a fair motive assigned for the treatment of any particular scene. For instance, in the carnival scene of *Venice* at Olympia, it was my aim to make the costumes reasonably suggest that they were burlesquing the types and modes of their own time; this gave the necessary touch of grotesqueness to the dresses without departing too far from the *vraisemblance* of the period and the situation; and without necessitating the introduction of pierrots and such folk – positively proposed by some, oblivious of the anachronisms they would have been importing into a fourteenth-century picture. In the Venetian fête of the final scene, the Masque (had it been carried out as I intended) should have represented the conquest of Day by Night, followed by the Heralds of Fame calling on Beauty and Wealth to surrender their mimic fortress, to which the troops of love lay siege. The occupants were to defend the assault with showers of roses, and when forced to capitulate, were themselves the victors' reward. A mania for 'a clear stage' shelved the fancy fortress, and the Masque, as presented with maimed rites, must certainly have appeared quite unintelligible to the spectators . . .

[Wilhelm gives accounts of a number of ballets for which he has been responsible, including an open-air production of *A Midsummer Night's Dream* at the Crystal Palace in Sydenham. The description of his designs for the ball scene in *Cinderella*, 'in the key of gold colour', is representative of his techniques.]

The palest primrose, ranging to citron and bronze; mahogany, paling into apricot tones; symphonies of orange and lemon; maize colour, cinnamon, ivory – all were pressed into the service. Tiger lilies and Gloire de Dijon roses, sunflowers and narcissus; fawn and leopard skins; leather and the sheen of gold, copper and brass; rich embroideries, and every conceivable fabric, entered into the design. Sumptuous brocades were woven expressly, and the costumes of the leading characters being carefully chosen in heliotrope, faint sea green, and vieux rose, no jarring note was present. The scheme was most thoroughly worked out; nothing was left to chance, and no detail was too insignificant to be studied . . .

[He concludes with a hope for the general acceptance of artistic values in ballet.]

May we not picture the three graces of Melody, Movement and Colour, animating an ideal world of beauty and fancy, in which the jaded nineteenth-century galley-slaves might find a respite from social and commercial wear and tear, and a stimulus to the imaginative fancy? Time will show.

NOTES

1 *pas de fascination*   Not a technical term, but used to describe a seductive solo dance.

2 *cap-à-pie*   From head to foot (archaic, probably referring to *Hamlet* I. ii. 200).

3 *Alias, Auguste . . . Miss Fisher*   Costumiers: Charles Alias, Soho Square; Auguste and Co., Wellington Street; Miss Mary Elizabeth Fisher, Bedford Street.

Part IV

Management

In his *Reminiscences* Macready pondered the mystery of managerial temperament:

> A theatre is like a little kingdom, shut out from intimacy and sympathy with the little world around it, in which the little monarch has his flatterers and courtiers, as sycophantic and subservient as in real courts. Upon his talents, his virtues, and even on his person, he receives the adulatory homage of those he employs; and with such an exalted opinion of himself, as this incense must excite, it cannot be a matter of surprise if he should not always hold the scale of justice with a steady and impartial hand. (p.76)

Theatre management underwent considerable changes in the course of the century, but the source of managerial power – financial control over the artists and their work – remained constant. Towards the end of the period the agitation for an uncommercial, subsidized theatre and the activities of such groups as the Stage Society offered an alternative to the more or less benevolent despotism described by Macready. In the popular imagination Victorian theatre management is dominated by the figure of the actor-manager, a 'guv'nor' with astrakhan collar, silver-topped cane and a tendency to call male colleagues 'laddie', but this music-hall and *Punch* parody conceals the variety of managerial styles and modes of operation. At the beginning of the century the country actor-manager, represented below in Macready's reminiscences (i) needed the resourcefulness that Dickens only slightly exaggerated in Vincent Crummles. The rhetorical flourishes that are so amusing in Crummles are entirely characteristic of the language of managerial announcements – examples will be found in the playbills reproduced as illustrations 23, 24 and 25.

Companies working provincial circuits in the 1830s perpetuated the system of the previous century, relying on markets, race-meetings and assizes for their biggest audiences, building up relationships with a series of local communities, cultivating whatever the fashionable life of each town might have to offer, and giving a series of stock plays leavened by 'novelties'. The life of a non-acting manager in a city was not so different, although the pressures came from different sources – Peake's description of a manager's day (iii) suggests some of them. It had become almost impossible to manage the two 'patent' houses with profit, and Alfred Bunn's desperate shifts in running Drury Lane and even (for a while) both theatres were partly to blame for his notorious quarrel with Macready (ii). Attempts to cater for a popular audience and at the same time to attract 'Society' demanded the deployment of enormous resources in such theatres. In the 1830s the parity of salaries between the London theatres had been broken and there was fierce rivalry between the patent and 'minor' houses for actors and audiences: the process has been described succinctly in Christopher Murray's biography of Robert William Elliston (see *Further Reading*). The dilemma of the London manager is represented fictionally in Thackeray's *Pendennis* (1849) in the person of Mr Dolphin. In chapter 14 he is visiting the little theatre in the country town of Chatteris:

> In spite of all his exertions, and the perpetual blazes of triumph, corruscations of talent, victories of good old English comedy, which his play-bills advertised, his theatre . . . by no means prospered, and the famous impresario found himself on the verge of ruin. The great Hubbard had acted legitimate drama for twenty nights, and failed to remunerate anybody but himself: the celebrated Mr and Mrs Cawdor had come out in Mr Rawhead's tragedy, and their favourite round of pieces, and had not attracted the public. Herr Garbage's lions and tigers had drawn for a little time, until one of the animals had bitten a piece out of Herr Garbage's shoulder; when the Lord Chamberlain interfered, and put a stop to this species of performance: and the grand Lyrical Drama, though brought out with unexampled splendour and success, with Monsieur Poumons as first tenor, and an enormous orchestra, had almost crushed poor Dolphin in its triumphant progress: so that great as his genius and resources were, they seemed to be at an end. He was dragging on his season wretchedly with half salaries, small operas, feeble old comedies, and his ballet company; and everybody was looking out for the day when he should appear in the *Gazette*.

Theatre Royal, Drury Lane.

☞ TO THE PUBLIC

The Success which has attended the production of the
New Grand Opera,

THE SIEGE
OF CORINTH!

has so surpassed even the most sanguine expectations
of the Management, that in deference to the unanimous
approbation of one of the most brilliant Audiences ever
assembled in a Theatre, it will be repeated EVERY
EVENING. But as such announcement would, under
ordinary circumstances, forestall every other Novelty,
and thereby interfere with

THE TRIUMPHANT CAREER
OF
Mr. EDWIN FORREST,

the Lessee of this Establishment has resolved on submitting to Public Patronage, without any regard to
the expence it will incur,

A COMBINATION OF ATTRACTIONS

which places the possibility of Competition out of the
question. The unprecedented result which attended a
similar experiment last Season, has led him to the conviction that any similar exertion to merit Public
Patronage will meet with a corresponding support;
and in such persuasion he begs leave to announce, that

The Performance of Mr. Forrest

will take place on the same Evening with that of

The Siege of Corinth!

and in order to afford as much variety as possible to each
Night's Entertainments, this celebrated Performer will
go through the range of his most popular Characters.
The Evening's Selection will be so arranged as to present the most diversified Entertainment hitherto introduced on one occasion, & will terminate at a reasonable
period of the Evening.

☞ In order to render every facility at the Box-Office,
owing to the great demand for Places, it will remain
open an additional hour daily; and a further number
of Agents have been appointed both in the City, and at
the West End of the Town.

W. WRIGHT, Printer, Theatre Royal Drury Lane.

23 Managerial style, 1836: handbill advertising performances by
the American tragedian Edward Forrest at Drury Lane.

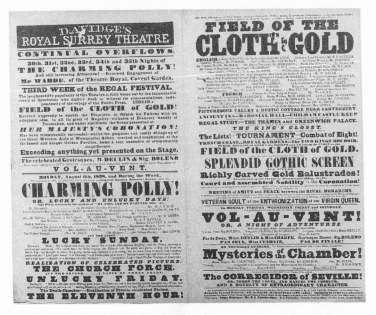

24 Melodrama, History and Spectacle causing 'continual overflows' at the Surrey, 1838: playbill for a nautical melodrama and a 'popular romance' in which furnishings from Victoria's coronation was used. The prices are 2s., 1s. and 6d., with half-price admission to boxes only.

Dolphin was now scouring the provinces to find some new talent whose attractions might stave off the day when he would be gazetted as a bankrupt. The sources of theatrical finance varied from the association of a group of backers to produce (in modern British parlance) plays to such enterprises as the establishment in 1874 of the Criterion by the catering firm Spiers and Pond. Covent Garden and Drury Lane were funded by a system of shares. The account of Sadler's Wells theatre given in the agent's prospectus for its sale (ix) indicates the kind of relationship common between company manager and theatre proprietor. When a 'star' toured on his own – or with a few colleagues – from theatre to theatre, acting with the resident companies, the local managers often found that delicate negotiations were needed. There has always been an intimate relationship between the actor's financial worth and his or her self-esteem (cf. Part II, no.ii). At the lower levels of the profession there were frequent instances of rogues getting together a company, playing a week and absconding before 'treasury' – the 'Managerial vampires' of no. v.

238

The shift to long runs of single productions was not absolute, but by the end of the period the stock company with its seemingly limitless repertoire was a historical curiosity. Bernard Shaw was among those unable to feel any grief for its loss: the stock company actor, he wrote in 1895, was notable for his 'universal readiness', which meant that 'in his incorrigible remoteness from nature and art it mattered nothing what he did.' (*Our Theatres in the Nineties* (1932) I, 271.) A desire for some accommodation with nature and art led to the establishment of what were effectively 'legitimate' repertory theatres by Samuel Phelps at Sadler's Wells and Charles Kean at the Princess's. The Bancrofts' régime at the Prince of Wales and Irving's at the Lyceum sought to achieve stability, continuity and an appeal to a coherent (and middle-class) clientèle. There were several new patterns of touring: the company with a fixed repertoire, organized round the star's show-pieces (the Compton Comedy Company, for example); the replication of a London success (often by several companies, reaching different parts of the kingdom); and the Shakespearean repertory companies of Ben Greet and F.R. Benson. The managers of large theatres in the regions might stage their own pantomime productions and, in some cases, Shakespearean 'revivals', and fill the rest of the year with visits from touring companies. Many managers outside central London – in the suburbs and the provinces – established close ties with their local audience, achieving a sense of common identity quite distinct from the atmosphere of the West End. John M. East, in *'Neath the Mask*, and Frances Fleetwood in her account of the Conquest family (see *Further Reading*), describe such relationships. When the Conquests finally took their farewell benefit at the Surrey Theatre, in 1904, a characteristically patriotic epilogue was delivered – the kind of managerial address not at all uncommon in the period – in which the audience were asked to recall 1881:

> When, with the dear old 'Guv'nor' in commmand,
> His crew a merry and devoted band,
> The good ship Surrey ventured on the seas,
> Spreading its sails to catch each fav'ring breeze.
> For twenty years his bulldog British pluck
> Brought him the best of fortune and good luck,
> And what to life a sweeter flavour lends –
> His kindly nature made him hosts of friends.
>
> (Fleetwood, *Conquest*, p. 173)

Much successful important work originated outside the metropolis: Charles Calvert in Manchester and Wilson Barrett in Leeds can be cited as actor-managers with a powerful local reputation who became exporters of their productions to other centres and even (notably in the case of Calvert's *Henry V*) to America and the Colonies. A vivid and well-documented account of life in this worldwide network of plays and companies is given in David Holloway's *Playing the Empire* (1979), which traces the Holloway Touring Company's life from Australia to South Africa and the British Isles. Theatre 'product' in the form of scripts, scenery and costumes, as well as the performances of individuals, changed hands across continents. The activities of such impresarios as Milton Bode (xvii) were not at all unusual.

There were always journalists ready to point out the 'errors' of theatrical managers (as in no. vi), much as editorials showing how to reform the English Stage were likely when leader-writers had nothing much else to offer. Within the profession one impresario, John Hollingshead (see no. xiii), was particularly vocal and also notably energetic in promoting 'the National Drama'. Under his management the Gaiety, primarily a theatre for burlesque (later transformed into musical comedy) was remarkable for its forays into 'legitimate' drama. After 1886, under George Edwardes, the Gaiety focused more narrowly on musical comedy, of which Edwardes became the most notable exponent: his productions were staged at several London theatres – including the Apollo, Daly's and the Prince of Wales – as well as on tour. At Drury Lane, Augustus Harris claimed to continue the traditions of the house while offering the public a diet of spectacular pantomime and melodrama – his defence of his 'National Theatre' (xiv) makes an interesting comparison with the proposals for an endowed theatre (see Arnold and Archer, xii and xvi). Bram Stoker, Irving's 'acting' (i.e. business) manager at the Lyceum, offers a spirited defence of actor-managers (xv). It was becoming difficult to ignore the connection between the internal politics of the theatre and its wider social and political significance. The most extreme kind of actor-manager, ruthlessly subordinating all else to the display of his own talents, survived well into the new century, but it would soon be impossible to claim that such figures represented the highest aspirations of the profession. The examples of the Comédie-Française (whose 1879 visit inspired Arnold's call for an organized theatre) and the Saxe-Meiningen company suggested alternative ways of organizing a 'national' troupe so as to secure a credible standing for the theatre as a cultural institution.

25 Legitimate drama (with Phelps and Macready) and pantomime at Drury Lane in 1842; prices at 5s., 3s., 1s.6d. and 1s., with corresponding half price.

Meanwhile the demands of radical playwrights and performers created a system of 'experimental' matinées and private (and consequently uncensored) performances.

In Shakespearean production at the turn of the century the demand for lavishly staged 'revivals' was satisfied by a number of metropolitan and provincial managements – the field was dominated by Tree and Irving in London and on tour. In theatrical commerce between Britain and the United States it had become common for whole companies and their productions to tour. An alternative to these often beautiful but invariably unwieldy and expensive operations was offered in the companies run by F.R. Benson and Ben Greet, who could offer Shakespeare under almost any conditions at home and abroad. Greet was an educator as well as a manager, offering tuition to would-be actors and actresses, and then employing the more promising pupils in his various companies. Benson operated a similar scheme of 'apprenticeship' in order to give the experience of a classical repertoire that work with (say) the Number Three Floradora company could not afford. Benson's idealism owes much to the educating spirit of Oxford in the 1870s, the ethos of William Morris and the enthusiasms behind the amateur and semi-amateur avant-garde drama associated with the Aesthetic Movement. He had learned much from Henry Irving through the experience of working in his company. As well as a sense of mission akin to that of Lilian Baylis's management of the Old Vic in the 1900s, Benson was able to give training through experience to a host of actors and actresses. He was instrumental in the founding of regular festival seasons at Stratford-upon-Avon and created a commercial (but hardly profitable) Shakespearean equivalent of the civic repertory theatres.

For many years a favourite adage of the commercial theatre had been 'Byron spells bankruptcy and Shakespeare spells ruin', intimating the eternal unprofitability of the 'legitimate'. By the end of the century means were being found to make serious drama profitable, if only by challenging the cruder definitions of 'profit'.

Macready's introduction to the manager's life, 1808-11

[This passage from the *Reminiscences* of William Charles Macready gives a vivid picture of the life of the actor-manager – as it existed well into the new century (*Macready's Reminiscences, and Selections from his Diaries and Letters,* ed. Sir Frederick Pollard, 2 vols., 1875). Macready junior had been to London, where he had taken fencing lessons, improved his knowledge of the world and the theatre. He returned to face the consequences of his father's bankruptcy.]

My visit, from which I derived considerable benefit, being ended, I returned to Leicester, and thence proceeded to Manchester, where by appointment I rejoined my father. We slept at the Bridgewater Arms that night, and the next day late in the afternoon I went with him to the house of the sheriff's officer, to whom he was to surrender himself. When I found him actually a prisoner, my fortitude gave way, and I burst into tears. He had evidently a struggle to collect himself, but he did so, saying, 'There is nothing I cannot bear but compassion. If you cannot command yourself, go away.' I remained with him whilst it was permitted, and the next morning he went with the officer to his sad prison, Lancaster Castle, and I with no less heavy a heart to take charge of the company of players still in his service at Chester. I was but sixteen years old, and 'the world was all before me.' My lodgings were not uncomfortable, but my situation was very dreary.

I was quite alone, and every performer in the theatre, of which I now entered on the direction, was a stranger to me; and what aggravated the difficulty of my undertaking, several were in a state of mutiny, their salaries being considerably in arrear. The slovenly manner in which the business of the theatre was carried on by the persons in office was apparent to me in the play I saw represented the night of my arrival. I was surprised and vexed to find that it was a novelty of some interest put forward without notice or due preparation – *The Foundling of the Forest,* which had been an attraction through the summer at the Haymarket theatre. I enforced more attention at the rehearsals; announced a piece upon the subject of the late jubilee [of George III's accession], which excited curiosity, and was attractive; received what were called 'bespeaks' from Lord Grosvenor and Egerton, the member for the city opposed to him, which were crowded houses; but when I had cleared off most of the claims upon the concern, the proprietors put in an execution for the remainder of rent due, and I was at my wits' end. I wrote to friends for the loan of what money they could afford me, and having conciliated the good-will of some of the best among the actors, I was enabled to discharge the rent, pay off the salaries in arrear, and at the close of the theatre pursue my journey with three of the company in a post-chaise to Newcastle-upon-Tyne. The money I had been able to provide was nicely calculated to carry us through. It was the week before Christmas, and regular December weather. My hopes of relief from the obligations which still embarrassed me, and of raising the credit of my father's theatres, rested on the approaching season at Newcastle. My whole dependence was there. The best performers from Chester were to meet there the *élite* of the Leicester troop, and together would form a very good provincial company.

We left Chester, where I had learned my first lesson of the world's difficulties, on Christmas Eve, and, with four in a chaise and luggage, could not expect in winter roads to move on very expeditiously. Travelling all night we reached Brough, a small town on the wild borders of Westmoreland, about noon on Christmas Day, where we stopped to lunch. Here I gave our last £5 Bank of England note to pay the post-boy who had brought us from Sedburgh. To our utter dismay the landlord entered the room with the note in his hand to say he did not like the look of it, that he therefore demurred to give change for it, and that he could not send us forward, from the state of the roads, without four horses! Here was a dead lock! all my cherished hopes endangered, if not ruined, unless I reached Newcastle in good time on the morrow . . .

[By offering three watches as security, Macready and his companions prevailed on the landlord to loan them the money they needed.]

The event of the season at Newcastle did not disappoint me. The company was very superior to the average of provincial theatres. Poor Conway, then a very handsome young man, with a good voice, great ardour in the study of his art, and evincing very considerable promise, was its hero, performing Hamlet, Othello, Jaffeir, &c., to good houses. The new play of *The Foundling of the Forest*, got up with new scenery, &c., under my most careful superintendence, was an attraction for many nights. *The Jubilee*,

Macbeth as a pantomime (*proh pudor!*),[1] *Valentine and Orson*, &c, added to our receipts, enabling me to remit regularly three pounds each week to my father in his melancholy duress at Lancaster. A little before the close of the season in the spring he obtained with his release his certificate of bankruptcy, with most complimentary testifications to his uprightness and liberality . . .

Omnia mutantur[2] is a familiar proverb of the oldest philosophy. In this world of changes the theatrical calling has undergone revolutions as complete as those of science or religion. Witness the difference between the present state of the stage and its condition when I entered on it. At that time a theatre was considered indispensable in towns of very scanty populations. The prices of admission varied from 5s., 4s., or 3s., to boxes; 2s. 6d. or 2s. to pit; and 1s. to gallery. A sufficient number of theatres were united in what was called a circuit, to occupy a company during the whole year, so that a respectable player could calculate upon his weekly salary, without default, from year's end to year's end: and the circuits, such as those of Norwich, York, Bath and Bristol, Exeter, Salisbury, Kent, Manchester, Birmingham &c., with incomes rising from £70 to £300 per annum, would be a sort of home to him, so long as his conduct and industry maintained his favour with his audiences. But beyond that, the regularity of rehearsal and the attention paid to the production of plays, most of which came under the class of the 'regular drama', made a sort of school for him in the repetition of his characters and the criticism of his auditors, from his proficiency in which he looked to Covent Garden or Drury Lane as the goal of his exertions. . . . The distance from London was then so great, and the expense and fatigue of travelling was such as to make a journey then more rare; and the larger towns, as York, Newcastle, Bath, Exeter, Norwich, were centres or capitals of provincial circles, to which the county families resorted for the winter season, or crowded to the public weeks of races and assizes, when the assembly-rooms and the theatres were the places of fashionable meeting.

---

1   *proh pudor!*   (Lat.) For shame!
2   *Omnia mutantur*   (Lat.) All things change.

Macready vs. Bunn, 1836

[One of the most famous theatrical quarrels took place at Drury Lane Theatre between William Charles Macready and Alfred Bunn, sometime manager of both Covent Garden and Drury Lane. It was a direct conflict between two incompatible personalities, and the rival interests of the actor's professional standing and the manager's need to draw up a good bill. In his two-volume apologia, *The Stage: Both Before and Behind the Curtain* (1840) Bunn puts his side of the case.]

The national theatres of this country are not, like those of the continent, supported by government – they are matters of private speculation; and although [a] manager must defer as much as possible to public opinion and taste, he should do it in a manner most calculated to repay such speculation. Having had so many seasons to provide amusement for, at least, two hundred nights in each, I have frequently turned my attention to that kind of entertainment an actor provides on the only night of the season when *his* ingenuity is so taxed, viz., HIS BENEFIT NIGHT; and I did so at the present time. On the 25th of January 1836 – (nothing like being particular) – Mr Macready performed, for his own benefit at Bristol, in one act of Shakespeare's Second Part of *Henry Fourth*, and, after the introduction of some trifling intermediate matter, in Knowles's play of *William Tell* as the afterpiece. In addition to my impression that what Mr Macready had selected for *his* own advantage was likely to be conducive to *mine*, I knew that I should thus be enabled to give this very play (then representing at the opposite house for 4s. to the boxes), for 3s. 6d., by placing it as the second piece, instead of the first.

This order of things was by no means uncommon, for most of the plays Mr Macready this year played in, were supported by the full Operas of *Gustavus the Third, The Bronze Horse, The Corsair, Fra Diavolo, Der Freischütz, Masaniello,* &c., &c. The point of degradation, therefore, which was attempted to be set up was 'sheer nonsense' – it could be no more degrading to Mr Macready to play after Mr H. Phillips, Mr Templeton, Miss Shireff and others, than it could be for them to play after Mr Macready. Mr Macready had, moreover, for his own benefit in this very theatre, in 1825, played in *Rob Roy* (a part, it will be remembered, he now stipulated *not* to play) AFTER *Henry Fifth*; and for his benefit in

1834, the full opera of *The Lord of the Manor* was played after his attempt upon the personation of King Lear. But precedent upon precedent of such arrangement could be furnished, if necessary; and, knowing that, it never entered my head, in announcing *William Tell* as the last piece – so recently performed by him as such – that any objection would arise. Nothing, however, would induce Mr Macready to perform the character in the situation announced, unless my stage manager undertook, in my absence, that he should never be called upon to do a similar thing . . .

[Bunn's stage manager, Cooper, gave the assurance, 'to preserve peace and quiet'. Unfortunately, a royal command came for *Henry IV*, Part Two, to be given as 'second piece', which Bunn could not fulfil because of this agreement. In order to 'diversify the entertainments' Bunn announced a bill consisting of three acts of *Richard III*, *The Jewess*, and *Chevy Chase*. He did not like having to give only a part of a Shakespearean play, but there was precedent in Macready's own career.]

I solemnly avow that, in making this selection, I had no more idea of wounding Mr Macready's feelings than if he had not been in the theatre. I never once thought whether it would please him or displease him, my object being solely to make out as effective a bill as possible.

On Friday the 29th of April, I was sitting at my desk, a few minutes before nine o'clock, and by the light of a lamp, so shaded as to reflect on the table, but obscure the room generally, I was examining bills and documents, previous to their payment on the following morning; when, without the slightest note of preparation, my door was opened, and after an ejaculation of 'There, you villain, take that – and that!' I was knocked down, one of my eyes completely closed up, the ankle of my left leg, which I am in the habit of passing round the leg of the chair when writing, violently sprained, my person plentifully soiled with blood, lamp oil, and ink, the table upset, and Richard the Third holding me down. On my naturally enquiring if he meant to murder me, and on his replying in the affirmative, I made a struggle for it, threw him off, and got up on my one leg, holding him fast by the collar, and finally succeeded in getting him down on the sofa, where, mutilated as I was, I would have made him 'remember *ME*', but for the interposition of the people who had soon filled the room . . .

[In his diary Macready describes the incident with some remorse as well as a sense of indignation against Bunn for the ill-treatment he felt he was receiving. (*The Diaries of William Charles Macready, 1833–1851*, ed. William Toynbee (2 vols., 1912).]

My spirits were so very much depressed, so overweighed by the situation in which I was placed, that I lay down to compose myself, and thought over the part of Richard as well as I could. Went to the theatre; was tetchy and unhappy, but pushed through the part in a sort of desperate way as well as I could. It is not easy to describe the state of pent-up feeling of anger, shame and desperate passion that I endured. As I came off the stage, ending the third act of *Richard*, in passing by Bunn's door I opened it, and unfortunately he was there. I could not contain myself; I exclaimed: 'You damned scoundrel! How dare you use me in this manner?' And going up to him as he sat on the other side of the table, I struck him as he rose a back-handed slap across the face. I did not hear what he said, but I dug my fist into him as effectively as I could; he caught hold of me, and got at one time the little finger of my left hand in his mouth, and bit it. I exclaimed: 'You rascal! Would you bite?' He shouted out: 'Murder! Murder!' and, after some little time, several persons came into the room. I was then upon the sofa, the struggle having brought us right round the table. Willmott, the prompter, said to me: 'Sir, you had better go to your room, you had better go to your room.' I got up accordingly, and walked away, whilst he, I believe – for I did not distinctly hear him – was speaking in abuse of me. Dow came into my room, then Forster and young Longman. They talked and I dressed, and we left the theatre together . . .

As I read the above lines, I am still more struck with my own intemperate and unfortunate rashness. I would have gone through my engagement in forbearance and peace, still enduring wrong on wrong, as for six years I have been doing, but my passions mastered me, and I sought to wreak them . . .

The theatrical manager's morning, 1840

[From an article by the dramatist Richard Brinsley Peake, in *Heads of the People, or Portraits of the English, drawn by* Kenny Meadows (1840).]

How little do various grades of the public dream (whether seated aristocratically and in perfect comfort in private boxes, respectably and equally comfortable in the public boxes, conveniently in the pit, or most commodiously in the gallery, where gentlemen may sit with their coats off, if they like it) of the toil, care, misery, and vicissitude, of the caterer for their pleasure . . .

His temper must be as equally mixed as a bowl of punch; but that is only a simple comparison. We must go to actual contradistinctions, to enable him to have a chance to pursue his course.

He must be firm, yet supple; bold, yet cautious; liberal, yet sparing; he must possess penetration, yet see no further than is necessary. Whether he is asleep or not, he must always be wide awake. He must be a man of education, and be able to calculate tenpenny nails; he should know Shakspere [*sic*] and the *Trader's Price Book* by heart. He should be accomplished as a painter, a musician and an author; and yet he must have achieved that point of knowledge of being able to tell how many tallow candles go to the pound, and how far that pound will go. His tact must be divided between judgement in the decision of dramas to be accepted, and Birmingham ornaments;[1] the merits of actors, and cotton velvets; the favourable notice of the press, and the foil-merchant's account.[2] He must have a pretty notion of tailoring, ladies' dressmaking, and the armoury; in short he must be a factotum.

We will endeavour to sketch his duties; in fact, as if the Manager himself had kept a journal: –

Arrived at the theatre at ten o'clock; not late, considering I was here until half-past one this morning. Look at rehearsal-call, stuck up in the passage: 'New ballet at ten: everybody concerned – properties, scenes, firework-maker, Mr Pingle, répétiteur.'

Very wet day. All the ladies of the corps de ballet, including coryphées,[3] assembled with their hair in papers, looking like ghosts with bad colds, being kept up so late every night in the frost scene in the pantomime. Sneezing and low grumbling in all directions; each person attending literally to the words of the call; everybody looking 'concerned'.

Groupings commence to a single violin, and the loud thumping of the ballet-master's stick to keep time. Most of the sylphs and fairies rehearsing in their street-clogs, some with umbrellas. Go to my room adjoining the stage, the chimney of which smokes; but obliged to keep the door closed, because I hate to be overlooked. The table covered with letters, and the daily papers. Peep at superscriptions of the letters, to guess whether or not they may be disagreeable; endeavour to open that likely to be least offensive first. D—n the fiddling and the stamping – but they are unavoidable; and read Note no. 1: –

My Dear Sir – On my return home yesterday, I cannot conceal my surprise and mortification on finding that the part of Lady Anne[4] has been sent to me. There must surely be some mistake, as it was expressly stipulated in my engagement that the Queen is my property. If any other lady in the theatre had been cast for the Queen but the one that has been so favoured, I might not have felt the injury so deeply; but, believe me, I never will play second to Miss —, who has, throughout her theatrical career, endeavoured assiduously to blight my prospects, and mar my success with the public; to the favour of which public I ever look forward with anxious pride, knowing that on their kind support I am to rest my professional welfare. You are at liberty to make this letter public, if you please. I have, therefore, sent the part of Lady Anne back, and shall in justice expect to perform the Queen.

I am, my dear sir, yours, most sincerely,

* * * *

P.S. The man omitted to leave the play-bills at my lodgings this morning: but it is the way I am generally used in this world.

Oh, ah! she objects to play Lady Anne. Very well, I will make her go on for the Duchess of York, and that will bring the lady to her senses. Read Note no. 2: –

Dear —, At your request I have read Mr Drudge's farce. It has some capital situations, and is throughout full of fun; it is also very original. But I think that the author has committed an error, in imagining for one moment that I would play the part you have named that he intended for me. You are perfectly well aware that, as *I* stand with the public, *I* must be *the* feature. Now, there are several other prominent and good parts in the farce, which would materially deteriorate from my 'peculiar effects'. If Mr Drudge will, however, take the farce back again, and cut these other characters down to ribands, I have no objection to look at it once more, and see what can be done. It is in my engagement to decline anything which I think will not contribute to my advantage; and you know I am inflexible on that point.

Is it true, that we all played to less than forty pounds, first and second price, last night? If so, heaven help you.

Yours always, faithfully,

* * * *

Open Note No. 3 (anonymous, enclosing a ticket): –

Sir – If you will take the trouble to go, or send somebody on whose judgement you can depend, on Thursday next, to Mr Pym's private theatre, in Wilson Street, Gray's Inn Lane, I think you would be much gratified with the performance of a young gentleman, who will act Barbarossa on that night. His friends impartially think his talents superior to anyone at present on the stage, Macready or Kean excepted; he is cleverer than Warde or Phelps, and has got a much louder voice than the late Mr Pope.[5] There is only one drawback (and that might not be particular) to his becoming a first-rate actor, and this drawback is candidly pointed out to you, *as you may not see it* – he has a club-foot. Begins at half-past seven.

You are quite right my friend; I certainly shall not see it.

(*A knock at the door:*) Come in. What is it? 'Can you see Mr Fatton?' What Mr Fatton? 'The master of the supernumeraries.' Send him in. Now, Fatton, what is the matter? Make haste, for I am busy. 'Sir, there's *a strike* with the children in the theatre.' So there ought to be, Mr Fatton, if you did your duty properly, and kept a birch rod. 'Yes, sir, but all their fathers and mothers come on me and threaten to punch my head; now you know it is not my fault.' Well, what is this strike, as you call it? 'The girls who are to fly in the new ballet won't have the wires affixed to them unless they are raised to eighteen-pence a night: their mothers won't let them endanger their lives under that sum! Now, sir, we should be in a great scrape at night, if this were to happen; worse than they were in at the other house, with the boys in the storm.' What was that, Fatton? 'Didn't you hear that, sir? Oh; there were sixty boys, who stood on the stage under a very large canvas, painted to represent the sea. Now these boys were placed alternately, and were to rise and fall, first gradually and then violently, to represent the motion of the waves in a storm; and in the first three nights of the piece it had a powerful effect; but, after that, the manager reduced the water-rate, that is to say, he lowered the salary of each wave to sixpence per night. The boys took their places under the canvas sea; and when the prompter gave the signal for the storm, the water was stagnant – instead of the ship striking it was the waves that *struck*. The sub-manager, in a fury, enquired the cause; when the principal billow said "We won't move a peg unless you pay us a shilling a night, for it wears out our corduroys so." Gad, I think that must have been the *deep* deep sea! Well, promise the girls the eighteen-pence; but I will be even with them, I will keep them dangling in the sky-borders in a thorough draught all the night. Tell them so. – (*Exit Fatton.*)

Take up newspaper; look to article under head of 'THE DRAMA'. Something agreeable, I dare say. (*reads*)

— Theatre. – If we condescend to call the attention of the public to the management, or rather mis-management of this theatre, it is only to express our utter contempt of the system at this period in operation. Does Mr — imagine that such miserable trash as that which was presented within these classic walls last night, can possibly attract an audience possessed of common sense? No; 'reform it altogether'. Shade of Foote[6] (here's another Foot)! Spirit of Sheridan! Ghost of Garrick! we almost imagine we listen to your lament and wailing for the for-ever-lost essences of our national Drama. The plot of the new piece brought forward was so confused and inextricable, that we will not attempt to detail it to our readers: the whole affair was insufferably dull, and was deservedly condemned.

Bravo! (*rings bell*) Send the free-list clerk to me. I rather think that the critic who wrote this precious paragraph was absent from the performance. Pray, did the * * * * card come in last night? 'No, sir.' Was Mr — here? You can tell by the signature on your book. 'No, sir.' He is too good a judge to *pay*. 'There was no one from that paper last night, sir.' I thought so; that will do . . .

[After dealing with various problems, including a singer who has sent in an untruthful sick-note and a dispute with the owner of a 'theatrical and masquerade warehouse', the manager receives a packet from the Lord Chamberlain's Office, returning a play on the subject of Wat Tyler. Money has been spent on the production, but now the licence has been refused, on the grounds that the play contains radical sentiments. The manager settles down to sign orders for payment before going home to his dinner.]

'What is this mass of papers?' Merely the weekly outlay, to be settled at the treasury tomorrow; only the salaries of the company – the band, the chorus, dancers, painters, property-makers, wardrobes, dressers, housekeepers, cleaners, watchmen, firemen, carpenters, copyists, soldiers, supernumeraries, children, bill deliverers, lampmen, gas-lighters, printer, advertisements, candles, oil, hair-dressers, military band, licences (Wat Tyler excepted), ironmongery, turnery, basket-work, colours, music paper, stationery, tinman, florist, drapery, hosiery, timber, laceman, ropes, canvas, brushes, authors, and law expenses, box-keepers, money-takers, check-takers, candle-stickers, police, call-boy, and coal-porter, besides a portion of nondescripts which cannot possibly be imagined anywhere else than behind the curtain of a theatre!

NOTES

1   *Birmingham ornaments*   Birmingham was a major centre of production for buttons, badges and costume jewellery.

2   *foil-merchant's account*   Metal foils were used to decorate properties and scenery (see Part III, xiii).

3   *coryphées*   Leading members of the *corps de ballet*.

4   *Lady Anne*   The play in question is *Richard III*.

5   *Warde . . . Phelps . . . Pope*   Samuel Phelps made his London début in 1837. The other actors are probably James P. Warde (d. 1840) and William Coleman Pope (d. 1868).

6   *Foote*   Apparently a reference to the wit, actor and dramatist Samuel Foote (1720–77).

The problem of free admissions, 1840

[Alfred Bunn, manager, describes the need to give out 'orders' for free admission in *The Stage: Both Before and Behind the Curtain* (1840).]

I come now to another alarming difficulty with which a director of these theatres has to contend, which, despite the resolution and the prudence every novice is bent upon adopting, will never be got rid of, and which is of more vital detriment than may at first be imagined. I allude to the free admissions, commonly called ORDERS – the very bane of the profession. Contend as you may against the issue of such privileges, there are so many to whom, in the mutual exchange of courtesies, they MUST be given, that it is almost hopeless to draw the line of distinction. Performers for the most part stipulate for them – limit the issue to a few members, and you sour the rest of the company. The press claim them on the score of reciprocity (the admission of your advertisements on payment of the duty); and although by such argument they should naturally be extended only to those Journals whose circulation can render a correspondent advantage; yet, if you omit a paper or periodical of the vilest description, your reputation is assailed by it, and your exertions misrepresented in the most shameless and mendacious manner. An indiscriminate distribution of these 'freedoms' is the most deceptive pivot upon which the fortunes of a theatre can possibly turn; a more manifest instance of which cannot be cited than the following. The disastrous season of 1828–29, terminated . . . in the seizure of all the property in Covent Garden theatre at the instance of the parish of Saint Paul; and as one proof of the misrule which led to such a calamity, this fact may be adduced, that at a preceding period of the management under which it occurred (*viz*: from the 17th of May to the 12th of July, 1824,) Mr Robertson, treasurer to Messrs. Kemble, Willett, and Forbes, wrote 11,003 orders; which, calculated at the rate of 7s. each (the admission at that time to the boxes), amounts to the sum of £3,851 1s. [Bunn quotes the list] . . .

In further evidence of the dangerous tendency of such practice, it very frequently occurs that the parties to whom you give orders, particularly if they happen to be performers, congratulate their manager on there being a fine house, at the very time a little reflection would convince them that the appearance such house assumed was created by the free admissions which they and others had received. Give an author a number of orders for the support of his play, and from the vociferation of his friends, by virtue of such orders, he not only dates its complete success, but maintains that it has been productive to the treasury – at least, FROM THE APPEARANCE OF THE HOUSE. Give an actor orders, and if hissed by every other person in the theatre, save those to whom he entrusted them, he will stoutly argue that he was applauded throughout the evening. Give them to a tradesman, and, seeing a full house, without reflecting that half of its audience paid the same admission money by which he got in himself, he will call the next day for his 'little bill', because there was so numerous an audience the night before.

It is an impression with many, that a given quantity of orders brings along with it a given quantity of money. I doubt it; and it is impossible, I should say, that it ever brings in the quantity it keeps away; for out of the £3,851 worth of admissions gratuitously distributed, according to the foregoing declaration, at least one half the amount might have found its way into the treasury of the theatre. Then the trouble entailed upon a theatre by these courtesies is beyond belief. Those who apply for them, seldom do so, unless the entertainments to be seen are attractive; and though at the moment such applications are made you happen to be very much occupied on matters calculated to add to the exchequer, if you do not instantly attend to matters that cannot aid it at all, you are set down for an ill-bred upstart, in every respect unfit for your situation. Taken altogether, the ORDER SYSTEM is one of the most thankless, troublesome and injurious of the many duties devolving on the manager of a theatre.

'Managerial vampires', 1847

[Under this headline *The Theatrical Times* (1 January 1847) quoted this instance ('from a bill') of a common kind of managerial fraud. The journal inveighs against 'those rascally cases of victimization, and ruffianly deception, on the part of speculative blackguards, and their equally culpable hireling agents, of which the . . . paragraph affords an example.' The 'bill' seems to be for a benefit performance which the actors hoped would meet their expenses.]

BOSTON THEATRE – *Unprincipled conduct of the Manager, Mr Robson Daniels. – Appeal to the Public.* – For the general benefit of the company, who in making this appeal, feel bound to state the circumstances that compel them to do so. Mr Robson Daniels engaged, or caused to be engaged *by Agency*, a company from London, (each individual bearing his own expenses) to open with him at Boston, for a season of *Six Weeks*, stating that at the end of that period he had other theatres *to take them to, which was false*; he also required and was to give a month's notice to the majority of the company in case of separation on either side; he however *abruptly closed the theatre* on Friday evening at the end of *Four Weeks*, without giving the slightest notice of so doing, save what appeared in the *Bills* of Wednesday last, and by that means, a number of persons were prematurely thrown out of employment, after coming a journey of 120 miles, independent of having the same number of miles to return. But the calamity did not end here, for on the Saturday morning, when the company assembled at the theatre to receive their salaries, his heartless conduct again appeared, by his causing a notice to be affixed to the green room door, stating the salaries would not be paid (he, the Manager, having taken the precaution to get his own benefit over and pocket the receipts). So much for the conduct of Mr R. Daniels. Three of the company only have gained means of leaving the Town, the rest have therefore no resources but of making this appeal, and sincerely hope it will be responded to, as it is the only means by which they can leave the Town with credit to themselves, and with the utmost disgust to Mr Robson Daniels.

'The errors of managers', 1849

[One of a series of articles in *The Theatrical Journal* (1849), offering definitions of the 'grand errors, which, if they do not peril the safety of the drama, retard its progress to perfection.']

Jealousy, the 'green-eyed monster' of which the great master of the human heart bids us beware, because 'it makes the meat it feeds on', is a serious stumbling-block in the way of a manager. Under its influence he suppresses talent in his own company and puts inferior pieces upon the stage.

Let us take an illustration. Mr Buskin is director of a company of comedians. He is himself an actor (always a misfortune, by the way), and if not first fiddle, at any rate secures himself a prominent position in the *corps dramatique*. Mr Lamp is a rising actor in the company – a 'utility' man, who can play Rosse in *Macbeth*, or Dicky Darling in *He Would Be an Actor*. A new piece is produced. Buskin has a part he is sweet upon and Lamp a 'little bit' which he is to make the most of. Buskin's name comes out strong in the bills. Lamp's appears in a line with two others – Buskin's part goes without a hand – Lamp carries off all the honours! He is the *bijou* of the drama – like 'a good deed in a naughty world' his light shines out to illuminate the surrounding darkness. Buskin bears it for a night or two, but he gets very bilious on the third or fourth performance, and begins to turn over in his mind, whether he shall hand over his own part to some other stick,[1] or create a pretext for getting rid of Lamp. He does the former, because he sees that Lamp's kit[2] draws people to the house. But Lamp has cooked his own goose in his zeal. Thenceforth, he gets no fat parts: he is put into a line,[3] which affords no scope for his ability, or is shelved altogether. His brilliancy is his ruin; he has 'paled' the manager's 'ineffectual fires',[4] and there is a yawning gulf thenceforth, established between them. Thus the manager's jealousy weakens the force of his own company.

Now let us see how it works in the other case. A drama of thrilling interest is brought out at the Porte St Martin, or the Gymnase in Paris. Buskin's agent sends him an early copy with the *mise en scène*, or plan of the whole business. He reads it with avidity, leaving unread scores of good pieces by English authors. Snooks, who manages another theatre, likewise gets a copy, and Snooks being a less careful and somewhat sharper caterer than

Buskin, brings out his version first. This is dreadful. What is Buskin to do to counter this 'nasty' move? Play his piece now as he may – get it up at what cost he will, the gilt has been taken off the gingerbread. Nothing, then, is left to him but preposterous placards, fierce underlinings in his playbills, insidious advertisements, and applications for injunctions. We dare say the rows about *Used Up* and *Le Diable à Quatre*[5] are fresh in the recollections of our readers. The consequence of this ebullition of jealousy is that the rival house is advertised, and Buskin's establishment suffers in attraction . . .

The evil of an indulgence in a passion for stars has been written about so much of late years, and to such little effect, that, while we can hope to say nothing new, we can scarcely expect to produce a lively impression. The mischief will, in time, cure itself; but, in the meanwhile, it is doing immeasurable harm to the stage. If A or B, lifted by transatlantic or provincial success, returns to London, he conceives himself entitled to rate his improved capacity at a high figure. Where he was accustomed to receive £10 a week, he now demands £25 per night, with certain privileges as to free admissions and a benefit, and insists upon typographical announcements of gigantic proportions.

The manager, building upon the public thirst for novelty, agrees to the stipulation of the self-created 'star', and thus pampers an appetite that grows the more voracious by what it feeds on. What is the consequence to the general interests of the drama? Why, that all other grades of the profession being underpaid, in order that the 'star' may be paid in excess, men of education decline to become candidates for histrionic honours. Nor is this all. The style of performance introduced by the 'star' becomes a model for aspirants; its vices are overlooked in the halo of brilliancy with which puffery has temporarily invested it, and in progress of time the stage is overrun with a mongrel race of artificial quacks, who have caught the manner without any of the spirit of the original . . .

We come to the last of the grand errors, on which we have felt it our duty to expatiate, *an absence of respect for the profession*. If managers would learn to consider their performers as members of a profession, which exacts a higher amount of human skill and a greater variety of mental and personal accomplishments than are requisite in any other line of life, instead of treating them as domestic servants or slaves, we should soon perceive a very marked change in the public estimation of the stage. No one but the *habitués* of green-rooms, or the authors who have attended rehearsals, can imagine the lofty airs which managers give themselves in their intercourse with the actors. The despotism of an African chief, or the autocrat of all the Russias is *égalité*, compared with the absolutism of the monarch of the lamps. The black man who protested against *preachee and floggee*[6] too, had a sense of the kind of tyranny to which the 'poor player' is subjected – plenty of bullying and poor salaries – miserable dressing-rooms, and considerable fines for small *laches*,[7] little heed of petitions and remonstrance, but much heed of trifling faults, that is about 'the size' of managerial treatment of a company. Let it be reformed altogether. Let men in brief authority learn that zeal is to be insured, talent fostered, the stage elevated, and *money gained*, by letting each actor and actress feel that they are considered worthy of gentleman-like consideration. We shall not then find the 'legitimate' deserted for the spurious, and English performances held at a discount, if anything in the shape of a foreign composition is to be seen elsewhere.

NOTES

1   *stick*   Stiff, unconvincing actor.

2   *Lamp's kit*   This seems to be an allusion or a catchphrase, but I have not been able to identify it.

3   *line*   The parts to which the actor was especially suited and which he expected to play (old men, comic leads, juveniles, etc.).

4   *'paled . . fires'*   Cf. *Hamlet* I. v. 89–90: 'The glow-worm shows the matin to be near,/And 'gins to pale his uneffectual fire . . . ' The article is peppered with Shakespearean allusions.

5   *Used Up . . . Le Diable à Quatre*   Both plays were translations from French originals, the former by Boucicault and Charles Mathews.

6   *the black man . . . floggee*   The words 'preachee and floggee' (the twin aspects of colonialism) are cited together by *OED* in an example from 1809.

7   *laches*   Errors (Fr.).

Charles Kean's principles, 1850–9

[Charles Kean's management of the Princess's was notable for elaborately staged melodramas (notably *The Corsican Brothers*) and 'revivals' of Shakespeare's plays. (See also Part II, ix, and III, v.) After the performance of *Henry VIII* on the last night of his regime, 29 August 1859, Kean made a farewell speech. From J. W. Cole, *The Life and Theatrical Times of Charles Kean, FSA* (1859).]

This night concludes my managerial career. The good ship which I have commanded for nine years, through storm and sunshine, calm and tempest, is now about to re-enter harbour, and, in nautical phrase, to be paid off. I may perhaps be expected on an occasion like the present to make some allusions to the principles of management I have invariably adopted. I have always entertained the conviction that in illustrating the great plays of the grandest poet who ever wrote, historical accuracy might be so blended with pictorial effect that instruction and amusement would go hand in hand. I find it impossible that, because every detail is studied with an eye to truth, such a plan can in the most remote degree detract from the beauties of the Poet.

I remember that when I produced the *Winter's Tale* as a Greek play, that is, with Greek dresses, Greek customs, and Greek architecture, and objection was raised by some that although the scene was situated in Syracuse – then a Greek colony, whose King consults the celebrated Oracle of Delphi – yet the play was said to be essentially English, and ought to be so presented, because allusions in various parts bore reference to this country, and to the period when the author wrote.

You would perhaps have been somewhat astonished and perplexed to see the chest containing the answer of the Greek Oracle to the Greek King, supposed to have been delivered above two thousand years ago, borne upon the stage by the Beefeaters of Queen Elizabeth. You would perhaps have been equally surprised to have witnessed at this theatre Leontes as a Greek King, in the last act, attired as Hamlet Prince of Denmark, and yet such an incongruity was accepted within the last twenty years.

But to carry out my system of pictorial illustration, the cost has been enormous, far too great for the limited arena in which it was incurred. As a single proof I may state that in this little theatre, where £200 is considered a large receipt, and £250 an extraordinary one, I expended in one season alone a sum little short of £50,000. During the run of some of the great revivals, as they are called, I have given employment, and, consequently, weekly payment to nearly 550 persons.

Having said thus much, I need not deny that I have been no gainer in a commercial sense. I do not now retire from the direction of this theatre through any feeling of disappointment, but from the remembrance of the old adage, 'The pitcher goes often to the well, but the pitcher at last may be broken.'

viii

'Value of theatrical property', 1860

[From *The Times*, 18 February 1860: the theatre shares were valuable in proportion to their privileges of admittance to performances.]

On Thursday, at the Auction Mart, Mr Robinson offered to public auction a renter's share in the Theatre Royal, Drury Lane, on which an annual dividend is now paid, with a free admission, transferable annually, held for a period of 36 years – sold for 49 guineas; five £100 joint-stock or proprietor's shares in Drury-Lane Theatre, entitled to a personal free admission, for 25 guineas; a free admission to the same theatre for the present season, ending September next, sold for £2 5s.; a free admission to the Lyceum Theatre, from April to October next, sold for £1 10s.

Sadler's Wells for sale, 1862

[The estate agents' 'further details' of Sadler's Wells Theatre, issued when the lease was for sale in 1862 (prospectus, Sadler's Wells Collection, Finsbury Public Library). The description, even allowing for agents' licence, suggests how Phelps had turned a disreputable theatre into the opportunity for 'a sound and lucrative investment of capital', and indicates the extent of the property and the terms on which the lease was held. The eventual purchaser of the theatre was Robert Edgar. Phelps's term as manager finished in 1862.]

Particulars and Conditions of the sale of the lease of the highly popular establishment and favourite resort of the public known as the Theatre Royal, Sadler's Wells, situate in a densely-populated and respectable neighbourhood, not exposed to competition, in the full zenith of its fame and success, for an unexpired term of fifty years from midsummer last; the use of which is granted to Mr Phelps for seven years from Lady Day, 1860, at the annual sum of one thousand pounds per annum, subject to deductions for ground rent, insurance, etc . . .

PARTICULARS

The first-class long leasehold property known as the Theatre Royal, Sadler's Wells, covers a large area of ground, in a very populous and respectable neighbourhood, and it has excellent access from St John Street Road and Arlington Street, with a large area or court yard, affording unusual facilities for Carriage Visitors. The Theatre is brick-built, slated and tiled, admirably arranged, tastefully embellished and approached by a portico, the auditory is planned so as to secure a good view of the stage, as well as acoustic facilities, and comprises:

The Dress Circle, with seats for 102 persons,
The Boxes, to accommodate 150 persons,
Six Private Boxes,
Roomy Pit, to accommodate 1,000 persons,
The Gallery, to hold 800 to 1,000 persons.

There are two refreshment saloons, and a good box office.

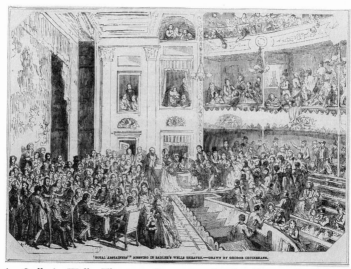

26 Sadler's Wells Theatre, 1852: engraving by George Cruikshank showing the auditorium and stage during a temperance meeting.

[BACKSTAGE FACILITIES]

The stage is ample and lofty (the width from fly rail to fly rail being 32 feet 9 inches) with handsome proscenium, orchestra, and every facility for producing pieces involving scenic effects, and the introduction of a large corps of performers. Over the stage, etc., are the upper and lower flies, carpenter's shop, and barrel loft; and conveniently disposed are the Green Room, Music Room, Ladies' Private Dressing Rooms and Gentlemen's ditto ditto, private and general wardrobe rooms, property room, cellarage, and other conveniences.

[TERMS OF THE MANAGER'S AGREEMENT]

The property is held on a lease for a term of sixty years from Midsummer, 1851, at a ground rent of £277 per annum; the lessees paying the insurance and other outgoings; and its use is granted to Mr Samuel Phelps, with such of the properties as belong to the proprietors, for 7 years from Lady Day, 1860, at the yearly sum of one thousand pounds, payable by 10 monthly payments of £100 each, to be made in each and every month excepting July and August; the Proprietors reserving to themselves the exclusive right to the use of 2 private boxes, the right to introduce 20 visitors before the curtain on every night of performance, except on benefit nights, and also to introduce a limited number of persons on the free list. Mr Phelps is bound to do repairs except to the main walls, timbers and roof. The proprietors are under covenant to pay the ground rent, insurance, rates and taxes. Also to allow Mr Phelps a sum not exceeding £350 for permanent repairs and improvements (not decorations) to be made by him; of which sum not more than £116 13s. 4d. is to be deducted in any one year, and to be deducted in equal parts from the several monthly payments; and such permanent repairs and improvements to be subject to the certificate of the Proprietors' surveyor.

The annual income derivable from this property may be estimated thus:

Rent payable by Mr Phelps, per annum	£1,000
Subject to the following outgoings, viz.:	
Ground rent, per annum	£277
Insurance	£90
Sewers' rate, taxes, etc.	£43 6s. 8d.
Poor's rate	£50
Watchmen (18s. per week, half of which is paid by the proprietors)	£5 8s. 11d.
Net improved or profit rental:	£510 16s. 5d.

The high character of the present tenant of the property, and the prestige long attached to it, may be considered as ample security for the safe realization of the above handsome improved rent, and the present opportunity afforded is of infrequent occurrence, enabling as it does a purchaser to effect a sound and lucrative investment of capital, in combination with the acquisition of the the attractive privileges above mentioned, as reserved to the Proprietors.

Such of the fixtures, properties, looking glasses, gas fittings, meters, manuscripts as belong to the vendors, will be included in the sale . . .

London theatre rents, 1866

[In evidence before the Parliamentary Select Committee on Theatrical Licences and Regulations (1866), the author and journalist John Hollingshead (subsequently himself a manager) argued that legal restrictions were limiting the number of theatres available to dramatists, and cited the high rents commanded in the West End in support of his argument.]

5217. In what way do you consider that the existing legislation concerning theatres operates as a restriction upon the industry of dramatic authors? – I ground my opinion chiefly on the extraordinary rise of rent alone in most of the London theatres during the last 25 years. I believe that at the Princess's Theatre the rental, until the year 1841, was £1,200 a year; in 1848 it went up to £1,800 a year; in 1851 it went up to £3,000 a year; in 1862 it was £3,800 a year; and in 1863 the present manager paid £4,000 a year for it. With regard to the Lyceum Theatre, in 1844 it was let for £2,000 a year, in 1846 it was £2,500 a year, and in 1863 it was £4,000 a year. Drury-Lane Theatre was let to Mr E.T. Smith, in 1860, for £4,500 a year, and in 1862 he sold his lease for a premium of £6,000 to Messrs Falconer and Chatterton. I consider that those facts, and I believe others can be brought forward of the same character, prove that the existing system must have been restrictive, for no other property has risen in equal proportion.

Financing a country theatre, 1860s

[W.T. Simpson's evidence before the 1866 Select Committee includes this account of the tribulations of country managers, at the mercy of local magistrates.]

[5404] . . . At Dudley, in Worcestershire, a man laid out his all to build a very nice theatre in a place where there are 60,000 inhabitants; he got a licence; it was his native town; he had been acting there 40 years; he built this theatre, and it was opened; it played the whole season, and never had one complaint against it; he went for his second licence, but in the interim some gentleman who was on the bench had been taken ill, and had made all the magistrates promise that they would never grant a theatrical licence until he was gone: the next season [the manager] was refused his licence, and he had to pull down his theatre and carry it away like old bricks and mortar. Mr G.V. Brooke* played in that theatre. [5408] . . . There was no harm in that theatre. It says in the old Act that any person opening a theatre shall be bound in a penalty of £500 or less if the magistrates think fit; that is the 6th and 7th Victoria. There happened to be a barrister, bearing the name of Kenealey, at Birmingham, and he happened to be in the court, when he started up with an opposition for this licence; they had only called one of the names, and he said, 'Mr Bennett, are you worth £500?' He said, 'No.' Then he says, 'Your worships, this cannot go on.' He says, 'How so?' 'Why,' he says, 'you might put him in a penalty of £500,' and so he lost it on account of that. That was a great deal to lose for a country manager, trying to get his bread and cheese in the country.

5409. What is the average cost of a theatre in the country? – The Northampton Theatre, which is small, that is, about £150 a year rent, and £50 a year taxes; a man has got his 12 months' rent to pay, and he has got £100 to start in his business; he thinks that will do, and he does not see why he should have that £500 too, and that is what prevents him from getting a licence.

5410. Is it possible to conduct a theatre fairly with less than £500? – Yes, those little theatres, if they have got a little local connection, can do it.

5411. When you pay £150 a year for a theatre, does that include properties? – There are very seldom any in a country theatre.

5412.   How do the actors dress themselves? – Every manager has a wardrobe of his own. You may find some scenery, but you are better without it, and you have your own in those little places; but Mr Saville has had that theatre for a considerable time, and it is in very excellent repair now.

NOTE

*   *G.V. Brooke*   Cf. note 6, p.33 above.

xii

Matthew Arnold's call for reform, 1879

[From 'The French play in London', occasioned by a visit from the troupe of the Comédie-Française, first published in *The Nineteenth Century*, 6, August 1879, and reprinted in *Irish Essays* (1882). Arnold observes that after the Civil War 'the English theatre reflected no more the aspiration of a great community for a fuller and richer sense of human existence', and that in pleasing the 'Town' it no longer appealed to the middle class.]

I remember how, happening to be at Shrewsbury, twenty years ago, and finding the whole Haymarket company acting there, I went to the theatre. Never was there such a scene of desolation. Scattered at very distant intervals through the boxes were about half-a-dozen chance comers like myself; there were some soldiers and their friends in the pit, and a good many riff-raff in the upper gallery. The real townspeople, the people who carried forward the business and life of Shrewsbury, and who filled its churches and chapels on Sundays, were entirely absent. I pitied the excellent Haymarket company; it must have been like acting to oneself upon an iceberg. Here one had a good example, – as I thought at the time, and as I have often thought since, – of the complete estrangement of the British middle class from the theatre.

What is certain is, that a signal change is coming over us, and that it has already made great progress. It is said that there are now forty theatres in London. Even in Edinburgh, where in old times a single theatre maintained itself under protest, there are now, I believe, over half-a-dozen. The change is due not only to an increased liking in the upper class and in working class for the theatre. Their liking for it has certainly increased, but this is not enough to account for the change. The attraction of the theatre begins to be felt again, after a long interval of insensibility, by the middle class also. Our French friends would say that this class, long petrified in a narrow Protestantism and in a perpetual reading of the Bible, is beginning at last to grow conscious of the horrible unnaturalness and *ennui* of its life, and is seeking to escape from it. Undoubtedly the type of religion to which the British middle class has sacrificed the theatre, as it has sacrificed so much besides, is defective. But I prefer to say that this great class, having had the discipline of its religion, is now awakening to the sure truth that the human spirit cannot live aright if it lives at one point only, that it can and ought to live at several points at the same time. The human spirit has a vital need, as we say, for conduct and religion; but it has the need also for expansion, for intellect and knowledge, for beauty, for social life and manners. The revelation of these additional needs brings the middle class to the theatre.

The revelation was indispensable, the needs are real, the theatre is one of the mightiest means of satisfying them, and the theatre, therefore, is irresistible. That conclusion, at any rate, we may take for certain. We have to unlearn, therefore, our long disregard of the theatre; we have to own that the theatre is irresistible.

But I see our community turning to the theatre with eagerness, and finding the English theatre without organization, or purpose, or dignity, and no modern English drama at all except a fantastical one. And then I see the French company from the chief theatre in Paris showing themselves to us in London, – a society of actors admirable in organization, purpose, and dignity, with a modern drama not fantastic at all, but corresponding with fidelity to a very palpable and powerful ideal, the ideal of the life of the *homme sensuel moyen* in Paris, his beautiful city. I see in England a materialized upper class, sensible of the nullity of our own modern drama, impatient of the state of false constraint and of blank to which the Puritanism of our middle class has brought our stage and much of our life, delighting in such drama as the modern drama of Paris. I see the emancipated youth of both sexes delighting in it; the new and clever newspapers, which push on the work of emancipation and serve as devoted missionaries of the gospel of the life of Paris and of the ideal of the average sensual man, delighting in it. And in this condition of affairs I see the middle class beginning to arrive at the theatre again after an abstention of two centuries and more; arriving eager and curious, but a little bewildered.

Now, lest at this critical moment such drama as the *Sphinx* and the *Etrangère* and the *Demi-monde*, positive as it is, and powerful as it is, and pushed as it is, and played with such prodigious care and talent, should too much rule the situation, let us take heart of grace and say, that as the right conclusion from the unparalleled success of the French company was not that we should reverse our old notions about the tragedy of M. Victor Hugo, or about French classic tragedy, or even about the poetic drama of the great Molière, so neither is it the right conclusion from this success that we should be converted and become believers in the legitimacy of the life-ideal of the *homme sensuel moyen*, and in the sufficiency of his drama. This is not the occasion to deliver a moral discourse. It is enough to revert to what has been already said, and to remark that the French ideal and its theatre have the defect of leaving out too much of life, of treating the soul as if it lived at one point or group of points only, of ignoring other points, at which it must live as well . . .

What, then, finally, *are* we to learn from the marvellous success and attractiveness of the performances at the Gaiety Theatre? What *is* the consequence which it is right and rational for us to draw? Surely it is this: 'The theatre is irresistible; *organize the theatre.*' Surely, if we wish to stand less in our own way, and to have clear notions of the consequences of things, it is to this conclusion that we should come.

The performances of the French company show us plainly, I think, what is gained, – the theatre being admitted to be an irresistible need for civilized communities – by organizing the theatre. Some of the drama played by this company is, as we have seen, questionable. But, in the absence of an organization such as that of this company, it would be played even yet more; it would, with a still lower drama to accompany it, almost if not altogether reign; it would have far less correction and relief by better things. An older and better drama, containing many things of high merit, some things of surpassing merit, is kept before the public by means of this company, is given frequently, is given to perfection. Pieces of truth and beauty, which emerge here and there among the questionable pieces of the modern drama, get the benefit of this company's skill, and are given to perfection. The questionable pieces themselves can be rationally attempted. 'Forget,' – can we not hear these fine artists saying in an undertone to us, amidst their graceful compliments of adieu? – 'forget your clap-trap, and believe that the State, the nation in its collective and corporate character, does well to concern itself about an influence so important to national life and manners as the theatre. Form a company out of the materials ready to your hand in your many good actors or actors of promise. Give them a theatre at the West End. Let them have a grant from your Science and Art Department; let some intelligent and accomplished man, like our friend Mr Pigott, your present examiner of plays, be joined to them as Commissioner from the Department, to see that the conditions of the grant are observed. Let the conditions of the grant be that a repertory is agreed upon, taken out of the works of Shakespeare and out of the volumes of the *Modern British Drama*, and that pieces from this repertory are played a certain number of times in each season; as to new pieces, let your company use its discretion. Let a school of dramatic elocution and declamation be instituted in connection with your company. It may surprise you to hear that elocution and declamation are things to be taught and learnt, and do not come by nature, but it is so. Your best and most serious actors' (this is added with a smile) 'would have been better if in their youth they had learnt elocution. These recommendations, you may think, are not very much; but, as your divine William says, they are enough; they will serve.* Try them. When your institution in the West of London has become a success, plant a second of like kind in the East. The people *will* have the theatre; then make it a good one. Let your two or three provincial towns institute, with municipal subsidy and co-operation, theatres such as you institute in the metropolis with State subsidy and co-operation. So you will restore the English theatre. And then a modern drama of your own will also, probably, spring up amongst you, and you will not have to come to us for pieces like *Pink Dominoes*.'

No, and we will hope, too that the modern English drama, when it comes, may be something different from even the *Sphinx* and the *Demi-monde*. For my part, I have all confidence, that if it ever does come, it will be different and better. But let us not say a word to wound the feelings of those who have given us so much pleasure, and who leave to us as a parting legacy such excellent advice. For excellent advice it is, and everything we saw these artists say and do upon the Gaiety stage inculcates it for us, whether they exactly formulated it in words or no. And still, even now that they are gone, when I pass along the Strand and come opposite to the Gaiety Theatre, I see a fugitive vision of delicate features under a shower of hair and a cloud of lace, and hear the voice of Mdlle Sarah Bernhardt saying in its most caressing terms to the Londoners: 'The theatre is irresistible; *organize the theatre*!'

NOTE

*   *they are enough . . . serve*   *Romeo and Juliet,* III i.98 (Mercutio's death speech).

xiii

'Dealing in theatricals', 1880

[In this essay from his book, *Plain English* (1880), John Hollingshead, manager of the Gaiety from 1868 to 1886, expounds, with some sarcasm, the philosophy of commercial management. His claim that the customer has a right to 'the same comforts that he leaves at home' reflects the desire of most contemporary managers to attract a middle-class audience and to give it what it wanted rather than attempt to lead it.]

There is no brick-and-mortar investment more profitable in London than that of building theatres, and there is no occupation more easy and agreeable than theatrical management. The happy landlord of a London theatre builds in odd holes and corners – in back-yards and blind alleys, in slums and dust-holes; and when his temple of the drama is nearly complete, he obtains a narrow

entrance and a frontage in a public thoroughfare sufficient to carry
a flaming gas 'device', and immediately lets his property at fifteen
per cent rental, reserving various privileges, and taking the fullest
security. His choice of tenants is ample and varied. At one end of
his list are a host of penniless showmen; at the other are half a
dozen belted earls with what are called 'theatrical proclivities'.
Undeceived by the Micawberism of one class, or the dazzling
brilliancy of the other, he demands and obtains those material
guarantees which make business a pleasure and earth a paradise.

The theatrical manager's occupation is easy and agreeable, far
beyond that of most occupations, because he has so many people
to advise him and take an interest in his affairs. The soap-boiler in
the City and the Government clerk at the West-end have no
misgiving as to their power of directing his faltering footsteps.
Sixty newspapers, more or less, seem to be written, printed, and
published for no other purpose than to point out to him the many
pitfalls in his path . . .

If the manager is a practical man – and no man who is not
practical ought to have the direction of a theatre – his first duty,
when he takes possession of his theatre, will be to supervise the
work of his architect. He will sit in every seat in his house, and
look at the stage from every point of view from which the
audience will have to look at it. If any Corinthian capital,
caryatides, gurgoyle [sic], or other architectural ornaments come
in the line of anyone's sight, from a sixpenny boy in the gallery to
the holder of a ten-shilling stall, he will sacrifice those ornaments
without a moment's hesitation. If any columns threaten to prove
obstructions of a similar nature, he will fill their places with
girders with the least possible delay, until he has made his theatre
a place in which all his audience can see all the performance.
When the Surrey Theatre was rebuilt after the last fire [on 30
January 1865], a splendid architectural ceiling was displayed on
the first night, which had only the trifling defect that it prevented
half the gallery from seeing the stage. The house had to be closed
and half this ceiling cut away before the manager could fairly
commence his business.

The next duty of the manager will be to ascertain whether his
audience can hear as easily as they can see, and on this point he is
more at the mercy of the brute force of matter. What are called
the 'acoustic properties' of a playhouse are largely the result of
accident. Until the first word is spoken, no one can say whether a
whisper will penetrate to the farthest corner of the building, or a
pistol-shot be scarcely audible. If the manager meets with good

luck in this respect, so much the better for the manager; if he meets with bad luck, he must try to improve it by every means in his power.

His next duty will be to ascertain whether the audience can breathe in his theatre, a matter that is very difficult in many playhouses. He must not bake his audience on one side and freeze them on the other, but he must so temper the wind to the shorn lamb that the shorn lambs may not suffer from neuralgia or old toothache. Whilst on the subject of ventilation he must thoroughly examine the sanitary condition of his property. A theatre ought not to play into the hands of the Mawworm[1] class, and become, what they say it is, a 'whitened sepulchre'.[2] No manager ought to invite a visitor to the play without offering him, as near as possible, the same comforts that he leaves at home . . .

The alliance which has been formed of late between the gin-shop and the theatre of England is one that requires careful supervision. In this respect the French theatres are models to copy. In some London theatres a gaudy bar and a flaunting barmaid meet you at every turn; the placards of the great brewers and distillers stare you in the face on every wall; while the programmes of the performance are carefully hidden until you produce a shilling. Hungry waiters prowl about and suggest drinks to people who are not thirsty or object to stand at a bar, until it is difficult to say where the public house ends and the theatre begins. Protected by a clause which was smuggled into an Act of Parliament, this theatre-bibbing is not bound by the go-to-bed legislation of the last few years; and as long as the actors fret their late hours upon the stage, the gin-shop in front of the theatre can sell its fire-water. On the memorable first night of *Oonah* at Her Majesty's Theatre the performance lasted till a quarter to three on Sunday morning; and up to this hour refreshments (sorely needed) were partaken of freely by the much-tried critics.

. . . It is customary at too many theatres for the management to let the bars to some half-amateur publican at a rental which almost compels the vendor to sell bad articles at exorbitant prices. It is also customary at too many theatres to let with bars the right of worrying the public for the custody of their coats, hats and sticks, of demanding fees for showing them into seats which they have paid for, and of forcing on them programmes at twenty times the value of paper and printing. These are evils that should be vigorously stamped out, not only by exhibiting placards warning the public not to give fees, but by discharging without mercy any servants found guilty of taking bribes, though these may have been forced upon them by weak-minded members of the public.

[The manager must remember that people come to the theatre for many different reasons, and have widely differing tastes and capacities.]

He must not forget the fact that many people are attracted by clean seats, civil servants, soft carpets, punctuality, and straightforward management. He may forget many things, but he must never forget the great fact that, no matter what persons may form his audience, they have a much clearer idea as to the article they want to see than he can possibly give them. He must never attempt to make his taste their taste. His business is to open his shop, and to serve them with what they want, and not with what he probably would like to give them. He must never commit the folly and impertinence of suggesting to a customer who asks for a baked potato the propriety of selecting a rose or a volume of poems. He is not a director of public taste any more than an editor is a director of public opinion. He is only a follower. He must have no theories and no prejudices. He must never sit at his own theatre and watch the pieces he gives to the public. Few men can do this without becoming prejudiced either for or against such pieces. He must only look at the financial results, and watch these carefully night by night, with all disturbing influences – rain, snow, strikes, commercial depression, and other evils. His idea of a good piece must be a piece that pays; his idea of a bad piece must be a piece that does not pay. When he finds he has got the first, he must carefully nurse it; when he finds he has got the latter, he must strangle it with as little remorse as providence shows for the poor beetle. He must take a lesson from the billiard-room, and be able to fluke with superhuman serenity. When he has made a success, either with a piece, an actor, or with both, he must look as if he were reaping the reward of a scheme which he had been maturing half his life. He must ignore the fact that, like all his tribe, he lives on a hand-to-mouth policy, always waiting for something to turn up. He must gently insinuate that he selects his authors after years of deliberation; that his pieces are written to order many seasons before they are wanted; and that his actors have been selected in the same way and trained for him, and him alone, by ages of study and tuition.

When he has to descend from this lofty pedestal, and really select the exponents of his dramas, he will find two courses open to him. He may engage what are called 'stars', who are rapacious, but popular; or he may surround himself with a group of well-drilled mediocrities. He must not be astonished if he is asked to pay the salary of an Under-Secretary of State to a young man who has just stepped out of society on to the stage, and whose chief merit may be his ability to act as a clothes-horse. If he asks one of these actors to play a recognized part in the standard drama of his country, he must not feel surprised if six months' rehearsal is demanded. The days have long passed when every actor had a repertory of twenty parts, in any one of which he was ready to appear at an hour's notice. Each actor in our time only plays about one part a year, is drilled by machinery, and goes on till the springs run down, like a piece of Swiss clockwork.

In the selection of his plays, or rather authors, his choice will be much more limited. If he shows any hesitation, it cannot arise from the variety of material at his disposal. He will find that there are fifty theatres, more or less, in London, and only about three dramatic authors. He will treat these gentlemen with great respect, and wait his turn to be served, like a duchess at a Civil Service store.[3] He will buy his dramatic pigs in a poke, and pay what is asked without a murmur. Occasionally he will get a piece from a French source, which he will either steal or pay for in a prodigal manner; and, having secured it, he will place it in the hands of one of the two recognized English adaptors. If he spends much money in placing it upon the stage, he will be told that he is a fool and an upholsterer; and if he starves it in the production, he will be told that he is a shortsighted niggard. If he flies to the old drama as a refuge, he will have to plunge into Shakespeare and legitimacy, as there are not more than three comedies out of a thousand, from the time of Queen Elizabeth to that of Queen Victoria, that are worth the trouble of acting. Being in for theatrical management, however, he will do his best according to his lights, and at the end of a few years he will find that he has either lost ten thousand pounds by hard work, or made double that sum by a series of inexplicable flukes. He may probably hold his peace in the market-place; but in the privacy of his study he will admit that no particular training in literature and art is necessary for the good government of a theatre, but precisely those qualities that make a successful cheesemonger.

NOTES

1   *Mawworm*   The title character of Isaac Bickerstaffe's *The Hypocrite* (1769).

2   *whitened selpuchre*   Matthew 23:27: 'Woe unto you, scribes and pharisees, hypocrites, for ye are like unto whited sepulchres, which indeed appear beautiful outside, but are within full of dead men's bones and of all uncleanliness.'

3   *a Civil Service Store*   Department stores, originally set up for the use of government employees (especially those posted abroad) by the Civil Service Supply Association.

xiv

'The National Theatre', 1885

[Augustus Harris, 1852–96, was manager of Drury Lane from 1879 to his death, and became known as 'Druriolanus'. In an article published in *The Fortnightly Review*, n.s., 38, November 1885, he describes his obedience to 'the unerring law of supply and demand' in the context of his theatre's history of managerial failures.]

[By the 1850s] theatrical speculators had come to look on Drury Lane as almost a drug in the market. Circus horses had pranced sacrilegiously in its precincts, and three administrations had lasted just three weeks, when Mr E.T. Smith, in 1853, managed to secure it at a very low rental. Mr William Beverley about this time invented transformation scenes, and his beautiful effects made the annual pantomime the sheet anchor of the new manager. The success of *The Peep o' Day* at the Lyceum persuaded Mr Edmund Falconer (who like many authors before and since fondly imagined that a solitary triumph gave him almost oracular authority), that he had a special mission to regenerate the drama, and he lent a willing ear to the proposals of Mr Smith, who was anxious to dispose of his lease on conditions favourable to himself. A bargain was struck, but Mr Falconer's illusions were of short duration. His experience was dearly purchased. Mr Chatterton first became his partner, and then replaced him as sole lessee. Mr Chatterton (wise in his generation) trusted to Mr Andrew Halliday[1] and Mr Dion Boucicault, who understood the public taste, and catered for it accordingly. *The Great City, Formosa, Amy Robsart*, and *Ivanhoe* drew large houses; and these successes, coupled with the burning of Her Majesty's [in December 1867], which brought the Italian company on remunerative terms to fill up the dullest part of the year at Drury Lane, the popularity of the Vokes family,[2] and the talents of the leading member of that troupe, who admirably united the qualities of a clever contortionist and capital comedian, all combined to convert the old show into a transitory 'El Dorado'.

It was not, however, to last. The opera went back to its home in the Haymarket; the public, wearying of the Vokes's, began to want some fresh features in the pantomimes; and, to make matters worse, the patrons of the 'legitimate' were as ungrateful for the revival of the *Winter's Tale*, with Mr Dillon[3] as Leontes, as they had been blind to the beauties of Mr Halliday's modernization of *Antony and Cleopatra*, and the declamatory force of Mr Anderson[4] in the principal *rôle*. History at last once again repeated itself, and another melancholy meeting took place in the saloon of Drury Lane. The appeal to the tender mercies of the actors to accept a reduced salary met with the same result as a like request did some sixty years before; and on a dismal evening in February the pantomime-goers from all parts of the metropolis found themselves confronted with the comfortless announcement, 'Theatre closed in consequence of unavoidable circumstances.' The proprietors took possession, and the gloomiest rumours were current as to the future. The doors remained shut, and the speedy absorption of the site in a projected enlargement of Covent Garden Market was confidently predicted. It was at this juncture that I conceived the bold idea of becoming the lessee of Drury Lane. My temerity was, perhaps, not excusable, but I was firmly convinced that the theatre might be made what is described in common parlance, 'a paying concern'; and having obtained a promise of financial support, I answered (not without misgivings) the advertisement of the committee for a tenant. My age told terribly against me, and the negotiations which ensued were long, tedious, and difficult. At last, to the astonishment of everybody, the lease in my favour was signed. My best friends only gave me a month's respite from discomfiture; some of my enemies said I should not open at all, while others, more charitably disposed, foretold the certain addition of my name to the list of administrators who had held sway for a single week.

Six years have elapsed since then; the prophecies of friends and foes alike remain unverified, for my most sanguine hopes have been more than realized. The policy I have pursued at Drury Lane from the commencement has undergone no change. It was planned before I asked the proprietors for the lease, it was adopted from the time I took possession of the theatre, it is maintained today. My constant aim has been to gauge the taste of the theatre-going public with the greatest possible accuracy, and to follow intelligently in the matter of dramatic entertainment the unerring law of supply and demand. To carry out my programme, certain experiments were necessary. Fortunately for me, Mr George Rignold,[5] fresh from his triumphs in America and Australia, decided to revive *Henry V* at Drury Lane. I let him the theatre. The critics treated him with generosity, but a deficit was the result. I thus learned by experience at the outset the dangers of the 'legitimate'. *Blue Beard* restored pantomime to its old home, and in the following autumn the charming performances of Marie Litton[6] in *As You Like It* fared no better than *Henry V*

By this time I had become more and more convinced that popular drama was best suited to the public taste, and the triumph of *The World* proved my surmise to be correct. No such success had been scored at Drury Lane for many years; the play was eagerly sought for in every country where the English language is spoken, and is even now making money for the fortunate purchasers of its acting rights. Its strong situations and striking spectacle was, I believe, a relief to the great mass of playgoers satiated with the ceaseless dialogue and unimpassioned acting of the 'cup and saucer' school. They wanted drama, but a powerful class amongst them once more clamoured for the 'legitimate'. Mr John McCullough's[7] anxiety to gain in London, on the historical boards of Drury Lane, the same successes as had attended his performances in the United States, enabled me to make arrangements for the production of *Virginius* and *Othello*. He reaped golden opinions on all sides, but he failed to fill the house. A week after the curtain fell on the last representation of *Othello*, the company of German actors maintained by the Duke of Meiningen, and admirably stage-managed by Herr Ludwig Chronegh,[8] made its appearance in *Julius Caesar* under the personal patronage of the Prince of Wales. The archaeological knowledge and exquisite taste of the Grand Duke, the wonderful *mise en scène* of Herr Chronegh, and the perfect training of every class of the actors, excited the most profound sensation.

The expert handling of the crowds in their most important plays revolutionized the functions of the super for the future in this country. Managers flocked to Drury Lane along with the general public to learn all they could from these talented foreigners. Nevertheless these famous classical revivals were, as far as the treasury of Drury Lane is concerned, but a magnificent *succès d'estime*.

The next drama I placed on the stage was *Youth*, which crowded the house, and gave a large profit. If my opinion as to the only policy possible at Drury Lane needed any further confirmation, I found it in the following year in the disasters of the German opera, the cold support given to the splendid genius of Madame Ristori, and in the delicate flattery administered to me by the imitation of my tactics by some of my colleagues. Since then the presence each year in the national theatre of Mr Carl Rosa's company[9] has been the only tribute I have paid to what is commonly described as high art, and I trust that our joint efforts have a little contributed to the increased appreciation of English opera in London.

For the financial success of Drury Lane I am more than ever convinced that my guiding star must be wholly and solely the taste of those I endeavour to please. If the public at large really wanted to see Drury Lane the home *par excellence* of the 'legitimate' they would have given a far more constant support to the various efforts of my predecessors and myself in this direction. They have failed to do so, and the only inference to be drawn from past events is that the demand in question comes rather from the dissatisfied minority than from the great mass of British playgoers. Experience is an unerring master, and experience teaches precisely what the public ask for at Drury Lane. Leaving the ever-popular yearly pantomime out of the question, the requirements of an average Drury Lane audience are sufficiently clear. They demand a performance which must be, above all things, dramatic, full of life, novelty, and movement; treating, as a rule, of the age in which we live, dealing with characters they can sympathize with, and written in a language they can easily understand. It must be well mounted, well acted, and should appeal rather to the feelings of the public at large than to the prejudice of a class.

The successful dramas of today must be realistic, for to be realistic is to be true to nature, and to be natural is artistic. If the powerful minority still insists on a national theatre (in their sense of the word) at Drury Lane, I am ready, nay, more, it will be my greatest pleasure, to oblige them, but I am unwilling to ruin myself in satisfying their caprice. If they are in earnest a sufficient subsidy would render my daily task – the constant gauging of the public taste – superfluous; or perhaps they may be influential enough to secure the realization of their hobby at the expense of the State. I am far from treating lightly the wishes of the supporters of the 'legitimate', but I desire to indicate the real extent of the demand they create. Mr Irving succeeds admirably in supplying their wants; he is the tragedian who seriously commands the attention of London audiences, and the dimensions of his theatre are exactly suited to his requirements.

Tragedy, like the town of Brentford,[10] never acknowledged but one king. When Fechter[11] and Phelps played on alternate nights, during my father's management, at the Princess's, the one filled the house, while the other emptied it, although the relative merits of the two actors are still a matter of controversy. The limited extent of the demand, the success of Mr Irving, the great space to be filled at Drury Lane, and the annual productions of pantomime, are sufficient to make any further experiment of the kind, under existing circumstances, almost out of the question.

But I must not for a moment be supposed to admit that the modern drama, which the majority prefers to pay for, is either missionless, or devoid of merit, or that it needs any apology to justify the place it now occupies. Lessons of honesty, thrift, and generosity may be taught by its means. Men may learn, from what they see on the stage, to know one another, and to sympathize with the sufferings of their fellows. The visitors of the stalls, transported in imagination to the homes of the poor, may understand, more forcibly than they otherwise would do, the terrible hardships and struggles which are constantly undergone, as well as the anguish of the starving and the trials of the wronged. On the other hand, the occupants of the gallery may realize the fact that masters and employers have also their troubles, and that the rich and the powerful have their trials to contend with and their duties to perform.

Literati and antiquarians may long for Shakespeare, aesthetes may fail to enjoy alike the jests and glories of pantomime, and bishops may denounce the ballet, but the practical and prudent theatrical manager will ever learn a lesson from the eventful history of Drury Lane, and carefully frame his programme in accordance with the majority of his paying patrons and the old law of supply and demand. I have, I think, said enough to show that, as a matter of fact, the National Theatre during the last few years has, on the question of high art production, done something more than its share. The material results, however, have been invariably discouraging. The time may possibly arrive when a change of public opinion will justify a revolution in the class of entertainment the managers of Drury Lane are called on to furnish. Till then we must be content to wait, but the causes which will bring such a state of things into existence must arise from the march of education and other influences entirely outside the drama, and will not depend, at any rate directly, on the theatrical manager, who is, after all, only the servant of the public.

NOTES

1   *Edmund Falconer . . . Andrew Halliday*   With E.B. Chatterton, Edmund Falconer managed Drury Lane from 1863. After Falconer left, Chatterton continued alone until 1879, when Harris took over. Andrew Halliday wrote many scripts for the theatre during this period, including several adaptations of novels by Sir Walter Scott.

2   *the Vokes family*   Popular pantomimists, consisting of four members of one family and a fifth performer who adopted their name, active 1861–84.

3   *Dillon*   Cf. note 2, p.173 above.

4   *Anderson*   James R. Anderson (1812–95), actor.

5   *George Rignold*   (1826–1904), actor; he toured extensively in Charles Calvert's production of *Henry V*.

6   *Marie Litton*   Actress and manager, 1847–84.

7   *John McCullough*   (1832–85), actor.

8   *the Duke . . . Chronegh*   Cf. note on p.208 above. Ludwig Chroneg (1837–91) was stage-manager at Meiningen from 1866.

9   *Mr Carl Rosa's company*   Founded in 1875 to promote English opera, by Karl August Nicolaus Rose, a German musician. He died in 1889, but the company bearing his italianized name continued to tour Britain until the late 1950s.

10   *the town of Brentford*   In Buckingham's burlesque *The Rehearsal* (1672) *two* kings of Brentford appear in the tragedy that is being prepared: Mr Bayes, the author, claims that there are two monarchs for one place 'because it's new; and that's what I aim at.'

11   *Fechter*   Charles Albert Fechter (1824–79), Anglo-French actor, whose Hamlet caused a stir in 1861 and who managed the Lyceum for a while from 1863.

Defending the actor-manager, 1890

[Bram Stoker, Henry Irving's Acting (i.e. business) Manager, speechwriter and apologist, contributed to a symposium in *The Nineteenth Century* (June 1890). After an opening section in which he outlines the rise of the actor's status and claims that the management of theatres by actors was an inevitable and desirable development, Stoker defends the system against its detractors. The final paragraph seeks to justify the actor-manager and defend him against comparison with European examples of subsidized theatre, by reference to British *laissez-faire* economics. In the same issue of the periodical articles by Irving and Charles Wyndham defended their role as actor-manager in similar terms.]

Indeed, if we take the succession of actors from Shakespeare down, we shall fairly find that the one who was crowned by public favour wore the golden circlet of his own kingdom quite as worthily as even the Monarch of the State in succession. It is in this very fact of public favour that we find the rationale and the genesis of the actor-manager. The public has its own discrimination; and its judgement, being the resultant of various needs and interests and wishes, is sure to be in the main correct – *vox populi vox Dei*[1] has a basis of truth which wise statesmen and students of men do well to consider. Public favour, when bestowed on a producer of work of any kind, is a valuable commodity; and to a player it is especially valuable, since his work is purely personal and cannot be reproduced or multiplied, like literature or music or work in the plastic arts. Thus, when the player has won his place, fortune follows, and his power can be turned into wealth, influence, position – that which he may aim at and which it is in him to achieve. Why, then, should he not use this power in the best direction and in the manner most serviceable to himself? . . .

    Let us now, acknowledging the fact that actors have become managers, and with some understanding of how they have achieved the position, consider of what value are the arguments which have been of late advanced against the wisdom of the system. It has been asserted that the reign of actor-managers is responsible for the following: – (1) the exclusion, through personal jealousy, of players of superior excellence; (2) excessive expenditure on the mounting of plays to the starving of the outlay on the company; (3) the acceptance of inferior plays when suitable to the idiosyncrasies of the manager; and (4) an insufficiency of new plays.

First, then, as to the jealousy which excludes good actors. The charge when made is a general one, and, so far as I have found, is unsupported by a single instance of any kind: therefore, as it cannot be refuted in detail, the answer must be a general one. Let it suffice that the same cry has always been made, and will always continue to be so long as there are inferior artists . . .

We may well ask, Where are the good actors who 'never get a chance' through jealousy or from any other cause? A very little examination of the facts will throw a somewhat sad light on the subject, for the unsuccessful ones will be found to fail from some defect of their own in the way of conduct, of self-value, or of personal equipment for the task which they have undertaken. We must not accept a man as justly aggrieved because the world does not take him at his own valuation . . . There is no royal road to success in theatrical management. The matter is a business which must be conducted in a suitable manner and with due knowledge; and as a skilled actor is more or less of an expert in stage matters the probability of his success is greater, *ceteris paribus*,[2] than that of a less skilled person undertaking the same venture.

The second allegation concerning excess of decoration, to the detriment of the salary list, is best met by the simple fact that since the number of theatres has increased – the leading ones coming into the hands of actors – salaries of capable actors have, on the average, nearly doubled. The young people of promise now get, at almost the start of their working lives, larger salaries than were formerly obtained by players on the hither side of greatness . . . In the face of such facts as are within the knowledge of every person in connection with the stage or concerned in the management of a theatre, it is actually absurd to say that the salary list suffers *because* the production is complete. On the contrary, the perfection of one aspect of a play as given shows up any weakness that may exist elsewhere in it, and in every actor-managed theatre in London today it will be found that small parts are, almost of necessity, played by a class of capable actors which a few years ago could only have been found in the second or third ranks of the cast.

Thirdly, any question of the influence of the system of management under consideration on the play-writing of the time touches both the acceptance of plays by managers and the material in the shape of new plays annually produced. The statement that managers only accept plays which suit their individual capacities as actors is really hardly worth serious consideration. Of course a manager only accepts plays suitable to his company, if the company is made up before the play is accepted; and it must not be forgotten that in actor-managed theatres the manager is presumably, at the least, one of the best actors in the theatre, and that, consequently, in the selection of plays the fact has to be borne in mind. It would be silly for any manager to accept a play which could not be properly performed, and, indeed, the first person to object to such a thing would be the author, who would thus see his work imperilled. It is actually now a custom with some authors, when arranging for the production of their plays, to retain the right of a veto on the cast. A manager committed for a season to one company cannot profitably engage another; economic requirements must, as a rule, restrain such business arrangements. When a good play is nowadays accepted a company to suit it is engaged; but this is done at a time and in a manner to suit the policy of the management and the length of its purse. Were a manager to refuse a good play simply because parts in it were too good for others of his company to suit his own vanity, the result of such unworthy and suicidal action would not be uncertain. The house so divided against itself would soon fall.

Fourthly, with regard to the alleged insufficiency of new plays, it must not be forgotten that even dramatists and actors are not always of one mind with regard either to plays or characters in them. . . . But the fact remains that under actor-management good plays increase, and lacking it they decrease. From the time Garrick ceased to manage Drury Lane the production of plays declined. Moreover, there never was a time with regard to the immense output of plays like the present, when the system complained of is in vogue; so that we can only wonder at the abysmal ignorance which underlies the charge. Roughly speaking, from an average of the past few years, a new play of some sort or another is produced for each working day of the year in England, though out of these there is not one, on the average, in each month which makes a success – either financially or *d'estime*. During the good months of the year in London, new plays are produced in large numbers. Certain theatres are conducted with regard to *matinées* for the purpose; plenty of capable actors are always available; stage managers with all the requisite knowledge abound, and costumiers are ready to supply dresses at reasonable cost. There is then no possible difficulty in any author having a play produced on his own account; and a good play when once produced will not have long to wait for a purchaser, or for some manager who will pay fee or royalty. If his wishes and aims be modest the author can easily fulfil them, for, even if he have no capital of his own wherewith to pay expenses, he may obtain the help required by the ordinary method of poor inventors. Where, then, is the difficulty? For what part in the great negative result complained of is the actor-manager responsible? I fear that the answer is too sadly simple to please the carpers. Actor-managers, as a rule, know their business, and will not produce bad plays. Too often the seeker after dramatic honours is not content to avail himself of the means of testing his work open to all. He wants to secure the services of the best artists and to have all done under the most favourable conditions; and he would pick a theatre whose record is such that the public will accept the work of its manager blindfold – partly, indeed, because that manager does not produce anything which is not good. If such manager will not see sufficient merit in a play to warrant its production, the writer is aggrieved. . . . In fact, the unknown aspiring dramatist wants too much; he wishes to share, without any risk or equivalent whatever, a part of the fortune or distinction which other men have won for themselves. It seems *prima facie* unfair to ask that the manager, whose position has been partly assured by discretion in his choice of work, should imperil his acquisition by a divergence, without adequate cause, from his habitual policy. It is, of course, not a pleasure for any man to thwart budding genius, or even to disappoint springing hope; but the serious matter of business must be considered in its proper place and sequence.

As to the influence of the control of theatres by actors on the other arts there is nothing to argue, for the complaint is made by the modern critics themselves that the stage is overladen with scenic effect. This same charge has been in existence ever since the very dawn of the English Drama. . . . That there is large expenditure on the appointments of a modern production is manifest, and that the arts benefit thereby is equally apparent. From time to time some of our best painters and composers are engaged in work for theatres. Alma Tadema, Marcus Stone, Seymour Lucas, Edwin Abbey and Keeley Halsewelle,[3] Sir Arthur Sullivan and Dr Mackenzie[4] are amongst the instances. Beyond this, again, literature itself owes much to the Stage and the player . . .

If any side light be required on the efficiency of the system of actor-management, let us look at the progress of other countries. The modern critics are perpetually quoting the French method as an exemplar in management. Certainly the Comédie Française is a great corporation, and one which has done splendid work; but then in it the plays are selected by the actors. It requires, however, certain improvements to be effected. So long, also, as mere talent is held in corporate esteem without the discriminating admiration which the public has for genius, so long will the Rachels and Bernhardts and Coquelins[5] secede from its ranks, unless accepted under their own conditions. The Germanic nations, too, which have a principle of subsidy in the Court and State theatres, are beginning to find out that genius has an explosive force of its own. When we find already the best theatre in Berlin controlled by an actor – Barnay[6] – we may well look for further development . . .

It is in things theatrical as in all other affairs of life – put matter in solution and it will crystallize if such be its nature, or it will become a sediment in its own way. English freedom has, despite all troubles, evils, and mistakes, made England what she is, and has invariably worked out in time its own economic salvation. Why then, should there be this one exception to all its rules? The natural result of power cannot be denied the men who have passed through the *Sturm und Drang*[7] of artistic endeavour, and who by their knowledge and their gifts can, without losing touch with the people, help to direct public thought. No good object can be achieved by carping at natural laws which fix direction as well as strength in the resultant of multitudinous forces.

NOTES

1 *vox . . . dei* (Lat.) The voice of the people is the voice of God.
2 *ceteris paribus* (Lat.) Other things being equal.
3 *Alma Tadema . . . Keeley Halswelle* Sir Lawrence Alma-Tadema (1836–1912); Marcus Stone (1840–1921); John Seymour Lucas (1849–1923); Edwin Austin Abbey (1852–1911); Keeley Halsewelle (1832–91): prominent figures in the fashionable world of art.
4 *Sir Arthur Sullivan . . . Mackenzie* Sir Arthur Sullivan (1842–1900); Sir Alexander Mackenzie (1847–1935). Irving sought the *cachet* of employing eminent (and expensive) composers for Lyceum productions. Sullivan's *Macbeth* overture (1888) has remained in the concert repertoire.
5 *Rachels . . . Bernhardts . . . Coquelin* Sarah Bernhardt (1845–1923) and Constant Coquelin (1841–1909) appeared with the Comédie–Française in London in 1879; Rachel (1820–58) belonged to an earlier generation.

6   *Barnay*   Ludwig Barnay (1842–1924), principal actor with the Meiningen Company.

7   *Sturm und Drang*   The 'Storm and Stress' element in German Romanticism, particularly associated in the theatre with the work of Goethe and Schiller.

xvi

William Archer on the need for an endowed theatre, 1897

[William Archer (1856–1924) was dramatic critic for *The World* from 1893 to 1898, wrote an important essay on the theory of acting (*Masks or Faces*, 1888) and was one of Ibsen's earliest translators and advocates. In an introduction to a volume of dramatic criticisms, *The Theatrical 'World' of 1896* (1897), Archer set out the arguments for subsidized theatre. He points out that *laissez-faire* economics dictate a narrow artistic policy in the theatre and require that star actors appears in excessively long continuous runs of mediocre plays: 'I take my stand upon the plain facts of political economy, or, in other words, of human nature.']

ART FOR THE MULTITUDE MEANS MEDIOCRE ART

Can there be any plainer fact than that the highest art does not, in its novelty at any rate, appeal to the greatest number? or, in other words, that delicate artistic perception is not a universally, or even a very widely, diffused gift? If, then, a certain form of art is compelled, as the first condition of its existence, to make immediate appeal to a vast multitude of people, it follows that, do what they will, the practitioners of that art cannot possibly rise above mediocrity.

This is precisely the situation of the English dramatist. He is at present compelled, on pain of sheer extinction, to enlist the immediate suffrages, or, in plainer English, to gather in the punctual half-crowns, of a far larger body of people than can possibly be expected to have any relish for the most delicate forms of art. On the other hand, in a community like ours, there exists, beyond all question, a public within the public, which is capable of enjoying and paying for the very best that theatrical art can do. Under present conditions, the dramatist has no means of getting at this public, this public has no means of bringing its demands to bear upon the dramatist. The Repertory Theatre, which must at first be to some extent an Endowed Theatre, is required to afford a meeting-place for the artist-playwright and the art-loving (as opposed to the merely show-loving) public.

THE MANAGERS POWERLESS

Pray observe that I am not attacking or criticizing the actor-manager or the commercial impresario. Cases do, no doubt, occur in which they seem to conduct their business with insufficient intelligence; but, taking our leading actor-managers as a body, one gladly admits that they do for art all that can reasonably be expected of them. They are the slaves of their conditions. They are forced to bid for great successes, because small successes are no successes at all. So inert, unwieldy, and unselective is our overgrown public, that, practically speaking, either everybody or nobody goes to see a given play. You must run your hundred nights at the very least, or you have scored a failure, – you have probably lost money, certainly prestige. And so deplorable are the conditions that a manager cannot even, on the strength of a great success, treat himself to a little artistic experiment. If he ventures upon a 'trial matinée', his evening receipts at once fall off. It is the old story: 'To him that hath shall be given'; success only comes with a rush, and no sooner does the sapient public suspect that the rush is over than it loses interest in a play, and the rush is over indeed. How far I am from holding the managers responsible for the existing state of things may be seen in the very fact that I look for salvation only in a new mechanism, or, more precisely, a new fulcrum for the application of a new leverage. If individual intelligence were sufficient to break the vicious circle, there would be no need to agitate for co-operation and endowment.

'THE LAW OF THE HUNDRED THOUSAND'

Let us deal in round numbers, and suppose that a 'good house' at a theatre like the Haymarket or the St James's means 1000 people. To rank as a success at all, a play must run, to good houses, at least 100 nights. That is to say, it must in the course of less than four months be seen by 100,000 people; and a great majority of these people must take considerable pleasure in it, else the first audiences will advise others not to go to it, and, after dragging on for a month or six weeks, the play will be withdrawn, a confessed failure. Now, it is absurd to imagine that there are in London, at any one time, 100,000 playgoers of keen intelligence and delicate artistic perception – capable, in short, of appreciating the highest order of drama. If there were such a public, London would be the most artistic city on record – a modern Athens in very deed. Nowhere and at no time has the best work found so large a public centred in one spot and waiting to acclaim it. Even in Paris, with its cosmopolitan population of theatre-goers, it may be said, roughly, that the maximum of immediate success ever attained by a serious play is about equivalent to the minimum demanded of an English author . . .

THE LAW OF THE HUNDRED THOUSAND MUST BE ELUDED

If we are to make any substantial and permanent advance beyond this point – and there is no alternative between advance and retreat – we must enable dramatists to appeal to a public consisting of (say) a tenth part of the Hundred Thousand, with some fifteen or twenty thousand more recruited from the class which now very rarely goes to the theatre, simply because it takes no interest in *Red Robes* and *Circus Girls*. Can any one doubt that there are in London at the present moment 25,000 people capable of relishing really delicate dramatic work, if only they knew where to look for it? Now 25,000 people at an average of four shillings a head mean £5000 – a sum which would scarcely spell ruin for the entertainment or beggary for the author. And of course this 25,000 would be merely the nucleus of the public which a Repertory Theatre would gather round it. This is the minimum which could be relied upon for any play that was not an absolute artistic failure. The theatre neither could, would, nor should restrict itself to the production of plays that are above the heads of the multitude. Both in the classical and in the modern drama it should aim at 'great successes' – productions which should have their three or four repetitions a week until they had reached eighty or a hundred performances in the season. The point is not to have *no* runs but to have no *unbroken* runs, and to establish as the standard of honourable success something less heroic than the instant conquest of the Hundred Thousand . . .

The reader may have observed, not without suspicion of some logical thimble-rigging, that the theatre we are discussing appears under three designations, now as an Endowed or Subsidized Theatre, again as a Repertory Theatre, and in the last paragraph as an Artistic Theatre. Let me assure him that I am blameless, in intent at any rate, of any dialectical sleight-of-hand. The three terms are, to my mind, absolutely synonymous. We cannot have an Artistic Theatre, in the large and permanent sense of the word, which shall not be a Repertory Theatre, where unbroken runs are barred; and we cannot have a Repertory Theatre without an Endowment or Subsidy to enforce its constitution and bar the runs. The three epithets represent three aspects of one and the same thing. 'Artistic' points to the end, the other epithets point to the conditions and means. Let us now disregard, for a moment, the conditions and means, and simply ask ourselves what an Artistic Theatre should be and do – what is implied in the idea?

(i) IN RELATION TO THE ENGLISH CLASSIC DRAMA

An Artistic Theatre, in the first place, should keep alive as much of the national drama of the past as is found to have any abiding theatrical vitality. All Shakespeare is in a certain sense vital simply because it *is* Shakespeare. The fact of his transcendent genius lends interest even to his prentice-work and his failures; the glory of his great achievements is diffused over even his lesser efforts. Thus the whole of his actable plays (and the qualification excludes, I think, only *Titus Andronicus* and perhaps *Troilus and Cressida*) should be passed in review every ten years or so; while the great masterpieces should be constantly re-studied and reproduced at intervals of two, three, four, at the outside five years. Then a series of judicious experiments would presently bring together a representative acting-list of Elizabethan, Jacobean, Restoration, and Georgian plays, in which the history of the English drama – not inglorious, after all, even apart from Shakespeare – should be illustrated and brought home to us. It could then no longer be said that no modern nation has so rich a dramatic literature and so poor a theatre.

(ii) IN RELATION TO FOREIGN CLASSICS

An Artistic Theatre ought to have on its acting-list some representative classics of the foreign and even the antique stage. It is true that the drama is of all forms of literature most difficult of transplantation, and that English, as compared with German at any rate, is a refractory medium for the translator. Our stage, perhaps, could never become so eclectic as that of Germany, and there would be no use in attempting to force the national genius in that direction. Still, we are not so hopelessly insular as to be unable to relish in the theatre a few representative works of Calderon and Molière, Schiller and Goethe. In dealing with the foreign as with our own classical drama, judicious experiment would soon discriminate the plays which still live from those which (for us) are dead. Heaven forbid that we should persist in haling corpses to the footlights, however great the names attached to them!

(iii) IN RELATION TO THE MODERN DRAMA

An Artistic Theatre should above all things foster every kind of artistic effort in contemporary drama. It should exclude nothing except pedantry, stupidity, and vulgarity. The touch of the artist may reveal itself in farce no less than in drama, in romance no less than in realism. Form, classification, matters very little; it is the amount of specifically dramatic talent infused into the form that gives the work its value. No form is quite hopeless. A great genius might even put fresh life into the five-act tragedy in blank verse; though this indeed seems to touch on the outer verge of the improbable. An artistic theatre should no more seek to galvanize plays that are born dead, merely because their form is ambitious, than it should seek to resurrect plays that have died of old age. Life – that quality which no one can define, but which sane and sincere perception can always recognize – should be the first and last essential to be insisted on. But in practice, no doubt, the modern plays which would for the most part come within the sphere of the theatre we are conceiving would be of a more or less serious order. Lighter pieces, farcical or idyllic, would not be excluded, if only they showed the artist's touch; but as such plays can generally secure a hearing at the ordinary theatres, they would only in exceptional cases come in the way of this particular institution. The plays which would find in it their natural home would be those of a too high seriousness or too subtle humour to make immediate appeal to the multitude. These, as I have tried to show in the foregoing pages, are the plays which require an Artistic Theatre, and which an Artistic Theatre requires . . .

[Archer suggests that more than one auditorium may be found necessary – citing the Residenz and Hof theatres in Munich. He envisages the beneficial effect of the new regime on young actors, given greater range and more strenuous practice in different kinds of play, and then turns to consider the effect on the public.]

(v) IN RELATION TO THE PUBLIC

An Artistic Theatre, finally, should aim at becoming, in a certain sense, the established rendezvous of artlovers of all classes. It should gradually, yet not *too* gradually, gather around it a public, critical but sympathetic, which should take a personal interest in its fortunes and pride in its successes. And it should offer every possible hospitality to such a public. The abonnement[2] system, which obtains at all the great theatres of the Continent, but which the long run renders impossible, should be introduced and carefully fostered. Artistically it is most desirable, bringing the actors into a human and sympathetic relation with their audiences; and financially it is a tower of strength. Even to non-subscribers, prices should be moderate. As it would not be necessary to squeeze the last farthing of profit out of the space at disposal, the seats in all parts of the house should be roomy, and the rows wide enough to enable people to leave and return to their places with moderate comfort to themselves and others. The tedium of entr'actes to an audience packed into its seats like the pieces in a mosaic is at present one of the chief deterrents from theatre-going. Everything should be done to remove this drawback. Spacious corridors and comfortable crush-rooms[3] should be provided; ladies as well as men should be enabled and encouraged to leave their places between the acts; and these intervals, devoted to fresh air and conversation, should not only cease to be deterrent, but should take a distinct place among the attractions of an evening at the play. The theatre, in short, should be a sort of art-club or intellectual hostelry, where the bodily comfort of the members or guests should be in every way consulted, and their minds predisposed to a genial receptivity.

NOTE

1   *Red Robes and Circus Girls*   i.e. romantic dramas and musical comedies: *Under the Red Robe* by Edward Rose (1896) and *The Circus Girl* by J. Tanner and W. Palings (1896).
2   *abonnement*   (Fr.) subscription.
3   *crush-rooms*   Foyers.

A provincial impresario, c.1900

[From 'A chat with Milton Bode', *The Era*, 2 February 1901. Bode's interests included the ownership of theatres and the management of music-hall stars, as well as touring companies with productions – mainly musical comedies and melodramas – in which he held the provincial rights. His opinions on the relationship between London and the provinces are particularly interesting.]

Mr Milton Bode is thirty-eight years of age, and he speaks about the provincial stage with twenty years' varied experience, neither more nor less. He has worked his way steadily through 'fit-ups' and 'second rights' to the position of distinction that he now occupies among provincial managers. There is not a yard of the United Kingdom, but is known to him – with its theatrical value; and there is not a vicissitude of the actor's life that he cannot speak of . . .

[At the age of sixteen he left home to join the circus.]

Mr Bode's first employer in the theatre was the late Mr Fred Nelson, then a prominent south country manager, with whom he remained for several years. A later employer was Mr Balsir Chatterton. Eventually Mr Bode reached the Adelphi in the capacity of second low comedian, about the time that the run of *London Day by Day* was in progress. But Mr Bode, who has never had his whole heart in the work of acting, was at the same time using his unique knowledge of the provinces for the purpose of booking tours. He also transacted Mr George Alexander's provincial business for him. As his work extended Mr Bode ceased to act, and now regards himself as a manager exclusively. Naught comes amiss to him – he ran *Dr Bill*, *Liberty Hall* and *Lord Anerley* in the provinces; he has been a great purveyor of pantomime; now he is running *Gentleman Joe*, *The French Maid*, *Tommy Atkins*, *Women and Wine*, *Lights o' London* and *Saved from the Sea*.

But in regard to comic or serious pieces, Mr Bode has deliberately arrived at the conclusion that the playgoer, and especially the provincial playgoer, would rather laugh than weep.

What is more, he does not think that the means by which laughter is provoked should be too elegant or subtle. Broad fun – not meaning thereby improper fun – is the saleable commodity at this moment . . .

Before the provincial production [of the musical comedy commissioned by him, *Gentleman Joe*], Mr Bode was brought into communication with Mr Roberts, who sought a piece for the Prince of Wales's Theatre, and in these circumstances the comedy was leased to Mr Roberts and his partners, who produced it with a success that is well known. 'I believe,' says he, 'in engaging the very best people that my means will allow me to engage, treating them well, and particularly in not superintending them, except for urgent reasons. A provincial audience is very sharp in noting a change of cast between one visit and another, and if the change has been dictated merely by the desire to economize, resents this depreciation in the value of the entertainment.'

Mr Bode strenuously refuses to admit that theatrical business is bad in the provinces. He stoutly avers that there are more playgoers in the provinces than ever there were, and that a really good travelling company is in a far better position for money-making than ever before. But there is always room at the top – good companies find employment readily, at liberal terms. Mr Bode's operations have acquired a considerable magnitude. At the present moment he is running panto-mimes in Glasgow, Dublin, Chester, Cardiff, Newcastle and Grimsby.

One asks Mr Bode how far a preliminary success in London is essential to a success in the provinces, and he explains that it varies greatly in different circumstances. For instance, much more reliance is placed on London taste and judgement in the south of England than in the north of England. As to the phrase 'London Success', Mr Bode is fain to return it for particulars. There are so many varieties of London success. For example, a melodrama that has the cachet of Drury Lane, a burlesque that has the cachet of the Gaiety, and a comic opera that has the cachet of the Savoy are assured of approval in the provinces. But the vague bluff of the showman that his piece has achieved a triumph (for a week) at a second-class London theatre has ceased altogether to deceive the provincial playgoer. There are certain provincial managers who have established an independent reputation, and whose visits are awaited with pleasant expectation in various towns. Mr Bode has, by the way, theatres at Carlisle, Reading, Chester, Eastbourne, Pontypridd, London, Huddersfield, and Llandudno under his management; also Mr Dan Leno,* whom he pays £200 per week, commences his third tour under his management July 22nd this year.

NOTE

*   *Dan Leno*   (1860–1904), music-hall comedian.

Part V

The Author's Work

The improvements in payment and working conditions of Victorian dramatic authors reflect directly the other changes in the status of the theatre. The prosperous and respected men of letters who dominated the late Victorian and Edwardian stage seem to have little in common with the poorly paid hacks of the 1830s and 1840s. Some degree of just dealing was introduced by the legislation of 1833 and the founding of the Dramatic Authors' Society (see ii) but this amounted to a protection of rights rather than an increase in the fees themselves. In his *Life and Adventures* (1895) the playwright and journalist George Augustus Sala remembered that Reynoldson, the 'stock author' at the Princess's in the 1840s, under Maddox's management, received not more than £3 a week. In 1853 Sala and his brother were paid the 'prodigious' sum of 25s. a night by the Surrey Theatre for their version of *The Corsican Brothers*: Sala recalls the manager beginning an interview with the words, 'Well, sir, we have given as much as five pounds for a farce.' (I, 310.) Few dramatists could expect to make a living by their plays alone: most were active in other branches of the literary industry, several (including W.S. Gilbert) were barristers. With so many playwrights involved in journalism it is not surprising that there were frequent accusations of favouritism and corruption in dramatic reviewing (see vi, on John Oxenford).

Towards the end of the century there were instances of considerable wealth derived in large part from writing for the stage. The judicious sale of American and provincial rights and advantageous percentages for London runs benefited successful authors. In 1898 Arnold Bennett recorded in his journal that an indiscreet friend in the Income Tax office at Somerset House had told him that the assessment of the popular melodramatist George R. Sims had recently gone up from £3000 to £5000 – at a time when the rate was about one shilling in the pound (*The Journal of Arnold Bennett*, I, 81–2). At Pinero's death in 1934 his gross estate was reckoned at £63,310 16s. 10d. Both W.S. Gilbert and Henry Arthur Jones were wealthy men when they died.

One man's career, spanning six decades, is emblematic of the century's changes. Dion Boucicault (1820–90) was an engaging and successful actor and a jobbing dramatist. After the success of *London Assurance* (1840) he was associated with Benjamin Webster at the Adelphi and Charles Kean at the Princess's and was responsible for a number of successful adaptations of French melodramas (notably *The Corsican Brothers*, 1852). According to Sala, Boucicault's salary at this time did not exceed £15 a week. His labours were rewarded with a 'meagre weekly salary and the deprivation of authorial rights.' (Sala, I, 307, iii.) After a period in the United States, where he worked for the reform of dramatic copyright, he returned to London with the first of his Irish melodramas, *The Colleen Bawn*. Because this play had proved itself in New York he was able to insist on advantageous terms for his rewards as actor and author and for his wife as leading actress. Boucicault is particularly associated with the establishment of the royalty system for authors and the practice of long runs rather than the alternation of plays in repertory. When *Arrah-Na-Pogue* was staged at the Princesss's in 1867 Boucicault was billed as author and actor, and the public was informed that his own French translation of the play had been given in Paris – a satisfying reversal of the author's earlier position as a drudge translating French originals. In the course of his energetic career as actor, author and manager Boucicault earned and spent enormous amounts of money, but it was not so much his prosperity as his artistic control and assertion of the author's rights that give him his importance in the development of the profession.

Like Boucicault, Tom Robertson secured responsibility for the staging of his own plays. Under the old dispensation, the playwright was likely to be asked for a play to fit scenery or costumes – as happened to J. R. Planché when he was told that the management's acquisition of Scottish dresses made it necessary to set a vampire melodrama (as its French author had) in Scotland, a country historically free from any allegation of vampirism.

The same movement towards ever greater historical realism that brought about the Shakespearean 'revivals' set standards of consistency and realism that some managements extended to the dialogue and incidents of the plays produced. Robertson's stage-management, his gifts as a writer of domestic drama and the talents and social ambitions of the Bancrofts chimed together. W.S. Gilbert was remarkable for the high standards he demanded from the interpreters of his work, and for working out moves and business on a model stage. At the same time, Carte's managerial policy catered for a taste that was veering away from conventional production values for burlesque and comic opera: the settings for the Savoy Operas were tasteful and accurate in their depiction of local colour. As the success of their plays brought them leverage in the theatrical world, Arthur Wing Pinero and Henry Arthur Jones dealt on equal terms with the managers. In one remarkable letter to George Alexander, Pinero (who had been an actor) stated quite frankly the terms on which they could work together: 'To put the case shortly, there is not room for two autocrats in one small kingdom; and in every detail, however slight, that pertains to my work – though I avail myself gratefully of any assistance that is afforded me – I take to myself the right of dictation and veto' (*Collected Letters*, ed. Wearing, 1974, p. 181). Wilde's artistic and financial relationship with the same manager was less formal, but even when allowance is made for Wilde's customary pose of nonchalance, a letter to Alexander in the summer of 1894, when he was contemplating *The Importance of Being Earnest*, reflects the sums of money in question and the author's bargaining power:

> The real charm of the play, if it is to have a charm, must be in the dialogue. The plot is slight, but I think, adequate. . . . Well, I think an amusing thing with lots of fun and wit might be made. if you think so too, and care to have the refusal of it, do let me know, and send me £150. If when the play is finished, you think it too slight – not serious enough – of course you can have the £150 back. I want to go away and write it, and it could be ready in October, as I have nothing else to do . . . In the meanwhile, my dear Aleck, I am so pressed for money that I don't know what to do. Of course I am extravagant. You have always been a good wise friend to me, so think what you can do.
>
> (*Letters*, ed. Hart-Davis, 1962, p.389)

Wilde's presence in rehearsals allegedly became bothersome, but he was responsive to Alexander's requests for revision, even to the point of reducing the play from four to three acts. In an interview at the time of *A Woman of No Importance* in 1893 the actress Mrs Bernard Beere commented on Wilde's readiness to 'alter and cut down his work to suit stage purposes.' (*Sketch*, 26 April 1893.) In other letters Wilde gives Alexander detailed (and sometimes corrective) notes on staging. Successful playwrights of Wilde's generation had more power in the author–actor–manager triangle

27   The commonest form of printed play: French's and Dicks' editions.

than most of their predecessors. In selling the rights of their plays to American managers they could demand good terms and exert a degree of control over staging and casting – the letters from Jones (xvi) are representative of similar correspondence by Pinero, Shaw and Wilde. Shaw's contract with the American actor Richard Mansfield for *Arms and the Man* (1894) stipulates that the text 'as contained in the prompt copy supplied by the Author to the Manager' shall be performed fully (*Letters*, ed. Laurence, 1965, p. 442). With the exception of some authors who produced and acted in their own plays (à la Boucicault) the situation of the dramatists of the 1890s represented the most radical alteration possible within the framework of an unsubsidized theatre.

By the same token, authors were now anxious that their plays should be published in a form resembling that of 'respectable' literary works. The US Senate's ratification of International Copyright in 1891 made it profitable to publish plays for the general book trade. The popular series issued by Lacy's (subsequently French's), Dicks' and other publishers catered primarily for a market of theatrical amateurs and professionals, and had no pretensions to elegance or permanence (illus. 27). Better paper, clearer print and more generous margins were required. Authorial prefaces would now replace the brief summary of the play's salient points and the list of costumes and scenes that were provided in the 'acting editions'. The most extreme manifestation of this tendency is Shaw's provision of lengthy descriptive stage directions, designed to give readers as much information on the appearance of characters and scenes as they would find in a novel, and the prefaces in which he elaborates the point of view that informs each play. Henry Arthur Jones collaborated with French's on a style of presentation in which the technical directions required by amateur producers ('L.U.E.' for Left Upper Entrance, 'D.S.' for Downstage, etc.) were banished to a margin, allowing a free, uncluttered flow of text.

In all these aspects of the author's rising artistic and social status, the concept of control and unity is a key element. By the turn of the century the 'straight' play – what would once have been referred to as a 'legitimate' drama – with any pretensions to artistic standing, was expected to exhibit a degree of unified, harmonious effect in which the author's part was given considerable prominence. The cruder spectacular melodramas and most pantomimes still relegated the author to a subsidiary position: the spectacles staged by Augustus Harris were thought of primarily as 'Drury Lane' dramas.

But the more fashionable theatres gave their authors a prominence second only to that of the leading actors and actresses. Sometimes – as with many Shakespearean productions and most of the Lyceum's repertoire under Irving – the claim to be serving an author's purposes was more diplomatic than true. But such sagas as Shaw's struggles with performers over the interpretation of his plays are of a different order from the tribulations of the young Boucicault. Although interpretation of their work may be focused more profitably away from whatever we know of the individual playwright's identity and intentions, the Victorian perception of 'progress' in this area of culture was firmly rooted in the dramatist's rise to power – his (or, rarely, her) achievement of the status of independent, authoritative artist. Writing for the theatre, it was argued, had to offer the dignity and rewards that would attract the best intellects, and the intelligent middle class must feel able to lead the rest of society to the temples of the new art. The failure of the theatre in the 1800s to fulfil the needs of the Romantic poets must somehow be expiated.

But legislation failed to keep pace with the need for adaptation to new circumstances. The author was still the primary victim of pre-emptive censorship by the Lord Chamberlain's Office – a practice that did not cease until 1968 (see xv, and Pinero's remarks on the subject in xxi). Although, strictly speaking, any physical or vocal aspect of a theatrical performance was subject to the censor, it was the text that received the most thorough inspection. The Lord Chamberlain's readers were anxious to detect any immoral, indecorous or blasphemous tendency, and to prevent the impersonation of political or other well-known personalities on stage. Biblical subjects were taboo, including that of Wilde's *Salomé*, although such sanctimonious religious dramas as Wilson Barrett's *The Sign of the Cross* were acceptable. Allusion as well as debate was stifled. Although he may have been unfair to the individual (whose death was the occasion of his article), Shaw's vituperative description of the tastes and preoccupations of one examiner of plays, Edward Pigott, gives a sense of the gap between what some authors wished to discuss through the theatre and what censorship wished to keep out of it:

> He had French immorality on the brain; he had the womanly woman on the brain; he had the Divorce Court on the brain; his official career in relation to the higher drama was one long folly and panic, in which the only thing definitely discernible in a welter of intellectual confusion was his conception of the English people rushing towards an abyss of national degradation in morals and manners, and only held back on the edge of the precipice by the grasp of his strong hand.
>
> *(Our Theatres in the Nineties*, 1932, I, 49)

That Shaw was not wide of his mark may be gathered from Pigott's evidence in the 1892 Report of the Select Committee on Theatres and Places of Entertainment. His aim was 'to guard the credit and dignity of the profession' against unscrupulous speculators. 'As a servant of the Crown [the Lord Chamberlain's office] prevents scandals of which public opinion would otherwise demand a vigorous repression.' And Ibsen?

> I have studied Ibsen's plays pretty carefully, and all the characters in Ibsen's plays appear to me morally deranged. All the heroines are dissatisfied spinsters who look on marriage as a monopoly, or dissatisfied married women in a chronic state of rebellion against not only the conditions

which nature has imposed on their sex, but against all the duties and obligations of mothers and wives; and as for the men they are all rascals or imbeciles.

(Question 5227)

At least there was some consolation in Pigott's belief that pre-emptive censorship was hardly necessary in the case of Ibsen, as his plays would never attract significant numbers of the population.

Quite apart from its iniquities as a denial of civil freedom, the censorship was a formidable obstacle to the development of a serious theatre, a strong disincentive to any writer who might contemplate using the play rather than the novel as a vehicle for debate.

i

The author's poor rewards, 1832

[Douglas Jerrold's plays were enormously popular, but brought him little financial reward. In evidence before the 1832 Select Committee he described his fees for *Black-Eyed Susan* (1829), his most enduring success. The actor T.P. Cooke (1786–1864), who played William in Jerrold's melodrama, specialized in portraying nautical heroes. *The Rent Day* (1832) was a domestic drama inspired by Sir David Wilkie's painting *Distraining for Rent*. Asked why he thought that a fairer system of payment would result in less translated and more original plays, Jerrold told the committee that 'it would be worth the while of men of original talent to devote their energies to the theatres.']

2790. Do you think that you should obtain much remuneration from the provincial theatres, or from the other theatres in the metropolis [if legislation were to enforce authors' copyright]? – I think in the agggregate, I might obtain a great deal by receiving a small sum from each theatre. I will instance *Black-Eyed Susan*, which was played 400 nights in the course of the first year after its production.

2791. In different theatres? – Yes, 150 nights at the Surrey, I think; perhaps 100 nights at Sadler's Wells, 100 nights at the Pavilion, 30 nights at Covent Garden theatre, and at other houses, as the West London and the Olympic, a few nights. For that piece I received altogether as much as Mr T.P.Cooke has informed the committee he received for six nights' acting at Covent Garden theatre.

2792. Sixty pounds? – Yes.

2793. That was from the first theatre? – Yes.

2794. Do you suppose if the other theatres had had to remunerate you, they would have acted it? – Certainly. It would have amounted to a great sum to me if it had been paid even on the humble terms of 5s. a night throughout the country.

2795. Was it published? – It was.

2796. Then the Surrey theatre has lost all control over it? – Yes, but I could have had no control over it, if it had not been published.

2797.   Did you receive anything from the publisher? – I received £10 for the copyright, which, with £50 I received from the theatre, make the £60 altogether. If it had not been published I should not have received more money, as in the instance of *The Rent-Day*. That piece was played in the country a fortnight after it was produced at Drury Lane, and I have a letter in my pocket in which the manager said he would very willingly have given me £5 for a copy of the piece, had he not before paid £2 for it to some stranger.

2798.   Some stranger? – Yes, I have no doubt where he got it from. There is an agency office where they are obtained.

2799.   What agency office? – Mr Kenneth,* at the corner of Bow Street, will supply any gentleman with any manuscript on the lowest terms.

2800.   How does he procure them; is it by a short-hand writer in the theatre? – He steals them somehow; he has no right to them.

2801.   This is previous to publication? – Previous to publication.

2802.   It must be done by a short-hand writer? – I do not know how it is done. I offered to sell copies of the *The Rent-Day* for £5, because an author receives a double injury: in the first place, they are not paid for their pieces, and in the next place, they are represented by the skeletons of their dramas; so that, as it was emphatically said by a sufferer, the author was not only robbed but murdered . . .

2805.   Do you consider the remuneration to dramatic authors is not sufficient to attract first-rate talent to that branch of composition? – Certainly not, when periodical writing and novels are so highly paid for. A gentleman will get £1000 for a novel, and Mr Sheridan Knowles only got £400 for *The Hunchback*.

2806.   Did you apply to Covent Garden for additional remuneration for *Black-Eyed Susan*? – I did; and I received a letter from Mr Bartley, the manager, in which he expressed something more than surprise at the request, and said the representation of that piece at Covent Garden theatre had done me a great deal of good. I have not yet discovered that.

2807.   In point of reputation, he meant? – The reputation I acquired did not give me sufficient influence to get a piece brought out the next season at Covent Garden.

2808.   But certainly the reputation of being the author of a piece which had been played so many nights would do you good? – Not at Covent Garden. It was played 30 nights there, and Mr Cooke left Covent Garden to play at the Surrey.

2809.   On what stage did it appear to most advantage? – On the Surrey, certainly; in fact, it was infinitely better played at the Surrey than Covent Garden.

2810.   What did you receive for *The Rent-Day* at Drury Lane? – £150.

2811.   How many nights has it been acted? – I am not certain, for I was out of town towards the close; I believe either 43 or 44.

2812.   Did you receive the £150 at the close? – On the twenty-fifth night.

NOTE

*   *Mr Kenneth, at the corner of Bow-Street*   Apparently the William Kenneth listed in contemporary trade directories as a bookseller at 22 Great Russell Street, Covent Garden.

ii

The Dramatic Authors' Act, 1833

[From James Robinson Planché's *Recollections and Reflections* (2 vols., 1872).]

On the 10th of June, 1833 . . . the Royal assent was given to the Dramatic Authors' Act, and a society was immediately formed to facilitate the working of it, with the least possible inconvenience to managers; for the clear and simple words of the Act, about which there could be no mistake, certainly placed the proprietors or lessees of provincial theatres in a very awkward situation. The performance of any sort of dramatic entertainment, 'or any portion thereof', without the consent in writing of its author or his assignee, 'rendered the parties representing or causing it to be represented, liable to a penalty of not less than forty shillings for every offence, or an action for damages either to the amount which it could be proved the author had suffered, or of what the manager had gained by the representation, at the option of the author, with double costs of suit.' The director of a theatre any distance from London, therefore, could not, under sudden and unexpected circumstances, change his bill, and put up a protected drama, without incurring the penalty, or exposing himself to an action for damages according to the terms of the statute, as it would be impossible for him to obtain, in the course of two or three hours, the written permission required; and in any case he would be compelled to correspond and make separate terms with every individual author whose pieces he was desirous of producing.

It was, consequently, as much to the interest of the managers as to that of the authors, if indeed not more so, that some arrangement should be made by which the obvious difficulty could be avoided.

By the establishment of a society in London, with a secretary who should be authorized by the members generally to grant conditional permission as the agent of the author, and the fixing of a scale of prices, according to the size of the theatre, for every class of protected dramas, managers were enabled to play whatever they pleased without fear of legal proceedings, and could calculate exactly the expenses they were incurring. Accustomed, however, for so many years to ignore the rights of authors, the recognition of them by the law of the land was anything but palatable to managers in general, and it was really as pitiable as ludicrous to observe the mean shifts and dishonest practices to which many resorted to escape the payment of a few shillings to a poor dramatist, while they would have considered it disgraceful to quit the town without paying the butcher or butterman's bill, or to leave their landlord to whistle for the rent of his lodgings.

Of course there were freebooters, in this as well as other professions, who had a more lofty disdain for the distinctions of *meum* and *tuum*, and who, not being worth powder and shot, carried on their depredations openly and with impunity. These unscrupulous persons were thorns in the side not only of the authors, but of respectable managers, under whose very noses they opened portable theatres or booths, in which they played for nothing the pieces the others honestly paid for, frequently anticipating their production at the regular theatre, and therefore diminishing their attraction. This was a very reasonable cause of complaint to the society from honourable managers with whom we were in regular communication. Unfortunately, however, we had no power to protect them, as these offenders were, like the ghost in *Hamlet* – 'here', 'there', and 'gone' before a writ could be served upon them; so we were, and still are, obliged to grin and endure it . . .

On the first introduction of our Bill, an outcry was raised by the country managers of their inability, in the depressed state of theatrical affairs, to bear any, the smallest, additional burden. Upon the same ground it might have been argued, that a man who could not afford to purchase goods to retail, was entitled to steal them.

The great champion of these dissentients, Mr Wilkins, an architect, and proprietor of several provincial theatres, declared before the committee of the House of Commons, that in his opinion no modern dramatist, Mr Knowles perhaps excepted, deserved to be paid; while, in the same breath, he admitted that nothing but the melodramas and other pieces successfully produced in London by the writers he was insulting would draw money in the country. On being examined before the same committee, I commented on his self-convicting evidence, and contended that if the performance of a drama merely lessened the loss of the manager one penny, the author of it was entitled to a farthing. The manager was not compelled to play the piece, and assuredly would not unless he believed he should profit by it; and if he did not, by what right did he cause the author to be a sharer in his speculations? On the passing of the Bill, a dinner was given by the newly-formed society at the Thatched House Tavern in St James's Street, to Mr Edward Lytton Bulwer[1] and his brother Henry (now Lord Dalling); and in the first year of the operation of the Act, the money sent up from the various country theatres to the agent of the Society amounted to nearly £800, independently of the payments merged in Mr Knowles's own engagement as an actor, which must have added considerably to his portion. Trifling as this sum was, compared with that drawn from the provinces during the same period in France (M. Scribe[2] alone receiving more than three times that amount), it was at least so much gained by those who would not otherwise have got a shilling, and established a system which, I trust, may one day produce to the widow or child of a deservedly popular dramatist an income, which the precarious nature of his profession renders it all but impossible he should bequeath to them in the more satisfactory form of 'Three per cent. Reduced' in the Bank of England.

NOTES

1   *Mr Edward Lytton Bulwer*   See note 1, p. 26 above. The name appears in various forms.
2   *M. Scribe*   Eugène Scribe (1791–1861), French dramatist and one of the chief originators of the 'well-made play.'

iii

An author's terms, 1830s

[Letters from the actor and dramatist John Baldwin Buckstone to Frederick Yates, co-manager of the Adelphi Theatre. The letters are quoted by his son, the journalist Edmund Yates, in his *Recollections and Experiences* (1879; 4th edn, 1885). Both plays referred to were attributed publicly to Buckstone as sole author.]

1838
As we have had no decided arrangement about *The Rake*, and as whatever terms we can agree upon about that piece will influence my future doings, I wish to state a few matters for you to think about: £50 was mentioned by you for it, and afterwards an additional £10 for securing the acting copyright in the provinces for twelve months. I was allowed £60 for *Henriette*, and really, with the prices I can now command, I am working at a very low rate in letting you have three-act dramas at that sum. For a successful three-act play you ought, I think, to afford me £70, such sum securing to you the sole acting right for ever in London, and to you alone for one year, or, say, to the 1st October following its production.

1839

I will do your piece for the opening, and a new three-act drama for Mrs Yates, company, and self, for my old terms for the pair, viz., two seventies. I really cannot say less. I now get £100 for a three-act piece, when it only runs a few nights. I bring out a full three-act comedy at the Haymarket immediately on the close of Covent Garden, and am now cogitating a farce for Power* and myself.

[Edmund Yates comments:]

So we see that at his increased rates Buckstone received £70 for a three-act drama, and £10 for the provincial rights for twelve months. Now I have been furnished by a worthy friend of mine, a writer of melodrama of the present day, whose name, for obvious reasons, I shall not mention, with a return of the fees which he has received for one piece alone, which at the time of writing are within £150 of a total of *ten thousand pounds*, and which are still rolling in at the rate of £100 a week! In this return, America, really unknown in the earlier days as a money-producer for the English dramatist, figures for £800 more than London; the provinces, valued by Buckstone at a £10 note, yield nearly £3000; while Australia, at that time chiefly known as a receptacle for convicts, yields more than double the amount paid by my father for the whole acting copyright.

NOTE

*   *Power*   Tyrone Power (b.1795), Irish actor; drowned at sea on his way back from America, 1841.

Macready and Bulwer-Lytton prepare *Money*, 1840

[Bulwer-Lytton's comedy of modern life, *Money*, was staged with the precise and conscientious realism that Macready brought to his historical pieces – including Shakespeare. These two letters from Charles H. Shattuck's edition of the correspondence of actor and author illustrate the kind and degree of detail sought by both. Macready's letter is given in full, the author's in part: the eccentricities of spelling and emphasis in both have been kept, but contractions have been expanded in Bulwer-Lytton's.]

Macready to Bulwer, 1 November 1840
I would have written you yesterday, but I wanted two important things – health & time. I am now driven up to a few minutes – Imprimis – about the Club-room – it is needful the scene *Act 3rd Scene last* & *Act 5th Scene 1st* should be the same – that the *Club* – the locus in quo should be ascertained. *What room is it* to be? – the drawing-room – or the Coffee-room – Qu. – *Drawing-room.* – Say definitively for the working of the scene stops, till I know. It will be important to *discover the Club-scene*, that the drawing-room – Act 3rd Scene 1st – should change to a room as if of Lady Franklin's – nearer to the proscenium. – This can be very well done, by the Servant – entering after – 'approach of the Honeymoon is to the Human Race' & saying 'My Lady will see you now, Sir:' – Will you give Graves a few lines to take him off with the servant – *change scene.* – *Enter Servant & Graves – Servant* – 'I thought My Lady was here, Sir: – I'll tell her you're waiting' – exit. *Graves.* 'My heart beats,' &c &c. – to the End. *We get much by this.* – Will you do it? –

Is Evelyn to be pronounced Evelyn or Ev-e-lyn? What Bank will you substitute for Hammersleys? Ransom's? Will you have the play announced (I SUPPOSE SO) with *your name*? It is of course advisable. – Will you give a hint of your wish as to *Toke's dress*? – and as to the women's dresses? – We are progressing, but slowly on the stage – it is too much for some of the actors.

What do you think of a *Prologue*? – It is so long since a Comedy was produced. –

Will you re-consider the speech on '*Battledore*' which *ought* to be an effect, but does not seem to me up to the mark – in its close – of effect – Forster thinks it a coup manqué. –

Qu.? – Should Evelyn say – is it not ungenerous in his

situation – 'Ah madam you would accept me now!' –

Can you give me – (I have not the old copy) – a line or two for Tabouret in *Act 2nd Sc. 1st* –

Mr Wrench wishes, but I do not see the need, to have a line more in his first scene. – Are you aware that Forster has transferred Smooth to him? He also proposes a white coat & light blue trowsers for his first dress – but *I do not see that.* – I like your sketch of the dresses very much – Voici tout! . . .

Bulwer to Macready, [3 November 1840]

Yours is received today. Regarding the Prologue & Epilogue. I have a superstitious horror of such things. I shall never forget the cold damp thrown over the Theatre when Mr H. Wallack in black shorts stepped forward to freeze the the Audience with the prologue to *La [Duchesse de la] Vallière*.[1] Besides – the Play is already long & the 10 minutes occupied by Prologue & Epilogue it's to be spared. I will think over it, but not with a good heart. There are no persons to whom such things could be trusted except yourself – and out of the rest, perhaps Miss Faucit? Eh! Give me your idea on this – as of course the kind of composition depends on who is to be the Oracle.

With regard to Smooth's white coat (I suppose great-coat), there is one objection. It is the London Season that is Summer – & besides it is a very dangerous article of dress unless the figure carries it off well. If he likes to wear it, Jackson must make it – in the present fashion – no buttons behind.

I will see if another line can be added to his part in the first scene, when I get the proofs thereof, having no copy here. – Toke should have black shorts[2] & silks – powder – smart showy waist-coat & his butler's jacket on (when he has his scene) – to shew what he is. When he comes on to you – a blue coat & gilt buttons. – You did not tell me how to smooth over the difficulty that Clara, knowing Evelyn had been led to suppose Georgina wrote to the Nurse, would of course have foreseen that he must suspect Georgina to have paid him the money. There is another difficulty. Evelyn bribes Sharp to say the Codicil contained £20,000. Now all such evidence would have to be filed at Doctors' Commons.[3] I fear it could hardly be settled legally in the off-hand manner Evelyn does it on the Stage. Let me know these 2 points – what could be said to smooth them . . .

With regard to the Club-room. Since they must be both, Act 3 & Act 5, be the same, it must be a drawing-room – in that case Smooth in Act 5 can't breakfast there – but he may be munching a biscuit with a glass of sherry – omit the egg. But we may as well be as accurate as we can, could you quietly find out thro' D'Orsay[4] or any member of Crockford's, without saying for what purpose, whether whist & piquet would be *ever* played in the great Dining-room at Crockford's – or in some other room set apart for the purpose. If it should turn out to be against the Fundamental rules of the Club to play in the great drawing-room why we must have the legitimate card-room for the scene. But if it should happen that – tho' not frequent or customary – yet that it occasionally does happen that a Table is made up in the great Drawing-room, that is all we want.

I would write to some member – but I think it better that they should not guess what the inquiry is for. Besides I should not like it to seem as if I had made the Manager put Crockford's on the stage. There is no objection to do so, but it might seem a clap-trap[5] for me to dictate it.

NOTES

1   *La Duchesse de la Vallière*   Bulwer-Lytton's play, produced in 1837.
2   *shorts . . . silks . . . powder*   Knee-breeches . . . silk stockings . . . powder used for a wig or for dressing hair.
3   *Doctors' Commons*   The site, near St Paul's, of ecclesiastical courts, specializing in marriage licences and wills. The courts were not held after 1858 and the building was demolished in 1867.
4   *D'Orsay*   Count d'Orsay (1802–52), French artist, supporter of the Bourbons and – in London – arbiter of a fashionable circle.
5   *clap-trap*   Behaviour designed to elicit applause.

The author's duties: a quarrel at the Adelphi, 1849

[Dion Boucicault writes to Benjamin Webster, complaining about an incident during a rehearsal at the Adelphi, when Webster's co-manager, Madame Celeste, 'so far forgot herself as a lady, as to address me before the company in a tone to which as a gentleman I could not reply.' In fact, as he admits later in the letter, Boucicault had been keeping away from rehearsals so as to avoid his creditors, and was in debt to Webster. The letter is dated Saturday, 24 November 1849 (MS letter, University of Pennsylvania Library), and the play appears to have been *The Willow Copse*, which opened on 26 November.]

Madame Celeste stated that my absence from rehearsal was an insult to the Adelphi company – but although I have seen the lady several times during the last three weeks she never discovered the *insult* until I declined to write the tag* which she desired to speak. I told her and I told you some time ago that I could not attend the rehearsals – I said I wd. leave it in your hands – I have however attended three rehearsals – I have not interfered with *the arranged business* although diametrically opposite to my written instructions in the piece – I have only suggested inflexions of voice & manners of utterance.

Madame Celeste had the indelicacy to tell me, that 'I had been paid for the piece. *I took my money* and ought to *do my duty*.' I informed her that an author is under no positive obligation to attend rehearsals.

I now ask you if Madame Celeste would have *dared* to utter this language to Mr Oxenford or Mr Jerrold – No – but she is aware of the unfortunate *dependence* which my necessities have kept me in *to you* – on this fact she relies – but *you yourself* would despise me if I could submit to it.

NOTE

*   *the tag*   The final line or phrase of a play, traditionally not spoken until the first performance.

John Oxenford, critic and author in the 1850s

[In *My Lifetime* (1895) John Hollingshead recalls the veteran author and *Times* drama critic John Oxenford.]

John Oxenford was what is generally called 'a character'. He was loaded to the muzzle with 'reserved force'. He often grasped a play, and certainly a plot, in ten minutes, which cost other people an hour. He was trained for his craft by a knowledge of the dramatic literature of the universe. When he was in a theatre there was little need to rush home and consult Genest and *Biographia Dramatica** for dramatic history. He had a habit of talking loudly in his box (the managers always gave him a box) which in little theatres like the Strand and Prince of Wales's annoyed the audience sometimes, and often provoked them to say so. He never 'slated' a play. If he could not say anything good of a piece or a performance, he gratified the management by giving a column notice, which on close examination proved to be the story of the play, told elaborately from one end to the other. He had the fault of his generation. Nearly every theatre had one of his adaptations – either to play the people in or play them out, and sometimes to find them their solid meal in the middle of the programme. Some managers did all they could to spoil him, by sending handsome retainers for him to read a piece, and give an opinion, or to edit a piece before it was put in rehearsal.

NOTE

* *Genest . . . Biographia Dramatica*   The Rev. John Genest's *Some Account of the English Stage, from the Restoration in 1660 to 1830* (1830), a standard work of scholarship and bibliography; Isaac Reed's *Biographia Dramatica, or, a Companion to the Playhouse* first appeared in 1782.

Employing an author at the Princess's, 1854

[Letter from Charles Kean, manager of the Princess's, to an unnamed correspondent, 13 September 1854 (Folger Shakespeare Library, Washington, DC).]

You agreed to complete the Pantomime [*Blue Beard*] comic scenes and all for £70 – *not* £80 – Our terms are to be these.

£40 for a one act piece
£70 for a two
£100 for a three
£15 an act for writing up –

The money to be paid weekly at £8 per week for 50 weeks.

Author sues manager, 1867

[A case, Leslie vs. Simpson, in the Court of Common Pleas, reported in *The Era*, 16 June 1867. This shows the kind of arrangement a manager might make to have a play written for his theatre, and the complications ensuing from the manager's failure to accept the restriction on the sale of rights that was required by the playwright's membership of the Dramatic Authors' Society. The subject of the play was appropriate because of a recent pit explosion. The case was settled by an award of £10 damages to the author, and an agreement not to proceed with a cross action by the defendant to recover the £20 already paid on account.]

In the opening speech it was stated that the plaintiff was a dramatic author, and had written works which had been performed with considerable success at some of the London theatres. Among these were *The Orange Girl*, which ran for 150 nights at the Surrey Theatre; *The Mariner's Compass*, brought out at Astley's; and *Time and Tide*, at the Surrey. Mr Simpson was a highly respectable gentleman, he was the proprietor of the Theatre Royal, Birmingham. Mr Leslie was a member of the Dramatic Authors' Society, and Mr Simpson was a subscriber to that Institution, or, to use language technical in the Profession, he was 'assessed' to the Society. On the 6th January, 1867, Mr Leslie inserted an advertisement in the *Era*, and headed it *The Orange Girl*, the work by which he was best known. . . . In this advertisement he announced his willingness to furnish managers with new pieces, and the consequence was that he got into communication with the defendant, who wrote – 'I should be happy to enter into an arrangement with you to write for me two or more new original dramas or adaptations' and added that he had ideas about the alteration or adaptation of two pieces, one *The Sea of Ice*, and another *The Colliery Strike*, which he did not mean should trench in any way upon *The Long Strike*. The plaintiff replied – 'I should, on my part, be happy to enter into the arrangement indicated by your favour of this morning. I like your idea of *The Colliery Strike* very much.' The plaintiff, in another letter, said that he should be ready to write the piece on terms, which he stated in this way – 'I have a general outline of the plot, which I can readily adapt for the purpose you require; and I will come to Birmingham and write the piece in the district, and watch the character of the people. I will do this if you will send me a preliminary cheque for £10, in the nature of binding the bargain, and give me £5 a week for four weeks while in your town, making in all £30.' For this the defendant was to have the exclusive right of representation in Birmingham, the right of representation in other towns to remain the plaintiff's property. On the 16th of January the defendant wrote – 'I accept your terms as regards Birmingham, but I should like, if the piece is successful, to have the right of purchasing the exclusive right in it, or, if you prefer it, to give you a percentage on whatever is received from other towns,' and the plaintiff answered, 'So far as Birmingham is concerned, the bargain is concluded, and you can send the cheque at your convenience. With regard to the other rights, I am quite willing to leave them matter for subsequent negotiation.'

The contract thus having been entered into, Mr Leslie proceeded to Birmingham, went down several coal mines, and took all necessary steps to make himself *au fait* upon the matter. Several conversations took place between the parties in reference to the defendant acquiring a more extensive right in the piece, but Mr Leslie said that he had no power to sell more than the right of representation in Birmingham, because he was bound, by the rules of the Dramatic Authors' Society, not to part with any more extensive right, and, further, was bound to place the piece upon the Society's list. Mr Sterling Coyne,* the Secretary of the Society, was appealed to, and he sent down the rules, which showed that the plaintiff was right in the view which he had taken in the matter. The plaintiff set to work to write his piece, which he called *The Black Country; or, Little Jem, the Collier's Son*, and he advertised in the *Era* that the piece would be placed upon the Dramatic Authors' Society's list, and that managers could have the right of playing it upon paying the usual charges. He received on account £20 from the defendant, and sent him the first act of the drama. The defendant, however, expressed his surprise at this advertisement, and said that he was called upon to pay £30, whilst other managers would have the same advantage by paying only the amount at which they were assessed by the Dramatic Authors' Society's list, and, under these circumstances, he declined to complete his contract . . .

NOTE

*   *Sterling Coyne*   Joseph Stirling Coyne (1803*–68), dramatist, author of the popular farce *How to Settle Accounts with your Laundress*.

Authors and managers, 1879

[From an article by F.C. Burnand in *The Theatre*, February 1879. Burnand, a playwright and (from 1836 to 1906) the editor of *Punch*, proposes a plan for fairer dealing over payment for original and adapted plays. The specific scheme was not taken up, but the use of fixed percentages in regulating an author's profits from an entertainment was becoming general. The article also reflects the debate concerning the economic reasons for the great number of plays adapted from the French – held to be an obstacle to the development of the native drama.]

What I offer are a few suggestions towards settling a difficult question between English dramatic authors and managers. Premiss – A piece is worth what it will bring. I think this will be at once admitted. A piece is worth to the proprietor and producer what it will bring them. Who are the proprietor and producer? The author and the manager. Of course, the proprietor is not necessarily the author; but with that I have nothing to do. Putting aside all question of literary merit, putting aside all question of time and labour given to the production of an original English work, or of an adaptation of a foreign one, I simply assert that a piece is worth what it will bring. The composition of an original work must, ordinarily, take the author months, a year, or even years. An adaptation will, ordinarily, occupy an author days, weeks, or perhaps a couple of months. Some men can do equally well in a day what will take others a week. The result I am supposing to be the same. I am not a great arithmetician; arithmetic is decidedly not my *forte*. Give me, however, a sum in addition, and in an hour I will give you the correct total. Give that same sum to a practised counting-house clerk, and he will give you the same result in five minutes. Give it to the calculating boy,* and in half a second he will give the correct result. So with the adaptation of a foreign play. Some men are born adapters; others have adaptation thrust upon them. If, therefore, the premiss is granted, that 'any play is worth what it will bring', it is clear that, as an original play, whose property is in its author, is worth to the author and the manager what it will bring to them, so an adaptation is worth what it will bring to its author, its adapter, and the manager who produces it. I do not, of course, consider any payment to author or adapter as 'what it produces'. What it produces is what it brings into the treasury of the theatre when it is brought out, *i.e.*, what the public pay to see it.

Now, a manager is a shopkeeper, and must display the goods best calculated to attract the public. He is no more bound to deal exclusively with English material than I am to eat English mustard. If the manager thinks that a French piece, doctored for the English market, is more profitable than what native talent can produce, he is quite right to deal in French pieces, and to employ native talent in so doctoring them. But as the doctoring required varies from five to two hundred per cent, so that in some, and indeed, in many instances, very little of the original material remains, the adapter's work is more often that of an English author writing as *collaborateur* with the French or German author, than of a mere adapter by way of translation, or, if I may use the term, by way of 'transferation' – by which I mean a process of transferring the French original to the English stage, on which the doctoring will be about forty per cent. But it will be granted that in no case of adaptation from a foreign original will the English author's work be equal to the exhausting hours required by the original creation. In an adaptation, plot, characters, construction, and dialogue are brought ready to the adapter's hand. Therefore, a very natural objection arises against an adapter's receiving for a successful adaptation the same remuneration as the author of an equally successful creation. Now, supposing it admitted that a play, whether adaptation or original, is worth what it will bring, how is this evident difficulty to be adjusted? Here are the suggestions towards a remedy:

Managers should agree to pay ten per cent on their gross receipts, or ten per cent on the receipts after a certain reduction, (but this is a matter for future arrangement) for *their entire evening's entertainment*. If one author provides the whole entertainment he alone takes the ten per cent. If two, or more, they share the percentage in a certain fixed proportion, acts counting as shares, and burlesques of five or more scenes reckoning as the acts. The English Dramatic Authors' Society should be in correspondence with the French Dramatic Authors' Society, and the two societies should be bound to act as each other's agent to the exclusion of all direct dealings with managers. The French dramatist would select his English author for any required adaptation, and according to the work required so should the shares of French authors and English adapters be fixed. Broadly they might be estimated as equal, the adapter (whether French or English) paying the fees for copying and the percentage due to the society. This would make no difference to the manager who pays ten per cent on his gross receipts for the entertainment, whatever it may be. It would, indeed, be an advantage, as no sum down would have to be paid to the original author. The English manager would merely deal with the English Dramatic Authors' Society for his piece, and his payments would be made straight to the society which is responsible to its members. Then, supposing this at work, the adapter would be in precisely the same position as a *collaborateur*. M. Chose, the French author of the original, and Mr Smith, the English author who had adapted M. Chose's work, will divide their ten per cent or their proportion (if there are other pieces not by them in the manager's programme) of the ten per cent. This scheme supposes all authors, whether novices or professed, to be members of the Dramatic Authors' Society. There will be no haggling or bargaining, even in the case of young authors; for a piece, no matter by whom it is written, is worth what it will bring. Where a manager takes £7000, the author whose work has brought this in – and the author is the *raison d'être* of the manager, theatre, actors &c. – will take £700.

I merely state this broadly. I am perfectly aware that there are other considerations which may go towards the modification of this scheme, such as arise from the manager's expenses of production. But to this point it is evident the managers must address themselves, as it only concerns them. I want to see an arrangement which shall be fairly adjusted and mutually beneficial. At present authors are underpaid, and it suits them better, far better, to adapt foreign plays provided by managers than to devote time and labour to original work. In France collaboration is the rule. And why? because there is an uniform system of payment by percentage, as I have here suggested. In fact, I am doing little more now than 'adapting' the plan from the French. English authors will not work together as *collaborateurs*, because at present it is not worth their while. How greatly the national drama would be benefited by the collaboration of those who are good at plot and construction with those whose *spécialité* is dialogue is very evident.

NOTE

*   *the calculating boy*   Possibly a reference to George Parker Bidder (1806–78) whose phenomenal powers of mental arithmetic had become evident at an early age.

'A bed of thorns': the tribulations of the author, 1879

[From an article by the dramatist J. Palgrave Simpson in *The Theatre*, October 1879. An earlier article by Sydney Grundy had described the dramatist's life under the ironic title 'A bed of roses', but Simpson claims that Grundy was not nearly harsh enough in his account.]

A well-known dramatic author, of more or less ability, is commissioned by an actress of great and acknowledged talent to construct for her a play in which she can perform certain characters of an exceptional type. He sets to work and invents his plot. He draws up an elaborate *scenario*, which meets with the entire approval of the talented artist. But then she desires to have a child introduced, on whom she can lavish maternal tenderness. In vain the poor author remonstrates that this child will hamper and disjoint his play considerably. She insists; and the author foolishly gives way, entirely against his own judgement and dramatic instinct, and 'lags in' the child with much trouble, and with every effort of ingenuity in his power to round-off an obvious excrescence. But still the actress is not content. Now she wants a drunken, or semi-drunken, scene. Again the author protests that such a scene would materially diminish the sympathy of her character in the eyes of an audience, and would be repugnant to his own feelings; and again the author is 'fool enough' – the term must not be spared him – to give way. Alas! that he should have done so; for these two points – the interpolated child, and the repulsive and irrelevant drunken scene – are exactly those which the critics, in the sad eventualities of the drama's fate, most strenuously condemn. It is to be hoped that there are not many authors so weak and foolish as this one in his concessions to wrong-headed demands of an actress.

Well! the elaborate *scenario* is complete. It meets with the unmitigated approval of the commissioning artist, who expresses her delight. The author, or rather the inventor and constructor of the drama, is too much hampered by his other avocations to give the necessary time to the composition of the dialogue. He calls in the aid of a friend, on whose literary ability and dramatic instinct he has the greatest reliance. The dialogue is written; and again the actress expresses not only her approval, but her admiration of it. So far the relations between the artist and the authors chime as pleasantly as 'marriage-bells'. The union appears most satisfactory.

Weeks, months, almost years of labour have been bestowed on the play. The actress is most anxious to produce it. She proposes America, but to this intention the authors object; as, by the first production of the play in the States, the English copyright would be lost to herself as well as to them. With difficulty she obtains a first-rate theatre in London, and rents it for a period for the sole purpose of producing the drama, on which she has the most unqualified reliance. Again, 'so far, so good!'

The time comes for the arrangement of 'terms' between the parties. The authors make every concession to the actress; they reduce their requirements to the lowest extent; they are 'beaten down' to a minimum. The contract is drawn up by the actress's own solicitor for the full protection of *her* interests; but it would appear that she does not content herself with the terms finally agreed upon by her own legal man of business and old friend; for immediately afterwards she designates one author as 'a scoundrel' before a stranger, and when the other expostulates warmly in defence of his friend, declares that she does not call *him* 'a scoundrel' as she 'respects old age'. But she still stamps him as the intimate associate of 'a scoundrel', and wonders that he should resent the obvious implication.

Thus bad begins, but worse remains behind.

It would be as well, perhaps, to finish with the mention of 'the actress' now. This designation is merged in that of 'the management'. The sufferings of the authors from the conduct of 'the management' begin from the very first rehearsal. It ('the management') grossly insults one of the authors at every turn. If he ventures to open his mouth to explain the meaning of his words, he is violently assailed with the term 'objectionable person', as interrupting the rehearsals and interfering with the stage-management – little as the mere interpretation of words can have any bearing in theatrical minds on the stage-management, as properly understood. At every moment he is treated with the most barefaced insolence. Anxious to avoid all open rupture with the management, he is obliged to subside into a forced nonentity, and bears the repeated insults still heaped on him with a gentlemanly forbearance which seems impossible to mortal nature . . .

So far all is seemingly done with openness. The authors have still to find that *surreptitiously*, without their knowledge and against their will, important alterations have been made, to their confusion and to the detriment of the play. It is only at the last moment they discover that the language of the principal part has been cut out by the management and its own bald balderdash substituted – that sentences in the same strain have been written in profusely without their knowledge, and, of course, without any attempt to obtain their consent. At this last moment – the night dress-rehearsal – they begin to have an inkling that a sensation scene, on the invention of which the contriver of the *scenario* had (perhaps foolishly – his folly has been already admitted) prided himself, was to be ruthlessly omitted; that firearms were to be used, contrary to the authors' express prohibition, in a medieval play, and that a variety of incongruities had been foisted in.

The play is naturally a failure; as naturally it is mercilessly 'slated' by the dramatic critics of the day. In face of the adverse criticisms – the word 'adverse' is the mildest which can be given – the authors have nothing to do but humbly bow their heads. Critics can do no more than judge a play as they see it represented on the stage. But they little know how much the intentions of the authors may be perverted and their efforts mangled. They could scarcely even dream of the injustice done them by the management – to say nothing of the insults to which they may have been daily compelled to submit on the stage – and even setting aside the crowning one of the withholding of the fees due for the few nights during which the piece was played until the receipt for them is *preciously* handed over.

xi

An author's complaint, 1881

[Sydney Grundy tells William Archer about his comedy *Over the Garden Wall*, produced by the popular comic actor J.L. Toole at the Folly Theatre, 20 July 1881. The letter is dated 'Thursday' (Archer correspondence, British Library). The 'tag' (second paragraph) is the final line of the play.]

When I tell you that 25 minutes were cut out of the piece at rehearsal, you will not wonder that the action is hurried. Actors have no idea of general effect, they only look at isolated lines, & they do not understand the value of the little connecting links which bind a piece together and at the same time regulate its action. In my MS, the action was perhaps unduly quick, but the proportion was artistic throughout, & there was no hurry. There is a great difference between haste & hurry, bustle & confusion.

I thought my tag was neat enough, but Toole wanted the present ending and asked me to write words up to it. I did so, and he did not take the trouble to learn them. He admits that the end now does not convey his idea, & that a suggestion I have made to him will improve it.

In my last 3 pieces, I have suffered cruelly from the imperfection of my interpreters.

Terms for a melodrama, 1881

[In *My Life. Sixty Years' Recollections of Bohemian London* (1917) George R. Sims quotes the 'principal portion' of his contract with the actor-manager Wilson Barrett for one of the most successful melodramas of the decade, first staged by Barrett in 1881.]

It is agreed between us that you cede to me [Wilson Barrett] and I take from you the sole right of producing your new play, now entitled (provisionally) *The Lights o' London*, in all English-speaking countries on the following terms: I agree to produce the said play at the Princess's Theatre and elsewhere, and will pay you the following fees as consideration of this agreement:

In London:
    If the sums taken as receipts do not exceed £600 per week of six performances, £2 2s. per performance.
    If over £600 up to £700, 5 per cent. of the gross receipts.
    If over £700 up to £800, 7½ per cent of the gross receipts.
    If over £800, 10 per cent of the gross receipts.

In the Provinces:
    Five per cent of all sums up to £50 per night, and 10 per cent of sums after £50 per night have been taken by the theatre.

This agreement to remain in force for three years after the first production of the play.

[Sims comments:]

I have said that Barrett might have bought all my rights for a thousand pounds, and if he had made a cash offer probably for less. My first week's royalties were a hundred and fifty pounds, and within a fortnight a thousand pounds had been paid down on account of American rights, and in the States the play ran for many years, and the receipts were then a record. In England the travelling companies toured the provinces with it, and the No. 1 company would stay for a month or six weeks playing to record business.

Terms for a tour and the strategy of a revival, 1883

[Ada Cavendish played Mercy Merrick, the leading character, in the first production of Wilkie Collins' *The New Magdalen* (1873). On 23 June 1883 Collins writes agreeing that she should have the touring rights at a preferential rate of £3 a performance, but finds himself in a quandary over her proposal to take the play to London (MS letter, Harvard Theatre Collection).]

If the contemplated performances are supported by a capitalist who finds the money, I will at once send you a draft of agreement, stating the conditions on which I will consent to a new series of representations in London next year.

But – if the responsibility of the speculation is yours, I don't like making *you* answerable to me (or to my executors?). To insist on a guaranteed 'run' and on stipulated payments – with you – if the venture turned out to be less successful than we had hoped, would (as I am sure you know, my dear) be simply impossible. And, in that disastrous case, what would my position be? After having refused over and over again to allow the piece to be prematurely revived – I should be left with a worthless dramatic commodity on my hands for years to come. This (after the pecuniary sacrifices I have made in keeping the play in my desk) is a prospect which I cannot afford to contemplate. In one word – I *must* be paid, and I *won't* say 'must' to you.

Authors, managers and critics, 1885

[From an editorial in *The Entr'acte and Limelight*, 31 January 1885.]

Speaking for myself I cannot bring my mind to believe that honest criticism is to be obtained from writers who are pecuniarily interested in the object criticized. Human nature is not equal to absolute honesty under such trying circumstances. Writers of newspaper criticisms don't care to slash the work of a brother journalist; for, in the first place, if they are continually rubbing shoulders with him, anything like outspoken condemnation would breed unpleasantness; while, secondly, they may have some intention of producing a play themselves some day, when they would want the good words of their newspaper friends.

Something like sixteen or seventeen years ago I remember that the late Tom Robertson had, in the *Daily News*, pitched into some piece the late Leicester Buckingham* had written for one of the London theatres. Like all playwrights, when their weaknesses are laid bare, the last-named was highly infuriated, and, as a matter of course, attributed the attack to envy, malice, and all uncharitableness. 'But,' said he, 'my chance will come.' These men were enemies from this time, and the gap was widened when Buckingham's chance arrived. He himself supplied the *Morning Star* with dramatic notices, and when Robertson's *Shadow-Tree Shaft* was produced at the Princess's, Buckingham slated it mercilessly in his journal. If these worthies had been authors only, it is most likely they would have been friends to the end.

Authors have no business to be newspaper critics, and when newspaper critics develop into authors, and carry on both businesses, they invariably, it is my opinion, ply an illicit trade. The critic of an important newspaper can always get the ear of the manager [of the theatre]; and the latter wishing, for well-known reasons, to keep on friendly terms with the journalist, is afraid to treat him as he would an ordinary producer.

When actors or musicians tell me that they advertise in the *Dutchoven* because the proprietor thereof also writes the notices in the more important *Gridiron*, I feel sure that this diplomacy reflects an iniquitous state of things. If ever I should write dramas – I don't think this is likely, for I am under the impression there are now too many dramatic tinkers in the market – I certainly should not think of writing dramatic notices again.

I have been told that the managers of our London theatres, before accepting a drama, now make a point of submitting it to one or two of the critics of our principal daily papers. Whether these luminaries are paid for pronouncing an opinion I have never heard. Should they vote in its favour, however, a manager by such means secures their good word; and this is something.

NOTE

*   *Leicester Buckingham*   Leicester Silk Buckingham (1825–67), dramatist.

xv

'The censorship of the stage'

[Authors were not the only victims of the censorship conducted by the Lord Chamberlain's office, but the submission of scripts for licensing put them in the front line and resulted in a general timidity in handling 'difficult' subjects. In this unsigned article, published in the *Westminster Review* (n.s., 65) in 1884, William Archer discusses the institution in the light of its history and gives examples of its consequences in the work of some modern dramatists.]

Let it be thoroughly understood by those who believe in the censorship as a bulwark of public morality, that it was established in its present form as a shield for political immorality. Combining the qualities of King Stork and King Log,[1] it has been alternately tyrannical and futile, odious and ridiculous. By its own confession it is inconsistent, and has admitted today what it prohibited yesterday, with no change in the circumstances to justify the change of front. By its own confession it is futile, having no power to enforce some of its most important directions. It can suppress a play which touches upon an ethical problem, but it cannot prevent an indecent 'gag' or an immoral double-meaning conveyed by the actor's look or gesture. It is anomalous, since it is the one irresponsible and secret tribunal in the land. It is unjust, since like the Jedburgh judges[2] of border history, it first hangs the prisoner and then tries him, or rather lets him do what he can to obtain a trial elsewhere. It is destructive, since it takes out of the people's hands a power which they alone can rightly wield, and thus deadens their feeling of responsibility for the morals of the stage. The first result of its abolition would be a quickening of the moral sense of theatrical audiences. Prudery rather than licence would probably be the order of the day.

'Good manners, decorum, and the public peace' are placed by the statute[3] under the censor's aegis. Religion, morals, and politics – these are, in fact, the subjects of his tutelage. He is a watchman to ward off the drama from the serious interests of life, swinging his fiery sword in blinding circles around the tree of the knowledge of good and evil. Let us see what terrible results would ensue if our autocratic and invulnerable angel-guardian were relieved from duty.

Would religion suffer? Would the tenets of Mr Bradlaugh, or even of Mr Matthew Arnold,[4] find exponents on the stage? We think not. It is possible, on the contrary, that one or two attempts might be made to hold up these doctrines to ridicule, which would at once and signally fail. The public is as determined as any censor can possibly be that such burning questions shall not be brought upon the stage. . . . England, the favoured land where religion and the public peace are guarded by official omnipotence, is the only country where a play has been produced of recent years in which the religious question was crudely and rashly handled, and which threatened to lead to a breach of the public peace. To do the censor justice, it must be admitted that, if *The Promise of May*[5] had been the work of an unknown and struggling playwright, whose career, perhaps, depended upon its chance of success, he would never have thought of licensing it. As it was by a great poet, whose name appears next to his own in the list of Her Majesty's Household, he thought, perhaps, of the fate predicted for a household divided against itself, and determined to stretch a point in favour of the Laureate. The result was a stormy first night, and, at a subsequent performance, a scene of indigant protest. This experience will probably teach managers, for some time to come, to let Agnosticism alone; but, even if it does not, if another

Promise of May were to be produced tomorrow with the same result, would there be any great harm done, any such evil as to justify the maintenance of an irresponsible official who should, but does not, prevent it? The great body of the theatre-going public is conventionally religious – witness the watery piety which found favour in *The Silver King*[6] – and is much less likely than the censor to tolerate anything which endangers their religion . . .

Let us take politics next, leaving to the last the more important subject of morals. What has been said of religion applies in a less degree to politics – namely, that pieces of strong political tendency would very rarely be produced, because they would be almost certain to fail. But supposing such a play to be produced, is England a country in which it is likely to lead to revolution, serious disturbance or even the much-dreaded 'breach of the peace'? We are accustomed to strong political argument and invective in the press; but that, say the defenders of the censure, is not to the point, since an invective delivered in print to a thousand people, at their thousand breakfast-tables, does not produce the same effect as it would if delivered by a skilled actor to the same thousand people assembled in the electric atmosphere of a theatre. Perhaps not; but a public meeting possesses this electricity of numbers, and a great orator is a skilled actor, using in deadly earnest the same weapons of satire and denunciation which are held so perilous in the mimic warfare of the stage. A public meeting, it may be objected, is sometimes – very rarely – riotous. True, but why should the excitement, which in a public hall is considered a healthy sign of political life, be held dangerous and destructive in a theatre? . . .

As for political persiflage after the manner of *The Happy Land*,[7] it is hard to see why it should be given extreme licence in the comic papers, and should be utterly repressed on the stage. Speaking of the play in which Mr Buckstone was to have represented Lord John Russell,[8] Mr Shirley Brooks[9] said, 'I do not feel sure that the Aristophanic drama would be such a very bad thing to restore.' It would surely be an excellent thing if we had but an Aristophanes. The only possible plea for repressing it is the old bugbear of the public peace, which was not in the least endangered by *The Happy Land*, or on the numerous other occasions when would-be Aristophanisms have eluded the censor's ken. John Bull's traditional phlegm is not so easily disturbed. On the music-hall stage, as we all know, songs of violent political tendency are nightly sung with no fatal results. One of these, at a crisis of our history, took such a hold on the public mind that it added a word to the English language.[10] Had Mr Macdermott been a playwright, instead of a poet, he would have been informed that a drama of such strong tendency was calculated to arouse the angry passions of the peace-party and consequently could not be 'recommended for licence'.

We come lastly to the great question of morals. Here there is a distinction to be drawn between the different senses in which the word 'immorality' is commonly used. It is applied on the one hand to indecency, obscenity, pruriency, and on the other to any form of thought or action, however conscientious, earnest, and high-principled, which transgresses the conventional rules of social decorum, or even touches upon matters which society has tacitly determined to wink at and let alone. Vulgar sensualism, and devotion to ideals more advanced than those of the crowd, are in popular parlance alike immoral . . .

[The censorship in fact fails to repress 'vulgar sensualism' but effectively excludes 'advanced ideals, nay the mere handling of any problem of delicacy and importance.']

Let us illustrate our conception of the true morality which the censorship fails to repress, and the false morality which it encourages. In Mr Pinero's much discussed play of *The Squire*, the heroine, supposed to be a noble and high-minded woman, is privately married to a man who believes himself to be a widower, but whose first wife afterwards turns out to be alive, just as the second finds herself about to become a mother. The situation is a painful one, and may give rise to various emotions in all concerned, while it opens many questions as to the best way out of the difficulty. The very last emotion which the heroine should experience is shame. That the discovery should diminish her self-respect, is a concession to a false ideal of conduct which may be justly described as immoral. If she had a spark of independence of character, she would see that the moral quality of an act committed in unavoidable ignorance of certain circumstances affecting it, is not in the least changed by the fact of these circumstances becoming known. Had this been clearly shown, the play would have been moral in the best, indeed in the only true, sense of the word – but it would probably never have been played. As it was, Mr Pinero never even suggested this view of the case. The heroine suffered agonies of shame, and was at last restored to self-respect and the esteem of the world, by the death of the first wife – a convenient circumstance no doubt, but one which did not alter by a jot or tittle the moral quality of her conduct. The fact that this end was accepted by the public shows how omnipotent is thoughtless conventionality in the judgement of conduct; and it is precisely this stolid conventionality which the censorship inevitably fosters . . .

NOTES

1 *King Stork and King Log* According to the fable the frogs asked Jupiter for a king, but found the log he threw down too docile; his response was to send a stork, which devoured them all.

2 *the Jedburgh Judges* Jedburgh in Roxburghshire, south-east of Edinburgh. 'Jeddart Justice' was proverbial and meant hanging a man first and trying him afterwards.

3 *the statute* Clause xiv of the 1843 Theatre Regulation Act.

4 *the tenets of Mr Bradlaugh . . . Mr Arnold* Charles Bradlaugh (1833–91) was a prominent secularist whose refusal to swear the customary oath on taking his seat as a member of Parliament caused a controversy. Matthew Arnold (1822–88), poet and man of letters, presumably represents cultural liberalism in this context.

5 *The Promise of May* Tennyson's play, produced in 1882, was the object of a demonstration mounted by the Marquis of Queensbury (later Oscar Wilde's persecutor) who complained that it misrepresented free-thinkers.

6 *The Silver King* Melodrama by Henry Arthur Jones and Henry Herman (1882), it shows a feckless man wrongly convicted of murder and escaping to redeem himself.

7 *The Happy Land* A burlesque by Gilbert À Beckett and W.S. Gilbert, produced at the Court Theatre in 1873, in which Gladstone and two members of his administration were impersonated.

8 *The play . . . Lord John Russell* Unidentified.

9 *Mr Shirley Brooks* Charles William Shirley Brooks (1816–74), humorist and dramatic author, contributor to and (from 1871) editor of *Punch*.

10 *it added a word to the English language* 'Jingoism', from the song made popular by the Great McDermott (1845–1901): 'We don't want to fight, but – by Jingo! – if we do . . . '

A new confidence: negotiating with America, 1880s

[Henry Arthur Jones had his first big success with *The Silver King* in 1882. The following extracts are from his correspondence with the American impresario Herbert Marshman Palmer (MS letters, Harvard Theatre Collection). The letters include descriptions (usually favourable) of the reception of Jones's work at home and proposals for the financial and artistic arrangements with America. The playwright's dealings with the manager reflect a sense of his worth: 'I am certain to have things a great deal my own way over here for the next few years, and it will be worth your while to work with me.' (30 October 1889.) This selection begins with terms for an American production of a play that opened in London at the Vaudeville on 3 November 1887. Thomas Thorne was joint manager of the theatre.]

30 January 1888
Yours of the 17th to hand. I have just seen Thorne and we agree to accept your proposed reduction of terms for *Heart of Hearts* – namely at Madison Square Theatre.

5% up to $4000
10% on all sums over $4000, up to $5000
15% on all over $5000.
in the provinces a straight 5% all round . . .

[Jones points out that a cable telling of the play's success was sent in good faith.]

Before its production I had very little faith in it as you may gather if you refer to my letters before it was played. But when I saw it received so rapturously I concluded that it was just what the public wanted and that it contained elements of popularity that I had overlooked. As you say it is not a piece of any great strength or originality but I have great faith in your management. . . . Upon the night of its transference to the evening bill the piece was received with the most frantic applause and all through its run I continued to receive the most extravagant praise of it from all quarters.

1 October 1889
I see you say '*Wealth* was a signal failure.' It was only a first-night failure – it makes money *every week* for the management, one

week a profit of £300. And this in spite of tropical weather. *The Middleman* is playing to splendid business. On Saturday *every reserved seat* in the house was sold before we opened. Yesterday Monday's booking was the biggest we have had and exceeded *Silver King* booking.

26 October 1889

I am afraid your terms will not be acceptable to Willard who has received so much higher offers elsewhere. This being the case – and I suppose the matter will be concluded before the reply to this letter reaches me – will you kindly cable me definitely about *Wealth* 'Yes' or 'No' – that is will you do it on the terms arranged either this season or next. If I do not get a cable from you before the 10th of November I shall consider myself free to deal with it. I am sorry about the *Middleman* as I should have liked you to have had it – we are doing magnificent business – every night money turned away and today (Saturday) every seat was sold before the box office opened this morning – and already the whole house is nearly sold for next Saturday.

30 October 1889

We are doing greater business than ever and turning them away every night – I send you the last return that has come to hand – Thursday £211 – Friday always a little below £201 – Saturday £241 – in reality the house at our prices will scarcely hold more than £200 but on Saturday they are content to stand more. . . . I send you these returns in confidence that you may know you have a genuine thing – the returns (6 performances) (Willard cannot stand the matinées) come to £1300 a week, the expenses now as we are *not* advertising anything except bare announcements – are only just £500, my fees another £130 – I hope to persuade Willard to come to you.

1 November 1889

[Willard has agreed to a contract with Palmer.]

I have throughout urged him to sacrifice a great deal in order to have the play brought out under your auspices – And I think you will both make a lot of money out of it. Of course you know the terms for the play are 10 per cent of the gross – The business keeps exactly the same £200 last night – this is practically all the house will hold. . . . There is no doubt we have the big success of the year – we are holding out and increasing so far as is possible. Of course at our prices – 3s. Upper Circle, 2s. Pit and 6s. Dress Circle – our houses represent £240 at Haymarket prices. But they are not keeping up with us.

12 November 1889

[*The Middleman*, opened on 27 August 1889 at the Shaftesbury, with E.S. Willard in the lead. In this and subsequent letters Jones tried to achieve the right terms for the play, for Willard and for another property, *Wealth*, produced on 27 April 1889 at the Haymarket.]

I received your telegram 'wait letter' and shall not settle anything till I see what you say. But I may tell you that *Wealth* will be done in New York next Autumn in any case, if not under your management then at another theatre. But of course I would rather have it done by you, especially as you are going to have the *Middleman* – Business keeps as firm as a rock – latest returns Thursday £209, Friday £196, Saturday £238 – but we turned away more on Saturday than we have ever done – had to refuse Duke and Duchess of Fife on Thursday afternoon – they sent for a box that night – we had none left.

19 November 1889

[*Wealth* became part of a combined deal over Willard and *The Middleman*, and Jones describes to Palmer the arrangement he has with Willard over acting rights. Willard had *The Middleman* for one year:]

. . . with the option of renewing for another year, and then again for a third. If he doesn't renew the piece will fall into my hands and I should think that even with the biggest success he will be anxious to return to London in 1891 so as to keep before his public here – But he has the piece only for such towns as he can play in himself and he has to give me a list of them within two months after he opens with you. Therefore in the event of a great success like *The Silver King* I shall be pleased to arrange with you for *The Middleman* in all towns that Willard does not visit, and for the piece after he leaves America. Therefore in arranging with him for certain towns you will remember that it is free for all other places . . .

[Terms proposed by Jones for *Wealth*:]

    5% of all sums up to $3000 weekly
    $7\frac{1}{2}$% of all surplus up to $4000 weekly
    10% of all surplus beyond $4000 weekly.

xvii

Money and the playwright, 1888

[From *Playwriting: A Handbook for Would be Dramatic Authors* by 'a Dramatist' – possibly Jerome K. Jerome.]

There are false impressions abroad concerning dramatic authors and their takings. It is popularly supposed that a successful play brings its author in from one to two hundred thousand pounds, and when I was young and used to believe this stuff, I used to wonder why it was that popular dramatists lived so quietly in little houses at St John's Wood or Brixton, instead of having two or three palaces each in different parts of the country. When I came to understand matters, however, I found that they did not receive such large incomes as I had imagined. Still, a very comfortable living may be earned by playwriting, and the returns to the author are certainly far in excess of those in any other branch of literature.

There are two methods of dealing with plays – one by sale, the other by 'royalties', the latter of which is by far the most generally employed.

Indeed, now that the author's share forms so large a proportion of the profits in a piece, it is hardly possible that any out-and-out sale of all his rights could be arranged. A successful play is a property well worth from £20,000 to £30,000; and an author would be foolish to part with all his rights in a piece he had any faith in, for anything under £3,000 to £4,000. On the other hand, the MS of a play, if a failure, is only worth $1\frac{1}{2}$d. a lb., so that a speculator would not care to risk so large a sum, especially seeing how impossible it is to say beforehand whether a piece, however good, will take with the public. One thousand pounds would be, I should say, the most that would ever be paid down for a piece; and a manager would need a deal of faith in an author before he parted even with that sum.

As a rule the only plays that are brought outright are dramas of the transpontine or provincial school, for which £50 or £100 would be considered a handsome price, and plays written specially to suit some artiste, such as *My Sweetheart* and *Hans the Boatman* etc., pieces which would be comparatively valueless if left to stand alone. Young authors also often sell their pieces outright, being only too glad to get it accepted anyhow, and rightly arguing to themselves that it is better for them to get it out, and have the advertisement, even if they have to let it go for an old song, as the saying is, than to lose a chance which may not come again for years . . .

The purchase of particular rights in a play, such as the American rights, the Australian rights, the provincial rights, &c., is a common enough thing, but this is after the play has been produced and proved successful. The American rights are of great value – almost as valuable as the English rights. There are special firms in America which make it their business to look after the works of English authors out there, and collect and remit them their fees. Nearly all the successful plays, and especially the melodramas produced in London, are played all through the States, and bring in the English authors very handsome returns. Still, if you can get anything like a reasonable sum, I would strongly advise you to sell the American right[s] out and out as soon as possible. They are an enterprising people across the herring pond, and it is not always easy to obtain your fees.

So also with Australia; £100 at your bankers in London is well worth £200 owing to you in New South Wales.

The provincial rights I hardly see the wisdom of ever parting with. You can never expect to get, in a lump sum down, anything approaching in amount to what 'royalties' would, under usual circumstances, bring you in; and, unless you are very hard up for ready money, I should say stick to any British rights, you cannot very easily miss your fees in England, Ireland, or Scotland.

The other system, the 'royalty' system of payment, may itself be subdivided into two methods, the one the payment of a stated sum per night, the other the payment of a percentage on the gross takings. The latter system is the one most usually adopted with regard to London, the former as regards the provinces. The payment per night, if a fixed sum, varies from £1 up to £9. One pound a night would be fair enough to pay for a country drama – that is, one written for and produced in the country; and £9 would be readily given for a 'London success' – that is, a piece that has had a moderate run and tolerable notoriety at some West-End house . . .

When a play is paid for by percentage, as is the usual method with all leading original plays, five to ten per cent on the gross receipts is the usual fee, and as a good draw will bring into the box office an average of £200 per night, and will run for from one to two years, and as a couple of provincial companies will be sent round with the piece at the same time, and bring in the author between them fees almost equal to those received from the London house, and as, in addition to this, there is the American and Colonial rights before referred to, and the piece will very likely be revived and have another long run before it is finally laid by, it may be seen that one play may easily be something like a fortune in itself.

If you can get five per cent for your early pieces, that is as much as you can expect; ten per cent is only paid to established popular writers. I have heard of twelve being asked, but that was for a piece that had already been successfully produced, and then they didn't get it. Two authors, of course, share the five or ten per cent, as the case may be, between them.

All the foregoing applies to three or four-act pieces, but curtain raisers are coming to the front just now, and can, if properly worked among the amateurs, be made a very respectable little property. *Uncle's Will*, I believe, brings in Mr Theyre Smith a steady income of £50 per annum; and a friend of mine tells me that a little play of his, written many years ago, has returned him an average of £20 a year ever since. The price paid by theatres for first pieces varies from 30s. to £6 a week, and as such pieces are often revived, and are played constantly round the provinces, they well repay writing. It is from the amateurs, however, that the chief income of a one-act play is derived, there always being a fair demand for such pieces among these ladies and gentlemen.

If your curtain-raiser is successful, when produced, take it to Mr French, of 89, Strand. He won't say much, being a comfortable-looking old gentleman of few words, but for 3s. a printed page he will publish it, and put it in his list, sending you fifty copies, which you can write pretty dedications in, and send round to all the girls you know. He will also collect your fees from the amateurs, and, after deducting his commission, hand you over the balance each month. As I have said, a good one-act play will be used pretty frequently by the various AD clubs and societies about the country, and, for each performance of it, Mr French will charge them ten or fifteen shillings, or a guinea.

Anything beyond a one-act piece, however, it is not safe to have published, because, under the American copyright laws, a play published over here in book form, can be sneaked and performed over there for nothing. One-act pieces don't matter. They are rarely used in America, and the American right of them is, consequently, next to *nil*. Of any big play, likely to be sought after by the amateurs, let Mr French have two or three neatly-typed copies, which he will loan round when required . . .

xviii

Rehearsals: an author's view, 1890

[From 'A stage play', by W.S. Gilbert, reprinted in *Foggerty's Fairy, and Other Tales* (1890). Gilbert's point of view is represented by Facile, the author of the play in production.]

Facile knows something of stage-management, and invariably stage-manages his own pieces – an exceptional thing in England, but the common custom in France. He is nothing of an actor, and when he endeavours to show what he wants his actors to do, he makes himself rather ridiculous, and there is a good deal of tittering at the wings; but he contrives, nevertheless, to make himself understood, and takes particular good care that whatever his wishes are, they shall be carried out to the letter, unless good cause is shown to the contrary. He has his own way; and if the piece is a success, he feels that he has contributed more than the mere words that are spoken. At the same time, if Facile is not a self-sufficient donkey, he is only too glad to avail himself of valuable suggestions offered by persons who have ten times his experience in the details of stage management. And so the piece flounders through rehearsal, the dingy theatre lighted by a T-piece* in front of the stage which has no perceptible effect at the back; the performers usually (at all events during the first two or three rehearsals) standing in a row with their backs to the auditorium, that the light may fall on the crabbed manuscripts they are reading from; the author endeavouring, but in vain, to arrange effective exits and entrances, because nobody can leave the T-piece; the stage-manager or prompter (who follows the performers) calling a halt from time to time that he may correct an overlooked error in his manuscript or insert a stage direction. The actors themselves pause from time to time for the same reason. Every one has (or should have) a pencil in hand; all errors are corrected and insertions made on the spot; every important change of position is carefully marked; every 'cross' indicated as the piece proceeds; and as alterations in dialogue and stage business are made up to the last moment – all of which have to be hurriedly recorded at the time – it will be understood that the 'parts' are in rather a dilapidated condition before the rehearsals are concluded . . .

There is much, very much, fault to be found (so Facile says) with the system – or rather the want of system – that prevails at rehearsals in this country. In the first place every actor and every person engaged in the piece should have a perfect copy of the piece, and that copy should be *printed*, not *written*. It costs from five to six pounds to print a three-act comedy, and in return for this trifling outlay, much valuable time and an infinity of trouble would be saved, not only to the prompter, but to the actors and the author. It is absolutely necessary that every actor should have the *context* of his scenes before his eyes as he studies them. He also says (does Facile) that it is a monstrous shame and an unheard-of injustice to place three-act pieces on the stage with fewer than thirty rehearsals, in ten of which the scenes should be set as they will be set at night, and in five of which every soul engaged should be dressed and made up as they will be dressed and made up at night . . .

In first-class French theatres this system is adopted. Parts are distributed, learnt perfectly, and then rehearsed for six weeks or two months, sometimes for three or four months. Scene rehearsals and dress rehearsals occupy the last week of preparations. Actors and actresses *act* at rehearsal: they have been taught and required to do so from the first, and the consequence is that a bad actor becomes a reasonably good actor, and a reasonably good actor becomes an admirable actor by sheer dint of the microscopic investigation that his acting receives from the stage-manager and

28 Rehearsing a burlesque, 1871: T-pieces illuminate the stage.

from the author. And until this system is in force in England; until the necessity for longer periods of preparation for rehearsals that are rehearsals in fact and not merely in name – rehearsals with scenery, dresses, and 'make-up' as they are to be at night; every expression given as it is to be given at night; every gesture marked as it is to be marked at night; until the necessity for such preparation as this is recognized in England, the English stage will never take the position to which the intelligence of its actors and actresses, the enterprise of its managers, and the talent of its authors would otherwise entitle it. At least, so says Facile.

NOTE

* *a T-piece* Gas standard-lamp used to light the stage for rehearsals (see illustration 28).

Dealings with authors, 1890

[From an article by Mrs Kendal reprinted in her *Dramatic Opinions* (1890).]

I have sometimes been asked to give the history of a play from the MS to the stage. I may begin by saying that very few plays indeed have ever been acted before the public in the state in which they were originally brought into the theatre. They undergo a thousand changes. It often happens that a MS is submitted which contains a very beautiful leading idea, but badly worked out. In such cases, the manager becomes, as it were, a collaborator with the author. Many plays are altered in this manner. The manager makes suggestions, and the actors do the same when they come to rehearse; receiving, of course, hints in their turn from the author; and so the work gets into shape.

Mr Kendal and I get quantities of plays brought to us and we make it a rule to read nearly every one of them. Of course, they are not all worthy of being placed before the public; but I am perfectly astonished at the amount of good there is to be found in the first plays of young playwriters, – unknown young men and women. There is perhaps one scene that is remarkably good, or it may be some leading idea or character, but so badly surrounded that the play will not admit of production. I always in such cases write back to the author, 'Go on; you have the germ. Do not spare paper and ink and trouble, and you will eventually find that the good fairy has touched you with her wand.' I should think in the course of a year we have hundreds of plays submitted to us. My working table is covered with them, and I have some cupboards full besides. A great many are comediettas in one act, sent me by young ladies – sometimes translated from the French or German – pretty little things often, but too light and flimsy for use; containing, nevertheless, decided germs of talent. I think the *matinées* which have come into fashion are a great boon. Of course, they are in some ways detrimental to art, but they have many advantages which more than counteract any harm they may do. I have seen some very bad plays produced at them, but I have also seen some very good ones. They afford an excellent means of making the work of a young author known . . .

As a rule Mr Kendal reads most of the plays sent to us. He is an excellent judge, and possesses the faculty of knowing exactly when there is money in a play. He is very difficult to please and very seldom wrong, his judgement is so cool . . .

I am sometimes asked whether we have ever made a success with a play that has been refused elsewhere. I could not be positive on the point, but I think it is more than probable that we have. Sometimes, what is finally submitted to the public is only half what the author originally wrote. A striking instance of this is Mr Smith's comedietta of *Uncle's Will*. We practically took only half the piece, but I think we picked out all the plums. Nearly the same thing happened with regard to *Little Lord Fauntleroy*. When the play was produced, Mrs Burnett said to me, 'You have cut it about rather severely.' I ventured to remark, that had I cut any flowers out of the play, I would humbly beg her pardon, but that I thought that I had only knitted my cloth a bit finer, and by that means brought out its brighter gloss. That is, of course, only what habit gives you the power of doing – that and the instinctive feeling of what will be more or less dramatic.

It is no easy task to 'cut' well, as we call it – that is, to be able to make judicious omissions; to leave all the beauty and only take out the weeds; to separate the wheat from the chaff; or, taking another metaphor, to gather the stitches together, as we do with crewel-work.

Sometimes authors will leave plays with us for three or four weeks, or for as many months, and then, after a little while, they write and ask us whether we have read them, and what our opinion is. We often write a very detailed opinion, which is sometimes shown to other managers, and used as a lever. The number of plays we manage to read in a given time of course depends on whether we are busy at rehearsal, or have other things to do. As a rule, my husband and I, every night of our lives, read something or other, or I go through a book that perhaps will make into a play. When a manuscript has been accepted it is in due course put into rehearsal. As a rule the authors are present at rehearsals, and are very nervous, which has rather a paralysing effect on the actors. Authors differ a good deal in the way they regard the interpreters of their work. It often happens that one finds one's part too long, and then one 'cuts' it oneself; or it is too short, and then one asks the author to 'write in' a speech, or to elaborate a scene, and generally such requests are granted readily enough. Some authors, however, boast of writing plays which they are pleased to term 'actor-tight', meaning that the play is independent of the artists who interpret it; but I think that this way of looking at things is dying out, and that most authors will acknowledge that they owe something, at any rate, a little something, to the actors.

My brother Tom always stage-managed his own plays, and I have always believed that he was a very clever stage-manager; every action and idea of his being followed by the actors and actresses of the Prince of Wales's Theatre, who believed in him, and of course, when people believe in you, you start fair.

xx

American copyright and the author, 1891

[From the preface to *Saints and Sinners* (1891) by Henry Arthur Jones.]

The passing of the American Copyright Bill is a fact of the highest import for English playwrights and for the future of the English drama, – that is, if the English drama has a future. It will indeed afford an accurate gauge of any individual playwright's pretensions, and of the general health and condition of the national drama. Hitherto the publication of an English play would have incurred the forfeiture of the American stage-rights, in many cases a very serious pecuniary loss. It would also have been attended with a very grave artistic risk. The best American managers – those who are capable of doing justice to the author in the production of a play – would naturally have refused to touch it unless their stage-rights were protected. It would have been presented, if at all, under the worst auspices, and with the worst and most haphazard stage management and surroundings.

Under these circumstances it is a question whether the placing of a play in the hands of the reading public would have compensated for the loss of its influence in its legitimate sphere on the stage, and for the discredit brought on the author by inadequate and irresponsible production and performance.

Further, in the present uncertain relations of English literature and the modern drama, an author may be excused for having some doubts as to whether the interests of either are to be served by the publication of plays whose perusal may only serve to show how sharp is the division between them. The American Copyright Bill removes these disabilities, and makes it inexcusable to yield to these doubts. If, from this time forward, a playwright does not publish within a reasonable time after the theatrical production of his piece, it will be an open confession that his work was a thing of the theatre merely, needing its garish artificial light and surroundings, and not daring to face the calm air and cold daylight of print. And further, if a custom does not now arise in England, such as prevails in France, of publishing successful plays, and if a general reading public is not gradually drawn round the drama, then it will be a sign that our stage remains in the same state of intellectual paralysis that has afflicted it all the century. Our drama will continue to be a 'Slough of Despond'[1] in the wide well-tilled field of English literature, an irreclaimable bog wherein, as in John Bunyan's, 'twenty thousand cartloads of wholesome instructions' have been thrown without improving the way.

But it will be urged that many successful plays will not 'read' at all, while in many others the passages that charm us most in the study are those that bore us most on the stage, and the passages that do not strike us at all in reading sometimes come out in letters of fire at the theatre. This brings me to remark what it is one of the chief objects of this preface to enforce and illustrate, namely, that there is a certain very strong antagonism between the literary and theatrical elements of a play. Very often this antagonism is more apparent than real, very often it is the just rebellion of the theatrical ass (I am speaking quite figuratively) against carrying a load of literary luggage that does not belong to him; very often it is his native friskiness refusing to carry any literary luggage at all – that is, to drop metaphor, it is the mere impatience of intellectual exertion in a theatre on the part of both entertained and entertainers. But whatever the cause of the quarrel, and whatever the various and debatable circumstances that may place the blame on the one side or the other, there does exist this very palpable antagonism, and jealousy, and desire of mastery between the two elements, theatrical and literary, that make up a play. So much so that on seeing some popular plays one is tempted to exclaim, 'The worst and deadliest enemy of the English drama is – the English theatre.'

It is not my province here to deal at length with the relation between English literature and the modern English drama, or rather with the want of relation between them. I am only concerned to establish the general rule, that the intellectual and art values of any drama, its permanent influence and renown, are in exact proportion to its literary qualities. Shakespeare and Sheridan are popular playwrights today, strictly on account of the enduring literary qualities of their work. They have admirable stagecraft as well, but this alone would not have rescued them from oblivion. The French drama has been operative intellectually and has commanded the respect of the civilized world because its authors have been men of letters, and because their works have always been available and recognizable as pieces of literature. There has been a definite literary standard below which it was impossible for any French dramatist of standing to sink. In England there has been no literary standard, and no ready means of marking the literary and intellectual position of the modern drama. The most amazing masterpieces of artificiality, extravagance, and theatricality have been rapturously received by the great British multitude without ever being examined as works of literature or studies of life. Every great literary critic of the age has contemptuously spoken of the modern drama, or has more contemptuously ignored it. If any little flame of authentic literary fire has arisen, it has quickly flickered out in the inane air. Perhaps the most accurate idea of the literary status of the modern drama can be gained from the style and form of presentation of those plays which for necessary business theatrical purposes it is considered advisable to print. Nothing could better express the frank contempt of the English theatre for English literature. In the first of Mr William Archer's volumes on the modern theatre, *English Dramatists of Today*,[2] will be found what will surely be a sociological curiosity of great interest in another generation or two – a transcript of the most popular scene from the most popular and money-making comedy of our time.[3] At present it is severely instructive reading. I shall doubtless be called to task for sneering at what has brought innocent delight to thousands. Innocent delight! Fireworks and Aunt Sally are innocent delights, and there is no deadly sin in an exhibition of chromolithographs.

Perhaps some of my remarks would be more applicable to the theatre of ten or twenty years ago. In quite recent days it may be gratefully acknowledged that in London at least a new spirit is kindling our audiences, and a new strong desire is openly expressed that the modern drama should take its rightful position as a national art in definite relation with literature and the other arts, with an acknowledged intellectual status and declared intellectual and artistic aims. The piercing light of science has been sprung upon us behind the scenes, and our worn-out old apparatus of theatrical effect and situation looks half-ghastly and half-trumpery in that cold cruel beam . . .

To return to the examination of the opposing literary and theatrical elements in a play. The comparative intellectual and literary degradation of the modern drama for two or three generations past is due to the fact that plays have been chiefly considered and exploited from their purely theatrical side, and as a vehicle for exhibiting the powers and peculiarities of an actor or a company. Now it is quite natural and just that an actor should have the highest opinion of his art, and that he should wish to subordinate the purely literary element in a play. I do not mean that he will wish to cut any literary speech that occurs in his part, or that he will not like to win the praise that is bestowed upon a literary production. But naturally and of necessity under our present system those plays, and those parts of a play, will be exploited which give the actor an immediate chance of dazzling the public . . .

Now the custom of publishing our plays at least offers a chance of escape from some of these difficulties and absurdities, if it does not open up a larger and higher sphere for the dramatist. . . . Perhaps if one searches a little into causes, the intellectual poverty of the drama of this century may be chiefly ascribed to the Puritan dread of the theatre, and to those other reasons which have kept the English from being a playgoing nation as a whole, and have also kept any considerable portion of cultivated playgoers from forming a body of sound dramatic opinion among themselves.

But the prejudices that have kept the English from being a playgoing nation are rapidly breaking up, and more encouraging still, a body of carefully discussed and examined opinion is being gradually formed amongst the more advanced section of playgoers. The intellectual ferment of the age has reached the theatre and has begun to leaven it. I have tried to indicate what appears to me one of the great hindrances to our advance to a higher level. While audiences are trained to regard the theatrical elements of a play as the essence of the matter, plays will succeed or fail mainly on their theatrical merits, and at best we shall remain in our present position. No very high literary or intellectual average will be maintained because the prizes are to be looked for in another direction, and for other qualities. . . . The passing of the American Copyright Bill will prove the mettle of English playwrights. It will show whether we are capable of seizing and holding our great legacy as the inheritors of our Elizabethan forefathers, or whether we are only fit to be the lackeys and underlings of French *farceurs*, supine, effete, disabled, and impotently dallying with the great issues of human life as with a child's box of wooden toy-men.

NOTES

1 *Slough of Despond*   In John Bunyan's *The Pilgrim's Progress* (1678).
2 *English Dramatists of Today*   Published in 1882.
3 *the most popular . . . comedy of our time*   H.J. Byron's *Our Boys* (1875) which ran for over four years.

xxi

The successful playwright, 1893

[From an interview, 'How I construct my plays: a chat with Mr Pinero', in *The Sketch*, 15 March 1893. Pinero had several successful plays to his credit, including *The Magistrate* and *Dandy Dick*. The new play referred to here, *The Amazons*, opened on 7 March at the Court Theatre. The author's comfortable surroundings and self-confidence and the respectful tone of the interviewer (who signs himself 'T.H.L.') are far removed from the situation of dramatists sixty years earlier. The patronizing, ultimately philistine, attitude to Ibsen and his supporters is consistent with Pinero's frequently expressed view that the theatre must advance by appealing to a broad public: similar views were expressed by Henry Arthur Jones, much to the exasperation of Shaw and Archer.]

The master of farcical comedy, the deft maker of crisp epigram and subtle jest, has exchanged the dreary little study, familiarly known among his intimates as 'The Tunnel', in his late abode in St John's Wood Road, for a handsome library in a brand-new house of red brick with stone dressings in Hamilton Terrace.

It was here that he gave me audience a few days ago on the eve of the appearance of *The Amazons*, which, fully printed, lay in its bright pink paper cover on his Davenport writing-table. Under the strict seal of secrecy he was good enough to give me an outline of the plot which, before these lines are in type, will have become public property.

'Now, tell me what you have to say about your new play, Mr Pinero,' was my first request.

'Well, it is a whimsicality, a little, unpretentious effort, a sort of digestive after dinner. In it I have attempted to find the poetry of farce. As a comic play I hope it is amusing, while I have endeavoured to import into it a suggestion of daintiness.'

'Does the play give you satisfaction ?' I ventured to ask.

'None of my work thoroughly satisfies the ideal to which I try to work up. I see faults in all; every play I write falls short of what I would wish to do. Perhaps that is the reason I am generally more in love with the work I next intend to take in hand, hoping to give it greater finish and to make it higher work. What I set myself to do is to break down the conventionality of the stage without going beyond the reach of the public.'

'Kindly tell me how you construct your plays.'

'Well, I never commence with a plot – I can tell you so much. The plot grows out of the men and women I conjure up. I make their acquaintance and familiarize myself with them, and I expect them to tell *me* the story. If they don't, and they prove uninteresting, I simply drop their acquaintance.'

'And do you set out for yourself any special hours for work?'

'Oh, dear, no! My work won't let me put it aside. I carry it about with me – in my head, I mean. I am completely led by it, and that is why I find play writing, or composing, very exhausting. When I sit down to my desk, I scribble right away what I have thought out previously. Then I rewrite and rewrite until I have given the work the highest finish I can. I think I wrote *The Amazons* pretty quickly, as I only commenced it in November.'

'Now, of all your plays . . . which do you consider your greatest?'

'*The Profligate*, I think. In that I made no concession to the popular taste. I introduced no comic relief, yet it was unquestion-ably a great success. But even that play is old-fashioned now. One has to move on in steps, you understand.'

'It has been said that the critic should reserve his critique till a play is a few days old. What do you say?'

'If you mean that the first night's performance should not be criticized, I should say it would be a great mistake. Mrs Kendal, for instance, an artist whom I greatly admire, never acts so well as she does at a *première*. Take Irving, again: I question if he ever rises to the same height of dramatic power as he does on a first performance, as he did in *Becket*, for example. Besides, the presence of the critics and of a keener audience than usual is in favour of the artists themselves. There is more enthusiasm, and the effect of the bursts of applause is to italicize the best points in the play, and it reacts undoubtedly on the minds of the critics,' said the playwright, as he walked up and down the room with his hands in his pockets, intent on answering my questions.

'And what are your views with regard to the office of censor, Mr Pinero? Would you dispense with him, as they do in America?'

'No, that is a mistake, I think; for, having no legalized tribunal to decide what is contrary to good morals, extreme prudishness is the result, and so vital things are not treated at all on their stage. What I would like would be to see the office of Censor made a department of the Privy Council, or of some such body, with a right of appeal to another court of judgement.'

'It would be interesting if you would give your opinion on the latest of Ibsen's plays before the public. What do you think of *The Master-Builder*?'

'Well, I cannot see that the interests of the Drama (spelt with a big D) are advanced by an appeal not addressed to the broad public. And although the play is now in the evening bill, it is really only a 'hole-and-corner' business; it cannot address itself to the public, but only to a very limited audience of cranks and experts. *The Master-Builder* is an obscure prose-poem, full of depths and subtleties. Even Ibsen students cannot explain his meaning satisfactorily. Mr Archer says he is content not to understand him, but it seems to me foolish to put a play before the public when the writer's meaning is confessedly not understood. When he has been interpreted it will be time enough to act him.'

'Criticism and the renascent drama', 1892

[From an article in *The Theatre*, June 1892. The author, W. Lewis Bettany, comments on the clash between 'Ancients and Moderns' that had been preparing long before the production of *A Doll's House* in 1889.]

The modern Peter the Hermit,[1] the preacher of the new crusade against the theatrical infidels, is, of course, Mr Clement Scott. He leads a band ever ready to repudiate his authority, but every member of which is madly, nay frantically, opposed to the 'New Movement'. The questions in dispute are well known and may be summed up as melodrama, the well-made play, and Ibsenism. In this battle of realism and unconventionality against so-called Idealism and stage convention, the virtues and failings of the older school of critics would best be discovered by selecting Mr Scott's published opinions as the data for our conclusions. But it would obviously be out of place in the pages of this magazine to discuss Mr Scott as a critic. Prejudiced and reactionary as his opinions on matters theatrical may seem to some people, Mr Scott has never been at a loss for vigorous and lucid expression, and whatever else he may or may not be, the *doyen* of English play-reviewers still remains unrivalled as a critic of acting.

Turning now to Mr Scott's followers on the press, we shall find that the *Times* critic need not detain us long. Mr J.F. Nisbet[2] is a gentleman of scant emotional susceptibility, a believer in the necessary conventionality of the stage, a great admirer of Mr Jones and, to a less extent, of Mr Pinero and Mr Grundy. But Mr Nisbet's views on the drama are too pessimistic, his style too unsympathetic and scientic [sic] to render him a very popular critic, while as an appreciator of histrionic ability, this gentleman is surely the least capable of all our metropolitan critics.

NOTES

1   *Peter the Hermit*   (1050–1115), preacher of the first Crusade.
2   *J.F. Nisbet*   (1851–99), chief dramatic correspondent of *The Times*, 1882–99.

Further reading

This list is a selection of books – for the most part modern, scholarly works. Among the periodicals that frequently print articles on aspects of the Victorian stage are *Nineteenth-Century Theatre* (formerly *Nineteenth-Century Theatre Research*), *Theatre Notebook, Theatre Research International and Theatrephile*. Unless otherwise specified, the place of publication is London.

General historical and reference works

Michael Booth (1981) *Prefaces to Nineteenth-Century English Theatre*, Manchester; (1965) *English Melodrama*.

V.C. Clinton-Baddeley (1954) *All Right on the Night*.

Gilbert Cross (1977) *Next Week, 'East Lynne' – Domestic Drama in Performance, 1820–1874*, Cranbury, NJ.

Joseph W. Donohue (1975) *Theatre in the Age of Kean*, Oxford.

Richard Foulkes (ed.) (1986) *Shakespeare and the Victorian Stage*, Cambridge.

Clifford Leech and T.W. Craik (eds.) (1975) *The Revels History of Drama in English*, volume VI, 1750–1880.

Robert W. Lowe, James Fullarton Arnott and John William Robinson (1970) *English Theatrical Literature, 1559–1900: A Bibliography*.

Allardyce Nicoll (1959 etc.) *A History of English Drama, 1660–1900*, vols. IV, V and VI (revised editions) Cambridge.

G.C.D. Odell (1920) *Shakespeare from Betterton to Irving*, New York, 2 vols.

Kenneth Richards and Peter Thomson (eds.) (1971) *Nineteenth-Century British Theatre*.

J.W. Robinson (ed.) (1971) *Theatrical Street Ballads*.

George Rowell (1978) *The Victorian Theatre, 1792–1914*, 2nd edition, Cambridge; (1981) *Theatre in the Age of Irving*, Oxford.

Richard Southern (1970) *The Victorian Theatre: A Pictorial Survey*.

J.C. Trewin (1976) *The Edwardian Theatre*, Oxford.

Ernest Bradlee Watson (1926) *From Sheridan to Robertson*, Cambridge, Mass.

Theatres for Audiences

Victor Glasstone (1975) *Victorian and Edwardian Theatres*.

Diana Howard (1970) *London Theatres and Music Halls, 1850–1950*.

Richard Leacroft (1973) *The Development of the English Playhouse.*

Richard and Helen Leacroft (1984) *Theatre and Playhouse.*

Iain Mackintosh and Michael Sell (eds.) (1982) *Curtains!!! or, New Life for Old Theatres.*

Ray Mander and Joe Mitchenson (1976) *Lost Theatres of London* (revised edition); (1975) *Theatres of London* (revised edition).

Paul Sheridan (1981) *Penny Theatres of Victorian London.*

The Actors' Life (see also Management)

Nina Auerbach (1987) *Ellen Terry: The Actress and her World.*

Michael Butler (1978) *The Rise of the Victorian Actor.*

Alan S. Downer (1965) *The Eminent Tragedian: William Charles Macready,* Cambridge, Mass.

Laurence Irving (1951) *Henry Irving: The Actor's Life.*

Roger Manvell (1968) *Ellen Terry.*

Margot Peters (1984) *Mrs Pat: The Life of Mrs Patrick Campbell,* New York.

Michael Sanderson (1984) *From Irving to Olivier.*

Mollie Sands (1979) *Robson of the Olympic.*

John Stokes, Michael Booth and Susan Basnett (1988) *Bernhardt, Terry, Duse,* Cambridge.

J.C. Trewin (ed.) (1967) *The Journal of William Charles Macready.*

—(ed.) (1968) *The Pomping Folk in the Nineteenth Century.*

Jane Williamson (1970) *Charles Kemble, Man of the Theatre,* Lincoln, Nebraska.

Behind the Scenes

Michael R. Booth (1981) *Victorian Spectacular Theatre 1850–1910;* (ed.) (1981) *Victorian Theatrical Trades: Articles from 'The Stage', 1883–1884.*

David Mayer (ed.) (1980) *Henry Irving and 'The Bells',* Manchester.

Martin Meisel (1983) *Realizations: Pictorial and Theatrical Arts in Nineteenth-Century England,* Princeton.

Terence Rees (1978) *Theatre Lighting in the Age of Gas.*

Sybil Rosenfeld (1974) *A Short History of Scene Design in Great Britain.*

Richard Southern (1952) *Changeable Scenery.*

A. Nicholas Vardac (1949) *Stage to Screen: Theatrical Method from Garrick to Griffith,* Cambridge, Mass.; repr. New York (1968).

Pieter van der Merwe (1979) *The Spectacular Career of Clarkson Stanfield, 1793–1867,* Gateshead.

Management

Shirley S. Allen (1971) *Samuel Phelps and Sadler's Wells Theatre*, Middletown, Connecticut.

William Appleton (1974) *Madame Vestris and the London Stage*, New York.

Peter Bailey (1978) *Leisure and Class in Victorian England*; (ed.) (1987) *Music Hall: The Business of Pleasure*.

Joseph Donohue (ed.) (1970) *The Theatrical Manager in England and America: Player of a Dangerous Game*, Princeton.

John M. East (1967) *'Neath the Mask: The Story of the East Family*.

John Elsom and Nicholas Tomalin (1978) *The History of the National Theatre*.

Frances Fleetwood (1953) *Conquest: The Story of a Theatre Family*.

J.M. Golby and A.W. Purdue (1984) *The Civilization of the Crowd: Popular Culture in England, 1750–1900*.

J.M.D. Hardwick (1954) *Emigrant in Motley: The Unpublished Letters of Charles and Ellen Kean*.

David Holloway (1979) *Playing the Empire: The Acts of the Holloway Touring Theatre Company*.

Alan Hughes (1981) *Henry Irving, Shakespearean*, Cambridge.

Christopher Murray (1975) *Robert William Elliston, Manager: A Theatrical Biography*.

John Pick (1983) *The West End: Mismanagement and Snobbery*, Eastbourne.

John Stokes (1972) *Resistible Theatre: Enterprise and Experiment in the Late Nineteenth Century*.

J.C. Trewin (1967) *Benson and the Bensonians*.

Wendy Trewin and J.C. Trewin (1980) *All on Stage: Charles Wyndham and the Alberys*.

Sir St Vincent Troubridge (1967) *The Benefit System in the English Theatre*.

Margaret Webster (1969) *The Same Only Different: Five Generations of a Great Theatre Family*.

James Winston (1974) *Drury Lane Journal: Selected from James Winston's Diaries, 1819–1827*, edited by Alfred L. Nelson and Gilbert B. Cross.

The Author's Work

William Cox-Ife (1977) *W.S. Gilbert: Stage-Director*.

Richard Ellmann (1987) *Oscar Wilde*.

Richard Fawkes (1979) *Dion Boucicault: A Biography*.

Rupert Hart Davis (ed.) (1962) *The Letters of Oscar Wilde*; (1985) *More Letters of Oscar Wilde*.

Michael Holroyd (1988) *Bernard Shaw: Volume One: The Search for Love*.

Dan H. Laurence (ed.) (1965) *Bernard Shaw: Collected Letters, 1874–1897*.

John Russell Stephens (1980) *The Censorship of English Drama, 1824–1901*, Cambridge.

Charles H. Shattuck (ed.) (1958) *Bulwer and Macready: A Chronicle of the Early Victorian Theatre*, Urbana, Illinois.

George Speaight (ed.) (1956) *Memoirs of Charles Dibdin the Younger*.

Jeavon Brandon Thomas (1955) *Charley's Aunt's Father: A Life of Brandon Thomas*.

J.P. Wearing (ed.) (1974) *The Collected Letters of Sir Arthur Wing Pinero*, Minneapolis.

Index of plays

General Index

Theatres which used the prefix 'Royal' or were styled 'Theatre Royal...' are here listed by the most significant element of their name. Unless otherwise indicated, theatres are in London.